Agatha Christie
A BIOGRAPHY

Agatha Christie

A BIOGRAPHY

Janet Morgan

COLLINS
8 Grafton Street, London w1
1984

William Collins Sons & Co Ltd
London * Glasgow * Sydney * Auckland
Toronto * Johannesburg

British Library Cataloguing in Publication Data

Morgan, Janet
Agatha Christie.
1. Christie, Agatha——Biography   2. Novelists,
English——20th century——Biography
I. Title
823'.912   PR6005.H66Z/

ISBN 0-00-216330-6

Printed in Great Britain by
St Edmundsbury Press, Bury St Edmunds, Suffolk

For Shiela

Contents

Illustrations

Preface

Agatha Christie valued her privacy. She rarely gave interviews and never put herself on display: 'Why,' she asked, 'should authors *talk* about what they write?' Her reputation, she believed, should stand or fall by her work, and that wish was respected by her family, friends and advisers. They were ready to assist serious analysts of her writing but kept at a distance those who sought to discuss her life. There have been, nonetheless, many biographies of Agatha Christie, in many languages. Some have been no more than fantasies. Others have relied on material from published sources – newspaper reports, reviews, books published by people who knew her or worked with her (though the better acquainted they were, the more circumspectly they wrote) – and have drawn on her own books, plays and poems, especially her recollections of Syria in *Come, Tell Me How You Live* and her *Autobiography*, and on her second husband's reflections in *Mallowan's Memoirs*.

In 1980 it was felt that the time had come for a full and thorough account of Agatha's Christie's life, and her daughter, Mrs Anthony Hicks, invited me to write it. Her view was that there was no point in embarking on this venture unless all her mother's papers were opened to me, with complete freedom to use them as I thought best. This book is based, therefore, on the letters Agatha wrote and received, on her manuscripts and plotting books, photograph albums and scrapbooks, diaries and address books, receipts and accounts, saved from well before her grandparents' time to the present day. My chapter headings, all quotations, are taken from these sources.

Biographers, however, do not look only at papers. Agatha's houses and gardens, furniture and possessions have been equally revealing; her family have given me generous access to all these, particularly to Greenway, her house in Devon. Here, with the books she read as a child still in the library, her china in the cupboards and the trees she planted in the garden, I have written most of this book. Mr and Mrs Hicks have been welcoming and hospitable; their greatest kindness has been to read every word of this biography, several times, to point out factual errors, chase references, and talk about Agatha Christie, without once insisting on a view of her character or work that might differ from my own. No biographer could ask for more and I would like to thank them here.

At Greenway, too, I first met many of Agatha's family and friends. There, and later at their own houses, they told me more about her. I am particularly grateful to her grandson, Mathew Prichard, his wife Angela and their children; to Mr and Mrs Archibald Christie, the son and daughter-in-law of Agatha's first husband, Archie and his wife Nancy; and to Mrs Cecil Mallowan, Mr and Mrs John Mallowan and Mr and Mrs Peter Mallowan, the family of Agatha's second husband, Max. I would also like to thank Lady Mallowan, who, as Miss Barbara Parker, first knew Agatha and Max on their archaeological expeditions to Iraq and who later married Max. She has not only described them both to me but has also explained a great deal about their work at Nimrud. Agatha's family have all spoken freely and thought carefully about my many questions; they have made letters, papers and possessions available without hesitation and smoothed my path towards other witnesses.

Apart from the odd name-dropper (and there are only a couple), people who knew Agatha have hitherto refrained from discussing her with strangers. Old friends kept their stories to themselves, professional colleagues and advisers confined their published remarks to diverting anecdotes about her books and plays, and, by and large, those who worked for her, however briefly or casually, maintained a silence as deep as that of any doctor, priest or lawyer. They knew her as a person, not as a phenomenon; they saw how she shrank from publicity and sympathised. Only the password 'authorised biographer' unlocked those doors. Reassured, Agatha's friends and acquaintances gave me their time, their recollections and their correspondence. Others, who did not know Agatha Christie but were interested in her work and character, guided me to new sources and gave me expert advice. My portrait of Agatha Christie is composed of these memories and reflections and I would like to thank the following people for their part in making it: Mrs Edward Allen; Jeffrey Andrews; Mr and Mrs Tom Ayling; Larry Bachmann; William W. Baxter; Dr and Mrs

Richard Barnett; Mrs J. Barrett; the Hon. Mrs Guy
Beauchamp; Guildford Bell; Sir Isaiah Berlin; Mrs Connie
Bessie; Miss Kathleen Bird; Mrs Anthony Boosey; the late Sir
James Bowker; Lady Bowker; Miss Christianna Brand; Richard
Buckmaster; Nigel Calder; Miss Elizabeth Callow; Lady
Campbell-Orde; Lady Camoys; Sir Simon and Lady Cassels;
Mrs Rose Coles; Lady Collins; Edmund Cork; Miss Jill Cork;
Miss Pat Cork; Denis Corkery; Miss Ann Disney; Sergeant
Durrant of the Surrey Constabulary; Jonathan Dodd; Edward
Dodd; Eiddon Edwards; Michael Evelyn; Mr and Mrs Peter
Fleming; Anthony Fleming; Richard Fletcher; Mr and Mrs G.
Gardner; Sir Julian Gascoigne; Mrs Raleigh Gilbert; Hugh
Goodson; Mrs D. Gould; Mr and Mrs Basil Gray; Miss
Deborah Greenep; Mr and Mrs Donald Griggs; Caroline
Grocholski; Mrs John Gueritz; Professor and Mrs Oliver
Gurney; Mr and Mrs C Hackforth-Jones; Dr Donald Harden;
Sir Peter and Lady Hayman; Sir William and Lady Hayter; the
late Sir John Hedges; Lady Hedges; Mrs Diana Helbaek; the
late Mrs Arthur Hicks; Brigadier and Mrs William Hine-
Haycock; Mrs Daphne Honeybone; Mrs Irene Hunter; Mr and
Mrs Peter Hulin; Sir Geoffrey Jackson; Mrs Frank James;
Dennis Joss; Denis Kelynack; James Kelly; Mr Rodney
Kannreuther and the late Mrs Kannreuther; Mr and Mrs
Austen Kark; Mr and Mrs Arthur Kellas; Mr and Mrs Richard
Kindersley; Sir Laurence and Lady Kirwan; Frank Lavin;
Richard Ledbetter; Mr and Mrs Maurice Lush; the late Mrs
Ernest Mackintosh; Harvey McGregor QC; Mr and Mrs
Richard Mallock; Mrs M. Marcus; Commander Marten and the
Hon Mrs George Marten; Mr and Mrs A.R. Maxwell-Hyslop;
the Hon Mrs John Mildmay-White; Dr and Mrs Philip
Mitchelmore; Charles Monteith; John Murphy; Professor and
Mrs David Oates; Miss Jennifer Oates; Miss Dorothy Olding;
James Paterson; S. Phelps Platt Jr; Sir John Pope-Hennessy;
Professor and Mrs Nicholas Postgate; Briton Potts; Mr and
Mrs J.B. Priestley; Dr and Mrs Julian Reade; Sir John and
Lady Richmond; Mrs Betty Rivoli; Miss Patricia Robertson;
Sergeant Geoffrey Rose of the Thames Valley Police; Mrs
Adelaide Ross; Raymond Ross; Lady le Rougetel; Sir Steven
Runciman; Mrs Herta Ryder; Sir Peter Saunders; Professor and
Mrs Seton Lloyd; Mr and Mrs Guy Severn; Mrs Reginald
Schofield; Madame de Soissons; Mr and Mrs J.C. Springford;
Dr Anthony Storr; Julian Symons; Miss Geraldine Talbot; Mrs

M. Thompson; Miss Barbara Toy; Lord and Lady Trevelyan; Dr Alan Tyson; John Vaughan; Algernon Whitburn; the late Mr Albert Whiteley; Stephen Whitwell; Mr and Mrs Michael Wildy; Professor Donald Wiseman; Mr and Mrs John Wollen; Nigel Wollen; Sir Denis and Lady Wright and Rolando Bertotti, the head waiter at Boodles. There are others, too, whom I would like to thank but their names are obscured by a blot where a raindrop has fallen on my pages. I will thank them properly when we next meet and in the meantime they have my apologies.

I am especially grateful to those who have allowed me to quote from letters to or from Agatha Christie and from family papers. Mrs Anthony Hicks, Mr and Mrs Mathew Prichard, John Mallowan and Peter Mallowan have been immensely helpful and I am also indebted to Edmund Cork and his family. I would also like to thank: Anthony Fleming, for permitting me to quote from the letters of his mother, Miss Dorothy L. Sayers; Mrs Frankfort, for an extract from a letter from her father, Professor Stephen Glanville; Lord Hardinge of Penshurst, whose reports to Collins are quoted here; Lady Kirwan, for quotations from letters from Agatha and Max; Mrs Anne McMurphy, formerly Miss Marple, whose letter from Agatha revealed the origins of that heroine's name; James Paterson, for extracts from his correspondence about the Churston window; Miss Dorothy Olding, whose exchanges with Edmund Cork I have plundered; Sir Peter Saunders, for quotations from letters and telegrams about plays; Professor Harry Smith, for allowing me to quote from a letter from his father, Professor Sydney Smith; and Miss Barbara Toy, whose correspondence I have cited in writing about *Murder at the Vicarage*.

I also wish to thank the directors of Agatha Christie Ltd, and the board of Booker McConnell Ltd, for allowing me to use their records; the BBC Written Archives Centre, and Mrs J. Kavanagh, Neil Somerville and Jeff Walden, for permission to quote from their records; the British Red Cross, and the archivist, Miss Margaret Wade, for details of Agatha Christie's service in the First World War; the directors of William Collins Ltd, for opening their files and allowing me to quote from them; Harrods Press Office, for their efforts to trace a letter Agatha Christie sent them in 1926; the *Harrogate Advertiser and Herald*, whose archive gave an illuminating picture of the town and its visitors in the 'twenties; the Home Office Library and the Departmental Records Officer, for their invaluable help in my search through the accounts of Agatha's disappearance; Hughes Massie Ltd, for permission to examine the records of Agatha's dealings with her agent; the Imperial War Museum for giving me access to the tape-recording Agatha made for their oral archive; the Trustees of the Allen Lane Foundation, and Dr Michael Rhodes, the archivist, for allowing me to cite extracts from Agatha's correspondence with The Bodley Head; the Trustees of the Mountbatten Foundation, for enabling me to quote from Earl Mountbatten's correspondence with Agatha about *The Murder of Roger Ackroyd*; the trustees of the Harold Ober estate, who made the correspondence of Agatha's American agent available to me, the Rare Books and Manuscripts Section of the Firestone Library at Princeton University, which houses it, and Miss Jane Snedeker, who guided me to it; the Surrey Record Office, and Dr Robinson, for their help in disentangling the events of 1926; and the University of Manchester Library, and Miss J. Sen, for supplying details of the careers of the doctors who attended Agatha in 1926.

There are others who, out of enthusiasm, curiosity or both, contributed to this book by producing new ideas and surprising references. I particularly wish to thank: Dr Marilyn Butler; Professor John Carey; Christopher Campbell; Stephen Hearst; Leofranc Holford-Strevens; Miss Frances Irwin; Edward Jospé; Mrs Cécil Jospé; Gordon Lee; Douglas Matthews; Mrs Alexandra Nicol; Miss Olivia Stewart; and Miss Anne Willis. I am equally grateful to those who interpreted, typed, arranged and copied my manuscript as I moved from one house, hotel, office and country to the next: Mrs Rigby Allen; Mrs Berry; Miss Michelle Cooper; Vincent Jones; Mrs Daisy Sasso; Mrs Jean Smith; and, as choreographers, Mrs Sheila George and Ray Walters. I would also like to thank Mr Bobby Burns and the Hon. Mrs Burns for their patience and hospitality while I cut and shuffled the text in their house in Jamaica.

The encouragement and guidance of my publishers have been indispensable and I am grateful to Bob Gottlieb of Alfred J. Knopf, Philip Ziegler of William Collins, Elizabeth Burke, Elizabeth Bowes Lyon and Elizabeth Walter.

This book is not only for people who like detective stories but also for those who are interested in a writer's development and experience, in Agatha Christie's character and the instinct which made her work a success. Like the lives of many writers, hers changed pace as she reached middle age. There was less incident, more consolidation. She was, moreover, quiet and reflective by temperament, and increasing age and fame made her more so. Though her energy remained immense, she gave most of it to her work. This book looks at the way in which she distilled her experience in her novels, plays and detective stories. Only in one case, however, does it reveal the solution to a plot and then only where Agatha Christie has done so in her own memoirs.

Agatha Christie lived to a great age and she was prolific. I have not given a chronological list of her work at the end of this book, for it is already long and readers who would like such a bibliography may find it in one of the interesting critical accounts of Agatha's writing. *The Agatha Christie Chronology* by Nancy Blue Wynne (New York: Ace Books, 1976) is particularly useful; less accurate but more daring is Charles Osborne's *The Life and Crimes of Agatha Christie* (Collins, 1982). Robert Barnard has published an excellent study in *A Talent to Deceive* (Collins, 1980); Gordon C. Ramsey's *Agatha Christie: Mistress of Mystery* (Collins, 1972) is thoughtful and was examined before publication by Agatha Christie herself. Sir Peter Saunders's autobiography, '*The Mousetrap Man*' (Collins 1972), gives a producer's perspective on her work for the theatre, while Tom Adams and Julian Symons have compiled a volume that is stimulating to look at as well as to read, by writing about the jacket designs for some of her paperbacks, in Tom Adams's *Agatha Christie Cover Story* (Paper Tiger, 1982). Those who need assistance in keeping track of the characters in Agatha Christie's work will find, as I have done, that Randall Toy's *The Agatha Christie Who's Who* (Muller, 1980) is painstaking and invaluable. Citations from the reviews of books and plays may be found in many books about Agatha Christie, notably Dennis Sanders and Len Lovallo's *Agatha Christie Companion* (Delacorte Press, NY 1984), which is devoted to this theme. I have preferred, however, not to draw greatly on such material, for, apart from their remarkable geographical spread, reviews of Agatha Christie's work are interesting mainly for their predictability.

There is one more group whom, at the end of this preface, I would like to thank: the secret army of those who gave good advice, pursued elusive references and raided libraries and bookshops across the world, so that they could telephone to Devon – and remoter spots – with answers to questions I thought urgent. Though these friends are anonymous here, I will write their names, with gratitude and affection, in their copies of this biography.

Janet Morgan.

I

'... the Millers, a family ...'

Even the beginnings were deceptive. To comfortable middle-class households in Torquay, the airy coastal resort in Devon where Agatha was born, the end of the nineteenth century seemed to be a Victorian afternoon. They did not notice that twilight was stealing over the terraces, the gardens and the pier. Agatha's own family, the Millers, looked equally prosperous and secure, but their fortunes, too, were imperceptibly growing shakier. And, like most families, the Millers were not as ordinary as they first appeared. In fact, they were decidedly unconventional.

Agatha was the youngest of three children. Madge, her sister, had a passion for disguise that exasperated her teachers and, eventually, her husband, as much as it entertained her friends and bewildered her visitors. Monty, Agatha's brother, had a different if related talent – for hitting on wild schemes into which he would draw harmless bystanders, to no one's profit but everyone's delight, particularly that of the women. Frederick, Agatha's father, was a charming, nonchalant American, keen on amateur theatricals, fussy about his health but not, until too late, about his investments; her mother, Clarissa, known always as Clara, was capricious, enchanting, and said to be psychic. She was also prone to spiritual and intellectual recklessness. Agatha adored them all.

Frederick and Clara had a romantic and complicated history. Clara's childhood was a mixture of comfort and insecurity that made her an especially possessive mother; this, in turn, fed Agatha's devotion, which for a time was to become obsessive. To understand Agatha, it is necessary to know her parents and, equally important, the two women who shaped their lives: her grandmother and step-grandmother, Mary Ann and Margaret.

The family was connected as neatly as characters in a detective story. These links are clearer if they are described like the settings for Agatha's plots, with the help of a plan:

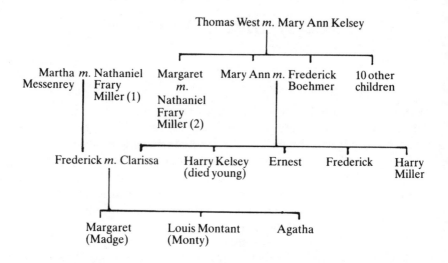

Mary Ann and Margaret West and their ten brothers and sisters were orphans and were brought up on a farm in Sussex by childless relations. In 1851 Mary Ann met Captain Frederick Boehmer of the Argyll Highlanders, who pressed her to marry him. Since he was thirty-six and she sixteen, her family demurred but Captain Boehmer argued that, as his regiment was about to be sent abroad, the wedding should take place at once – and it did. Mary Ann and Frederick had five children in quick succession (one died as a baby) of whom the only daughter, Clara, was born in Belfast in 1854.

In April 1863 Captain Boehmer, then stationed in Jersey, was thrown from his horse and killed, at the age of forty-eight, leaving Mary Ann, now twenty-seven, with four children to support as best she could. She was an excellent needlewoman and, by embroidering pictures and screens, slippers, pincushions and the like, augmented her husband's tiny pension. As Frederick had lost what savings he had in some vague speculative venture, Mary Ann had a great struggle to make ends meet. It is little wonder that in an entry in a family 'Album to Record Thoughts, Feelings, etc.' known as the 'Confessions,' written eight years after Frederick's death, she gave her state of mind as 'Anxious'.

Meanwhile, Mary Ann's elder sister, Margaret, had been working in a large hotel in Portsmouth, a post found by an aunt who had for many years been its forceful and greatly respected receptionist. Margaret, already formidable herself, married when she was twenty-six, in April 1863. Her husband, Nathaniel Frary Miller, a widower, had been born in Easthampton, Massachusetts, and had become a successful businessman, a partner in the firm of H. B. Chaflin in New York City. Nathaniel and his first wife, a hospital nurse, had only one child, a son, Frederick Alvah Miller. After his mother's death, Frederick was brought up mostly by his grandparents in America, but, after his father remarried and settled in England, where his firm had business in Manchester, Frederick visited Nathaniel and Margaret there. Here he met Clara.

It was a fortnight after Margaret's marriage to Nathaniel that Mary Ann lost her husband. Margaret wrote immediately to her younger sister, offering to take one of the four children and bring it up as her own, and Mary Ann, now despairing, decided that Clara should go to live with her aunt and uncle in the North. The little nine-year-old was lonely and homesick in her new surroundings and Clara always believed Mary Ann had sent her away because she cared more for the boys, rather than, as seems likely, because she felt it would be less easy for a girl to make a career for herself. Clara's chief consolation was her favourite book, *The King of the Golden River*, which she brought with her from Jersey. She would read aloud to her uncle Nathaniel the story of its hero, a lonely but determined little boy, who conquered his desolation by being sensible and considerate. Clara, quiet and imaginative, knowing her aunt and uncle were being kind to her but feeling bereft and misunderstood, treasured this book all her life, as Agatha did in her turn.

Clara's upbringing and tastes were those of an intelligent but sheltered late-Victorian girl. When she was seventeen, she too listed her likes and dislikes in the 'Confessions.' Her 'favourite qualities in man', she said, were 'firmness, moral courage and honour', and, in woman, 'refinement, frankness and fidelity'. Her favourite occupation was reading and talking, her chief characteristic 'a great love for children', and 'the fault for which she had most toleration' (in this case her own), 'reserve'. But the young woman whose 'present state of mind' was 'wishing for a long dress' and who admired Landseer and Mendelssohn, Tennyson, Miss Nightingale and the novels of Miss Mulock, nevertheless had a more robust and merry side. She gave her favourite food and drink as 'Ice-cream; American soda water', her favourite fictional heroine as Jo, the energetic tomboy in *Little Women*, and to the question 'If not yourself, who would you be?' she replied firmly, 'A school-boy.'

When Clara came to live with the Millers, Frederick, Aunt Margaret's American stepson, was seventeen years old and the cousins became fond of one another. Although there was only nine years' difference between them, it seemed a larger gap: Clara lived quietly at home in England, while Frederick, after school in Switzerland, had enjoyed a lively, to Clara a dizzy, time in America. As one of his friends later told Agatha, 'He was received by everyone in New York society, was a member of the Union Club, and was widely known, and there are scores of present members of the Union Club, mutual friends of ours, who knew him, and were very much attached to him.' After Frederick's marriage, his and Clara's names appeared in the New York Social Register; in his own copy Frederick's blue pencil ticked the names of his many New York friends and acquaintances and others in the best families of Philadelphia and Washington.

The sort of life Frederick led is described in the novels of Henry James and Edith Wharton. The American upper-class society in which he moved was small and intimate – some nine hundred families only are listed in the Social Register of 1892 – and much time was taken up with visiting friends and relations, reading newspapers and writing notes at the Club, dining, dancing, going to the theatre and (less frequently for those who were not devotees) concerts and galleries, playing tennis, croquet and cards, smoking (a serious pastime) and watching horses racing or, alternatively, yachts. Frederick Miller was not, however, one of the moody young fellows depicted in novels of the time, but, in Agatha's words, 'a very agreeable man'. Indeed, in his own joking entry in the 'Confessions,' written when he was twenty-six, he gave an accurate picture of his temperament – easy-going, philosophical, hardly energetic. His favourite occupation was described as 'doing nothing', his chief characteristic, 'ditto'. The characters in history he most disliked were Richard III and Judas Iscariot, his favourite heroes in real life Richard Coeur de Lion and 'a country curate'. His pet aversion was 'Getting up in the morning', his present state of mind 'Extremely comfortable, thank you', and to the question, 'If not yourself, who would you be?' he placidly replied, 'Nobody.' Only one question had a really enthusiastic answer and that concerned his favourite food and drink, where he crowded into a two-line reply: 'Beefsteak, Chops, Apple Fritters, Peaches, Apples. All kinds of nuts. More peaches. More nuts, Irish stew. Roly Poly Pudding', and, an asterisked afterthought, 'Bitter Beer.'

In the same entry Frederick described the characteristics he most admired in women as 'amenibility to reason' (his spelling, like that of Madge and, especially, Clara and Agatha, was often erratic), 'with a good temper'. These were his little cousin's qualities. She was devoted to Cousin Fred, who had been the first person to compliment her, at the age of eleven or so, on her beautiful eyes, and who sent her when she was seventeen a volume of Southey's poems, bound in blue and gold and inscribed: 'To Clara, a token of love'. Clara, for her part, sent Frederick letters and poems and, later, notebooks embroidered with daisies, monograms in gold thread, inscriptions and, most ambitious, a red heart stuck with two arrows. She took pains over these tributes; she was a much less skilful needlewoman than her mother and in one piece of embroidery was obliged to leave off the last letter of Frederick's name, having misjudged the space available. She also gave him serious and sentimental poetry; a maroon and gold album contains the verse, mostly about love and death, which she composed during their engagement. Occasional corrections in Frederick's hand show that he not only conscientiously read his cousin's poetry but here and there improved it.

The most lively verse in that collection was a satirical view of marriage, 'The Modern Hymen', which Clara described as being a purely egotistical arrangement: 'For the Bride, fair beauty, For the Bridegroom, wealth. Two in one united, And that one is – Self. . . .' Clara's and Frederick's marriage was not at all on these lines. She had refused his first proposal because she thought herself to be 'dumpy' and he, though believed to be rich because he was an American, enjoyed a comfortable but not enormous income.

The cousins were married in April 1878; Frederick was thirty-two and Clara twenty-four. A month later, in Switzerland, she wrote a long, rhapsodic poem for him, asking God to send her 'an angel friend', whom she could charge to protect and support 'her darling'; the gift to Frederick is the more touching because it has at the foot a slightly botched attempt at a drawing of an

angel and a request to 'excuse this piece of paper ... the only thin
piece I had left', as well as enclosing two dried edelweiss, a gen-
tian, a violet and some clover. These, with the notebooks, Frederick always kept by him.

Margaret Frary Miller, Frederick and Clara's first child, was
born in January the following year, in Torquay, where the Millers
had taken furnished lodgings. Soon after Madge's birth her parents took her to America, so that Frederick could present his wife
and baby daughter to his grandparents, and it was thus that the
second child, a boy, was born in New York in June 1880. This
was Louis Montant, named after Frederick's greatest friend. The
Millers and their two children then returned to England, where
they expected to stay only a short time before going back to
America to live. Frederick, however, was suddenly obliged to
return to New York to see to various business matters and suggested that while he was away Clara should take a furnished
house in Torquay. With the help of Aunt Margaret, now a
widow, Clara accordingly inspected two or three dozen houses
but the only one she liked was for sale, rather than for rent.
Despite – or perhaps because of – the restrained and ordered
environment in which she had been brought up, Clara was determined and impetuous, and she immediately bought the house,
with the help of £2,000 which Nathaniel had left her. She had felt
at ease in it at once and when its owner, a Quaker called Mrs
Brown, had said, 'I am happy to think of thee and thy children
living here, my dear', Clara felt it was a blessing. Frederick was
somewhat taken aback to discover that his wife had bought a
house in a place where he expected them to stay a year or so at
most but, always good-natured, he fell in with her wishes.

The house was Ashfield, in Barton Road. It has long been
demolished but some impression of it can be had from Agatha's
recollections and those of her contemporaries and from photographs taken at the turn of the century. Ashfield was large and
spreading, like other Torquay villas of its kind, built for the
sizeable families of the professional middle class, who needed
plenty of spacious rooms to hang with draperies, cram with furniture and stuff with interesting objects which they liked, or liked
to display. Such houses were no trouble to heat, because fuel was
cheap, or to clean and maintain, because servants were inexpensive, with enterprising and ingenious plumbers, glaziers, carpen-
ters and masons in abundant supply. Ashfield was an attractive
and unusual house; a rectangular two-storey part, with wide sash

windows, adjoined a squarish three-storey section, with tall windows, some of those on the ground floor having coloured glass in the upper part, while the lower sections opened on to the garden. There was a multiplicity of chimneys; trellis-work and climbing plants covered the walls. The porch, which was large and topped with window boxes, was entirely shrouded with creeper. Attached to the house was an airy conservatory, full of wicker furniture, palm trees and other spiky and exotic plants, and at ten-foot intervals along the edge of the lawn, where it bordered the gravel, were huge rounded pots of hyacinths, tulips and other plants in season. A second, smaller greenhouse, used for storing croquet mallets, hoops, broken garden furniture and the like, and known as 'Kai Kai', adjoined the house on the other side. (Towards the end of her life Agatha described this greenhouse in *Postern of Fate*.)

The garden seemed limitless to Agatha, most of whose childhood world it composed. She described it as being divided in her mind into three parts: the walled kitchen garden, with vegetables, soft fruit and apple trees; the main garden, a stretch of lawn full of trees – beech, cedar, fir, ilex, a tall Wellingtonia, a monkey-puzzle tree and something Agatha called 'the Turpentine Tree' because it exuded a sticky resin; and, last, a small wood of ash trees, through which a path led back to the tennis and croquet lawn near the house. Ashfield was, moreover, at the end of the older part of the town, so that Barton Road led into the lanes and fields of the rich Devon countryside. The houses and gardens seemed immense and that was how Agatha remembered them when she was grown up – but Ashfield was certainly big.

It was as well that the house was spacious, since Frederick had a mania for collecting. Torquay being a fashionable resort, patronised by people with money, taste and plenty of spare time, it had attracted a number of dealers, into whose smart shops he would make a detour on his daily walk to the Yacht Club. The shopkeeper who did best was J. O. Donoghue, of Higher Union Street, whose lengthy bills give a detailed picture of Frederick's purchases of coffee tables, card cases, plaited baskets, salts, oriental jugs and jars, china plates, cut-glass candlesticks, paintings on rice paper, muffineers and innumerable pieces of Dresden china. The stack of bills preserved among Frederick's papers also shows the extent of the Millers' domestic establishment and hospitality. Five-course dinners were prepared daily by Jane, the cook, with a professional cook and butler hired for grand occasions, when at each course a choice of dishes would be presented. Clara kept a book of 'receipts for Agatha', which indicates the richness and expense of the food that was served: fish pies, for instance, were made of filleted sole layered with oysters (though there was a footnote saying 'Best brand of tinned oysters "Imperial"') and directions were given for preparing truffles to add to meat or chicken, for making breakfast dishes of cold salmon and of kidneys and mushrooms, for dishes of quail, splendid savouries, and various complicated salads, smooth creams and junkets. The only really economical recipe, for macaroni cheese, instructed the reader to 'get the macaroni at a shop in Greek Street, Soho, kept by an Italian' and carried the terse comment 'Not very good.'

Into this well-equipped household Agatha was born on September 15, 1890. She was the much-loved 'afterthought'; her mother was thirty-six, her father forty-four and there was a gap of eleven years between Agatha and Madge and ten between Agatha and Monty. Madge was by now a boarder at Miss Lawrence's School in Brighton (later to become the celebrated girls' boarding school, Roedean) since this accorded with Clara's current view of what should constitute female education. Madge's letters to her baby sister – 'My dear little chicken ... Who do you get to make you a big bath of bricks in the schoolroom now that your two devoted slaves have left for school to learn their lessons?' – reflected her gregarious and comic nature. She was a tumbling, bouncing girl, not beautiful but with an attractive, mobile face and an engaging grin. The only wistful note in her entry in 'Confessions' was her answer to: 'If not yourself, who would you be?' to which she replied, 'A beautiful beauty.'

Madge adored jokes, pranks and disguises and Agatha was awed and delighted by her sister's exploits. She talked with amazed pride of the time when Madge dressed up as a Greek priest to meet someone at the station and of the occasion when, having come to Paris to be 'finished', she accepted a dare to jump out of the window and landed on a table at which several horrified Frenchwomen were taking tea. Madge would thrill her sister by spicing affectionate play with a dash of spookiness, saying solemnly, 'I'm not your sister,' looking for a moment like a stranger, or, in an even more terrifying version of this game, putting on the silkily ingratiating voice of the imaginary madwoman Madge and Agatha called 'The Elder Sister', who lived in a cave in the nearby cliffs, and uttering the horribly unreassuring words,

'*Of course* I'm your sister Madge. You don't think I'm anyone *else*, do you? You wouldn't think *that*?'

It is much harder to catch a glimpse of Agatha's brother, Monty. Here and there, in the first dictated draft of the part of her autobiography that deals with her childhood, Agatha alluded to the fact that 'at about this time, Monty disappeared from my life'; as it was, he hardly seems to have been there at all. This is partly because, when Agatha was young, Monty was at Harrow and when she was older he had vanished abroad. He was not a scholar – he left Harrow without passing his examinations – but his winning disposition helped him to survive. Agatha told the story of Monty's being the only boy allowed to keep white mice at school, since the Headmaster had been induced to believe that Miller was especially interested in natural history. Her picture of him was, as one would expect, of someone who, by virtue of his being a boy and ten years older, led a strange and exciting life of daring exploits in boats and later in motor cars, in which he would sometimes disdainfully allow his little sister to take part.

Things cannot have been easy for Monty, in a circle of four forceful women – his energetic and argumentative elder sister, shrewd impulsive mother, and two formidable grandmothers. A photograph shows him, in an ill-fitting buttoned uniform, with a sullen expression on his handsome face; he might be any age from nine to nineteen and he looks bored and unhappy. But other pictures show Monty at his most gay and irrepressible: we see him, in smoking jacket, top-hat and huge leather boots, sitting in 'Truelove', the tiny wheeled horse and carriage with which the children played, cheering on a puzzled goat which has been attached to the reins. Monty has a look that is simultaneously wild and self-indulgent.

In his portrait, painted when Monty was nineteen or so, he seems calmer but somehow unconvincing, as if he were not sure whether to look foppish, quizzical, or rakish. His entry in the 'Confessions' (which he forgot to sign) conveys a similar impression of uncertainty. His remarks were those of someone trying to be amusing, with neither the panache nor the wit to carry it off: 'Your favourite heroes in real life?' – 'Fenians'; 'Your present state of mind?' – 'Oh my!'; 'Your favourite qualities in man?' – 'Being a good fellow generally'; and – a clue to the fact it is Monty who is writing – 'Your idea of misery?' – 'Borrowing money.' There was something melancholy about Monty and, though his influence on his younger sister was much less direct and obvious than that of Madge, he nevertheless presented a worrying puzzle to Agatha.

Agatha Mary Clarissa was named after her mother and grandmother, the name of Agatha, she believed, being added by Clara, with her usual agility, as a result of a suggestion made on the way to the christening. (One of Clara's favourite novels was, moreover, Miss Mulock's *Agatha's Husband*.) During the course of Agatha's life, she was to acquire, or adopt, a number of different names and titles; to her friends and family (except those close relations who later called her 'Nima', her grandson's corruption of 'Grandma') she was always 'Agatha'. As her first publisher told her in 1920, it was an unusual and therefore memorable name – and that is what we will call her here.

Frederick's collection of bills also gives some impression of the furniture, books and pictures amongst which Agatha grew up. Some of the better furniture was sold in the years after her father's death, when her mother's circumstances were considerably reduced, but a good deal of it, including many of the lamps, screens and pictures, and much of the china, cutlery and glass, was used to furnish the houses in which Agatha subsequently lived. As she said herself, her father's taste in pictures did not match his discrimination in buying furniture. The fashion of the eighteen-eighties and eighteen-nineties was to hang as many pictures as possible on whatever wall space was available and this Frederick proceeded to do, with vague oils, Japanese caricatures, pastels on copper and masses of engravings, including one called 'Weighing the Deer', of which he was particularly fond. Certain cherished objects were assigned to those members of the family who would eventually inherit them. (Clara's Aunt Margaret would write names of the future beneficiaries on the backs of the canvases.) Agatha's particular inheritance was 'Caught', an oil of a woman catching a boy in a shrimping net, exhibited at the Royal Academy in 1884 and acquired by Frederick ten years later for the sum of £40. In the same year, when Agatha was four, her father commissioned a local artist, N.H.J. Baird, to paint the family dog, an exercise which was regarded as so successful that Mr Baird was subsequently invited to paint Frederick, Agatha, Monty, Madge, and Agatha's nurse. When, at the age of seven, Agatha was asked to name her favourite poets, painters and composers in the 'Confessions,' she loyally put Baird's name alongside those of Shakespeare and Tennyson.

The focus of Agatha's life as a small child was 'wise and patient Nanny', the cook Jane, and successive parlourmaids. Her recollections of these companions date from an early age. Unusually, too, her *Autobiography* described what Nursie and Jane looked like, her nurse with 'a wise wrinkled face with deep-set eyes', framed, as in Mr Baird's portrait, by a frilled cambric cap, and Jane, 'majestic, Olympian, with vast bust, colossal hips, and a starched band that confined her waist'. Nursie represented 'a fixed point, never changing'. For instance, her repertoire of six stories did not vary, whereas Clara's were always different. Clara, unlike Nursie, never played the same game twice; as Agatha wrote of her mother's tales and games, their unpredictability sometimes shocked her but she also felt the enchantment of the perpetually unknown. Nursie's religious beliefs were firm. She was a Bible Christian, devoutly keeping the Sabbath by reading the Bible at home. Clara, by contrast, experimented with various schools of religious thought: she had nearly been received into the Roman Catholic Church; next she tried Unitarianism, which in turn gave place to Theosophy and then, briefly but keenly, to Zoroastrianism. She was at one point deeply interested in Christian Science and occasionally attended Quaker meetings. Clara broke the rules – she and Agatha would gaily gather up all the towels in the house to play with – while Nursie enforced them. When Agatha was four or five, Nursie returned to Somerset. Agatha missed her desperately, for she had been the centre of order, calm and stability.

So was Jane, who presided over the kitchen. There she was, massive, placid, always gently munching on some delicious scrap, providing regular meals at regular times, and bits and pieces in between. It is not surprising that food was always a pleasure and a solace to Agatha and that she is remembered for the ample meals she offered, the expertise with which she would make éclairs and mayonnaise, and the delight she took in food that was served to her. Jane taught Agatha to make cakes, 'some with sultanas, and some with ginger,' as she wrote proudly to her father when she was eleven, 'and we had Devonshire cream for tea.' She was passionately fond of cream: Devonshire cream on its own, eaten with a spoon; double cream mixed half and half with thick milk and drunk from a cup; or clotted cream put together with treacle to make 'Thunder and Lightning'. This was real Devonshire cream, as thick as butter and as smooth, with a yellow crust and palest gold below, a simple but matchless taste, a slippery consistency and a flavour bland yet unlike anything else – just the sort of dish for which a lonely child might yearn.

Agatha was, moreover, energetic and intelligent; she got hungry and bored, in spite of the games and stories she invented, and she remained a skinny child. Monty called her 'the scrawny chicken'. Meals, punctually served, were benchmarks in the day and the ceremonies of presenting and consuming food were fascinating, especially since she was orderly and fond of ritual. Throughout her life she served formal meals as they were composed in her childhood, with silver and glasses correctly placed, flowers arranged, napkins folded, course succeeding course. A meal was a celebration.

Liking the way things were arranged, Agatha was also interested in the way people were ordered. She was to discover as she grew up the fine gradations of Torquay society but her first inkling of a hierarchy was in the household at Ashfield. With her sharp ear for words and phrases, she noticed forms of address: cooks were always 'Mrs,' housemaids equipped with 'suitable' names (even if they did not arrive with them), like Susan, Edith, and so on, and parlourmaids, who 'valeted the gentlemen and were knowledgeable about wine', had names sounding vaguely like surnames – Froudie was one of the Millers' parlourmaids – to go with their 'faint flavour of masculinity'. Duties, too, were clearly allocated and, while there were few complications in Ashfield's small household of three servants, from time to time Agatha would be aware of friction between the nursery and the kitchen. Nursie, however, was 'a very peaceable person'.

As the servants deferred to Agatha's parents (Jane, when asked to recommend a dish, would not dream of suggesting anything except, non-committally, 'A nice stone pudding, Ma'am?'), so the lower servants genuflected to those in higher authority. Agatha was deeply impressed, as a child, by the reproof which Jane (addressed by the other servants as Mrs Rowe) administered to a young housemaid who rose from her chair prematurely: 'I have not yet finished, Florence.' A sensitive child, she could spot where power lay and, as children do, grew skilled at managing complex relations with a number of adults with whom she had understandings of varying degrees of complicity. Agatha knew about the servants' world, not only because these were the adults with whom she spent a fair amount of time but also because she needed to keep her wits about her in order to avoid trouble and

interference, obtain attention and titbits, and know what was
going on.

Like most children, too, she was interested in the execution of
practical tasks – the way pastry was made, ironing done, fires
laid, boots blackened and, as Agatha observed, 'glasses washed
up very carefully ... in a papier-mâché washing-up bowl'. She acquired a proper respect for the efficient exercise of these domestic
skills, enhanced by Clara's instilling into her that servants were
highly trained professionals, versed not only in the intricacies of
whichever part of the household they managed but also in the
correct relations that should prevail between themselves and the
people for whom they worked. Agatha emphasised this point in
her *Autobiography*, since she was aware that the world before
1939 which she was describing was quite different from that of
many of her readers, who might be baffled by the nuances of
these domestic relationships.

To Agatha her mother was an extraordinary and magical
being. Now in her late thirties, Clara supervised her household
and her husband with natural authority, reinforced by experience.
She knew and thought about her husband and children sufficiently keenly for them to believe that she had second sight
(Madge once said to Agatha that she didn't dare even to think
when Clara was in the room), an impression that must have been
fortified by her fickle but profound interest in various bizarre
philosophies. She still wrote poetry; one of her stories, with Callis
Miller as a pseudonym, survived among Agatha's papers. The
narrator of *Mrs Jordan's Ghost* was the unhappy spirit of a dead
woman, manifesting itself whenever a particular piano was
played. The preoccupations of this forlorn soul-rippling music,
an ominous verse, guilt and purification, a vaguely apprehended
unknown Power, 'the unwritten laws of this mysterious universe'
– were exactly what one would expect in a story by Clara. An
exotic figure, looking in her later photographs drawn and astonished, she seemed to Agatha a charming mixture of waywardness
and dignity, certainty and vagueness.

Agatha saw her mother at special times: when she was ill or
upset; when she needed permission to embark on some rare adventure or wished to report on one; and after tea, when, dressed
in starched muslin, she would be sent to the drawing-room for
play and one of Clara's peculiar stories – about 'Bright Eyes', a
memorable mouse, whose adventures suddenly petered out, or
'Thumbs', or 'The Curious Candle', which Agatha later dimly

remembered as having had poison rubbed into it (this tale too, came to an abrupt stop). It was then that she could study her mother's ribbons, artificial flowers and jewellery. Small girls (as she recalled in *Cat Among the Pigeons*) are not immune to the spell of jewels and those belonging to an older woman are especially magical, for they represent all sorts of mysteries and transformations. In her *Autobiography* Agatha described Clara's ornaments, although her list is thin in comparison with the pile of jewellers' accounts among Frederick's bills: for lockets and stars, brooches and fans, buttons, rings, scent bottles and card cases, and two of the items Agatha remembered, a diamond crescent and a brooch of five small diamond fish, bought, endearingly, during the last weeks before Agatha's birth.

In Nursie, Jane, Clara and Madge, Agatha was surrounded by strong and influential women. Her father, kindly and interested in his daughter's progress, had his own detached way of life. In the morning after breakfast he would walk down to the Royal Torbay Yacht Club, calling *en route* at an antique dealer's, to see his friends, play whist, discuss the morning newspapers, drink a glass of sherry and walk home for luncheon. In the afternoon he would watch a cricket match, or go to the Club again and weigh himself (preserved among his papers is a sheet of Club writing paper, with such records of stones and ounces as: August 9th, p.m., blue suit, 14.0; September 13th, a.m., Pep. Salt., 14.0), before returning to Ashfield to dress for dinner. Frederick's photographs show him stout and contemplative, and, in part because of his fashionable moustache and beard, he looked older than his years.

There were two other important and impressive women in Agatha's childhood: her grandmothers Margaret and Mary Ann. Margaret, Clara's aunt and Frederick's step-mother, was known as Auntie-Grannie, while Mary Ann, Clara's mother, was known as Grannie B. It was at Margaret's house that the family gathered. After Nathaniel's death she had moved from Cheshire to a large house in Ealing, filled with a great deal of mahogany furniture, including an enormous four-poster bed curtained with red damask, into which Agatha was allowed to climb, and a splendid lavatory seat on which she would sit, pretending to be a queen, 'bowing, giving audience and extending my hand to be kissed', with imaginary animal companions beside her. 'Prince Goldie', named after her canary, sat 'on her right hand' on the small circle enclosing the Wedgwood handle of the plug. On the wall, Agatha recalled, was an interesting map of New York City. Throughout her life Agatha maintained that a well-appointed and efficient lavatory, preferably of mahogany, was an essential feature of a house or an archaeological camp; she was delighted to discover in her house in Devon a room fitted with wooden furniture almost as magnificent as her grandmother's.

Auntie-Grannie passed her days not in the drawing-room, 'crowded to repletion with marquetry furniture and Dresden china', nor in the morning-room, used by the sewing woman, but in the dining-room, its windows thickly draped with Nottingham lace, every surface covered with books. Here she would sit either in a huge leather-backed carver's chair, drawn up to the mahogany table, or in a big velvet armchair by the fire. When Agatha was tired of the nursery and the garden, full of rose trees and with a table and chairs shrouded by a willow, she would come to find her grandmother, who would generally be writing long 'scratchy-looking' letters, the page turned so that she could save paper by writing across the lines she had just penned. Their favourite game was to truss Agatha up as a chicken from Mr Whiteley's, poke her to see whether she was young and tender, skewer her, put her in the oven, prick her, dish her up – done to a turn – and, after vigorous sharpening of an invisible carving knife, discover the fowl was a squealing little girl.

This memory, like many of Agatha's other recollections of her maternal grandmother's house, was of fun and of eating. She described with great vividness each morning's visit to the store cupboard; Margaret, like her stepson, was a collector but, as well as hoarding lengths of material, scraps of lace, boxes and trunks full of stuff, and surrounding herself with a profusion of furniture, she also assembled quantities of food: dried and preserved fruit, pounds of butter and sacks of sugar, tea and flour, and cherries, which she adored. (The 'Confessions' gives Margaret's favourite food and drink as stewed cherries and cherry brandy and when she left Ealing thirty-six demijohns of home-made fruit liqueur were removed from her house.) She would dispense the day's allocation to the cook, investigate any suspected waste, and dismiss Agatha with her hands full of treasure – crystallised fruit like jewels.

Mrs Boehmer, Grannie B., lived in Bayswater but made frequent visits to her sister at Ealing. Here Agatha saw her, and always on Sundays, when the family would assemble at Auntie-Grannie's table for a large Victorian lunch: 'an enormous joint, usually cherry tart and cream, a vast piece of cheese, and finally dessert'. Two of Clara's brothers would be there, Harry, the Secretary of the Army and Navy Stores, and Ernest, who had hoped to become a doctor but, on discovering he could not stand the sight of blood, had gone instead into the Home Office. (Fred was with his regiment in India.) After lunch the uncles would pretend to be schoolmasters, firing questions at Agatha, while the others slept. Then there was tea with Madeira cake. On Sunday, too, the grandmothers would discuss and settle the week's dealings at the Army and Navy Stores, where they had accounts and where, during the course of the week, Grannie B. would make small purchases and take repairs for Auntie-Grannie (who, Agatha suspected, discreetly added a small present of cash when reimbursing her sister). Agatha joined her grandmothers on some of these expeditions, which are recalled in her description of Miss Marple's missions to the Army and Navy Stores in *At Bertram's Hotel*.

Agatha's *Autobiography* gives only the most general description of her grandmothers' appearance. As widows usually did, they dressed in heavy black. Both seemed to Agatha extremely stout. Grannie B. in particular suffered from badly swollen feet and ankles, as Agatha was later to do, and her tight-buttoned boots were torture. In fact their photographs show that they were small women but to Agatha, a thin and bony child, they and the silky stuffs in which they were swathed must have appeared imposing. It was their conversation she remembered and recorded most clearly: good-natured bickering between the two sisters, each teasing the other over who had been more attractive as a girl – 'Mary' (or 'Polly', as Auntie-Grannie called Grannie B.) 'had a pretty face, yes, but of course she hadn't got the figure I had. Gentlemen like a figure.' And Agatha drank in their gossip about friends who came to call: Mrs Barry, for instance, whom Agatha regarded with profound awe because she claimed to have been in the Black Hole of Calcutta. Though implausible, her story was so horrid that it fascinated the company.

These conversations were riveting to an imaginative child whose fancy careered ahead of her understanding and who was particularly susceptible to words. (On one occasion a farmer's angry shout 'I'll boil you alive,' when Agatha and Nursie wandered on to his land, stuck her dumb with terror). Especially interesting were the anecdotes of gallant colonels and captains, with whom Auntie-Grannie kept up 'a brisk, experienced flirtation', knitting them bed-socks and embroidering fancy waistcoats, and who made Agatha nervous with their heavy-handed archness and tobacco-laden breath. She remembered exceptionally clearly the remarks, deliberately made in her hearing, about the relationship between a retired Colonel in the Indian Army and the young wife of his best friend, who had retired to a lunatic asylum: 'Of course, dear, it's perfectly *all right*, you know. There is *nothing* at all *questionable* about it. I mean, her husband particularly *asked* him to look after her. They are very dear friends, *nothing more. We all know that.*'

Margaret seems to have been a more forthright and colourful character than her younger sister; certainly Agatha's autobiography contained many references to the opinions, precepts and warnings handed out by her Ealing grandmother, whereas she recalled little of the views of her quieter counterpart in Bayswater. But the serene and affectionate Mary Ann, who never remarried, busying herself with her needle and giving her attention to her three sons, and the more striking Margaret, with her pithy wit and scorn of humbug, thoroughly interested in what the world was thinking and doing, surrounded by cupboards and drawers full of bits and pieces, both provided models of what an old lady might be like. From their characters Agatha was later to draw much that was instructive and entertaining.

2

'... in private
and in your own time ...'

Clara's views on education were almost as inconsistent and 'advanced' as her religious opinions. Agatha was not only to be educated at home, unlike Madge, but Clara now maintained that no child should be allowed to read until it was eight years old, since delay was better for the eyes as well as the brain. This was too much to hope for in Agatha's case. She was fascinated by words and phrases, lived among talkative adults who were natural storytellers and was surrounded by books, many of which had belonged to Madge and Monty: Walter Crane's *Panpipes*, a wonderful book of songs like 'Willow, O Willow' and 'Early One Morning,' with swirling *art nouveau* illustrations of elves, flowers and wreaths; fairy tales like *The Giant's Robe* and *Under the Water*, the story of children who discovered an extraordinary world beneath a stream. One enduring memory was of reading *The Adventures of Herr Baby* while staying with Auntie-Grannie in Ealing. This book, written by Mrs Molesworth in 1881, had belonged to Madge; it is the tale of an irritatingly precocious four-year-old's travels abroad with his family and how he is lost, found and restored to them. Mrs Molesworth's children's books were popular during Agatha's childhood and she acquired them as soon as they were published: *Christmas Tree Land*, for instance, in 1897, and *The Magic Nuts* in 1898. At this time, too, Edith Nesbit was writing marvellous fantasies, all of which Agatha read: *The Story of the Treasure Seekers*, which came out in 1899, when she was nine, *The Phoenix and the Carpet* of 1903 and *The Railway Children* of 1906.

There was also the literature Clara had enjoyed as a child, exciting, simply written, illustrated books from New York, and the volumes she had been given later, like Louisa M. Alcott's unfussy, family-centred *Little Women*, which appeared when Clara was fifteen, and *Little Men*, which came out three years afterwards. Some of Madge's and Monty's books had also come from America, including a series of startling thrillers: *Mr Barnes of New York* (first chapter entitled 'A Vampire Brood'); *Cynthia Wakeham's Money*; *The Masked Venus*; and *Mr Potter of Texas* (Chapter One, 'The Deserted Hotel': 'Sir, I have something to tell you!' – 'My heavens! Is there a woman – an Englishwoman – in this accursed place tonight?').

An increasingly wide range of literature became available for children at the end of the eighteen-nineties and in the early nineteen-hundreds. For small children there were ingenious 'pop-up' books (Madge had a collection) and vividly-illustrated stories, like *Punch and Judy*, but until Beatrix Potter began to produce short books of simply worded tales with pretty drawings (*The Tale of Benjamin Bunny* appeared in 1904) there was little that children aged from four to seven could easily read for themselves. For older children, however, literature brightened up considerably, the work of Edith Nesbit and Frances Hodgson Burnett, for example, being perfectly suited to someone of Agatha's age and circumstances. The language is exact, the sentences uncluttered, and the ideas – missing fortunes from India, tyrannical schoolmistresses, adventurous children, secret gardens, magical cities, juggling with time – just the right mixture of the fantastic and the familiar. Agatha could look up strange words and puzzling references; the Millers' house was well-furnished with encyclopaedias, atlases and dictionaries. These late-Victorian and early-Edwardian children's books were, too, full of complex and extraordinary fantasy, reflecting the hidden themes of 'real life' – quests, adventures, transformations, the wish to make order out of chaos or to obtain justice, the curious effects of money, death and love. Agatha was brought up on such reveries – the weird sketches and mad verse of Edward Lear and the remarkable worlds created by Lewis Carroll (Frederick had bought *Through the Looking Glass* in 1885, when Madge was six), not just those explored by Alice but also the more baffling, yet perfectly comfortable territory of *Sylvie and Bruno*. Like dreaming, reading mirrored and assuaged a child's subconscious turmoil.

In spite of Clara's notion that premature reading was injurious, Agatha received presents of books from an early age. In 1893 Madge gave her *The Ballad of Beau Brocade*, difficult for a three-year-old but with a jolly swing to the lines ('Seventeen hundred and thirty-nine, that was the date of this tale of mine. First Great George was buried and gone, George the Second was plodding on ...'). When she was eight Auntie-Grannie presented

her with *Robinson Crusoe* and, two years later, with Frances
Hodgson Burnett's newly published book, *Granny's Wonderful
Chair* ('Chair of my grandmother, tell me a story ...'). Agatha's
family also encouraged her to read by sending her regular letters,
short and easy, whenever they were parted. Frederick, whose own
taste was for melancholy but uplifting American verse and for
the jauntier Thackeray, sent particularly charming notes. In January 1896, when Agatha was six, her parents took Madge to
America, and Frederick wrote from New York: 'Tell Grannie it
was three degrees below *zero* (thirty-five degrees of frost). You
see all the people in the streets with fur around their throats and
little covers for their ears so they don't get frozen!' Madge took
trouble to print her letters to her 'dear Pip', decorating them with
animals and palm trees, and during their absence Clara wrote
often to 'her sweet darling little girl'. Clara's letters invariably
bore only the vaguest of dates (Agatha inherited this habit) but
postmarks on the envelopes show that when Agatha was seven
she was receiving detailed instructions to help Nursie track down
missing photographs and ensure that Grannie rested properly. By
the time she was five, Agatha had taught herself to read by puzzling
out a text that had often been told aloud to her, L.T. Meade's
The Angel of Love, a long book, full of interesting words like 'monstrous', 'discomfited' and 'tirade'. She used a copy that Monty had
given Madge for Christmas in 1885; its spine is broken and it falls
open at the place where, taking pity on the little girl in the black
and white illustration, whose sisters are saying, 'We think her very
ugly,' Agatha or Madge has coloured her hair with purple crayon.

Frederick now declared that Agatha should also learn to write.
She started with pencil and by the time she was seven graduated
to ink and an italic nib, in which she wrote a large, legible hand,
joining up some of the letters. She had mastered reading by
matching meaning to the appearance of entire words, rather than
single letters, and for a long time she had difficulty in distinguishing B from R. Her spelling was always of the hit and miss sort
that characterises people who remember words by ear rather than
by eye. Madge encouraged Agatha to practise her writing, ruling
a copybook with pencilled lines and writing out sentences for her
sister to follow. Each sentence featured a different letter of the
alphabet and they all had Madge's special touch: for J there was
'Jealousy is a green-eyed monster,' P was represented by 'Pork
pie is made of pig and paste' and I had 'I was an idler, who
idolised play.'

Agatha liked arithmetic, which Frederick taught her every morning after breakfast. He soon moved her on to questions concerning the allocation of apples and pears and the diminution of bathsful of water, problems she enjoyed enormously. Like her father, Agatha had a tidy mind and was naturally quick at sums and tables; later, in her mid-twenties, when she qualified as a dispenser, she had no difficulty in mastering the basic principles of physics and chemistry or remembering the proportions of each substance required to compound a particular drug. Her natural grasp of such concepts as quantity, scale and proportion, together with the fact that she had an ear that was more discerning than her eye, also encouraged her aptitude for music. She learnt to play the mandolin and would practise on her grandmother's piano in the unheated drawing-room at Ealing. Frederick was very musical and could play anything by ear; with her father's help and that of a German music teacher, Fräulein Üder, and her successor, Mr Trotter, Agatha progressed from *The Merry Peasant*, by way of Czerny's *Exercises*, to Schumann and Grieg.

Apart from her music teachers, Agatha had no professional tuition at home but her general education was every bit as good as, if not better than, that of her contemporaries who were formally taught. She read voraciously, devouring Jules Verne's early science fiction and Henty's adventure stories, and tasting the sets of bound volumes Frederick had accumulated: complete editions of George Eliot's works, Mrs Henry Wood's novels, Scott, Dickens, Trollope, Byron and Kipling, sets of the *Cornhill Magazine*, the *Art Journal*, *The Nineteenth Century* and *The Lady's Magazine*, novels by the Brontë sisters and Marion Crawford, Oscar Wilde's poetry, the French classics, thirty volumes by British essayists, Pinero's plays and every novel of Disraeli. All these, save for some racy plays in French, she was allowed to read.

There was, moreover, a great fashion for question and answer books, compendia of general knowledge and books of lists. Dr Brewer's *Child's Guide to Knowledge* was one, full of useful information on which a child could be tested, as in the games played by Agatha's uncles. *The Home Book of Pleasure and Instruction* not only gave directions for such exercises as 'How To Make A Rag Doll Which A Baby May Put Into Its Mouth Safely', but also instructed the reader in 'The Twenty-four Classes of Linnaeus', 'The Synopsis of Seaweed Tribes', 'Hints on Heraldry', 'The Principles of Photography', 'The Classification of Shells', and so on. Such books also contained various games with words and numbers: acrostics, letter and figure charades (TELE-GRAPH: I am a word of nine letters; my one to seven is a Chinese plant; my five, six, seven, one, two, is a fireside requisite; etc.), inversions, rebuses, enigmas, arithmorems, chronograms, cryptographs, and the like. These riddles provided amusement and trained the mind in what is now called lateral thinking. To her interest in order, hierarchy and proportion, Agatha added a liking for manipulating letters and numbers, interpreting codes, and playing with arrangements and sequences to hide or uncover other meanings.

Although Agatha was always defensive about the fact that she had neither gone to school nor had teachers at home, in many ways an education of this sort was as valuable as school lessons would have been, and it was undoubtedly instructive and memorable. She acquired a great deal of general information, learnt how to look things up for herself, and browsed over all manner of subjects. For a short time, when she was about thirteen, she attended classes for two days a week at Miss Guyer's Girls' School in Torquay, where she studied algebra and sought to grasp the rules of grammar and spelling. But, perhaps because her early education had ranged about with such lack of discipline, she was intellectually wayward. She had not been trained to work at subjects that bored her, bother with fundamental rules of spelling and grammar, or follow an argument through logical steps to the end. In itself this was no hardship; there are many ways to be creative and to manage one's life and Agatha's native wit, orderliness and common-sense served her well. Indeed, she managed so well that she was inclined to think 'education' greatly overrated, a common view among highly intelligent, successful people whose formal education has been slender – particularly among women who, for reasons of health or because of their social class or sex, have been discouraged from taking much formal intellectual instruction. Pleasingly, it often goes hand in hand with a great admiration for people – generally men – who have achieved academic success. Agatha, for one, held these two views simultaneously.

She was also scathing towards those who observed, later in her life, that as a girl she had lacked the company of other children. From the age of five or six she was taken by Nursie to dancing classes, where marches, polkas and dances like Sir Roger de Coverley were taught and the children taken through Swedish exercises with silk and elastic chest-expanders. Later, there was Miss

Guyer's and, after that, when Agatha was fifteen, a succession of *pensions* at which she boarded in Paris. The first of these establishments was Mademoiselle Cabernet's, where Madge had crashed among the tea-things and where Agatha now learnt the history and the provinces of France and failed lamentably at dictation, having learnt French, like her native tongue, largely by ear. She made friends among the girls – French, Spanish, Italian and American. She took drawing lessons, at which she was hopeless, and an effete gentleman called Mr Washington Lobb instructed her in dancing and deportment. From Mademoiselle Cabernet's, which Clara judged unsatisfactory, Agatha moved briefly to Les Marroniers, a sound and 'extremely English' school at Auteuil, and from there to Miss Dryden's, a small finishing school in Paris kept by the sister-in-law of Auntie-Grannie's doctor. Here Agatha learnt and recited a great deal of French drama, worked seriously at singing and at the piano with an excellent Austrian teacher, Charles Fürster, and wrote essays on such themes as '*Qu'est-ce que les affections corporatives?*', '*Qu'est-ce que l'esprit de corps?*' and '*Le sublime est-il la même chose que le beau?*' – the sort of philosophical questions, simultaneously sweeping and precise, that were (and still are) typical of French education, and to which Agatha provided typical French answers: full of subjunctive verbs, following a standard pattern and falling into three parts.

It is nonetheless true that Agatha spent much of her early childhood without the companionship and competition of other children. Madge and Monty were away at school, so that for most of the time she was the focus of her parents' notice. She was devoted to her animals – her cat, her Yorkshire terrier, Toby, and Goldie, the canary – and it was with her pets and her imaginary companions – Mrs Benson and the Kittens, Dick and Dick's mistress, and later, a school of invented girls and a dynasty of make-believe kings and queens – that she entertained herself in the schoolroom and the garden at Ashfield and Ealing. Though she did see other children at her dancing class and when they came to tea, there were none in the houses neighbouring Ashfield and in her first ten years or so none with whom she could regularly play and quarrel, share adventures, books, toys, and the time and attention of adults.

When Agatha was five, she at last found some friends. Frederick, whose income was diminishing (it turned out that his business managers in America had made unfortunate investments and disbursements of the property that supported his father's trust), decided to let Ashfield for the winter and take the family abroad, where the cost of living was lower. The practice of moving to France or Italy was not uncommon among English upper-class people who felt the need to economise in a good climate and there were certain towns in France and Italy where it was fashionable to stay. Pau, in South-West France, looking out from a crest to the Pyrenees, was one of these. It had crisp, clean air, which in the early nineteenth century had given it the reputation of being particularly healthy, and the proprietors of its large and ornate hotels were accustomed to taking English and American visitors for long stays. There were English bookshops and tearooms, and even an English hunt. It was, in fact, rather like Torquay, with French food and, to Agatha's amazement, since no one had warned her, the French language. Instead of sea, there were mountains, and it was there when summer came, that at the little town of Cauterets she met three or four English and American girls of her own age, with whom she could romp and explore. Like other children, she found living in a big hotel particularly agreeable, with its huge public rooms, empty at certain times of the day, long corridors for racing, interesting lifts and surprising staircases. There was more forbidden territory than at home and, precisely because it was not home, more scope for mischief. Feuds could be sustained and alliances struck with pages, maids and waiters (one, called Victor, used to carve mice out of radishes for Agatha and her friends), pacts and contests more intense than engagements with the servants at home, because, being transient figures, hotel staff could be teased with less risk. All summer long Agatha larked about with Dorothy and Mary Selwyn – putting sugar in the salt-cellars, cutting pigs out of orange peel to decorate astonished visitors' plates – and, when the Selwyns left Cauterets, conspiring with Margaret Home, an English girl, and Marguerite Prestley, an American, whose chief attraction was her fascinating pronunciation and vocabulary and her possession of a good deal of inaccurate but ingenious biological information. In old age Agatha remembered this interlude clearly and affectionately.

When September came her parents moved on to Paris and then to Brittany. In Dinard they found some old friends and their two sons, but the boys took scant notice of the little seven-year-old, and Agatha's recollections were chiefly of their mother, Lilian Pirie, whom she greatly admired, and continued to see at intervals over the next forty years. Mrs Pirie's character and habits – she was well-informed, well-read, and decorated her houses in 'a startling and original manner' – in some respects resembled Agatha's own. The Millers' last stay was in the Channel Islands, not Jersey where Clara had spent her first nine years, but Guernsey, where Agatha once again found herself playing alone, constructing stories about three exotic birds she had been given for her birthday.

Nursie had long before retired and, after the failure of a number of unfortunate experiments with French governesses hired in Pau, Clara carried off, with one of her capricious master-strokes, the assistant at a dressmaker's establishment there. This was Marie Sijé, a sweet-natured, conscientious twenty-two-year-old, the middle sister in a family of five children. Marie spoke no English and it was from her that Agatha learnt her idiomatic and fluent French, never accurate on the page but always intelligible and convincing in speech. The two quickly became excellent friends, Marie depending on Agatha, as much as Agatha on Marie, for stimulus and reassurance, particularly when they came home to Torquay, where the other maids thought the French girl very odd, with her plain wardrobe and simple habits, sending home the greater part of her wages and saving the rest for her *dot*. Agatha, who noticed Marie's homesickness and unhappiness, admired her industry and good sense; the impoverished but determined young women who eventually appeared in some of her stories (in *The Hollow* one works for a sour-tempered dressmaker) are a belated compliment.

At Ashfield, however, Agatha saw less of Marie than during their months of companionship in France. It was then that she invented the School, not, she wrote later, 'because I had any desire myself to go to school,' but because it constituted 'the only background into which I could conveniently fit seven girls of varying ages and appearances ... instead of making them a family, which I did not want to do.' Their faces and figures were based on reproductions of pictures in the Royal Academy which Agatha found in Auntie-Grannie's bound volumes and on the representations of flowers in human form drawn by Walter Crane in *The Feast of Flora*, a book which now seems droopingly sentimental but which was very popular in Agatha's youth.

Agatha discussed 'the girls' at length in her autobiography. The one about which she said least was 'Sue de Verte', whom she described as 'curiously colourless, not only in appearance ... but also in character'. This, Agatha said, was probably because Sue really stood for herself, being the character the author assumed in order to take part in the story, 'an observer, not really one of the dramatis personae'. This was appropriate because, although she did not say so, when Agatha invented the girls she was naturally unclear about the sort of person she was or might become. Any tentative ideas she entertained were embodied not in Sue de Verte but in the seventh girl to be added to her collection, 'Sue's step-sister, Vera de Verte', aged thirteen, who was to grow up into 'a raving beauty', her 'straw-coloured hair and forget-me-not blue eyes' being already more impressive than the vaguer features of Sue. There was also a mystery about Vera's parentage (as girls of Agatha's age often wish there might be about their own). For want of any better ideas, Agatha 'half planned various futures for Vera of a highly romantic nature'.

More real girls, luckily, broke into Agatha's life when she was twelve. At the beginning of September 1902, Madge, now twenty-three, married James Watts, the quietest and steadiest of her many beaux but the one on whom the perceptive Marie, with whom Agatha used to assess their chances, had firmly placed her bet. In the unpublished first draft of Agatha's autobiography she recalled with much animation the fun and excitement she enjoyed with her fellow bridesmaids. All their names are there: Norah Hewitt, who dashed out into the garden, a mackintosh and tarpaulins protecting her from the rain, to cut marguerites and daisies for the church; Constance Boyd, another friend of Madge's; 'Little Ada', the adopted daughter of Great-Uncle Jack; and, Agatha's greatest discovery, the bridegroom's younger sister, Nan. It was with Lionel and Miles, Nan's younger brothers, and Gerald Boehmer, Agatha's cousin, that she and Nan inflicted 'every variety of torture' on the newly-married couple – rice in suitcases, a notice on the back of the carriage proclaiming 'Mrs Jimmy Watts is a first-class name' – and with these other children that she let off steam by steeple-chasing round the schoolroom. Nan, a tomboy of fifteen to whom Agatha had been held up as a model of politeness, and Agatha, to whom Nan had been presented as the epitome of wit and sociability, immediately liked each other; each went to stay with the other, Agatha acquired Nan's cast-off clothes, Nan learnt to drink a cup of cream.

From this moment, too, Agatha began to make a number of local friends. She saw, for example, a great deal of Dr and Mrs Huxley's five daughters, whom she joined in the singing class they shared with three or four other girls, under the tutelage of the happily named Dr Crow. The Huxley girls were unusual and enterprising, shocking older Torquay society by their lively behaviour, which included the fact that they did not wear gloves. They merrily carried Agatha along with their plans, inducing her to take part in *The Yeomen of the Guard*, of which three performances were given in the Parish Rooms, to the vast amusement of the family and friends in the audience. James Watts in particular never forgot this exhibition. 'Of course,' Agatha reflected years later, 'it must have been very funny. A large quantity of weak girls with squeaky breathy voices, producing the scene in the Tower of London, practically all in male roles.' She always remembered with special hilarity her own difficulties with the middle-aged governess, drafted into the performance at the last moment to replace someone who was ill, whom she had to clasp around the waist while addressing loving phrases to her – 'a kind of feeling of *lèse-majesté*' was how Agatha described it.

The Yeomen of the Guard, Agatha maintained, was 'one of the highlights of my existence'. Tall, with a clear, thin soprano voice, she played Colonel Fairfax, and her confident performance surprised her family. Agatha felt no stage-fright and later ascribed to this apprenticeship her lack of nervousness when it came to singing before other people. In all other respects, however, she remained very shy. It is difficult for people who are naturally outgoing to appreciate the agonies of someone who, as Agatha confessed, 'can hardly bring herself to enter a shop and has to grit her teeth before entertaining a large party'. Madge inherited Auntie-Grannie's chattiness, Agatha the reserve of Grannie B. and Clara. In her quiet childhood, she grew up to be a listener rather than a talker; obliged to show her paces before other people, she could be overcome by nervousness. Before the end of term concert at Mademoiselle Cabernet's she was beset by anxiety, dreaming at night of the piano being transmuted into an organ, of notes sticking, or of being late, and, self-protectively, fell ill with such high fever that she was forbidden to take part. The Gilbert and Sullivan performance with the Huxleys was different; it was delivered with friends before people she knew. Outside a circle of those she trusted, she would never be entirely comfortable and her early solitude had something to do with that. Agatha learnt to work by herself and to discipline herself; she liked to make her own pace. As she was later to write, 'the most blessed thing about being an author is that you do it in private and *in your own time.*' Perhaps the company and competition of other children would have changed her; perhaps not. At any rate, she made the best of her instincts and inclinations.

3

'. . . a possession that is yours to do what you like with'

Although Agatha lacked companions of her own age, her child-hood was happy and secure. The adults in her world were kind and thoughtful; her parents did not quarrel; the servants were equable and stayed for years; the household kept to a stable routine; her grandmothers, slow and massive, dispensed wise words and regular treats; birthdays and other anniversaries were properly celebrated and the progress of the seasons was marked with appropriate entertainments – sea-bathing, picnics, Christmas pantomime – and feasts – asparagus, strawberries and salmon, game, turkey and plum pudding. There was a comfortable order and predictability to life; in Agatha's recollections of her child-hood there are unexpected pleasures but no broken promises. Her world was private and safe: Ashfield and Ealing were large enough and the family sufficiently small for her to have her own quarters with her possessions around her. She was given responsi-bility for amusing herself and looking after her animals and birds, but the management of her surroundings was in the safe hands of sensible adults. She could see clearly where authority lay: her father was, as she put it, 'the rock' on which the family rested; her mother's wishes shaped the management of the house and its members' behaviour to one another; each grandmother was in charge of her domain at Ealing or in Bayswater; Nursie super-vised Agatha and the Nursery; Jane's sphere of influence was the kitchen; and the parlourmaid too had her own territory. These were, moreover, all adults whose authority Agatha could venerate because she respected both their characters and their professional skills. They took her questions seriously and considered her re-quests carefully; there were no absurd rules. Only when Agatha went to her *pensions* did she find regulations enforced for regu-lations' sake; by then she had some self-knowledge and the sup-port of more confident contemporaries to help her tolerate rather than be awed by people in charge. As a child she never found the grown-ups around her pettily tyrannical and the only example of injustice she later recalled was the scolding she and her friends in Pau were given when they were caught walking along a parapet at the hotel, an exploit that had not been specifically forbidden because no one had thought of it before.

Agatha was not entirely untroubled. From time to time she had a particularly disturbing dream, which she described in her autobiography and in the novel *Unfinished Portrait* which she published, as Mary Westmacott, in 1934. The nightmare varied only slightly: she would dream of some sort of festivity, a family party or a picnic, at which she would suddenly be conscious of the presence of someone who was not supposed to be there. This was the 'Gun Man', frightening not because he carried a gun but because of his strange and terrifying way of staring at her with his pale blue eyes. Originally the Gun Man had the look of 'a Frenchman, in grey-blue uniform, powdered hair in a queue, and a kind of three-cornered hat, ... the gun ... some old-fashioned kind of musket'. In later dreams Agatha, among her family and friends, would suddenly realise that, though they seemed familiar, one of them, perhaps Clara, was really the Gun Man. The manifestation described in *Unfinished Portrait* is even worse: 'You looked up in Mummy's face – of course it was Mummy – and then you saw the light steely-blue eyes – and from the sleeve of Mummy's dress – oh, horror! – that horrible stump.'

Agatha was never able to fix on the source of this nightmare, maintaining that it resembled nothing she had overheard or read. Perhaps the picture in her mind came from something she had forgotten, an advertisement on a hoarding, or the illustrations of 'The Man that Went Out Shooting' and the horrid 'Scissor-Man' in 'Little Suck-A-Thumb', two stories in her copy of Dr Hoffman's appalling *Struwwelpeter*. Her terrors may have been intensified by adults' talk, or Madge's game of the mad 'Elder Sister', but her dream must have had some underlying cause. Its form – of someone familar and loving suddenly transformed into a hostile stranger – suggests that she may have doubted whether those who were supposed to love her actually did. This may seem odd. Clara and Frederick did not neglect Agatha (indeed, according to Madge and Monty, she was petted and spoilt) and she herself emphasised how close she and Clara always were. But relationships between parents and children are intricate and strange: even when profound and genuine love is demonstrated in innumerable ways, one, both or all can feel insecure and excluded. Later in her life Agatha was often to write about the destructive power of love, about possessiveness, the relations between mothers and daughters and the nature of the maternal instinct, while the theme of an adopted son or daughter or a distant relation's joining the household occurs repeatedly in her detective stories. These are the preoccupations of someone acutely aware of the complexities of family life. Serene on the surface, Agatha's childhood was vaguely, but not unmanageably, disturbed beneath. Her idea of misery, as she wrote in the 'Confessions' at the age of four, was 'Someone I love to go away from me.'

Two shadows fell over the Miller household, of which Agatha was dimly aware: anxiety about illness and about money. By the time she was five, Frederick's business affairs had fallen into a sorry state, and it was then that the mishandling of Nathaniel's trust obliged the Millers to economise by letting Ashfield and spending a year abroad. On their return they found matters no better. Money that had been invested in leasehold property in New York City brought little or no income, being mostly swallowed up in repairs or taxation. One of the trustees, who wrote Frederick encouraging but baffling letters, eventually shot himself. Frederick took himself to New York to try to sort matters out but had no success; in any case, as Agatha wrote later, he was a trusting man whom it was easy to swindle. On one occasion, after the Millers' return from France, Agatha overheard her parents discussing their financial difficulties, which she not unnaturally compared to the catastrophes befalling the families described in the books she read. (Edith Nesbit's *The Railway Children* and *The Story of the Treasure Seekers* were two, with the father wrongfully arrested in the first story and losing all his money in the second.) She straightway announced to Marie that they were ruined. When this reached Clara's ears, she reproached Agatha and quickly dispelled her melodramatic visions, explaining that they were simply badly-off and would have to economise. This was disappointing because it was unsensational; it was also not entirely reassuring.

Where money came from and why it came at all were in any case mysteries to Agatha. As her father did not go off each day to any sort of business, her notion of the connection between the expenditure of effort and the earning of money was vague. The amount of her own pocket money fluctuated from day to day; it was not computed according to any obvious principle – so much for each year of her age, or whatever – but consisted of what copper coins Frederick turned out of his pockets. 'I would visit him in his dressing room, say good morning, and then turn to the dressing table to see what Fate had decreed for me ... Twopence? Fivepence? Once a whole elevenpence! Some days, no coppers at all. The uncertainty made it rather exciting.' Prosperity or penury, then, depended largely on 'Fate'. This was the theme of some of Agatha's own early inventions, like the story of Mrs Benson and the kittens, precipitated into direst poverty when the Captain went down at sea but, with his reappearance, restored to vast wealth 'just when things had become quite desperate'. As money arrived in some inexplicable fashion, so it could vanish away. Now Agatha could see that her parents were worried and that these anxieties were making her father ill.

Frederick had first felt seedy while the family was in France, where he had seen a couple of doctors, one of whom diagnosed kidney disease. His own doctor in Torquay disagreed and other diagnoses were then made by different specialists. He suffered from attacks of pain and breathlessness, exacerbated, it seemed, by worry about his financial affairs. None of the treatments prescribed – rest, a diet of hot water and hot minced beef, and so forth – produced any improvement. Clara, a keen reader of *The Lancet* and the *British Medical Journal*, found the variations in diagnosis and prescription extremely trying, but she continued to encourage Frederick by telling him how much better he looked.

Frederick, however, was very unwell. He methodically kept a list of 'Heart Attacks' – fifteen bouts between April 1899 and June 1901 and another thirty, mostly late at night, between June and September. He continued to seek treatment; in late October he stayed with his stepmother in Ealing and went again to see one of the most respected specialists. A letter to Clara from his Club shows how desperately they had been searching for remedies:

My darling Clara, I saw Sansom this morning & he told me very much the same thing as last time. He insisted that my trouble has more to do with the nerves of the heart than anything else and recommends very much the same thing as before – viz. plenty of fresh air, distilled water, milk after meals & later perhaps cod liver oil (emulsion) or Extract of Malt and moderate exercise. He says most positively that my heart is not dilated and is of normal size & there is nothing valvular wrong but that it is weak & irregular. ... He does not think the lying up system advisable but would compromise by having me lie on a sofa a part of the day with the window open &

fresh air blowing over me. I have felt wonderfully better the last two days – better in fact than I have for 3 weeks – scarcely any breathlessness & splendid nights. I don't know whether this is owing to a prescription of Taylor's with digitalin in it or to my doing much less walking ... I have decided to return on Wednesday next 30th if all goes well. I should much prefer – between ourselves, coming down now but Mother is so kind and good that I cannot bear to disappoint her. I can't tell you how nice she has been to me & I know she was greatly worried in the early part of the week. I didn't tell Sansom that I had been under homeopathy. ...

Ill though he was, Frederick never seemed to Agatha to become cross or irritable and, as far as he could, he lived much as before. One letter to Clara reported that he had lunched at the Naval and Military 'with the best appetite I have had for weeks – roast beef & spinach & rice pudding' and that his stepmother had taken him to *The Silver Slipper* – 'very pretty music and fairly amusing'. That letter ended cheerfully: 'I am now, please God, done with Doctors, & hope I may get better soon. Love to my dear ones. I hope Agatha is better today [she had a cold]. The weather is again vile today. I hope this letter will make you feel happier & I think you will see by its tone that I certainly am. God bless you, my darling.' Less than a month later, Frederick returned to Ealing, to see friends in London who might help him to find some sort of job. He caught a chill, which turned to double pneumonia; Clara and, eventually, Madge and Agatha, were summoned. On November 26th, at the age of fifty-five, he died.

Agatha, who was eleven, fixed that moment as the end of her childhood. Her world was vulnerable; for the first time she felt responsible for someone else: Clara. Her parents' marriage had been a good one. Hannah, the cook at Ealing, who took Agatha into the kitchen on the pretext that she needed help mixing the pastry, told her again and again, 'They were very devoted.' The rest of the household crept about and whispered, sighing over Clara's prostration. She was devastated by Frederick's death. In her autobiography Agatha spoke of Frederick's last letter to her mother: 'You have made all the difference in my life. No man ever had a wife like you. Every year I have been married to you I love you more.' With it Clara kept the notebooks she had embroidered for him, the order of service from his funeral, some beech leaves from Ealing Cemetery, the little account book in which he recorded his expenditure, with a few of his fine, pale brown hairs pressed between the pages, and the piece of Pears soap he had last used. On a card placed with this collection was written: 'There are four things that come not back to man or woman: 1. The Spoken Word. 2. The Sped Arrow. 3. The Past Life. 4. The Neglected Opportunity.'

After three weeks in France with Madge, Clara returned to Ashfield, where Agatha was waiting alone. Monty was now abroad with his regiment. He had worked in a shipyard on the Dart in Devon and afterwards in Lincolnshire but had failed in his efforts to become an engineer. The outbreak of the Boer War in 1899 settled his choice of career. He volunteered for the 3rd Battalion of the Royal Welsh Regiment and, at the end of the War in 1902, obtained a commission with the East Surreys and proceeded to India. Madge and James lived in the North, at Cheadle, near James's parents. Clara and Agatha were left together at Ashfield; as Agatha put it, 'We were no longer the Millers – a family. We were now two people living together, a middle-aged woman and an untried, naïve girl.' Her description of herself is illuminating: she was, after all, only eleven. Though written years later, it is a reminder of how vulnerable and responsible she suddenly felt. There was little money. Auguste Montant, Frederick's executor, explained to Clara that most of Nathaniel's estate had disappeared. H.B. Chaflin & Co., of which Nathaniel had been a partner, would continue to provide an income for his widow, Margaret, and a small income for Clara, while the three children, Agatha, Madge and Monty, would each receive an income from the trust of £100 a year. Sensibly, Clara decided to sell Ashfield and find a smaller house; she preferred cathedral towns to the seaside and rather enjoyed the prospect of living somewhere like Exeter. But her children violently protested; Monty writing from India, Madge and James offering to help with running expenses, and Agatha, especially, desperately begging her mother not to abandon their home. Agatha's attitude is particularly interesting. She wrote in her autobiography of Clara's unselfishness in bowing to her children's protestations and spoke of the anxiety and expense she herself was to reap from that decision. At no point, however, was she apologetic or defensive. On the contrary, she emphasised the deep importance of Ashfield in her own life and, having talked of her mother's feelings, her tone of voice changed and she wrote only of her own love for that house, the price she was to pay for it and her emotions at their eventual parting. It was as if, having had her father snatched away, she felt it only right for her to keep Ashfield. Her sense of responsibility for her mother seems to have been matched by a feeling that it was her particular duty to protect and maintain their home.

After Frederick's death, Agatha became increasingly anxious lest Clara should be run over by a tram or die suddenly in the night; she would creep along the passage and listen at the door to ensure that her mother was still breathing. Although, as Agatha admitted, children of twelve or thirteen do suffer such exaggerated worries, Clara's condition did give grounds for concern. She, too, had suffered a number of mild heart attacks and eventually Agatha took to sleeping in what had been Frederick's dressing room, next to Clara's bedroom, to be on hand to revive her in the night with brandy or sal volatile. This is not to say that Clara was a prostrate invalid. In many ways she was as lively as ever, suddenly carrying Agatha off to hear Sir Henry Irving ('He may not live much longer and you must see him, a great actor. We've just time to catch the train . . .') and, when she accompanied Agatha to Paris, going with her to the theatre and the opera.

Clara depended largely on Agatha for companionship and amusement. They could no longer afford to entertain at home and, partly for that reason, Clara did not often go out to lunch or to dine. In any case, the position of a widow, even a young one, was different from that of a woman with a husband to escort her, particularly if, as in Clara's case, she had not been accutomed to going about alone even before her marriage. In the evenings she and Agatha would read aloud from Scott, Thackeray and, their favourite, Dickens – Clara, who wanted light nearer than the gas jets, balancing a candlestick on her chest.

Clara's circle had been enlarged, however, by Madge's marriage. James Watts's mother, Annie Browne, had been a great friend of Clara's when they were schoolgirls and it was in this way that Madge and James had met. James came from a prosperous Manchester family, whose fortunes derived from a colonial export business founded by his grandfather, Sir James Watts. In his palatial warehouses Sir James stored the bicycles, alarm clocks, flannel trousers and other goods destined for the furthest reaches of the Empire. His house, Abney Hall, was an equally famous sight. An enormous Victorian Gothic mansion, it had been altered and extended at Sir James's direction and included a vast room that was used for religious and political gatherings, for Sir James was Lord Mayor of Manchester. The Prince Consort was entertained at Abney, while Mr and Mrs Gladstone and, on a separate occasion, Mr and Mrs Disraeli had stayed there. Madge's father-in-law, James Watts Senior, had inherited the house in the late eighteen-seventies. An antiquarian and amateur photographer, he had continued to embellish and enrich it until it almost overwhelmed the occupants.

Much of Abney's lavish ornamentation, including its carvings, carpets, furniture and hangings, was 'Gothic revival'; indeed, the work was based on designs by Pugin, architect of the newly re-built Houses of Parliament. There were innumerable staircases, alcoves, galleries and arches, all fancifully decorated. Windows of coloured glass were traceried, mullioned and ornamented with gargoyles. The main drawing-room had a frieze on which a proverb was endlessly repeated, the walls were hung with green damask covered with more hangings stencilled in bright colours, and the ceiling had octagon-shaped inverted pinnacles, tipped with gold, descending from each panel – 'like the Alhambra,' the children said. Another drawing-room, bursting with chintz-covered sofas, had a fireplace set in a huge curlicued marble chimney-piece. The woodwork and the papier-mâché carving of doorways and shutters was picked out in ultramarine, vermilion and green; ceilings and tiles were initialled; doorhandles, lock-plates and hinges, grates, candelabra and standard lamps were all specially designed. Agatha remembered Abney as having three pianos and an organ and, years later, when it was sold, harpsichords and virginals were discovered here and there (as well as half a valuable tapestry whose remainder had hung for centuries in a church in Bruges). Every corridor was crowded with oak chests and every wall hung with paintings, some by Madge's father-in-law. There was a room for jigsaws and in the garden a lake, a waterfall, a tunnel and a set of houses for children to play in, one a small fort with its own pointed windows and crenellations.

Madge and her husband lived at Cheadle Hall, a Georgian house nearby. Agatha and Clara spent part of every winter there, for after 1903, when Madge's son Jack was born, they would go north to look after him while his parents went to St Moritz for skating, and at Christmas they joined the whole Watts family at Abney, feasting gloriously with James and Annie, Madge and James, Madge's four brothers-in-law and her sister-in-law Nan. Christmas Day was especially strenuous, with a huge lunch, tea and supper, interspersed with quantities of chocolates, preserved fruits and confections from the store-room, to which, unlike its counterpart at Ealing, access was unrestrained. On Boxing Day there was an expedition to Manchester to the pantomime, while Abney itself was pervaded by charades and dressing-up, for all the Watts family, apart from James, were enthusiastic actors. Humphrey, James's brother, who was eight or nine years older than Agatha, had his own theatre in Manchester, while Lionel, another brother, acted professionally in London. Madge, too, never lost her mania for disguise. Once, late in her married life, she came down to dinner dressed as a cricketer, in black breeches, cricket cap and shorts. James disapproved, but she induced Agatha to show solidarity by assuming the appearance and manners of a Turkish woman; entirely swaddled in black, she sat through the meal making little belching noises, as Madge instructed. (Jack Watts, Madge's son, had the same trait. As an undergraduate at Oxford he is reputed to have dressed up in women's clothing, on one occasion as the Virgin Mary.)

From the day of his birth Jack gave Agatha great pleasure; she was then thirteen, still baffled as to how babies originated and ignorant as to how long they took to arrive, but enthusiastically assuming the duties of an aunt. Her autobiography has many descriptions of Jack's sayings and doings and her album pages of photographs of her playing with him, reading to him and, wearing a large oilskin cap like a pudding-basin cover, taking him bathing in the sea. Agatha liked small boys and from the age of twelve until her marriage at the age of twenty-four she saw a good number – the children of her mother's friends or of her own. One of these remembered, years later, playing at Ashfield when he was three and she was twenty. He had sprinkled someone's feet with a watering-can and, when Agatha told him he was a rascal, gleefully cried out, 'And you're a lady rascal.' She carried him off to the schoolroom, riding on her back, so he called her 'Lady Elephant', and, when she showed him the stuffed swans in two glass cases in the Billiard Room, he called her 'Lady Swan'. Agatha remembered this occasion too; nearly twenty years afterwards she brought back a lapis lazuli elephant from the East as a present for her former playmate, and the game they played is described by Mrs Ariadne Oliver in *Elephants Can Remember*.

From 1902 or thereabouts, Agatha's companions were not just little boys of her nephew's age. This was the time when she was sent for lessons first to Miss Guyer's and then to the succession of French *pensions*, in part, perhaps, because Clara did not wish that the two of them should become too exclusively dependent on each other's company. At home in Torquay Agatha was now old enough to go about independently with other young people – the Huxleys, Hoopers, Morrises, Lucys, Bushes and Thellusons: to the Fair, where they bought nougat from a stall and rode on switchbacks and gilded roundabout horses, the girls sitting side-saddle, balancing their fruit, flower and ribbon-laden hats; to the Regattas at Dartmouth and Torquay, where they watched the yachts from the quay and the fireworks in the evening. There were teas and suppers on neighbours' lawns and grand garden parties, with splendid ices and cakes, served by professional waiters, whom they knew because they also helped at dinner parties. Agatha's album has many photographs of young men in high starched collars and young women in muslin leg-of-mutton blouses or narrow-waisted, fur-trimmed costumes, their skirts only a few inches from the ground, playing croquet or manipulating the sticks and strings of the new game called Diabolo.

In the morning Agatha and the Lucys would take their skates and pay their twopences to go roller-skating on the pier; there is a picture of the five of them, holding hands in a line, just managing not to roll away. Agatha, tall and slender, with quantities of thick, pale hair, is wearing a splendid hat with three or four pheasant's tail-feathers sticking out at a dashing angle. Prim though Torquay society was at that time, with its careful segregation of the classes and the sexes, it afforded many amusements for the young – yachting and tennis, roller-skating, eating fresh mussels and oysters bought mid-morning, listening to the Royal Marines' String Band. It was also a healthy place; the train that steamed into Torre had reached the end of the line and, though horse-drawn cabs and broughams plied between the station at the top and the Quay at the bottom of the town, Agatha and her friends usually walked everywhere, up and down Torquay's seven hills, in the clear sea air. In the summer she would cheerfully walk the two or three miles to and from her favourite swimming place; she adored sea-bathing and continued to take every opportunity to swim until she was very old. It is not surprising that she and her friends had hearty appetites, nor that, despite them, they retained their elegant shapes. Artifice helped. In a list she drew up in the nineteen-sixties comparing the advantages and disadvantages of 'Then and Now', Agatha put first among the drawbacks of the early nineteen-hundreds: 'Boned collars of muslin blouses. Most painful, giving red sore places,' and, 'Corsets.

One was encased in a kind of armour of whalebone, tightened round the waist and coming up like a painful shield over one's bosom.' That, and the rest of the list, gave a crisp summing-up of her circumstances; the disadvantages continued with: 'Patent leather high-heeled shoes in which one went to garden parties. This entailed walking in them for anything up to three miles, holding up one's long skirts at the same time. A refined form of Chinese torture. Long skirts. A continual nuisance, though useful because one could dust one's patent leather shoes on the back of one's stockings on arrival at a party, and your skirt concealed all. Cold hands and feet, and chilblains. Agony in winter. Children's, and others', tight buttoned boots. (Probably the cause of the chilblains.) Hair dos. Elaborate and painstaking, and usually entailing the use of tongs.'

The advantages, though fewer in number, were as deeply felt: 'High standard of domestic comfort. Fire lit before you got up, cans of hot water brought at intervals all day. Luxurious train travel. Hot foot-warmers pushed in at stations at intervals, lots of porters to handle luggage, delectable lunch baskets, comfortable carriages and well cleaned. Leisure. Our greatest loss. The one really valuable thing in life – a possession that is yours to do what you like with. Without it, where are you?'

4

'... she will have to make up
her mind between them
some time ...'

Though Agatha was strong and happily occupied, Clara was unwell and her life emptier than before. Shortly after Agatha's return from Miss Dryden's in 1910, her mother fell seriously ill; no doctor could diagnose exactly what was wrong – they suggested, variously, gallstones, paratyphoid and appendicitis. Disenchanted with all of them, Clara took matters into her own hands. She believed she needed a change and, having found a doctor who advised her to try sunshine and a warm climate, settled on Egypt. This was not a bizarre choice. Near and Middle Eastern countries that today seem exotic and somewhat dangerous to Europeans were much less mysterious to the Victorians and Edwardians. They were in large part administered by the British (and, here and there, the French), there were regular sailings to and fro and Thomas Cook and Sons were used to making arrangements. Egypt was a particularly sensible place to spend the winter; it was dry and sunny and not too far away, Cairo had reputable hotels where English people stayed, several regiments were stationed nearby, there was polo to watch and a dance at one or other of the hotels nearly every night of the week. As Clara could not afford to give Agatha a London season of dances and afternoon parties like that which Madge had enjoyed in New York, Cairo was a perfect substitute. It was not expensive, there would be Englishwomen to give Clara some society and English girls for Agatha to mix with, but not so many and so smart that she would be daunted, and plenty of unattached young men with whom she could dance, flirt and go on expeditions and among whom she might even discover a husband.

They sailed on the SS *Heliopolis* and installed themselves for three months at the Gezirah Palace Hotel. Chaperoned by Clara, Agatha went to some fifty dances. She was profoundly irritated by the difficulty of putting up her hair, which was so long that she could sit on it; dressing it with an artificial knot of curls was almost impossible. She took, however, enormous pleasure in her first evening dresses: one of pale green chiffon with small lace frills, a plain one of white taffeta and a third of deep turquoise material, produced by Auntie-Grannie from one of her bottomless chests but so fragile that during the course of a dance it split in all directions. Its replacement 'bought from one of the Levantine dressmakers of Cairo' (a fashionable one, Agatha believed, since the dress was very expensive), was pale pink shot satin with a bunch of pink rosebuds on one shoulder. This wardrobe is described in *Unfinished Portrait*, whose heroine Celia, during her own season in Cairo, is obliged to pad the bodice with the 'delicate ruchings of net' called 'plumpers', being, like Agatha, tall and thin.

Agatha's photograph album shows how they passed the afternoons. There were the Cairo Races, attended by the Duke of Connaught, and Spring Manoeuvres (the pictures show the officers sitting on folding stools and the men on the ground); there was the Review, watched from a pavilion by the visitors, the ladies wearing muslin veils to protect them from the sun. Dashing officers mounted on beautiful horses brandished polo sticks and leapt over hurdles, and, with boaters and cigars at a rakish angle, perched on tables or lay languidly in wicker chairs during leisurely tea parties. There was an expedition to the Citadel and a picnic in the desert (at which the ladies in their whalebone sat heroically in canvas deckchairs). There was also, as at home, croquet and Diabolo.

Egypt was not yet the object of popular fascination that it was to become in the early nineteen-twenties, when Howard Carter's archaeological investigations were crowned with the opening of Tutankhamun's tomb. Some of the findings of early explorers were, however, to be seen in the Cairo Museum and Clara tried to persuade Agatha to accompany her there. Agatha, vastly enjoying her new acquaintances and social preoccupations, resisted her mother's entreaties. Nor did she wish to make an expedition up the Nile to visit Karnak or Luxor, although she was taken to see the Pyramids and the Sphinx, where she was photographed, sitting confidently on a donkey. It was not, then, this first stay in Egypt that stimulated Agatha's later interest in antiquities and archaeology but it was certainly a happy visit, her first association of the East with feelings of comfort, amusement and success.

At least one of the attentive young subalterns and captains immortalised in Agatha's photograph album asked Mrs Miller whether he might 'speak to' her daughter. The only men who stirred her heart, however, were a couple of bronzed colonels of thirty-five or forty, who conceded an occasional dance and teased the 'pretty young thing'. Agatha was, moreover, still shy, with no conversation. Indeed, one of the older men said as he returned her to Clara after a dance: 'Here's your daughter. She has learnt to dance, in fact she dances beautifully. You had better try and teach her to talk now.' This was Captain Crake, who had accompanied the party to the Citadel. From his photograph he looks a playful fellow, shown kneeling in his tartan trews and looking upwards at the tennis ball his fiancée is about to drop on his head. In *Unfinished Portrait*, Agatha made a joke of this remark, but, though justified, it was cruel.

During her stay, Agatha made friends with at least twenty or thirty young men and that, after all, was the main objective. In her autobiography she has much to say about the procedure by which girls of her age and class were launched into adult life, into a world where public affairs were with few exceptions managed by men, and older men at that. Her description is of a time of gaiety and freedom, the season in which girls who might have known few young men intimately, apart from their brothers and other male relations, might now meet large numbers of them from much the same background and with much the same expectations as themselves, while youths, hitherto confined to each others' company at school, in the Army or Navy, might at last encounter girls other than their sisters and female cousins. From a circle so dramatically enlarged, a suitable mate might be selected. Agatha was delightfully straightforward about this; several passages in her *Autobiography* explain what it was like to find herself, as she put it, in 'the world of females on the prowl', looking for 'their Fate'. She reminds us that, certainly before the First World War, when she was a girl, and arguably up to the Second, the career which middle and upper-middle-class women were exhorted to seek, the destiny promised them by mothers, grandmothers, sisters and aunts, nannies, popular literature and social convention, was marriage. 'No worry,' she wrote, 'about what you should be or do – Biology would dictate. You were waiting for The Man and, when The Man came, he would change your entire life.'

Here was a collection of young people, at their most healthy and attractive, primed with romantic anticipation, lacking sexual experience but not sexual exuberance: as Agatha later said, 'We didn't need pep pills; we didn't need sedatives.' They were not careworn or anxious; Agatha attributed this to the fact that neither examinations nor careers weighed them down. Their responsibilities were limited: the world's affairs were considered a matter for adults and the business of the young was held to be emotion, not facts. As for their own entanglements, shrewd social arrangements minimised risk. Chaperones were ever present and philandering men and 'fast' girls who flouted convention were as far as possible excluded from dances and weekend parties. Overall, a careful balance was struck. On the one hand the young were encouraged to indulge intensely romantic emotion; on the other, they were protected from the consequences of mistakes which, given their innocence and inexperience, they might easily make. Life was, as Agatha recalled, 'great fun'; it was also reasonably safe.

Agatha's own friends, particularly the younger married couples, rallied round to assist in this process of maximising choice while minimising risk. On her return from Cairo she found herself invited four or five times a year for country house visits, of which the centrepiece might be a local hunt or military ball, a race meeting, a regatta. Attractive young people to fill the house and help make up a party were much in demand and it was not necessary to be rich to enjoy friends' hospitality and do them credit. There were, of course, fares to find and the right clothes, though not necessarily many. Although the getting and spending of money was thought an inappropriate subject for conversation, people breezily acknowledged into which serviceable category – 'very rich', 'well-off', 'not well-off', 'poor' – their friends and acquaintances came. Hosts and hostesses ensured that impoverished girls were not induced to gamble for money at cards or at the races; once arrived at a house there would be no unexpected expenses, apart from small tips to the maid. What is more, certainly in the society in which Agatha spent her girlhood, there was little defensiveness about being badly off or, for that matter, rich, perhaps because in other ways – socially, morally, even as a nation – people felt easy and assured. There was no shame in retrimming a hat, recycling the same six dresses or wearing mended stockings; there was, moreover, time in which to do it.

Again, Agatha's album illustrates the weekends she spent with people she and Clara had met in Cairo: Mr Park-Lyle, 'the Sugar

King', and his kind, if artificially preserved, wife, with whom she stayed in Suffolk, where the party played tennis and croquet and gazed at the lake; Sir Walter and Lady Barttelot, at Littlegreen House in Petersfield, from which they went to the races at Goodwood; and the Ralston-Patricks, where Agatha nervously rode round a field (her previous experience being confined to ambling a dispirited horse about the lanes of Devonshire and scrabbling over an occasional wall), and, exhilaratingly, in a motor car. Agatha had first seen motor cars in France as a child and had been greatly excited by them. Robin Ralston-Patricks' motor was highly temperamental and to make an expedition in it exhausting, but she never forgot a fifty-mile trip they made to Banbury in 1909, equipped with rugs, scarves and baskets of provisions and seen off with tender farewells. More alarming was the occasion when she was driven back to Torquay from Petersfield by Lady Barttelot's brother. They charged along the lanes at what Agatha believed to be nearer fifty miles an hour than what was considered the 'safe' speed of twenty, with her driver, rather like Toad in *The Wind in the Willows*, dashing past the places where he believed the police to be lurking – 'Yes, the villains, that's what they do, hide behind a hedge and then come out and measure the time' – and then dropping suddenly to ten miles an hour – 'that dished him!' She found her driver disconcerting but she loved his bright red motor.

On one of these visits Agatha met Charles Cochran, the theatrical impresario, and his delicate and adoring wife, Evelyn. Some months later the Cochrans invited her to stay with them in London and here she particularly enjoyed hearing intimate theatrical gossip. Agatha had been taken to plays and musical comedies since she was a small child: her Ealing grandmother was especially fond of them and, fortified with half a pound of coffee creams from the Army and Navy Stores, would take her to matinée performances, buying the score to play at home afterwards. Frederick had taken a great interest in the local amateur dramatic society in Torquay, for which he had stage-managed (this, as Agatha wrote dryly, 'was then the term used for production and did not mean a harassed young woman in trousers being blamed for everything ...'), while Madge and Monty had initiated Agatha into going weekly to the pit stalls in the local theatre. (Frederick's account book shows that in 1901 a seat at the play cost a shilling, comparing well with one shilling and sixpence for a haircut and ninepence for a banana.) In Dinard, at the end of the year that had taken the Millers to Pau, Agatha had begun her own theatrical performances. Her parents' bedroom there had a large bow window, almost an alcove, across which the curtains could be drawn, and Agatha conscripted Marie into helping her present a version of various fairy stories, 'Sleeping Beauty', 'Cinderella' and so on, which Frederick and Clara patiently endured every evening after dinner. Now, as Agatha grew into her twenties, the amateur theatricals became grander, with a bigger cast: one set of photographs, taken in 1912 or so, shows her larking about with a dozen friends, the women in beads and veils and the men in baggy trousers, turbans and magnificent whiskers, for a performance of *The Blue Beard of Unhappiness*, an original work in part derived from *A Thousand and One Nights*, *Blue Beard* and light musical comedy. (Its nature is indicated by the title of Act 1: *Why Did They Bag-Dad?*) It was put on at Cockington Court, where Agatha's friends the Mallocks lived; Mrs Mallock played Scheherezade, and Agatha, in voluminous harem trousers, Sister Anne.

As well as concocting sketches with her friends, Agatha was by now doing a fair amount of her own writing. Much of this was poetry. With her liking for words and her ear for rhythm and patterns, she found it easy, particularly since she need not start cold but could choose a verse form to follow or a model to parody. Poetry, too, offered a convenient vehicle for an adolescent to express confused but deeply-felt emotions; being in a formalised code, it kept her secrets safe, and, being poetry, it could be opaque. Agatha read and bought a good deal of poetry. Amongst the volumes was a beautifully bound edition of Herrick, in olive green leather, tooled with a design of gold tulips. The edition, published in 1906, falls open at the poem called 'Discontents in Devon':

> More Discontents I never had
> Since I was born, than here;
> Where I have been, and still am sad,
> In this dull Devon-shire:
>
> Yet justly too I must confess;
> I ne'er invented such
> Ennobled numbers for the Presse,
> Than where I loathed so much.

A poem Agatha wrote at the age of eleven had been published in the local paper. The new tram service had been extended to

Ealing, much to the fury of the residents, and Agatha recollected her first verse as being:

> When first the electric trams did run
> In all their scarlet glory,
> 'Twas well, but ere the day was done,
> It was another story.

This poem, however, cannot be traced. Between 1901 and 1906 only three poems about trams appeared in issues of *The Middlesex Country Times* and *The Hanwell and Ealing Post*, none resembling Agatha's. Later, Eileen Morris, her closest and cleverest friend, suggested she send work to the *Poetry Review*, whose editor did accept some of Agatha's poems, for a guinea each. Though her early verse disappeared without trace, we can still read some of the poetry she wrote at the age of seventeen or eighteen, since it was printed in *The Road of Dreams*, the volume Geoffrey Bles published in 1924, and reprinted in *Poems*, published by Collins, in 1973. It is, apart from an occasional phrase, sentimental and derivative. One long sentence tells the story of Harlequin and Columbine, Pierrot and Pierrette, whose Dresden china figures decorated both Auntie-Grannie's house and Ashfield. The theme of magical Harlequin, the lover and protector of lovers, was to resurface twenty years later in Agatha's book, *The Mysterious Mr Quin*.

Agatha also set her 'Harlequin poems' to music. Her composition was, in her own words, 'not of a very high order', but it was competent and expressive. A waltz she wrote was published, despite the fact that, in her own view, it was trite. 'One Hour With Thee' ('a pretty hefty time for a waltz to last,' she later observed), depicted on its cover a young woman looking much like Agatha herself, with golden hair, sloping shoulders, and a bunch of pansies at her bosom. To Agatha's great pride, it was occasionally included in the repertoire of the local dance band.

By the time she was seventeen Agatha had set aside her musical ambitions, doing so with remarkable despatch. Her studies with Charles Fürster had led her to hope that with practice and hard work she might become a professional concert pianist but, after one disastrous occasion when she was bidden to play before a visitor and, on sitting down to the piano, found herself 'overwhelmed by inefficiency', she asked Fürster to be honest with her. 'He told me no lies,' she wrote. 'He said that quite frankly he thought I had not the temperament to play in public, and I knew he was right.' It is interesting that, although she was miserable for a while, she immediately accepted this verdict: 'If the thing you want beyond anything cannot be, it is much better to recognise it and go forward instead of dwelling on one's regrets and hopes.' Although Agatha did not know herself well, even then she recognised that public performance unnerved her. Rather than battling against her temperament, she complied with it.

Singing was, as we have seen, the one thing she could undertake confidently in public but here too her early hopes were disappointed. In Paris she had one of the most respected singing teachers of the time, Monsieur Boué, who trained her to make the best use of her soprano voice, taking her through Cherubini, Schubert and, eventually, arias from Puccini. At home, she studied with a Hungarian composer and an English ballad teacher. Agatha sang at local concerts and to fellow guests after dinner but her ambition to become an opera singer flowered in 1909, when Madge, who had become interested in Wagner, took her to hear *Die Walküre* at Covent Garden. Richter conducted and Brünnhilde was sung by an American soprano, Minni Saltzman-Stephens, whose performance enraptured Agatha, already overwhelmed by the power and beauty of the music. 'Although I did not deceive myself,' she wrote in the unpulbished draft of her autobiography, 'I used to go over and over in my mind the faint possibility that one day I might sing Isolde. It did no harm, I told myself, at any rate to go through it in fantasy.' An American friend of the Millers, who was connected with the Metropolitan Opera House in New York, came to hear Agatha sing, taking her through arias and exercises: 'And then she said to me: "the songs you sang told me nothing, but the exercises do. You will make a good concert singer, and should be able to do well and make an name at that. Your voice is not strong enough for opera, and never will be." ' Again, Agatha's reaction was brave and drastic. 'I came back to real life and put wishful thinking aside. I pointed out to Mother that she could now save the expense of music lessons. I could sing as much as I liked, but there was no point in studying singing.'

Here her disappointment went deeper. The 'cherished secret fantasy' was one she had taken seriously, although she tried to persuade herself that it had been no more than that; 'faint possibility' in the first draft of her autobiography becomes 'illusion' in the second and 'dream' in the last. 'I did not want to be a concert singer,' she wrote. 'It would not have been an easy thing to do anyway. Musical careers for girls did not meet with encouragement.' 'Yet', she declared, 'if there had been any chance of my singing in opera, I would have fought for it, but that was for the privileged few, who had the right vocal cords. I am sure there can be nothing more soul-destroying in life than to persist in trying to do anything that you will do badly and in a second-rate manner.' These urgent arguments show that she did mind; becoming an opera singer she saw as the pinnacle of attainment. Moreover, she continued to do so; towards the end of Agatha's life she startled a young friend by saying wistfully, 'If I'd been an opera singer, I might have been rich.'

'So,' as Agatha put it, 'let us take it from there.' Here was a creative and thoughtful eighteen-year-old girl, well-read, her days full of leisure, needing something to which to apply a good mind. One day as she sat in bed, recovering from influenza, bored with reading and playing Patience, she found herself reduced to idling with a silly game she had learnt in Pau and with which she always amused herself when she was ill. It consisted of dampening little pieces of bread and moulding them into tops which could be baked in the sun or a slow oven and then painted, so that they spun prettily as well as merrily. (In the second draft of her autobiography this long explanation is dispensed with; Agatha succinctly deals herself bridge hands instead.) Clara, thinking this a pathetic expedient for dealing with boredom, suggested that the invalid try to write a story, something which Madge had done successfully before her marriage, when a series of her tales had been published in *Vanity Fair*. After several false starts Agatha found herself 'thoroughly interested and going along at a great rate', and a couple of days later the story was finished. 'The House of Beauty', as she called it, was some 6,000 words long – about thirty pages. She typed a fair copy in purple ink on Madge's old Empire typewriter and signed it with the psuedonym 'Mac Miller Esq'. It is a powerfully imaginative story, about madness and dreams, echoing the novels about the occult that Agatha and her friends were reading at the end of 1908, by Edgar Allan Poe and May Sinclair – 'psychic stories', Agatha called them. There was at this time a great interest in mysticism and spiritualism; one of Agatha's friends constantly sought to persuade her to read theoretical books on the subject but she found the writing tedious and their assertions improbable. Nevertheless, she was interested in dreams and in the thin boundary between the real and the imaginary, and she was both fascinated and repelled by 'madness', a word which the Victorians had used to describe all sorts of instability and which was often believed to be hereditary.

These disturbing themes are all present in 'The House of Beauty', together with a happier but no less interesting thread, the search for a well-known but elusive place, in this case 'a strangely beautiful house'. Despite its infelicities of style (the word 'exquisite' is particularly hard-worked) and extravagance of treatment (everything is there: death, delirium, the jungle, madness, music, even a black-robed nun), 'The House of Beauty' is a compelling story, well-constructed and conveying with complete conviction how fragile and tenacious a dream can be. From the begininning Agatha demonstrated the two skills that characterise all her writing: she was an excellent story-teller and she could tap her readers' deeply-held fantasies. There are glimpses, too, of another characteristic that was not yet fully developed: she could be very funny. The snatches she gives of a dinner-table conversation (each person in turn opening his remarks with the proposition that it has been an unusually wet summer) have a nice comic touch, and her picture of one of the guests, a professor with an 'unpleasantly cadaverous countenance' and 'a big white beard that wagged with peculiar vindictiveness when he talked', is effective if not vastly original. 'The House of Beauty', drastically revised, was to be published as 'The House of Dreams' in *Sovereign magazine* in January 1926.

Agatha's next effort was 'The Call of Wings', later published in *The Hound of Death* in 1933 (and again in *The Golden Ball* in 1971). It describes how easily those who are disposed to believe in psychic phenomena can be manipulated, especially when new mechanical inventions – in this case, the wireless – are brought into service. Agatha then tried 'a grisly story about a séance', which, rewritten many years later, appeared as *The Sittaford Mystery*. Fourth came 'a dialogue between a deaf lady and a nervous man at a party', which has not survived. Agatha's papers do include a copy of her fifth try, 'The Little Lonely God', a story of the encounter in the British Museum between an explorer aimlessly passing the time in London, to which he has returned after eighteen years trekking about the globe, and an equally solitary young woman, in pathetically shabby clothes, whom he assumes to be a governess, alone in the world. It is sentimental, with a little twist at the end, and lacks the force of 'The House of Beauty'; there are no dreams and no deaths; unlike the description in her first story of the heroine's breakdown at the piano, nothing that appears to be based on Agatha's direct experience.

As 'Mac Miller', 'Nathaniel Miller' and 'Sydney West' Agatha followed Madge's example and sent her stories to various magazines, from which they were all promptly returned. Other early efforts have remained among her papers. They are all in purple ink and on the two submitted under the pseudonym of 'Sydney West', she wrote 'Both these written when I was about 17.' One, called 'In The Marketplace', reads like a parable. A man comes to the Salesman in the Great Marketplace of the World and, when asked what he desires, replies 'Everything.' He goes away, laden with rich gifts but unsatisfied, and twice returns for more. Only when, 'after long years', he passes through the Marketplace untempted and answers the Salesman's question, 'What do you desire?' with the one word 'Nothing', are all the Market's stores and treasures brought out and laid at his feet. This moral tale has a biblical ring, but what the moral is remains obscure.

It is interesting to compare 'Sydney West's' other offering, 'The Choice', with 'Callis Miller's' 'Mrs Jordan's Ghost', the tale Clara had written years before. Superficially the two stories are much alike. Both have at their centre the figure of a woman, most likely a projection of the author herself, who has 'sinned and suffered' but is ennobled by pity and repentance. Both are written in a deliberately naïve and declamatory style, with consciously rhetorical sentences ('it is in truth a smooth way...') and phrases repeated like an incantation ('The second shadow is like the shadow of a child, though not like that of any earthly child that I have ever seen'). Agatha's and Clara's stories also have deeper similarities. Both sound, or are written so that they sound, as if they originated in dreams. They are pure metaphor, their meaning wrapped in the fogs of sleep and the subconscious, the stories themselves attempt to expose the authors' hopes and anxieties. But there is a difference. Agatha's tale is more artful than her mother's. She cannot resist giving it a tweak: in 'The Choice', for instance, her narrator consciously makes the 'wrong' decision and, because that choice brings complacency, knows it to be the 'right' decision. In an otherwise prissy parable, Agatha has a joke at the narrator's expense.

Agatha next tried her hand at a worldly novel. Set in Cairo, it recalled three people she used to see in the dining room of the Gezirah Hotel – an attractive-looking woman and the two men with whom she had supper after the dance. 'One was a short broad man, with dark hair – a Captain in the Sixtieth Rifles – the other was a tall fair young man in the Coldstream Guards, possibly a year or two younger than she was. They sat, one on either side of her; she kept them in play.' This, and the overheard remark, 'she will have to make up her mind between them some time,' was enough to give Agatha a start but, after going a certain distance, she became dissatisfied and turned to a second plot. Again, it was set in Cairo but this time the heroine was deaf, a grave mistake, as Agatha soon realised, because 'once you have done with what she is thinking and whatever people are thinking and saying of her, she is left with no possibility of conversation with anyone.' Undaunted by her difficulties in bringing either novel to a close, Agatha ingeniously merged the two, called the resulting mixture *Snow Upon the Desert*, and despatched it to several publishers, using this time the pseudonym 'Monosyll -aba'. Not unexpectedly, they sent it back. Clara now hesitantly suggested that Agatha might ask the advice of their neighbour Eden Philpotts, a well-known writer himself, then at the height of his reputation, and a friend of the family. Adelaide, Eden's daughter, had attended the same dancing class as Agatha, who had once made her a pink frock. Eden Philpotts was gouty and kept to himself, so the Millers did not bother him with invitations, though they visited him occasionally to admire his garden. Shy though Agatha was about her writing, she asked him what he thought.

His reaction was splendid. He took her request seriously, reading her work and writing a careful, encouraging letter, which started with a word of praise and ended by giving her something to do:

> Some of these things that you have written are capital. You have a great feeling for dialogue. You should stick to gay natural dialogue. Try and cut all moralisations out of your novels; you are much too fond of them, and nothing is more boring to read. Try and leave your characters alone, so that they can speak for themselves, instead of always rushing in to tell them what they ought to say, or to explain to the reader what they mean by what they are saying. That is for the reader to judge for himself. ... I should like to recommend you a course of reading which I think you will find helpful. Read De Quincey's *Confessions of an Opium Eater* – this will increase your vocabulary enormously – he uses some very interesting words. Read *The Story of My Life*, by Jefferies, for descriptions and a feeling for nature.

Warning her that it was difficult to get a first novel accepted, he nonetheless sent her an introduction to his own literary agent, Hughes Massie. Agatha was sufficiently encouraged to go to see him; she found this 'large dark swarthy man' terrifying. Her recollection indicates how appalling that interview must have been for a nervous eighteen-year-old: "'Ah," he said, looking at the cover of the manuscript, *Snow Upon the Desert*. Mmm, a very suggestive title, suggestive of banked fires."' Hughes Massie returned her manuscript some months later, saying that the best thing for her to do would be to put it out of her mind and start again.

Magazine editors might reject Agatha's early stories and Hughes Massie be dauntingly dismissive, but she pressed on. Among her next efforts was 'Vision', a story inspired not only by May Sinclair's *A Flaw in the Crystal* but also by a detective story only recently published in English, Gaston Le Roux's *The Mystery of the Yellow Room*. Although Agatha put 'Vision' on one side after it was done, she was to make important use of it later on. Another offering was sent to Eden Philpotts for scrutiny, a story called 'Being So Very Wilful'. It has vanished, but his report, written on February 6th, 1909, survives. Again, his letter was shrewd and constructive.

> Dear Agatha,
>
> I need not go into technical detail with your story 'Being So Very Wilful', but I am glad to say that in its own plane it shows steady advance. You have worked hard & you have a natural sense for construction and balance. In fact all is going exceedingly well with your work & should life so fall out for you that it has room for art & you can face the up-hill fight to take your place & win it, you have the gifts sufficient. I never prophesy; but I should judge that if you can write like this now you might go far. However life knocks the art out of a good many people & your environment in the time to come may substitute for the hard road of art a different one. ... However these considerations are beside the question of the moment.
>
> For the present you must go on writing about these people and no doubt the more you learn of them the more interesting you will make them. But always remember the worth of people is to be judged by their aims, and this class will never lift you to anything really fine.
>
> They will do to practise on, but presently you will probe deeper into human nature & seek beautiful character & find it.
>
> Your own bent is to the fine & distinguished, & 'Society' of the sort you have so far written about is neither the one nor the other. The

average crowd of English abroad is just as you paint it. In fact you are lenient.

But if you go on you'll soon sicken of them & seek other themes & finer issues.

Never be flippant in the first person. Let your flippant characters be; but don't be yourself. And avoid all first-hand moralising. It is bad art. Of course great artists have done any amount of it; but not the greatest. If you are to take my advice you must go to the school of Flaubert for your models. The artist is only the glass through which we see nature, & the clearer & more absolutely pure that glass, so much the more perfect picture we can see through it. Never intrude yourself.

Presently re-write this story but not just yet. Don't put poetical quotations at the top of the chapters.

Make the heroine a little younger. Thirty-one is rather too old – don't you think? ...

The construction of the story is admirable, & shows a feeling for form which is very hopeful; but this is a difficult length for publication; too short for a novel & too long for a short story.

Some day perhaps you will publish it in a volume; but you'll want to re-write it first. I take it you may read what you please now & should advise that you read a few of the French men. If you can read equally easily in French as in English, then read them in French; Anatole France – the stories – & Flaubert's *Madame Bovary*. But this last is very strong meat & perhaps you had better wait till you have taken some lighter dose first of the more modern men. When you come to it, remember that it – *Madame Bovary* – is one of the greatest novels in the world.

Come & see me if you like & when you want to know anything, or have time for more books.

Try another short story – quite a new one of three thousand words – & we'll see if we can publish it. A little print is very encouraging I know; but I don't want you to be in too much of a hurry.

> Your friend,
> Eden Philpotts.

There was one more exchange. Agatha wrote to Philpotts to ask what she should be doing with her life and, firmly and sensibly, he put her problems into proportion.

Art is second to life & if you are living just now (we only live by fits & starts) then put art out of your mind absolutely. ... Tell me when I can be useful to you again.

Clara could not have directed Agatha to a wiser mentor.

5

'... he will change
your entire life'

Agatha's confusion arose largely from the romantic complications of her life. While staying with the Ralston-Patricks in War-
wickshire, she had been taken to 'a cold and windy meet', where
she had encountered a Colonel in the 17th Lancers, Bolton
Fletcher. That evening they met again, at a fancy-dress ball at
another house, The Asps, and on several other occasions. Agatha
had dressed for the ball as Elaine, in white brocade with a
pearl-covered cap, and three or four days after her return to
Torquay she received a parcel containing a small silver-gilt box,
engraved inside the lid with the words 'The Asps, To Elaine' and
the date of the meet. Bolton Fletcher was, like Agatha's later
portrayal of him as Major Johnnie de Burgh in *Unfinished Portrait*, a master of the love letter, and ardent notes, flowers, books,
chocolates and other tributes followed swiftly. On his third call
at Ashfield, he proposed. Agatha was dazed and almost, but not
quite, ready to be swept away: 'I was charmed like the bird off a
tree, and yet, when he was gone away, when I thought of him in
absence, there was – nothing there.' Clara was troubled. As she
told Agatha, she had prayed for a good, kindly husband to
appear for her daughter, one 'well-endowed with this world's
goods', for her income was now stretched very thin.

Somehow this suitor did not seem quite right. Handicapped by
the lack of husband or sons who might make inquiries, Clara
wrote to the Ralston-Patricks, who assured her that, apart from
a profuse scattering of wild oats, Bolton Fletcher was in every
way satisfactory. Clara did not mind the wild oats, nor the fact
that the candidate was fifteen years older than Agatha (after all,
there had been ten years between Frederick and herself), but she
advised him that her daughter was too young to be pressed for
an immediate decision and proposed that there be no letters or
visits for six months, 'which was probably just as well,' Agatha
remarked later, 'because I should have fallen for those letters in

the end.' When the moratorium was over, a prepaid telegram arrived: 'Cannot stand this indecision any longer. Will you marry me yes or no?' 'No,' she wrote and straightaway felt enormous relief. 'I turned over on my pillow and went immediately to sleep. So that was the end of that.'

Though Agatha's life temporarily lost some of its savour, she regained her high spirits a few months later, with the arrival of Wilfred Pirie, whom she had last seen in Dinard when she was seven years old and he, older and rather superior, had been a midshipman in the Navy. Now a sub-lieutenant, he served in a submarine that came often to Torquay. Relieved to settle into a tranquil relationship, fortified by the friendship their fathers had enjoyed and their mothers now shared, and, no doubt, attracted as much by the lovely and intelligent Mrs Pirie as by her son, Agatha agreed that she and Wilfred should have 'an understanding'. The friendship prospered; the romance did not. Agatha's description of the fading of her illusion that she shared Wilfred's tastes and enthusiasms (a phenomenon immediately recognisable to anyone who has ever sought to persuade themselves that they have met their perfect match) shows she was bored, especially when Wilfred talked about theosophy and spiritualism. It was not Wilfred's embrace Agatha coveted but his family's. His father was dead but in some respects Wilfred provided the masculine protection and challenge of which Agatha was deprived by her own father's death and Monty's elusiveness. It did not occur to her that she treated Wilfred exactly like a brother. Then there was Wilfred's mother, whose character was as tantalising to Agatha as her schemes of interior decoration. Lilian Pirie represented the sort of woman Agatha admired; well-read, well-informed, lively and assured, she was a more emphatic version of Clara. As Agatha was to write in *Unfinished Portrait*, where much of Wilfred is to be found in Jim Grant ('interested in theosophy, bimetallism, economics and Christian Science'), 'the thing Celia enjoyed most about her engagement was her prospective mother-in-law.' In marrying Wilfred, moreover, Agatha could believe that she would not really be leaving Clara: 'I liked the idea of marrying a sailor very much. I should live in lodgings at Southsea, Plymouth, or somewhere like that, and when Wilfred was away on foreign stations I could come home to Ashfield and spend my time with Mother.'

The tedium of the understanding dawned on Agatha when Wilfred telephoned to ask whether she would mind if he spent his leave treasure-hunting with an expedition in South America. Naturally she agreed and on the day after he sailed she realised – for the second time – 'that an enormous load had slipped off my mind.... I loved Wilfred like a brother and I wanted him to do what he wanted to do. I thought the treasure-hunting idea was ... almost certain to be bogus. That again was because I was not in love with Wilfred. If I had been, I would have seen it with his eyes.' Clara and Wilfred were disappointed but not devastated. A few months later Wilfred married someone else.

For this was the time when Agatha's friends and contemporaries were determinedly marrying. Twice a bridesmaid, she speculated about her own prospects. She and Madge would look about the room for the most unappealing-looking candidates for 'Agatha's Husbands', forcing her to choose between them. That was in play but in reality, too, Agatha appraised the eligible men around her. She said something about this in her *Autobiography*, in a passage discussing friendship between men and women:

> I don't know exactly what brings about a friendship between man and woman – men do not by nature ever want a woman as a friend. It comes about by accident – often because the man is already sensually attracted by some other woman and quite wants to talk about her. Women do often crave after friendship with men – and are willing to come to it by taking an interest in someone else's love affair. Then there comes about a very stable and enduring relationship – you become interested in each other as people. There is a flavour of sex, of course, the touch of salt as a condiment.
>
> According to an elderly doctor friend of mine, a man looks at every woman he meets and wonders what she would be like to sleep with – possibly proceeding to whether she would be likely to sleep with him if he wanted it. 'Direct and coarse – that's a man,' he put it. They don't consider a woman as a possible wife.
>
> Women, I think, quite simply try on, as it were, every man they meet as a possible husband. I don't believe any woman has ever looked across a room and fallen in love at first sight with a man; lots of men have with a woman.

At first glance, these observations seem naïve. While acknowledging that sexual chemistry plays a part in all relationships, it is unwise to generalise, given the differences in people's sexual proclivities, or their lack of them. It is also harder, in some societies at least, to understand Agatha's remark that, 'Men do not by nature ever want a woman as a friend.' From the context (she is talking about Eileen Morris), it is clear that by 'friend' she means a mixture of companion and confidant. In Agatha's youth the spheres in which men and women worked and lived were distinctly separate; fewer experiences were shared from an early age. There was less for men and women to talk about together and they were in some ways more baffling to each other. At the age of twenty, moreover, Agatha's perspective was particularly narrow. She fully expected to meet 'her Fate' at any moment, and, moreover, she was looking out for him. So far, her own exquisite infatuations had been short-lived and she had sensibly backed off from the ardent Bolton Fletcher and well-meaning Wilfred. There was to be one more false start.

This was Reggie Lucy, the elder brother of Blanche, Marguerite and Muriel, with whom Agatha played tennis, croquet and Diabolo, picnicked on Dartmoor and roller-skated on the pier. A casual, comfortable family, they had first taken Agatha under their wing when Clara and Madge had gone to France shortly after Frederick's death and she had stayed behind at Ashfield. The Lucys were a happy-go-lucky, devil-may-care collection, racy and informal – the two younger girls were known as Margie and Noonie and, apart from Jack Watts, they seem to have been the only people ever to escape with calling Agatha 'Aggie'. Reggie, a Major in the Gunners, now came home after his foreign service; he took Agatha's erratic golf in hand and, as time passed, proposed to her in an unemphatic and companionable way. As always with the Lucys, who were constantly missing trams, trains and meals, there was no urgency: 'Just bear me in mind, and, if nobody else turns up, there I am, you know.' Agatha immediately agreed. Reggie, however, insisted equably that they should wait a couple of years so that Agatha could survey the field before settling down with him. He returned to his Regiment and their courtship continued by post. Reggie, who is the model for Peter Maitland in *Unfinished Portrait*, assured Agatha that, despite their understanding, she should consider herself absolutely free. Agatha, like Celia, in that book, did not wish to be. 'Don't be too humble,' says Celia's mother to Peter. 'Women don't appreciate it.' Sadly, she was right. Agatha was carried away by someone more determined and impetuous.

Archie Christie (it is impossible to think of that engaging young man as Archibald) is also described in *Unfinished Portrait*, as Dermot, whom Celia meets at a regimental ball in York. He spirits her away from the partners to whom she is pledged and, within a few weeks, from her fiancé. As we know from Agatha's autobiography, and from her own and Archie's papers, the reality was only a little less dramatic. The dance was given by Lord and Lady Clifford of Chudleigh, who had invited some of the garrison at Exeter, and Agatha was taken by old family friends who lived near Chudleigh, about twelve miles from Torquay. She already had one friend among the Exeter garrison, Arthur Griffiths, and, although he could not be there himself, he took the trouble to write to ask her to look out for a friend of his. This was Archie. That dance is the first non-military entry in a record Archie made of the most important events of his life. It took place on October 12th, 1912; Agatha was just twenty-two, Archie (whose birthday was a fortnight after hers) twenty-three. His history and interests were romantic. He had been born in India, where his father was a judge in the Indian Civil Service, and he had one brother, Campbell, who like Archie was in the Army. Archie's father had become very ill after falling from a horse – the fall had affected his brain – and had died in hospital in England. His mother then married William Hemsley, a housemaster at Clifton College in Bristol, where Archie had been head of the school. He was re-sourceful and intelligent and, on taking the entrance examination for the Woolwich Military Academy, was placed fourth on the list. He was commissioned Second Lieutenant in the Royal Field Artillery in July 1909, joining the 138th Battery at Bulford Camp on Salisbury Plain. The Brigade had moved to Exeter early in 1912.

He was, however, fascinated not by soldiering but by flying; the aeroplane was just beginning to be regarded as more than a bizarre plaything and the farsighted saw it as a powerful weapon of war. In June 1912, Archie, who was practical and ambitious, paid the £75 fee ('including breakages') for a course of lessons at the Bristol School at Larkhill, on the 'Special Reduced Terms' offered to 'those desirous of qualifying for The Royal Flying Corps'. He took a month's leave and found where his heart and talent lay.

By June 27th he was flying solo, practising right and left hand turns, and on July 6th he flew alone for twenty-five minutes at the dizzy height of 300 feet in a five-mile-an-hour wind. The exercise was precarious; the official log made special mention of the fact that all landings were achieved 'without even breaking so much as a piece of wire ...'. By mid-July, flying a Bristol Box Kite, Archie qualified for the Royal Aero Club Aviator's Certi-ficate, a magnificent document, printed in English and French.

The ranks of qualified aviators were noticeably small; Archie's certificate was only No. 245. He thereupon applied to join the newly formed Royal Flying Corps and returned to his Brigade at Exeter.

It was three months later that he met Agatha at the Cliffords' dance. From his photographs we can see that he was tall and well built, with fair, crisply curling hair, cut short. He had strong features: an attractive mouth, a nose with a small crinkle in it, blue eyes, heavy brows and a look of slightly anxious intensity. He was very young and determined and fell in love with Agatha almost at once. They danced together a great many times. In his scrapbook Archie pasted the programme and next to it a newspaper cutting of a jolly verse, 'The New Romance', which began:

> When first she fell in love with Frank,
> 'Twas not the latter's youth and rank,
> Nor yet his balance at the bank
> That won the heart of Elsie;
> 'Twas not the whiteness of his soul
> That made her lose all self-control,
> But 'twas the way he kicked a goal,
> When playing 'back' for Chelsea. . . .

Whether in Archie's case it was his dancing or his heart-stopping profession as an aviator that attracted Agatha we do not know, but he felt sufficiently confident to appear at Ashfield shortly afterwards, on his motor-bike.

Agatha was playing badminton with the Mellors, who lived opposite; she used to go across to their house whenever their son was at home, to try out the latest intricate dance steps, a joke that had begun years before when they had practised waltzing, in the fashion of popular operettas, up and down the staircase. Clara, always exasperated at finding herself left to entertain Agatha's young men unaided, summoned her home on the telephone. Rather cross, because she thought this was the 'dreary young naval lieutenant who asked me to read his poems', Agatha returned. There was Archie, pink and embarrassed, with a story about being in Torquay and thinking he might drop in. (Agatha spotted that he must have gone to some trouble to ask Arthur Griffiths for her address.) The afternoon passed; Agatha, Clara and Archie continued to talk, evening came, and the two women silently telegraphed to each other that he was to be invited to stay for supper.

Archie did indeed come, like Dermot, 'in a whirlwind' into
Agatha's life. Her *Autobiography* describes this important meal
as taking place both 'a week or ten days' after the Cliffords'
dance (that is, on about October 20th) and 'soon after Christmas,
because I know there was cold turkey in the larder'. Archie then
roared off into the night, returning several times during the next
few weeks (or, in Agatha's understandably shaky chronology,
days). Books were exchanged, though not for reading, Archie
invited Agatha to a concert at Exeter, where they decorously
drank tea at the railway station (Clara judged an hotel to be too
compromising), and Agatha asked Archie to the New Year Ball
at Torquay. The dance was on January 2nd. Archie was moody
and Agatha puzzled. Two days later, after listening to Wagner at
the Pavilion, she learnt the reason. When they returned to Ashfield, Archie announced that he was soon to leave Exeter for
Farnborough, since his application to the Royal Flying Corps
had been accepted. He begged her to marry him. She explained
about her understanding with Reggie Lucy; Archie waved it
aside. He wanted to marry her immediately and Agatha knew she
wanted to marry him. They were 'poles apart in our reactions to
things', but she believed, and continued all her life to believe, that
this was what fascinated both of them. It was, she said, 'the
excitement of the stranger' and, as she remembered years later, it
was at this time that she had awoken from a dream to find herself
saying: 'The stranger from the sea, the stranger from the sea.' A
poem she wrote then, 'The Ballad of the Fleet', indicates her state
of mind. It is about the people who first inhabited the hut circles
of Dartmoor, living a spare but secure life, until the coming of
the Vikings in their galleys. In her verse the leader of the invaders
– 'the Stranger from the Sea' – takes their Priestess for his own,
and both die for it.

Agatha and Archie were mesmerised by one another; Clara,
taken aback by Agatha's announcement that 'Archie Christie has
asked me to marry him and I want to, I want to dreadfully,'
brought them back to earth. The understanding with Reggie was
ended but Clara insisted that they wait, since Archie could not
hope to support a wife on a subaltern's pay, supplemented only
by Agatha's allowance of £100 a year from her grandfather's
trust. Archie, determined they should not wait a day longer than
they could help, was momentarily bitter, but reflected that in any
case the Royal Flying Corps preferred its young men to be single,
in case they crashed. Agatha, too, was desperate at the thought

Auntie-Grannie taking the air at Torquay.

Agatha's mother shortly before the Great War.

Agatha, her father and Toby at Ashfield.

Madge and Clara in the conservatory at Ashfield.

Monty, among the coffee things
at Ashfield.

Agatha as a girl.

that they might have years of delay. She was twenty-two and full
of turbulent emotion. It is not surprising that for the next year
and a half their relationship was stormy, first one and then the
other wanting to break things off.

Archie, at least, had his training to occupy his time and attention. Shortly after the end of January 1913 he passed the RFC
examination and was posted to Larkhill, in a squadron com-
manded by Major Brooke-Popham. His flights became ever
higher (1800 feet on April 22nd, 2000 feet on April 24th), longer
(45 minutes on April 17th), further (90 miles on April 22nd),
gustier (20 miles an hour wind on April 29th), and more hazardous (April 2nd: machine wrecked; April 29th: dropped passenger
engine; May 5th: bent chassis strut, goggles oily). He described
his manoeuvres to Agatha: making spirals, observing artillery
fire, swerving, firing double rockets from a Verey pistol. She was
appalled. On that first afternoon at Ashfield, when Archie had
described his chosen career to Agatha and Clara, they had been
enchanted. It was new and thrilling, and Agatha was fascinated
by the aeroplane. She had enjoyed the hair-raising drives in fast
motors; the magic of flying was still more entrancing. She had
herself already flown in one of those rickety early machines, for
in May 1911 Clara had taken her to see a flying exhibition where
for the sum of £5 visitors could be taken up in the air for a few
minutes. As Agatha acknowledged, Clara was wonderful, not just
for agreeing to spend what was then, and for them, an enormous
sum, but also for subduing her fears that the aeroplane, and
Agatha, might hurtle to the ground. Agatha never forgot that
experience. Her small straw hat firmly wedged on her head, she
was taken up, the plane circled round and round and then, 'with
that wonderful switch-back down', it 'vol-planed' back to earth.

None of this, however, resigned her to the perilous activities
Archie was undertaking as his daily routine. She wrote begging
him to give it up. Archie replied with a charming, though not
wholly reassuring, letter:

> I was so glad to get your note today, but I can't give up flying yet.
>
> For your sake, more than my own, I am taking no risks and feel
> perfectly confident that no harm can come to me. That poor fellow
> who was killed was not safe in any machine and the Cody biplane is
> very unstable and carries much too great a weight on the elevator. He
> hated flying it but did not like to refuse when he was asked to,
> showing a lack of moral courage.
>
> I am terribly sorry for his family - so much so that I will give up

this Corps if you really are unhappy about it but I know I am perfectly safe – I always carry St Christopher with me. It does make one morbid reading about these accidents – still more so seeing them – but confidence soon returns.

He came to see Agatha whenever he could, first from Larkhill and then from Netheravon, to which he was posted at the end of 1913. His letters to his 'dearest Angel' reflected the doubt and despair they were both feeling. 'The reason why I was unwell last week,' he wrote, 'was that I was so worried because I thought that it would be best for you if I never saw you again and hated telling you so. Now I have not a trace of pessimism left and feel sure that all must come right .... I was only doing in a clumsy way what I thought would be best for you ...'. Then, more cheerfully, 'To return to Aviation ...'.

At other times their spirits were more buoyant. After three days' leave with Agatha in Torquay, Archie wrote that 'One day we will have our cottage which will be heavenly happiness and will never say goodbye again. You will have to be poor but I will have you to love and look after for ever so all will be well.' They plunged into despair and out of it again. Some of their fears were exaggerated; Agatha, for instance, wrote breaking off their engagement when she learnt that Clara might lose her sight. Archie persuaded her that this was foolish, since it might not happen for years, by which time a cure for cataract might be found. But their financial insecurity was not misplaced. Archie's pay was minuscule and, after his stepfather's only rich relation unexpectedly left his fortune to the Charing Cross Hospital (who sent Mr Hemsley a handsome walking stick as a token of thanks), their hope of help from that source expired. Agatha's situation was even more precarious than before. The crash of H. B. Chaflin was now complete and Clara depended for her income on an annual allowance from the private fortune of the son of one of the partners. An indication of the economies the Millers now practised is given by a letter that Clara sent in February 1914 to the Greenwood Cemetery in Brooklyn, where Frederick's father was buried in the family plot. The site was valuable and its tending expensive, and Clara enquired whether the title might be sold: 'the lot being of no further possible use to the family, they do not wish to pay for its upkeep, and also desire the money for its sale, as they are in England, and never likely to be in America and in extremely low financial circumstances.' The application, however, was not sent off; Clara and Agatha somehow made ends meet.

As it turned out, the engagement lasted less than two years, but the delay seemed interminable to both Agatha and Archie, not least because they did not know when its end would come. Suddenly, however, in August 1914, they were swept into a drama far bigger than their own.

6

'This waiting is rather hard but all is ready ...'

It is difficult to appreciate how unexpected the First World War actually was, especially to people like Agatha and her mother, who did not read between the lines of politicians' speeches or bother with dissecting the ambitions of the Kaiser. There had been no major European wars for a generation – colonial imbroglios were not the same. True, there were those who perceived that German interests and Balkan quarrels would lead to trouble but even those responsible for running the country were surprised that things came to a head when they did. The summer months, a time when politicians and officials, like the rest of the English middle and upper classes, went to the country, the sea, Scotland, the spas, were in 1914 gloriously sunny; it seemed, afterwards, as if those weeks had been the last miraculous moment, like the pause before a wave topples over, of a world that for many had been golden and assured. Not for all; support was swelling for economic and social change. The Labour Party, formed in 1900, was growing in strength; the Liberals, despite Lloyd George's programme of reform, were losing their grip; the House of Lords, for what was not to be the last time, teetered on the precipice of abolition. There was trade union agitation, rebellion in Ireland and disruption by women demanding female emancipation and the vote. Some time the wave would break, but not yet, not in these languid days and glowing evenings. The assassination of the Archduke Franz Ferdinand in Serbia at the end of June was the catalyst, and war came.

The Royal Flying Corps was among the first forces to be mobilised. Archie's last letter from Netheravon, written as they were waiting for orders to move, describes his own attempt to swell the size of the Expeditionary Force:

On Friday I took my recruit to Devizes to get him enlisted and there heard of a bankrupt Russian Baron, who was in need of a job, so as he was a good mechanic and could speak Russian, French, German and English perfectly I persuaded him in the end to enlist in the RFC too.

He tried to reassure Agatha:

This waiting is rather hard but all is ready.

I have a revolver in a holster and an ammunition pouch full of bullets, just to please you.

The last time I shot off my gun was after travelling all night from Cheadle and I fired 96 rounds and averaged 19 out of 26 so I may hit a large German if I see one which is unlikely ...

You will be very brave won't you Angel, it will be very hard to sit at home and do nothing, and I am afraid you will have money troubles too but it must all come right if we are steadfast and I will always love you more than anything on earth.

Two days later Archie's squadron learnt that it was to move to Southampton to embark for France. He immediately wired to Ashfield for Agatha to come to Salisbury, if she could, to say goodbye. She and Clara set off straightaway; the banks were closed and all the money they had was in five-pound notes, which Clara, well-trained by Auntie-Grannie, always kept for emergencies. But no one would take a five-pound note and they were obliged to leave their names and addresses with ticket collectors all over Southern England (a trail vividly described in *Unfinished Portrait*). After endless complications and delays, they arrived in Salisbury on the evening of August 3rd, where Agatha and Archie had only a little time together before his departure. The next day she and Clara returned to Torquay.

On August 5th Archie left for Southampton and on the 12th crossed the Channel with the British Expeditionary Force. On landing he sent a postcard to Agatha; muddling her chronology again in the rush and turmoil of those first weeks, she maintained that it arrived three days after their parting. In fact she did not receive it until mid-September. Agatha later learnt how quickly Archie had been pitched into action. His logbook traces his progress across Northern France, until on September 12th his squadron, No. 3, moved with three others to Fève-en-Tardenous, where there was a heavy storm (which Archie and two of his friends missed, having fallen asleep on the floor of an inn). The German invaders, defeated by French and British forces at the Battle of the Marne and obliged to retreat some distance, now dug themselves into Belgium and much of the coal and iron-bearing part of France. The allied armies, retaining their direct communications with the Channel ports, poured men and weapons into that flat, muddy, occupied territory, seeking, yard by yard, to oust the Germans. This bloody trench warfare began in mid-September 1914 and was to last for four years.

Archie's dash and bravery were soon proved; on October 19th he was mentioned in the first despatch from Field Marshal Sir John French to Field Marshal Lord Kitchener, Secretary of State for War, describing the battles of Mons, the Marne and, particularly, the Aisne, and emphasising the great strain to which the RFC was subjected. In mid-November Archie was gazetted Flight Commander and Temporary Captain. More important, he was still alive and neither wounded nor shell-shocked. For the lists of dead and missing that were to mark the passage of those years were beginning to appear in English newspapers, and a dreadful procession of the physically and psychologically maimed started to make its way home. Agatha saw these men; she was now working with the Voluntary Aid Detachment (VAD) in Torquay, to which came many of the boats carrying the wounded. She had been going to classes in bandaging and first aid for some time before the war started and now she began at the hospital as a ward-maid, cleaning and scrubbing, and, like the other novices, being more of a hindrance than a help to the trained nursing staff. She learnt to grit her teeth and inflict painful treatment, assist in the operating theatre, cheer up wounded men and humour the doctors. It was hard, messy, evil-smelling, tiring work, which she later described in the novel *Giant's Bread*. Nightmarish though this transformation was, Agatha was at least busy, with distractions sufficiently exhausting to prevent her from being overwhelmed with anxiety for Archie. She was, moreover, a good practical nurse, and the companionship of the wards and her patients' dependence supported her. With her noticing ear and fascination with hierarchy and routine, she had a good deal of entertainment from hospital life: the deference shown by ward-maids to nurses, nurses to Sisters, and by everyone to doctors, the variations in forms of address and in manners (amicable badinage among the VADs, who called each other by their surnames, genteel whisperings by Sister This and Sister That) - all interested and amused her as much as the conventions observed in the household at Ashfield and in the carefully graded society of Torquay.

This was Agatha's first responsible job and she enjoyed being able to do it well. Like Archie, she was wiser and wearier when they were reunited at the end of the year, on his first period of leave. They met in London, as Agatha put it, 'almost like strangers', for both of them had not only been living through an entirely new kind of experience, of death, uncertainty and fear, but had been doing so alone. Archie's reaction was to behave as casually, almost flippantly, as possible, while Agatha had become more serious. The insecurity of the times had made her all the more anxious that they should be married and Archie all the more convinced they should not: 'You stop one, you've had it, and you've left behind a young widow, perhaps a child coming – it's completely selfish and wrong.' Archie's leave began on December 21st. The plan was that Clara should stay with them in London and, when she left for Devonshire, they should go to Clifton to stay with Archie's mother and stepfather. Agatha was uncomfortable with Mrs Hemsley, who was kind but gushing and possessive, and it may have been her nervousness at the prospect of spending Christmas with her, coupled with reaction to the tension of the past five months, that caused her to quarrel violently with Archie. The immediate cause was his Christmas present, a luxurious fitted dressing-case: 'If he had bought me a ring, or a bracelet, however expensive, I should not have demurred ... but for some reason I revolted violently against the dressing-case.' It is not difficult to see why. The gift represented frivolity – indeed, that was why Archie had bought it, in his determination to recapture some of the light-heartedness the war had swept away. Agatha, grave and responsible, was particularly touchy about any implication that she was not dedicated, serious, professional, that she did not have battles to fight as well: 'What was the good of my going back home to hospital with an exciting dressing-case ...?' The present also disturbed her in another way. 'A ring or bracelet' would perhaps have represented something permanent and binding; a dressing-case, however beautiful and well-appointed, suggested transitoriness, impermanence. That was what Archie was feeling; it was what Agatha wished to dispel. But these subtleties do not dawn on people when they give and receive presents. Archie had been clumsy, Agatha was tactless, and a tremendous row ensued, of such magnitude that it reunited them far more effectively than anything else could have done.

Clara departed and they left on the difficult and tiring journey to Clifton, where Agatha went almost immediately to bed, only to be roused by Archie, urgently arguing that they should marry before his leave was up. This time it was Agatha who foresaw the difficulties; separated from her mother, ill at ease in her prospective mother-in-law's home, she was doubtless terrified by Archie's intensity and impassioned determination. He talked wildly of special licences and the Archbishop of Canterbury; Agatha gave in and agreed that they should be married next morning, Christmas Eve.

Mrs Hemsley was, as Agatha predicted, greatly upset but Mr Hemsley, always sympathetic, urged them on. Archie and Agatha scrambled about for a licence to marry: a fortnight's notice was required for an ordinary £8 licence and a special £25 licence was unobtainable for December 25th. Then a kindly registrar, stretching a point, issued one on the strength of Archie's being a local resident. The vicar agreed to perform the ceremony that afternoon; the organist, who happened to be practising in the church, to play the wedding march; and Mr Hemsley and a passer-by, who turned out to be a friend of Agatha's, to act as witnesses. On the afternoon of Christmas Eve Agatha and Archie were married. With some difficulty, they managed to book a room at the Grand Hotel, Torquay, in order to be on their own together. The dressing-case, which Archie had hidden, was brought out again for the wedding journey, its devil exorcised. At midnight, after an even more horrendous train journey, they arrived at the Grand Hotel. They spent Christmas Day with Clara and Madge, now recovered from the initial shock they had felt when, on a bad line from Clifton, Agatha had telephoned to announce her news. On Boxing Day Agatha travelled to London with Archie to see him off; she was not to see him again for six months. She comforted herself, and sought to amuse Archie, by making him a New Year present, 'The AA Alphabet for 1915'. (AA stood for Archie and Agatha and also for Ack Ack, as the anti-aircraft guns were called.) It is full of private jokes and wistful references:

> A is for Angel, by nature (?) and name
> And also for Archibald, spouse of the same
>
> K for the Kaiser, of Kultur the King!
> (Indirectly the cause of a new wedding ring!)

The immediate and lengthy separation was as hard to bear married as unmarried. Archie was still exposed to great danger and the future was as uncertain as before. The casualty lists grew longer, friends and sons of friends were killed, the hospital was full of wounded. Everywhere Agatha saw death and decay. Her mother was frail, and, though Mary Ann was cheerful and robust, her other grandmother, Margaret, found living at Ealing a struggle, since her sight was rapidly failing and she suspected the servants of robbing her. By 1915 her eyes were so bad that she was obliged to come and live with Clara and Agatha at Ashfield. Much of her vast mahogany furniture came too, together with quantities of food – sardines and hams with which (despite her distrust of tinned goods) she had stacked her shelves and now hid on the tops of wardrobes, against the day when the Huns should seek to starve her out. It was particularly dreadful to Agatha to see the fate of that part of Margaret's hoard which was not immune to the passage of time – mouldy jams, fermented plums, butter and sugar nibbled by mice, moth-eaten velvets and silks, lengths of print rotted by the passing of the years, papers crumbled to dust. Margaret wept among the waste. What, Agatha wondered, was the point of being thrifty and prudent? She was deeply troubled by the discovery and destruction of those bags of weevily flour, fine linen garments gone into holes, deliquescent preserves; it seemed a universal omen, disintegration like that described in Kipling's story, 'The Mother Hive'. Just as Margaret's provisions were shown to be useless and her defences vulnerable to erosion and attack, so the familiar, ordered pre-War world was decomposing and collapsing into ruin.

In July 1915 Archie had three days' leave. He had been promoted to Captain in the Royal Field Artillery, to which he had been seconded, since trouble with his sinus made it impossible for him to fly. Agatha was relieved but still tense. They spent the time together in London, trying to forget the war, but it passed in a flash. Agatha then arranged to get herself to Paris, to be nearer him, only to find on arrival that further leave had been indefinitely postponed. Though Miss Dryden offered her a temporary job, Agatha felt she should return to England and the hospital, even though it was unlikely that she would obtain another permit to travel to France. Frustrated, lonely, tired by her two o'clock hospital shift and the chilly walk home, she succumbed to influenza and bronchitis and had to leave the hospital for three or four weeks. She returned to find that a dispensary had been opened, with Mrs Ellis, a local doctor's wife, and Eileen Morris in charge. Agatha joined them as assistant and began to study for the examinations at Apothecaries' Hall which would qualify her to dispense medicine for a medical officer or a chemist.

The hours were better, alternate mornings and afternoons, ending at six o'clock, which made it easier to fit in her duties at Ashfield. There was now a good deal of housework, since the two strong girls who had acted as cook and parlour-maid had been replaced by two elderly maid-servants. Auntie-Grannie also needed encouragement and attention, especially when she dropped stitches in her knitting and sat despairing at her failing sight. (A 'List of shawls and scarves she has crocheted during the Great War' nonetheless had 144 entries.)

Though Agatha eventually found dispensing monotonous, it was calm and orderly and the dispensary an oasis in the chaos that otherwise engulfed her. Mrs Ellis taught Agatha the practical side, while Eileen instructed her in the theory of physics and chemistry. She found it difficult at first but she was helped by her talent for mathematics, especially algebra, and her liking for codifying and classifying, symbols and signs, lists and measuring. In carefully ruled notebooks she described in alphabetical order the appearance and properties of various substances, the sources from which they may be derived, their active principles and the substances with which they are incompatible – aconitine, cascara, cannabis indica, quinine, gentiana ('looks like Russian chocolate') .... She made lists of substances to be recognised: 'Extract of Ergot liquid: smells of bad meat extract; Collodium: smells of ether – white deposit round cork.' There were notes on alkaloids, tables summarising the preparation of antimony, belladonna, digitalis, morphine, etc., with recommended doses. The most endearing entry had nothing to do with pharmacy. It was a pencilled list of names – Archibald Christie, Reggie Lucy and Amyas Boston (a former beau, who had acted in *The Blue Beard of Unhappiness* and whose name Agatha was later to give the victim in *Five Little Pigs*). Each name was paired with Agatha's own married name, and the letters common to each pair were crossed out. It was the game girls play, counting up the remaining letters and chanting formulas which show which man they should marry. Most interesting and touching is the last pair, coupling Clara Miller and Agatha Christie, in an attempt, presumably, to discover what, now Agatha was married, their relationship would be.

Archie's next leave was in October 1915 and they spent it in the New Forest. They celebrated their wedding anniversary, and Christmas, by post. Archie wrote:

Many happy returns of the 24th (and incidentally Christmas). You were really rather a dear last year, entrusting yourself boldly to me, but you will never really regret it and I shall love you as much as then – more I think. I wish I could get home for the anniversary celebrations but alas my 3 months hard labour is not up till nearly the end of January. Still then when I come home as a temporary major with about £700 a year pay we will revel in the flesh pots .... Blast the War, which keeps me here ....

His promotion to Squadron Commander and Temporary Major was gazetted on January 27th; on New Year's Day he had again been mentioned in despatches for especial bravery. In his letters to Agatha, he still tried to be frivolous. One, sent in July 1916, was an official paper stamped in large red letters, 'Secret':

Dear Miss, in response to your request I forward herewith your character and trust you will find it to your satisfaction. We are never wrong. Our fee is only £1.1s.

Yours faithfully, The OMNISCIENT ONE.

Character of Miss A. M. C. Miller

A kindly and affectionate disposition; fond of animals except worms and cockchafers; fond of human beings except husbands (on principle). Normally lazy but can develop and maintain great energy. Sound in limb and eye, wind not good up hill. Full of intelligence and artistic taste. Unconventional and inquisitive.

Face good especially hair; figure good and skin still excellent. Can wheedle well. Wild but if once captured would make a loving and affectionate wife.

Archie was again mentioned in despatches in January 1917 and the following month promoted to Depot Commander and Lieutenant Colonel. To Agatha's delight he was also awarded – she never knew why – the Order of St Stanislaus Third Class, with swords, a medal so pretty that she always longed to wear it as a brooch. Altogether 1917 was more bearable for Agatha, although the War seemed never-ending. Archie had three periods of leave and in between she worked for the Apothecaries' examination. She had no trouble in passing two out of the three parts, chemistry and materia medica (the composition of medicines, doses and so on). The practical part, however, reduced her to the same ham-handed state she had displayed when asked to play the piano in public at Miss Dryden's, but at her second attempt she passed, largely, she believed, because, rather than rolling pills or making suppositories, she had only to mix medicine and wait for the appropriate reactions to occur.

It was during this practical training that Agatha encountered a person of memorably strange demeanour, the more creepy because he was so ordinary. This was one of the principal pharmacists of Torquay, to whom she had been sent for coaching. Having demonstrated the making of some sort of suppositories and shown Agatha how to turn them out of the mould, he left her to box them, telling her to prepare labels stating that the dose contained a drug in the proportion of one part to a hundred. Agatha, however, was certain that the pharmacist had miscalculated, his actual mixture being ten times as strong. Sure enough, the decimal point in his calculations was in the wrong place. Agatha knew how easily such errors could be made. (She had once awoken at three o'clock in the morning with the vague recollection of putting a carbolic-contaminated lid on a pot of ointment and had immediately got up and gone to the dispensary to check.) She had been horrified by the casual manner in which an experienced pharmacist mixed this and that with the utmost confidence, compared with the prudence of the amateurs in her dispensary. This time she knew the pharmacist had been dangerously careless. Agatha's reaction is interesting. She did not think it wise to point out the mistake; this man was not, she thought, the sort of person who would admit to having made an error, especially to a student. She deliberately tripped, upset the tray on which the suppositories were cooling and firmly trod on them, apologising profusely. That episode was only part of the story. Its sequel came on another occasion, when, trying to impress her, the pharmacist took from his pocket a lump of stuff and asked her whether she knew what it was: 'It's curare,' he said. 'Know about curare? Interesting stuff, very interesting. Taken by the mouth, it does you no harm at all; enters the bloodstream, it paralyses and kills you ... do you know why I keep it in my pocket?' 'No,' she said, 'I haven't the slightest idea.' It seemed to her an extremely foolish thing to do. 'Well, you know,' he said thoughtfully, 'it makes me feel powerful.' The pharmacist was to reappear in Agatha's life: as Mr Zachariah Osborne, in *The Pale Horse*.

The Red Cross record card showed that during the war Agatha worked a total of 3400 hours, unpaid from October 1914 to December 1916 and, thereafter, as a dispenser, at an annual rate of £16 until the end of her service in September 1918. Her unofficial record was a sixty-page hand-made volume, illustrated with coloured drawings, bound in card and tied with pink and gold ribbon, which she and Eileen Morris devised between them. The contents of *What We Did in the Great War* included an opera, *The Young Students*, by 'AMC', complete with score, an 'Agony Column', 'Hints on Etiquette' ('Sister: "never omit to say 'Doctor' at least once after every third word ..."'), and a parody, 'The Chemist and The Pharmacists,' by 'AC', after Lewis Carroll:

> ... The centrifugalizing force
> Was whirling fast on high,
> No leucocytes were there, because
> No leucocytes were nigh;
> But many epithelial cells
> Were passed up high and dry.
>
> The Chemist and the Pharmacist
> Were writing their reports,
> They wept like anything to see
> Such quantities of noughts –
> (Correct to seven places too!)
> Percentages of sorts ....

Archie's preoccupations were more serious; one of the letters he sent in 1917 gives some indication of his duties:

> My darling Angel
>
> All is activity for the moment. I was glued to a telephone till 11pm last night and my temper is not so sweet today in consequence. I sentenced a man to 28 days of what the *Daily Mirror* used to call 'crucifixion' i.e. being tied to a tree and undergoing other punishments and fatigues because he refused to work, went absent without leave and pretended to be sick when he was not ....

At the beginning of December Archie was mentioned in despatches for the fourth time. On New Year's Day 1918 he was awarded the Distinguished Service Order and became a Companion of St Michael and St George. There was one more leave, in June, and then, to Agatha's joy, in September he was posted home, as a Colonel, to the Air Ministry. She left the hospital at once, joined him at an hotel and began to look round for a furnished flat.

Archie was just twenty-nine and Agatha twenty-eight. They had both grown used to tiredness, pain and grief, seen suffering and death, and were in different ways more mature. But for most of those crucial four years they had been apart and, while they had learnt how to sustain each other in difficult and precarious times, they were used to meeting and parting rather than being together for weeks at a stretch. The beginning of Agatha's married life – for when she left Ashfield she felt it had really begun – was not what she would have envisaged five or six years before. The country was still at war, and they and their microscopic flat at 5 Northwick Terrace, in St John's Wood, were looked after not by a maid but by Archie's batman, Bartlett. Archie worked long hours at the Air Ministry and Agatha, missing the hospital and her friends, filled in her days with a course of shorthand, where she struggled, and book-keeping, which she enjoyed and did well. It was as she left the secretarial school that she saw one of the most curious sights she had ever seen:

> Everywhere there were women dancing in the street ... laughing, shouting, shuffling, leaping even, in a sort of wild orgy of pleasure, an almost brutal enjoyment. It was frightening. One felt perhaps that if there had been any Germans around the women would have torn them to pieces. Some of them I suppose were drunk, but all of them looked it. They reeled, they lurched, shouted.... I got home to find Archie was home from his Air Ministry. 'Well, that's that,' he said, in his usual calm and unemotional fashion.

It was November 11th and the Armistice had been declared. The Great War was over.

7

'... menace and murder and sudden death ...'

It was in the middle of the War that Agatha had first tried her hand at a detective story. In retrospect an important moment, it did not seem significant at the time. For one thing, writing crime fiction was far from being her main preoccupation. The War, Archie's survival, her mother's and grandmother's failing health, the difficulty of keeping up Ashfield and the demands of the dispensary were such serious matters that, by comparison, writing a book was no more than a trivial pastime. Writing was in any case neither a new nor a surprising hobby for Agatha. Clara and Madge had written stories; so had she. For a long time she had been interested in the mysterious and sinister, as she showed in one of her earliest poems, 'Down in the Wood', of which the second verse ran:

> Bare brown branches against a mad moon
> (*And Something that stirs in the wood*),
> Leaves that rustle and rise from the dead,
> Branches that beckon and leer in the light
> (*And Something that walks in the wood*).
> Skirling and whistling, the leaves are alive!
> Driven by Death in a devilish dance!
> Shrieking and swaying of terrified trees,
> A wind that goes sobbing and shivering by ...
>
> *And Fear – naked Fear passes out of the wood!*

The dispensary, moreover, encouraged throughts of murder and malpractice, inspiring the poem 'In a Dispensary', published in 1924 in *The Road of Dreams*, (but not reprinted). The potions on its shelves were enough to cause a shiver:

> From the Borgias' time to the present day,
>   their power has been proved and tried!
> Monkshood blue, called Aconite,
>   and the deadly Cyanide!

Here is sleep and solace and soothing of pain
- and courage and vigour new!
Here is menace and murder and sudden death
- in these phials of green and blue!

There was more than the contents of the dispensary – and the
unnerving habits of the local pharmacist – to incline Agatha to
write a murder story. The Victorian and Edwardian press had
always relished a mystery and every opportunity was taken to
place before the reading public the details of sensational murder
trials, with ingenious solutions propounded by special correspondents and lofty summings-up from moralising editors. These
were the items Auntie-Grannie liked Agatha to read to her.
Agatha herself may not have enjoyed these reports but she was
certainly fascinated by problems and puzzles, by aberrant behaviour and the reasons why people departed from normal
routine. Perhaps, too, she liked to learn how people kept their
secrets hidden, for she herself was secretive. As a child she had
been teased about her frosty proclamation, 'I don't care for parting with information,' when asked why she had not reported that
a parlourmaid had been seen tasting soup from the tureen before
her parents came into dinner. It was the sort of phrase Agatha
must have heard from some adult and, although she admitted it
was pompous, she was proud of the fact that it stuck. Unlike
Madge, who could and would make a good story of anything,
Agatha resembled Frederick, who, when asked what he had done
with his day, would say, 'Oh, nothing.' She kept her own counsel
and occupied herself with private fantasies. She was interested in
techniques and stratagems for keeping secrets safe, in musical
patterns and mathematical codes, her aptitude enhanced by practice with puzzle-books, riddles and, eventually, theoretical studies
in elementary physics and chemistry.

In her childhood there was plenty of fuel for those who were
entertained by mysteries and paradoxes, for the end of the nineteenth century and the beginning of the twentieth saw the publication of an increasing number of ever more ingenious detective
stories. As a child Agatha read Dickens's *Bleak House* and Wilkie
Collins's two detective stories, *The Woman in White* and *The
Moonstone*. With Madge, she had enjoyed Conan Doyle's early
Sherlock Holmes stories, and, at the age of eight, she was fascinated by Madge's reading aloud of Anna Katharine Green's detective story, *The Leavenworth Case*. In 1908, as we have seen,

she had been particularly caught by *The Mystery of the Yellow Room*, a long, melodramatic tale of the attempted murder, by what appeared to be a fiendish supernatural agency, of a beautiful young woman sleeping in a sealed chamber, a heroine who, it emerged, was hiding some dreadful secret. *The Mystery of the Yellow Room* had a particularly attractive hero, the journalist Joseph Rouletabille, a young man of persistently mysterious origins, whose pursuit of the murderer was the more enthusiastic because he was competing with a disdainful and sinister professional detective, Frederic Larsan, 'the great Fred'.

It was while they were discussing one of these detective stories that Madge had challenged Agatha to write one herself. This suggestion was at the back of Agatha's mind when dispensary work began to become monotonous and she decided to try, adopting what was to become her standard practice: beginning by deciding upon the crime and settling on a procedure which made it particularly hard to detect. What she sought was a plot that was simultaneously commonplace and surprising: 'I could, of course, have a very *unusual* kind of murder for a very *unusual* motive, but that did not appeal to me artistically.' She wanted a riddle: 'The whole point was that it must be somebody obvious but at the same time, for some reason, you would then find that it was not obvious, that he could not possibly have done it. But really of course he had.' She next settled on the characters, discovering the difficulty of basing fictional characters on people she knew and breaking the creative log-jam only after seeing some striking people in a tram. It was not so much that they were odd-looking; rather, as with the three people in the Gezirah Hotel who had been the models in *Snow Upon the Desert*, that their relationship and their behaviour made Agatha begin to speculate.

Next came the question of the detective. She wanted someone like Rouletabille, a detective of a type which had not been used before. She eventually decided that he should be a Belgian refugee; as she recalled in a memorable sentence of her autobiography, Torquay was full of Belgian refugees, bewildered and suspicious, who wanted to be left alone, 'to save some money, to dig their garden and manure it in their own particular and intimate way'. The detective was to be clever, meticulous, with an impressive name and some knowledge of crime and criminals. Agatha made Hercule Poirot a retired Belgian police officer. Like Larsan, he was in his way an artist, with a high opinion of himself. There have been a number of theories as to Poirot's origins in Agatha's imagination. Some have pointed to Hercules Popeau, a former member of the Sûreté in Paris, who had been created well before the War by Mrs Marie Belloc Lowndes, or to Hercule Flambeau, G. K. Chesterton's criminal-turned-detective. Others have drawn attention to the fictional Eugène Valmont, formerly 'chief detective of the government of France', a character of overweening vanity and tolerant, good-natured contempt for the English people and, particularly, the English police. Valmont was the creation of Robert Barr, who published his stories in 1904 and 1905. Another critic, François Rivière, has connected Agatha's interest in food and cooking with the fact that Poirot's name is almost the same as the French word for a leek. Towards the end of her life Agatha was asked what she thought of some of these theories. She had only a vague memory of Eugène Valmont and certainly did not recall anything that might have directly influenced her creation. In fact, Poirot was very much her own invention; he was not a Frenchman because she had spent enough time in France for its citizens to be familiar to her, and she wanted something exotic. Belgians, at the time of Poirot's first manifestation, were the object both of respect ('Gallant little Belgium', overrun by Germany) and of some condescension, being thought to be neither as intellectual as the French nor as commercially astute as the Dutch. Poirot was clever, and equipped with a pompous character, ridiculous affectations, a luxuriant moustache and a curious egg-shaped head – in contrast to Rouletabille's bullet-shaped one. His creator could admire him without having to be so deferential that she felt unable to manipulate him. It does not matter whether certain of Poirot's features were derived, a fragment here, a morsel there, from other works that had contributed to the rich mulch in Agatha's subconscious; in his extravagance of personality he was sufficiently plausible to stand and survive by himself.

Agatha worked on and off at her story, writing it out in long-hand and, as each chapter was done, typing it on Madge's old machine. She was distracted by it but, at the half-way point, became tired and cross at wrestling with the exposition of her plot. Clara then suggested that she should take it away to finish during her fortnight's holiday, so *The Mysterious Affair at Styles* was largely completed at the Moorland Hotel at Haytor on Dartmoor. Agatha wrote all morning, walking over the moor to think out the next part of the book in the afternoon. Then she dined, slept for twelve hours, and set to work again the following morning. With a dozen of these concentrated bursts the back of her work was broken; she brought the draft home, tinkered with it – adding 'love interest' on the model of popular detective novels – and sent it away to be professionally typed. It went first to Hodder and Stoughton, came back, went elsewhere, was returned, was sent to Methuen, came back once more, and, last, was despatched to John Lane at The Bodley Head, where it appeared to sink without trace.

Agatha quickly forgot about it. Archie came to work at the Air Ministry in London, her real married life began, the War ended, and she found herself expecting a baby. Though astonished at the discovery, she was thrilled. 'My ideas of having a baby had been that they were things that were practically automatic. After each of Archie's leaves I had been deeply disappointed to find that no signs of a baby appeared. This time I had not even expected it.' She consulted a sensible doctor in Torquay, unhappily named Dr Stabb (his colleagues were Dr Carver and Dr Quick) and, although she suffered nine months of morning sickness, on August 5th the baby was born with little trouble. Agatha's daughter was called Rosalind Margaret Clarissa; she was born at Ashfield.

Agatha was still deeply attached to Ashfield. It was near the sea, it had trees, many of the belongings she had grown up with were there, and at its centre was Clara. Few of Agatha's friends were in London and she and Archie were not sufficiently well off to entertain very much or to amuse themselves with more than an occasional supper in town or visit to a dance hall. In Torquay, however, things were easier. Ashfield was large and, though some of Agatha's contemporaries, now married, lived rather grandly, there were still enough cheerful young people to enjoy a picnic on the moors or an impromptu party. On one occasion, for instance, Agatha gave a 'Poodle Party' at Ashfield, which all the guests attended dressed as dogs; a concession was made in Clara's case and she was allowed to come as a butterfly. Agatha wore a headdress of astrakhan and Archie's dinner jacket. She had cut a hole in the trousers and inserted the spring from a Captive Pencil (the sort held by a spring so that it would bend for use but bounce back when released), having substituted a pom-pom for the pencil itself.

What did Archie make of these proceedings? As his letters show, he had been a gay and light-hearted young man, and he was to amuse his daughter and later her school-friends with jokes,

games and wonderful presents. But he also succumbed easily to
anxiety. Agatha spoke of his unemotional manner but to some
extent that may have been a mask. Archie could be edgy, his
sinus gave him trouble and his digestion was delicate: there were
many evenings, Agatha wrote, when he came home from a taxing
day at the Air Ministry unable to eat, until, after some hours
groaning on the bed, he would suddenly say, to Agatha's constant
amazement, that he felt like trying something with treacle or
golden syrup. Archie had fought courageously in the War – the
repeated acts of bravery that had brought him his medals and so
many mentions in despatches also suggest quick reactions and
finely-tuned sensitivity to the needs of the moment – and it had
been a long, depressing, noisy, filthy campaign, whose effects he
had tried to conquer while on his leaves by being frivolous, but
which had still left him grave and serious. He had been obliged
to grow up too fast. Like a schoolboy, he demanded the smooth,
sweet viscosity of golden syrup to comfort his nervous stomach
and, with a sudden infusion of sugar, refuel his slender, exhausted
frame.

Not that Agatha overlooked this. She understood Archie and
was later to describe in her books the sort of difficulty that men
of his age and temperament found when they returned to everyday life after an heroic war. In many ways – as that unexpected
pregnancy shows – she was able to settle down more quickly to
changed conditions and a new pace. After a fortnight with the
newly-born Rosalind at Ashfield, she returned to London to secure the services of a nurse and a maid of all work, and to find
furnished accommodation in which they could live while she
looked for an unfurnished flat they could decorate and arrange
themselves. With much expenditure of time, energy and emotion,
all this was accomplished.

Archie had left the Air Force at the end of the War, determined
to go into the City to make some money. It was not too difficult
to find an opening, since City firms, whose usual recruits had
gone from school to the battlefield, there to be wiped out in
swathes, were naturally anxious to offer posts to brave and enthusiastic young officers. This did not mean, however, that Archie
earned a large salary; his first job brought him £500 a year, which,
with his gratuity and savings giving another £100 a year, and
Agatha's £100 annual income from her grandfather's trust, was
just enough. Rent and the price of food had risen enormously
compared with costs before the war but to employ a nurse and

cook/housemaid was not considered a luxury. Owning a motor car, however, would have been an immense extravagance.

Nonetheless, Agatha was perfectly happy. By a stroke of luck, she heard of an unfurnished flat, No. 96, in the same building – Addison Mansions – as the furnished one, No. 25, in which they were perching, and its ordering and decoration gave her a great deal of pleasure. She always enjoyed acquiring and embellishing houses; this time she and Archie papered and tiled the bathroom in scarlet and white, with the help of a painter and decorator. With a friend from the Air Force and his sister, they painted the sitting-room with shiny pale pink walls and, to the professional decorator's eventual grudging approval, covered the ceiling with black glossy paper decorated with hawthorn blossoms. Rosalind's nursery was washed with pale yellow paint, with an animal frieze around the top of the wall. The curtains were made elsewhere but Agatha bravely assembled loose covers for the furniture, though, she remembered, she 'did not attempt to do any piping'. She kept careful records of the furnishing and decorating expenses, some of which were assigned to her and some to Archie's account. Archie, for instance, bought Rosalind's frieze and a bed from Maples, Agatha a mattress and a mincing machine. The installation of a telephone (£4) was put down to Archie and purple quilts to a general housekeeping account. There was no piano, another reason why Ashfield remained important.

1919 was a good year for Agatha. She had found and was furnishing a pretty flat, she enjoyed her interesting and equably-tempered daughter, delighted in her husband and got on well with her servants. She was young and attractive and her family's health was good; she was not greatly worried about bills. Her spirits became even more buoyant with the next welcome surprise: just before she and Archie moved into the new flat, John Lane asked her to come to discuss the typescript of *The Mysterious Affair at Styles* which had been sent to The Bodley Head two years before. It was a moment of great significance in Agatha's life and her recollection of it is like a scene on the stage or in a picture. Indeed, she describes John Lane, 'a small man with a white beard', sitting behind a desk in a room full of pictures, looking Elizabethan, as if he should have been a portrait himself, with a ruff around his neck. Her memory has framed that encounter between the young amateur author and the shrewd professional publisher. At the time Agatha was delighted with the outcome. John Lane liked her book, though he suggested various

minor alterations and a major change in the ending. He would
publish it, and would give her a ten per cent royalty on any
English sales over two thousand copies and on American sales
exceeding one thousand copies, together with half of anything the
book earned from serial or dramatic rights. The Bodley Head
was to have an option, at only a slightly increased rate of royalty,
on her next five books. In later years, when Agatha knew her
work was popular and her name valuable, she would feel that
John Lane had taken advantage of her inexperience – as indeed
he had.

The relationship between writer and publisher is studded with
traps but at this first meeting, matters were relatively simple. John
Lane drove a hard bargain with an untried author, who was
overjoyed at the thought of her book's being published and who
had not contemplated this as a way of earning money. She agreed
to alter the last chapter, changing it from a court scene to a
conversation in the library between Poirot and Hastings, his
amanuensis and well-meaning but blundering colleague, and she
modestly celebrated her success with Archie. The serial rights of
The Mysterious Affair at Styles were sold to the *Weekly Times*
for £50, of which Agatha received half, and the volume was
published in America in 1920 and in England, at seven and sixpence, in 1921. Agatha dedicated it to Clara.

Soon after Rosalind's birth in 1919, Auntie-Grannie had died
at the age of ninety-two, of heart failure after an attack of bronchitis. With her death went part of the income salvaged from the
wreck of H. B. Chaflin, and Ashfield accordingly became even
more difficult for Agatha, Clara and Madge to keep up. Archie
first proposed that Ashfield be sold, to enable Clara to live more
economically and conveniently, but, when Agatha vigorously
protested that the idea was unthinkable, he suggested that she
should write another book. Although she did not believe she
would earn much money this way, she did draw some encouragement from Archie's remarks, which seemed to indicate that (like
Dermot in *Unfinished Portrait*) he did not wholly disapprove of
his wife's literary efforts.

Agatha next produced a thriller. Its catalyst was a discussion
overheard in an ABC teashop, in which the name 'Jane Fish'
struck Agatha as particularly odd and interesting. Jane Finn, as
she became, is an elusive figure, who has been entrusted in the
middle of the War with the delivery of certain important documents, which various individuals and factions are attempting to

obtain. The hero and heroine of the novel are a pair of 'young adventurers' (one of the titles Agatha originally tried), unemployed after leaving the Forces, ingenious, affectionate, unsophisticated and irrepressible and, particularly in the case of the girl, arch to the point of being irritating. The novel is especially interesting, however, not so much because it introduces Tommy and Tuppence Beresford, but for the first appearance of two important themes that were to figure in much of Agatha's work: the search for the mysterious possessor of some valuable secret or special knowledge – who may be a courier, a conspirator, the perpetrator of a crime, and who is as likely to be a woman as a man – and the identification of some powerful figure, able to buy unlimited information and arms, to travel anywhere and influence anyone, bent on domination. Sometimes, as in the story of the pursuit of Jane Finn by the 'man behind the Bolshevists', the two characters are opposed; in other books they are one and the same. The person who seeks to dominate is, without exception, evil at worst or of deplorable character at best; the possessor of secrets, on the other hand, may be either a sinister presence, an innocent pawn, or, as in the case where it is a detective with insight and experience, a force for good.

John Lane accepted *The Secret Adversary*, as Agatha eventually called her second novel, for publication in 1922. It earned her £50, although what proportion of this came from the sale of serial rights and what from an advance on royalties is unclear from the ambiguous sentence in her draft autobiography. More encouraging than cheques from John Lane and the *Weekly Times* was the praise she received from Bruce Ingram, editor of the *Sketch*, who commissioned her to write a series of Poirot stories for his paper. She began to compose these in 1921, together with another full-length detective novel, *Murder on the Links*, which was based on her recollection of a complicated case of murder that had happened in France not long before and on a number of French detective stories she had been reading. At this point, however, there were two interruptions.

The first was the prospect of the return to England of Agatha's brother Monty, who had been living in a precarious, harum-scarum way in various parts of the Empire. After Frederick's death in 1901 he had come home on leave and had then gone back to his regiment in India, where, having come of age and into his inheritance under Nathaniel's will, he proceeded to enjoy his legacy. It was quickly exhausted. Monty seems to have resigned his commission when his debts became too embarrassing and, unable to settle down, to have taken himself to Kenya to try his hand at farming, where, however, he neglected the tract of land he was granted, preferring to spend his time hunting elephants and other game. Apart from sending his mother and sisters lavish presents of silks and embroidery on his departure from India, and occasional telegrams requesting the urgent despatch of funds to Africa, Monty communicated rarely with his family. At the end of 1910 they endeavoured to trace him and learnt that he had moved to Uganda, where he was 'enormously popular' and frequently destitute. In 1911 he conceived a brilliant scheme for running small cargo boats on Lake Victoria. He sent Madge letters of support from enthusiastic friends and appealed to her to stake him. Thinking that at last a career for Monty had been found, Madge wired him his fare to England, and did what she could to help him finance the building of the first boat, the *Batenga*, in a boatyard in Essex. Monty threw himself into the project with alarming keenness: the *Batenga* was fitted with teak, ebony and ivory, special fireproof china and engraved wine glasses were designed, and a captain's uniform for Monty ordered from the tailor. Between visits to supervise progress on the boat's construction Monty would come to London and stay in an expensive hotel in Jermyn Street, lavishing treats upon himself – sets of silk pyjamas, a *bonsai* tree, and the like – and upon his family – a sapphire bracelet for Madge, and a *petit point* evening bag, acquired, of course, with the money she had put up in the first place. His family despaired of the *Batenga*'s ever being completed, let alone its arriving on Lake Victoria.

The venture might have succeeded but war broke out just as the boat was to be shipped to Africa, and it was sold for a song to the Government. Monty returned to the Army and enlisted in the King's African Rifles. He was known to his fellow officers as 'Puffing Billy' and, years later, Agatha heard from one of them about his exploits in the war. Monty had nearly been court-martialled for insisting that his convoy of mules halt at a spot which he declared a perfect place for battle with the Germans. His commanding officer disagreed and was protesting against Monty's insubordination when a large force of Germans actually arrived, was engaged and decisively defeated in what became known as 'Miller's Battle'. There was no court-martial. Monty was wounded in the arm during the African campaign and was later transported to hospital, with great difficulty, since he repeatedly climbed out of the ambulance train; according to the Colonel, who told Agatha about him. 'Every time they put him in one side he got out of the other. ...' He escaped from the hospital after three days and, though frail, eventually resumed his rough and tumble existence: 'mad as a hatter,' said Agatha's informant. Now, four years after the end of the War, Monty was coming home and preparations would have to be made for his reception. It seemed, however, that Agatha would not be there to welcome him, for the other interruption to the smooth course of her life with Archie and Rosalind was a scheme that would take her out of England: a tour of the Empire, lasting an entire year.

8

'... First Class! Good oh! Right here ...'

The Empire Tour was, in retrospect, richly comic. It was not so much that the Empire itself was entertaining, though the places to which Agatha was conveyed were certainly outlandish and exotic and the methods of transportation various and unpredictable, as that the inhabitants of the Empire were wonderful to behold. Their appearance and manners were bizarre, they were perfectly unselfconscious, and all a little larger than life – not just the people Agatha and her companions met on their travels but also the members of the Empire Expedition itself. Its style was set by its central figure: Major E. A. Belcher. Had Major Belcher been a less colourful character, less a caricature of himself, the Expedition might have been more humdrum, even-tempered, less prone, perhaps, to catastrophe and unexpected changes of plan. But with Belcher at the helm, gloriously temperamental, marvellously disorganised, extravagant in his demands, everyone and everything associated with him became more violent in temper, more extreme in behaviour, more exaggerated in attitude. Belcher brought out the worst in nature and in people – and the best in Agatha's writing. The account of the tour in her *Autobiography* is fluent and funny but it is not half as hilarious as the diary she kept, the sequence of letters she sent her family, and the two large albums of photographs and souvenirs she assembled when, at last, she and Archie escaped from Belcher's clutches.

Major Belcher had been a master at Clifton, where he had conceived a liking for Archie, whose efficiency he came to respect and for whose wife he now felt affection, not least because she listened while he talked. His genius appears to have lain in successfully persuading people to appoint him to positions of authority, where a flair for organisation was required. During the Great War, for instance, he had first invented and then accepted the post of Controller of Supplies of Potatoes; as Agatha wrote later, the production and distribution of potatoes was fraught with complication: 'At the hospital, I know, we never had them. Whether the shortage was entirely due to Belcher's control of them I don't know, but I should not be surprised to hear it.' For Belcher was in fact unimaginably inefficient, his true bent being for what is nowadays called 'public relations'. He was very good at self-promotion; as he had said of the potato job, 'I didn't know a thing. But I wasn't going to let on. I mean, you can do anything – you've only got to get a second-in-command who knows a bit about it, and read it up a bit, and there you are!' He would volunteer, full of self-importance and high expectations as to salary and conditions, for one undertaking after another where there were bound to be difficulties and disagreements. The Empire Exhibition was one of these.

It was to be held in London in 1924 as a showcase for the products of the British Empire, rather as the Great Exhibition in 1851 had been. Belcher had been appointed Assistant General Manager and invited (probably at his own suggestion) to lead a mission to the Dominions – Australia, New Zealand, Canada and parts of South Africa – to drum up interest among the political and business leaders of the various provinces and territories. The Expedition would take nine or ten months, the costs of railway and steamship travel being met by the countries the Mission was to visit. Belcher now asked Archie to join the team as Financial Adviser: 'You were Head of the School at Clifton, you've had all this experience in the City. You're just the man I want.' Archie's expenses would be paid and he would receive a fee of £1,000. If Agatha were to come, her travelling expenses would be covered and Archie's fee would just take care of her part of the hotel bills and the cost of a month's holiday in Honolulu for the two of them.

It was a gamble, since Archie's employer would not promise to hold his job open. The riskiness of the proposal was, however, part of its attraction. Archie was bored, for the demands of the City compared poorly with his wartime responsibilities; he disliked and distrusted his employer, and he was impatient for more authority. Agatha, for her part, pottered along comfortably until she was offered a test, but, energetic, perceptive and interested, she liked challenges and rose to them. She also longed to travel to the strange and remote places she knew only from explorers' tales and watercolours and from the exotic articles and fabrics of curious design and workmanship which her family and their friends had pounced upon. Travel in the nineteen-twenties and thirties was slow (that was part of the joy of it) and Agatha had believed that the brevity of the annual holiday Archie was allowed would prevent her from realising her dream of going to faraway places. Now, thanks to Belcher, they had the chance. There was little difficulty in contemplating a long separation from two-year-old Rosalind, who could be sent with her nurse to Madge or Clara. Nor did Agatha feel more than passing guilt at the prospect of leaving England just as Monty was about to return. Madge, who was closer to him in age, berated her sister for wishing to leave at this important moment but Agatha, supported by her mother, was adamant. 'A wife,' said Clara, '*ought* to be with her husband – and if she isn't, then he feels he has a *right* to forget her.' Agatha did not in fact feel that, if she did not accompany Archie, she would lose his affections, but Clara's convictions usefully buttressed her inclination to go with her husband rather than stay for her brother.

The Mission set off on January 20th, 1922. As well as Agatha, Archie and Belcher, the party included Mr Francis W. Bates, a tall, cadaverous young man, with heavy brows, and a wide and anxious mouth, who was to act as Belcher's secretary; Mr Hiam, an East Anglian potato king and friend of Belcher's, in the guise of agricultural adviser; and his wife and daughter Sylvia. They departed in some style: Belcher had secured for himself an audience with the King, who gave him a farewell present of two brace of pheasants from the Royal estates, and *The Times* had a photograph of the party on the platform at Waterloo. They are wrongly labelled, so that the nervous and diminutive Sylvia, huddled in furs and clutching a number of small packages, is designated Mrs Christie, while Agatha, beaming from beneath a cheerfully decorated hat, her coat embellished with a large bunch of violets given her by Clara and another bouquet in her arms, appears as Sylvia. Bates looks apprehensive: Archie, holding a pipe and leaning backwards, sceptical; Mrs Hiam smart, stout and ready for the rigours of the journey and the eccentricities of foreigners; Mr Hiam, with dog, solid and successful; and Belcher, a presence in a well-tailored overcoat, the model of a confident tycoon.

The Mission embarked on a ship of the Union Castle line, the RMS *Kildonan Castle*, pictured on the cover of the passenger list as a galleon, fully-rigged, breasting enormous waves and fighting a gale. This, indeed, was how the seas seemed to Agatha, who was immediately prostrated by the most violent and prolonged sickness, so uncomfortable that she resolved to get off at Madeira. She wrote to Clara, on the little Corona typewriter she carried with her:

> The day before we got there, I was very bad, sick without ceasing, having tried everything from champagne and brandy to dry biscuits and pickles, and my arms and legs were all going pins and needly and dead, so Archie fetched the doctor along, and he gave me teaspoonful doses of something or other, chloroform stuff, which stopped the sickness, and nothing to eat for twenty-four hours, and then Brand's beef essence. When we got to Madeira, Archie got me up on the deck, and fed me with it, whilst I almost wept because Madeira looked so beautiful! I'd no idea of it.

From then on she recovered, her stomach lurching only occasionally when the sea was rough. She watched porpoises leaping and, to her delight, flying fish. There was plenty of ship-board entertainment – impromptu dances and concerts, a trapeze act on the struts holding up the lifeboats, a cricket match between first and second-class passengers, an after-dinner concert by 'The Nickelodeons', sports, and a fancy-dress dance, to which Agatha went as a Bacchante, and Belcher, in a costume hired from the ship's barber, as Chu Chin Chow, for which he won first prize. Belcher, not surprisingly, was made chairman of the Sports and Entertainment Committee. Archie and Agatha, who entered bravely for everything, 'had our first contest yesterday, when to our utter surprise, we knocked out two Belgians who have infuriated the ship by hanging on to the quoits and practising all day long. It was a most popular victory. Everyone kept coming up to us and saying, "I hear you've knocked out the Dagoes! Splendid.'"

The Mission dined at the Chief Engineer's table and the King's pheasants were served, together with Belcher's description of his visit to the King. Belcher had promised the Queen an album of photographs of the Mission and his doings, so he solemnly noted everything in a diary, including conversations with those anti-British Dutch passengers on board, of which an 'Extract', typed by Bates, was to be sent to the Palalce.

They landed at Cape Town in the evening of February 6th and were escorted to the Mount Nelson Hotel. Agatha was enchanted by the gardens – 'Most lovely flowers climbing up the houses, lots of mauvy *blue* ones, great morning glories and a kind of hawthorn hedge' – and by Table Mountain and delicious juicy peaches Best of all was the sunshine – she adored the heat – and surfing, or 'bathing with planks', as she called it in her first long letter home, written on February 8th. Agatha and Archie slipped away whenever they could to Muizenberg for surfing, or to a white sandy beach, edged with mountains, at a place called Fish Hoek. It was a far cry from the bathing machines of Torquay, but even in these blissfully primitive surroundings the visitors behaved modestly: 'No bathing huts (and no cover!) but a kind young man offered us a hutch where he kept fishing tackle ... swimming is a little tame after surfing. We are going to buy light curved boards (that don't jab you in the middle) and absolutely master the art.'

Belcher, who had already displayed an ominous temper by complaining that African peaches were unripe, was growing irritable. He had a septic foot: 'the doctor says he must lie up and rest it, and he says he can't afford the time. Bates had forgotten to get him more carbolic, and he'd had a tight boot on all day, the food in the Hotel was atrocious, and the doctor has cut him down to one whisky and soda a meal, so matters nearly reached a climax last night.' Poor Bates was having a difficult time. 'He has been convinced ever since leaving England (which he has never left before) that he is going into deadly peril and will never return alive. He insisted on the BEE insuring his life before he started. ...' The others teased him. 'We sent him a pc yesterday with a picture of a Puff Adder on it, and an earnest warning purporting to come from the "Society for the Protection of Visitors" and Bates has been busily looking them up in the Telephone Directory, and cannot understand why no-one seems to know where their offices are!'

Agatha was enjoying herself hugely. She went to a garden party at the Archbishop's Palace (looking, according to the local newspaper, lovely, 'in pale yellow beaded on the bodice with steel beads and a big black bow and ends on the left hip'), to the opening of Parliament by the Governor General, then the Duke of Connaught, and to a luncheon at Government House: 'Belcher and Archie got on heroically with the Princess, and quite cheered her up. Belcher told her his famous lion story, and she and Archie agreed that they both hated getting up early and could never remember people's names, to which Archie added cheerily, "But that must be rather awkward for you in your line of business." ' The most interesting visit Agatha paid was to the Cape Town Museum. She wrote enthusiastically about prehistoric rock carvings and wall paintings and about the Museum's collection of models of skulls, on which the director lectured at length; 'altogether one of the best afternoons I have ever spent.'

Agatha had hoped that the Expedition would reach India and Ceylon but sailings proved too complicated to include this diversion in their itinerary, so Belcher decided that at the beginning of April the party should go on to Australia. First, however, the Christies, Bates and Belcher were to make an excursion to Rhodesia – that is, until Belcher discovered that he and his companions were not to be treated with appropriate deference:

> Grand crisis last night. The Union Government has given us free passes and a saloon on the Railways, but Rhodesia has been pigheaded and would only dole out three passes, and declined to have our saloon running over their lines without payment of a farthing a mile (which would work out at about £140) and ... this rather tore things. The ultimatum arrived last night, and Belcher flew into a really magnificent rage, and after a few preliminary remarks as to its being everybody else's fault for not handling the Railways properly proceeded to draft and send off vitriolic telegrams, Bates taking them down in shorthand, typing them, and dashing off to the PO with them in a taxi, and returning to do it again as Belcher thought of fresh things to say. ... Our itinerary (for the ninth time) was again completely revised by the perspiring Archie, and we are now leaving by RMS *Briton* for Durban on Tuesday next, and working through the Transvaal from there.

A day later, however:

> Rhodesia has climbed down utterly, will do anything we want! Great success of Belcher's fierce tactics. Grand revising of the itinerary, everything being now fixed up for Durban. I think we shall do that first and Rhodesia afterwards, returning ... to catch the *Aeneas* on the 7th April.

As it turned out, only Archie left on the *Briton*, for a terrific south-easter got up and Agatha decided to travel with Belcher and Bates by train to Pretoria. It was a ghastly journey:

> the hottest day I have ever known. Table Mountain seemed to get red hot and you just breathed red hot dust. ... The first night in the train was quite all right. When I woke up the following morning we were in the Karoo – all dust and stones and tiny bushes and little hills – rather wild-looking and desolate – and attractive from that point of view – but it got steadily hotter and hotter till the train was like an oven or a peach house in summer. Belcher and I played piquet most of the day and drank lemon squashes without ceasing!

On through the hills to Durban, where they were reunited with
Archie. Here there was another outburst:

> Belcher had been charming on leaving Cape Town, but at Bloemfon-
> tein General Hertzog had refused point blank to meet him, and his
> temper suffered in consequence. Also a new BEE pamphlet, sup-
> posedly written in Afrikaans, turns out be be in High Dutch and the
> wretched Bates was nearly slain in consequence. In fact, he was
> officially dismissed and told he could return to Southampton at once
> by the first boat – but the sentence appears to be commuted to separ-
> ation from the High War Lord, to be attached to Archie and myself
> for Johannesburg and Rhodesia. Belcher is not going to Rhodesia –
> he is returning by the *Briton* to Cape Town and sailing on the *Sophoc
> les* if he can get through in time. But Archie and I fear he won't, and
> that we shall have him with us on the *Aeneas* after all!!

After a brief look at Durban's tropical gardens ('like all really
beautiful places – just like Torquay'), Archie, Agatha and Bates
set off together for Johannesburg and Rhodesia, a journey more
hazardous that they had expected, for they found themselves on
the fringe of the Rand Rebellion (provoked by the efforts of the
Chamber of Mines to cut costs by increasing the black workforce
in the goldmines at the expense of the better-paid whites).

> At Germiston a wire was handed in from the Trade Commissioner
> ... saying Jo'burg was unsafe, he would meet us on the platform there
> and had arranged accommodation for us at Pretoria instead. ... All
> the Hotels had shut down that afternoon with their waiters etc. on
> strike – and there was no meat and no bread, as the bakers had come
> out, and the strikers had stopped all taxis and pulled out the drivers.
> They were throwing hand grenades in the street. ... Today they have
> proclaimed Martial law in Jo'burg – and all the bars are shut here. It
> seems an idiotic moment for coming to try and talk about an exhibi-
> tion that is to be held in two years' time – but we are off to Rhodesia
> on Tuesday, so must do what we can. They don't think the Railways
> will come out, and this place is pretty quiet.

Agatha had by now recieved letters from home – Clara had
bought Monty an invalid chair, there were various questions
about the purchase of Chinese Bonds, Rosalind had a cough.
From the Grand Hotel in Pretoria Agatha wrote to her daughter;
her letter has a sentence or two about butterflies and 'choo-choos'
but is less of a message to a two-year-old than a reminder to
Auntie Punkie (as Madge was now called) and a reflection
of Agatha's own anxiety that Rosalind might forget her: 'I

Agatha in a feathered hat rollerskating
with the Lucys on the pier.

Madge with Jack on Matilda.

On the pier at Torquay.

With Archie after his investiture in 1919.

Rosalind, aged six, with Peter.

The Mission setting sail:
Mr Hiam, Belcher, Bates, Archie,
Agatha, and a bystander

expect you love Uncle Jim and Auntie Punkie very much now, but if anyone asks you "who do you love?" you must say "Mummy"!'

Agatha and Archie were marooned in Pretoria for almost a week: 'Once there, we couldn't get away again, the strike having turned into a young revolution.' There were armoured cars in the town and bombs could be heard in the distance. Agatha, Archie and Bates passed the time swimming, playing bridge and examining the archives, but after five days they began to worry that they might never reach Rhodesia. They badgered their hosts but permission to leave was refused, until suddenly one morning, while Agatha was still in bed, a government representative arrived to say a car would be at their hotel in twenty minutes.

> Frenzied toilet and packing! We just took suitcases, all we could cram in, and left trunks with Bates who was to rejoin Belcher at the Cape as soon as a train runs. Had a splendid run into Jo'burg, stopped once or twice by cheerful-looking City gentlemen, smoking pipes, with bayonets tucked rakishly under their arms. Our train was due to leave at 10.45 and it got off at 11.30 to the sound of artillery and shrapnel, as the great attack on Fordsberg, which was to end the war, was just beginning.

The Rebellion was crushed by the Army and its ringleaders, members of the Third International, condemned to death. Agatha and Archie were now able to leave for Rhodesia, via Bechuanaland, where at every station natives were selling rugs, beads, baskets and small carved animals, which Agatha bought in vast quantities for Rosalind. Their overnight journey to Bulawayo was disturbed at three o'clock in the morning when 'an exquisitely dressed young man, looking like a musical comedy hero of the Wild West, entered our compartment and asked Archie where he was going. Disregarding Archie's first murmur of "Tea – but no sugar in it", he repeated his question, laying stress on the fact that he was not a waiter but an immigration officer. Archie, still fast asleep, replied: "Australia – at least, no, I'm going to Salisbury first."'

After a couple of days in Salisbury, playing bridge and examining citrus estates, they at last came to the Victoria Falls, with which Agatha was entranced. She wrote to Clara from the Victoria Falls Hotel:

> I can't bear to leave. It's not just the Falls themselves, although they are very wonderful – especially the width of them, I didn't realise that

they stretched for a mile and a quarter – but the whole place. No road, only paths, just the Hotel, primeval woods for miles and miles stretching into blueness. A delightful Hotel, long and low and white, with beautifully clean rooms, and wired all over like a fine meat safe against malarial mosquitoes.

Even here, however, there was a reminder of worldly responsibilities. 'An urgent telegram arrived from Belcher, telling us to return to Capetown via Johannesburg and "complete original programme" and demanding an answer by wireless, so he really has gone on the *Sophocles*, for which the Lord be thanked.'

Returning reluctantly to Cape Town, they found letters from Archie's family and John Lane. Agatha fired off a complaint to Madge: '*Do write*. The only letters that arrive are from Mrs Hemsley, Joab and Campbell [Archie's stepfather and brother] – all my family might be dead. Write me about my baba. It's a *month* now without a word – the first three weeks I got letters from Mother. Also, I want to know about Monty and everything – but especially my Rosalind.' There was, however, some news about the critics' reception of *The Secret Adversary*: 'Two batches of press cuttings from John Lane – *all* good – not one bad one. I'm very pleased with the *Punch* one. ... No grateful thanks from the people to whom I sent copies of the *SA* (NB even my nephew has not responded!!).' One stroke of luck was the discovery of a 'very nice ex-naval man, Captain Crowther', travelling in South Africa for what turned out to be Wilfred Pirie's firm. Agatha persuaded him to take the collection of wooden animals – elands, giraffes, hippopotamus, zebras (three cases altogether) – home to Southampton for posting to Torquay.

The SS *Aeneas*, of the Blue Funnel Line, sailed from Cape Town on April 9th. When they arrived at Adelaide, the 'Wild Man', as Agatha had taken to calling Belcher, was not there, but he had left a trail of messages, informing them that he had gone on to Melbourne and that they were to join him before setting off to Tasmania. In Melbourne, Agatha and Archie found Belcher 'laid up with a bad leg again and quite tame for the moment!' The trip to Tasmania reminded Agatha and Archie of how obnoxious Belcher had become: 'Wild Man worse than ever this morning. He is in his room darkened like a primeval cave, eating bread and milk, and growling at everybody. I offered to bandage his leg for him, and his polite reply was, "Why can't I be left alone?" He would not say whether he was going to Tasmania or not, and would not advance any money for anyone else

to go. ...' When they arrived at Launceston there was more
trouble.

> We went into the Town Hall and were kept waiting a few minutes
> while they looked for the Mayor. Fresh explosions from B. When
> found, he genially asked Belcher who and what he was – I thought he
> would have apoplexy! We then adjourned to the Commerical Travel-
> lers Club for ginger ale and 'squash lemons', Belcher muttering:
> 'There's only one thing to do! I shall go back to Melbourne the first
> thing tomorrow morning!' Fortunately, he was asked to make a short
> speech, which slightly restored him, but a further crushing blow
> awaited him at the station. No saloon – merely a first class reserved
> carriage! He really does think he is a King, or Lord Northcliffe – it's
> a sort of – do I mean meglamania? [sic] ... Australians will *not* stand
> 'side' – they are extraordinarily nice and kind, and awfully hospitable,
> but 'swank' does not go down well.

On arrival at Hobart, their duties began once more – an excursion to a jam factory and, for Archie, Agatha and Bates, an
exhibition of Tasmanian goods: 'We explained B's absence as
best we could, exaggerated his leg, and calmed everyone down,
and Archie made quite a good speech, without mumbling, speaking quite distinctly. ...' Agatha liked Tasmania, where the air
was chilly but invigorating, and especially a visit to a power
station, three thousand feet up and very cold, 'but through beautiful country, all silvery blue gums. All Australian scenery that I
have seen has a faintly austere quality, the distances all a soft
blue green – sometimes almost grey – and the white trunks of the
blue gums give a totally different effect, and here and there great
clumps of trees have been ringbarked and have died, and then
they are ghost trees, all white, with white waving branches. It's
all so – virginal – if there were nymphs in the woods, they would
never be caught.' The next day was interesting, too, for she
looked over the museum, to learn more about skulls and skele-
tons and Aborigine history. 'There were death casts of several of
the Aborigines, and a great collection of sketches and water
colour drawings of the Tasmania of a 100 years or so ago – some
of them perfectly lovely – done on that pale yellow and grey
paper and just tinted.'

Back in Melbourne, the Mission discovered a parcel of mail,
which Belcher and Archie had been carrying about in the belief
that it was cigarettes. The package contained the news that
Madge, who had been writing a play, had found a producer.
'Awfully exciting,' wrote Agatha, 'and I shall be furious if she

arrives "on the film" before I do. It seems as though there was such a thing as an agent who is some good. I've been rather idle – but have written a Grand Guignol sketch and a short story.' In fact, she made good use of scraps of time, writing long letters and short stories and drafting her next book, in interludes between tea parties, ladies' luncheons, official dinners and expeditions. Belcher's latest requirement was that the Mission should be given a tour of the bush, and this duly took place, the party sitting on bags of sawdust, travelling in horse-drawn trucks. The pace never slowed. Next day there was a tour of a brick field, a freezing works, a 'dried milk place', a lunch, a ride on a 'bush tram', Agatha travelling part of the way on the engine, and each night 'the usual Australian meal, a plate with a slice of beef, a slice of turkey, a slice of ham, some parsnips, some carrots, two kinds of potatoes always, bread sauce, horseradish and stuffing and a portion of Yorkshire pudding, and a good strong cup of black tea. Then apple pie and enormous jugs of cream.'

Belcher returned from Tasmania in parsimonious mood. 'He dined at the club (to save a shilling, but as he forgot to give up his room on leaving, and they kept it for him, the saving will not be appreciable); a fresh economy has occurred to him (since he is now a teetotaller), that all members of the Mission shall pay for their own drinks! We are resisting to the last ditch!' Since Agatha loathed the taste of alcohol and disliked its effect, in her case the objection to Belcher's proposal was entirely altruistic.

It was now late May. Agatha, whose stamina was always impressive, continued to enjoy herself enormously and in a picture in the Melbourne *Herald* she looked well and happy. The photography session, 'rather like Mr Pecksniff and Salisbury Cathedral, "From the North-East, from the North-West, from the East, from the South, from the South-East etc." ', was part of an interview she gave to an Australian journalist, who wrote a pleasant if earnest piece: 'Mrs Christie's early girlhood was spent in trying to decide on a career. She had thoughts of a convent. ...' It was the first time, but not the last, that Agatha was to find how different casual remarks can look when they are embellished in a newspaper article. Spurred on by these attentions, however, and by Madge's success, she did manage to write some short stories and, far away though she was, remembered to instruct Monty in his duties at Ashfield: 'Look after Mother, and see she changes her clothes after she's been hosing the garden. She's always sopped through.' She also put to good use her visits to innumerable canneries, writing in a letter to Clara: 'If you are buying canned peaches, Shepperton Packing Co. Green Label "Fancy" are good.'

It was while the Expedition was at Brisbane that Agatha made friends with some young women who were not only to remain close to her but whose influence at that particular moment was important. She had now been travelling for nearly six months, some of the time quietly with Archie but for the most part with three men who were all in different ways demanding – Bates, who needed to be teased but reassured, Archie, who had to be given special wifely attention but without fuss, and Belcher, who required good-humoured deference. Constant travelling, conversations, official meals and visits of inspection, too much time spent at close quarters with the same people – all this was making Bates more moody, Archie nervy, and Belcher explosive.

If Agatha's own temper was becoming ragged, she managed not to show it in her letters, which remained good-tempered and cheerful. But she welcomed the solace she received one evening, when, while dining alone in the hotel, she was invited by a Major Bell, 'whom Belcher and Archie had been confabbing with on cattle the night before', to meet his sister, who was also staying there. This was Miss Una Bell, who lived with her parents and brothers and sisters on an enormous farming station at Coochin. Miss Bell and her brother reminded Agatha of that large, affectionate, energetic and easy family, the Lucys in Torquay, and she immediately felt at home. Una asked Agatha to stay and, after 'a somewhat dreary garden party at Government House', Agatha set off the next evening for Coochin, leaving Archie to carry out a heavy programme of engagements. It was, she told Clara, 'a long deadly journey of about six hours in a train that crawled. We arrived at ten o'clock after motoring five miles, and the room seemed full of tall energetic girls cooking scrambled eggs over the fire and all talking at once! I went to bed dazed ... I was to stay two days, but I stayed a week ... I sorted out the Bells at last! Mrs Bell is delightful, full of character, and intent on her garden. ... They seem to own most of the cattle in Australia, and are really rather like a royal family with a little country of their own, and look after all their people with great seriousness. ...' There were many reminders of the happy, frivolous times Agatha had known in Torquay before the War:

They were getting up a show for their small village on the Friday

night, and we made costumes and rehearsed etc. Doll and I did imit-
ations of Moving Pictures and 'Film Dramas' and really had the
greatest fun, and I sang and had a great success – possibly owing to
Aileen and Victor who went round the village in the morning carefully
creating the impression that I was Melba's latest pupil and discovery!
They were all over in England during the war. The boys were training
at Beverley and they had a house there – so of course we knew all the
same people. ... I felt quite one of the family by the time I left! And
quite sad to leave.

The Bells were just the right people to recharge Agatha's batteries, taking her into their warm embrace and making a fuss of
her, welcoming her to a home after so many weeks in hotels. She
was attracted to them partly because they were a large, gregarious
family, but also because the sisters were unlike any set of people
she had ever met. Tough, vigorous and independent, they took a
significant interest in the management of the station and the
supervision of their cattle-farmers. They strode about in breeches,
rode miles over the scrub, and expressed their opinions as decidedly as the men. At the same time, they were attractive and
much sought after in society – London society as well as Australian, for they had entertained the Prince of Wales at Coochin
and spent a good part of the year in Europe. The 'beautiful Bell
sisters' were to Agatha an example of what women could be like:
independent, confident and, simultaneously, feminine and gay.
Furthermore, they showed her to herself in a new light, as someone now sufficiently well-travelled and sure to accept an invitation to a strange house, who was not in the least shy of joining
in a local concert and dance, ready indeed to follow the first item,
Miss Una's Jazz Band, with various songs and 'Moving Picture
Stunts.' For weeks Agatha had been an auxiliary member of the
Mission, vital to the team's happiness and general welfare and
probably its most conscientious and genuinely interested partici-
pant when it came to inspecting canneries, saw-mills and so forth,
but she had thought of herself as an appendage to the main force
of speech-makers and negotiators. Suddenly she was the centre
of attention – an adventurous, experienced woman of thirty-two,
who had been on the edge of a revolution in South Africa, was
full of amusing stories, married to a war hero, had published
poetry and two detective novels, who entered into the spirit of
dressing-up and acting, and enjoyed the family's jokes. She was
unaccompanied but she could shine. She returned to Sydney, and
to Archie, greatly refreshed.

The Mission's next stop was New Zealand; they travelled on the *Manuka*, a three-day voyage remarkable mainly for the propaganda of a fellow-passenger whom the Mission called the Dehydrator. He had patented a device for drying food, 'never looked at anything in the food line without thinking how he could dehydrate it', and at every meal sent over platefuls of tasteless dried food to Belcher's party, who felt obliged to control their feelings and do their best with it, as the Dehydrator 'was very rich and powerful and could prove of great benefit to the Exhibition'.

Their first engagement was at Parliament House, 'where a gentleman was making a speech boasting about "borrowing at par," which aroused Archie's financial contempt.' Archie, incidentally, had been mistaken for the Governor of the Bank of England by one South African newspaper – he was, as it happened, as lean as Montagu Norman, though younger and less lugubrious in appearance – and this error persisted throughout their journey. Agatha played golf and bridge with local ladies, visited a woollen factory, and – the worst ordeal! – was guest of honour at what a local newspaper called, 'a delightful little impromptu morning tea' given by the Committee of the Canterbury Women's Club. The same newspaper reported that Agatha wore 'over her mole coloured marocain frock, a charming loose Paisley wrap, with mole collar and a small mole hat of hatter's plush, with upturned brim trimmed with pastel tinted ribbons that toned with the wrap.' Though fortified against the cold, Agatha was unprepared for the request that she make a speech. 'Horror!' she wrote to Clara, but she clearly performed satisfactorily, being reported as speaking 'most enthusiastically of the scenic beauties of New Zealand'. Agatha's compliments were genuine. She thought this country the loveliest place she had ever seen, particularly Otiri Gorge, which she explored with the rest of the Mission, and the hot springs and geysers at Rotorua, which she visited alone, 'a wonderful place – the air full of sulphur fumes and boiling steam coming up from the ground and great quaking boiling mud pits, and all the Maoris bathing and washing clothes in the hot pools.'

Having left Belcher with friends and Bates to his own devices, Agatha and Archie at last set off for their longed-for and hard-earned holiday in Hawaii. They arrived on August 5th. Agatha was ecstatic and wrote from the Moana Hotel to Clara:

Rosalind is three years old and we have arrived at HONOLULU. It
is exactly as stated. You arrive early in the morning, take a taxi, and
go along a road between palms and *lovely* flowers – hedges of hibiscus,
red, pink, white oleanders, blue plumbago and great laburnum trees
and poinsettias, like laburnum only blood red – till you get to a green
and white palace of a Hotel with a courtyard behind with a great
banyan tree (which they light up at night with coloured lights) and
the sea washing right up to the steps – with Hawaiians standing on
great surf boards flashing in from the reef to the shore.

Overjoyed to be free of the Mission, Agatha and Archie dashed
into the sea as soon as they had unpacked, but their surfing
experience in South Africa was no use here. At the end of the
first week, Agatha wrote to Clara:

Still enjoying ourselves, though we've had our troubles! The first day's
bathing so burned us that we were in real agony! Archie was much
the worst – his skin came up in huge blisters all over his back and
shoulders and the backs of his legs. He could hardly bear his clothes
rubbing against it. ... We have tried all remedies – anointing ourselves
with coconut oil, whitening, peroxide cream, etc. Finally A. has taken
to bathing in pyjamas, to the intense amusement of the natives who
roll about in ecstasies of mirth!

Hawaii was more sophisticated – and expensive – than they
had expected: 'There are also magnificent roads everywhere –
tarred and oiled, and a constant stream of motors – *everyone* has
a motor! You hear them passing in a stream up till 3 in the
morning. It's also pleasing to see nice-looking, well dressed
people again, after the drab bourgeoisie of the Colonies!!' After
five days they decided that the Moana, all very well for a week,
would be ruinous for a longer period. They hunted round and
found the Donna Hotel 'half way between the town and Waikiki
– but on the trams', where they had a little cottage to themselves
and spent all their time '(a) on the beach, (b) in the town drinking
ice-cream sodas and buying new remedies and preventatives for
sunburn'. A friend arranged for them to become members of the
country club, where they could laze and drink 'the ubiquitous
ice-water of Prohibition' and enjoy the local food, about which,
particularly the varieties of fresh banana, Agatha wrote home
enthusiastically. Out of habit, perhaps, they also allowed themselves to be taken on a tour of a pineapple cannery.

This idyllic existence was, however, disturbed by several minor
disasters. 'A tremendous shower of "liquid sunshine" came down
from the mountains and wet us to the skin and Archie has now

got a bad cold! Also he stayed in the sea too long at the beginning of the week and has all blistered up and peeled – back and shoulder nearly raw again.' One catastrophe which brought unexpected benefit was the destruction of Agatha's handsome and expensive silk bathing dress, which she had brought from England. To her embarrassment, the waves tore it from shoulder to ankle, almost dividing it in two, and she was obliged to buy at the hotel shop 'a wonderful, skimpy, emerald green wool bathing dress, which was the joy of my life, and in which I thought I looked remarkably well.' Archie thought so too, and sent a photograph to Clara, with a letter whose stiltedness is striking after Agatha's racy correspondence, since it consisted mainly of remarks about the complications of packing luggage.

Much more unfortunate was a sudden attack of neuritis in Agatha's left arm, so painful that she could hardly move it. She ascribed it to surfing: 'You "paddle" with your arms very vigorously when you surf, and that does it, I suppose.' This agonising pain could not have come at a worse time, for September had arrived and Agatha and Archie were obliged to end their holiday and join Belcher and Bates in Canada. They braced themselves for the reunion and for stringent economies, since Archie's £1000 fee was dwindling fast and they still had Agatha's living expenses in Canada to meet. Agatha did not mention this in her letters home; indeed, she urged Clara to look to her for any necessary help with keeping Monty's native servant: 'I can pay Shebani's wages. I've got far more money now than I ever dreamed I should have after this trip – my March a/c from John Lane is £47 for "Swedish rights", and things like that, of *Styles* – and I shall get a good lot of Tommy and Tuppence money this Sept – and all my dividends pouring in at home, so do do what you'd like.' In Canada she was obliged to adopt various parsimonious expedients; her chief scheme was to eat everything on the hotel's breakfast menu, which cost a dollar, supplementing her diet by sending for large jugs of boiling water, with which she made a soup from spoonsful of meat extract, the most useful present she and Archie had been given in New Zealand. She thought ruefully of missed opportunities: 'I also wished heartily that I had flattered the Dehydrator to the extent that he would have pressed large quantities of dehydrated carrots, beef, tomatoes and other delicacies upon me.' By these means, and by eating enormous meals when civic dignitaries entertained her, Agatha managed to keep body and soul together, and to sustain herself for the exertion of the trip from Victoria, on the West coast, across Canada to Ottawa.

By now the Expedition was weary. 'From Calgary we went to Edmonton and from there to Regina and from there to Winnipeg. We stayed a day in each place, usually sleeping in our faithful private car. . . . All the towns are much the same, set in the middle of flat endless prairies, the "bald headed Prairie" indeed – interesting to those interested in wheat – but not otherwise.' In Winnipeg, they were struck by another catastrophe. Archie had been taken with Belcher to inspect a grain elevator and his sinus, always sensitive, became so badly inflamed that he collapsed with congestion of the lungs. It developed into bronchitis and a doctor declared that he should not be moved. This infuriated Belcher, who had already had an attack of 'Wild Man' in Winnipeg: the Governor General had arrived on the same day, so that Belcher was overlooked. He refused to move and sat in his room dictating to Bates an article to the *Daily Telegraph* on 'Winnipeg the Yankee City', before departing in a rage, taking Bates with him. Agatha, woefully short of money, was left to nurse her sick husband. She did tell Clara about their ordeal:

> His temperature was up to 104 for days and finally a terrible bout of nettle rash came out – all over him – so that he was almost screaming with pain and irritation. . . . He was very bad one night and the doctor said he would like another opinion and brought another old idiot along, who appeared to be a King of the '99s' and kept mislaying his stethoscope. But the nettle rash is abating a little and he's had an hour or two of sleep today, so I feel much relieved about him.

When Archie recovered, they joined Bates and Belcher for a trip to the Rockies and to Banff, where Agatha soaked herself each morning in hot sulphurated water from the springs, running a current on to her painful neck and shoulder. She doubted it would do any good but to her relief the neuritis disappeared. There was a triumphant moment for Belcher, too, when he disembarked from the train to find a huge crowd, far outnumbering the plenipotentiaries on the platform, ready to welcome him. Sadly, he discovered that the gathering had assembled in the mistaken belief that Mary Pickford and Douglas Fairbanks, also touring the Rockies, were on the same train. Archie's illness had meant that he and Agatha had to change the remainder of their itinerary. Still weak, he went with Bates and Belcher to Newfoundland, while Agatha took the train to New York City, to stay with her Aunt Cassie, sister-in-law of Mrs Pierpont Morgan. She still worried lest Archie should catch pneumonia – winter had set in and it snowed all the time – but she was glad to be done with the Expedition. 'We are both sick of the Mission and longing to get home,' she wrote to Clara, and she even contemplated sailing earlier than the rest of the party, so anxious was she to see her mother, Rosalind, Madge and Monty. Staying with Aunt Cassie was extremely comfortable and great fun; Agatha learned about her father's doings in New York as a young man, and she was taken to restaurants to be restored to her former well-nourished state. After a week, however, she began, as she put it, to feel a little like a caged bird, since her aunt would not let her explore the city alone, although she was allowed a final treat – to go to a drugstore, or, as Agatha put it, 'a cafeteria'.

Archie, Belcher and Bates, all exhausted, managed to finish their work in Canada in time to come to New York to take up their passages on the RMS *Majestic* (not, as Agatha mistakenly recalled in her autobiography, the *Berengaria*). They left New York on November 25th and arrived at Southampton on December 1st. As the Mission was decanted from the train at Waterloo, 40,000 miles and ten months since it had embarked, Archie told *The Times*: 'The tour has been a great success. We were enthusiastically received everywhere, and are completely satisfied with the result of our work. We have had a strenuous time and are glad to reach home again, but it was worth it.' Less diplomatic but more telling were the remarks written on the *Majestic*'s menu for the last night at sea, which was, appropriately, Thanksgiving Day. Around the list of dishes – oysters, cream of tomato soup, poached turbot, sweetbreads, roast turkey and cranberry sauce, salad, mince pies and dessert – Major Belcher and his colleagues gave a franker verdict. Over his dashing signature, underlined twice, Belcher wrote: '*Forsan et haec olim meminisse juvabit*': a quotation from the first book of *The Aeneid*: 'Perhaps it will one day be a pleasure to remember these things.' Archie, more modestly but following his former schoolteacher's example, put '*Finis Itinerum*': the end of the journey; Agatha, remembering the slang she had picked up in Australia, put '1st Class! Good oh! Right here'; while beneath the signature of Francis W. Bates appeared, feelingly, 'RIP'.

9

'... The next I write will be the 5th ...'

In the five years after the Empire Tour Agatha was transformed from a little-known contributor to magazines and newspapers, writing imaginative stories for amusement rather than for money, to a professional author who earned her living by writing and who was so well known that it was a misery to her. As she found, acquiring and perfecting professional skills is a time-consuming process and so is the business – for it is a business – of maintaining a professional reputation for working to reliable standards and fulfilling the terms of a contract even when its first enchantment has worn off. Agatha, however, did not set out to become a professional and no one encouraged her to turn herself into one. It is easy to understand why she started to write; character, skills and circumstance all inclined her in that direction. It is more difficult to explain why she became a professional writer. Her practical nature had something to do with it; her skills were applied skills – cooking, gardening, arranging flowers. There was no point in writing stories simply to put them away. She was also, though reticent, a generous person, who most easily expressed her feelings obliquely, with a gift, a service, a performance. It was not so much that, as her family put it, 'Agatha doesn't like parting with information', as that she could not part with it spontaneously but would wait for the appropriate framework – wisely, because in that way an audience was more likely to be attentive. She liked an audience and she wanted to display her craftsmanship.

At the time when Agatha had, at Clara's suggestion, showed Eden Philpotts her work, she had no idea that she might become, like him, a professional writer. She was merely curious to know his opinion and she was also vaguely aware that there were flaws in her writing which he might help her correct. But from his first words of advice she learnt that writing was a craft as well as an art and that there were methods and tricks for overcoming stylistic and technical obstacles. She began to learn not just technique but also that, to satisfy herself, her writing had to meet other readers' standards as well as her own. With practice she became increasingly confident that she knew what her readers required and could produce work which would please them. Her correspondence with her publisher showed a growing firmness. It also illustrated other characteristics which propelled her along the way: efficiency and conscientiousness. Orderly and methodical, she had a sense of duty, as she had shown by remaining good-tempered during the long days with the exasperating Belcher.

There are, moreover, few things more certain to galvanise a shy amateur than the discovery that he or she is more efficient and resourceful than the professional people engaged to act as advisers and intermediaries. The mystique of professionalism vanishes for ever and the amateur realises that he is himself just as much of an authority. So it was with Agatha during the early nineteen-twenties, as, more and more sure of herself, she gradually put her publisher in his place. She discovered that The Bodley Head was dependent on her and not the other way round, that she had an unusual talent and that by exercising it she could earn money. She found she must maintain expected standards and manage her work and affairs intelligently. Her attitude to her writing became professional.

This is not how Agatha herself described it in her *Autobiography*, where her account focusses on domestic preoccupations. Not that these were trivial. When Agatha and Archie returned to England at the end of 1922, they were faced with two immediate problems. Archie had to find a job, since his old one had gone, and something had to be done about Monty. He was as unmanageable as ever, as Agatha had discovered when, just before their departure with the Mission, Archie had been dispatched to Tilbury to meet Monty and Shebani and bring them to rooms he had found in London. Though a sick man – his old wound had become infected and he had been given no more than six months to live – and heavily dependent on sedatives, Monty had retained his charming and airy guile, inducing Archie to deposit him not in his new apartments but at his favourite, extremely expensive hotel in Jermyn Street; 'Somehow,' said Archie, 'it seemed so reasonable the way he put it.' 'That is Monty's strong point,' Agatha informed him. A course of treatment by specialists in London so restored Monty's health that his mother and his sisters could hope that by living quietly he might last a good number of

years. He was accordingly moved to Ashfield, where Clara had
converted several rooms and built a new bathroom for him, as
well as persuading her two elderly maid-servants that they need
entertain no anxiety about sharing their quarters with an African
(an exotic and perplexing phenomenon in Torquay in the
nineteen-twenties) but could take this opportunity to convert him
to Christianity.

Agatha frequently asked about Shebani in her letters; she and
Madge between them paid his wages. He was an immense success,
listening patiently as the maids read the Bible to him and paci-
fying his master when his demands – for grilled chops one hour
before sunrise, for instance – were particularly unreasonable.
Monty himself, however, refused to settle down and, the better
his health, the more difficult it became for him to fit into Ashfield's sedate routine. He took to discharging his pistol from the
window (just 'keeping his eye in', he explained to the police),
terrifying those who sought to call at the house. Clara was exhausted. When, a few months after Agatha's return to England,
Shebani announced that he must return to his family in Africa,
it was clear that some new scheme must be devised for Monty's
care. The solution turned out to be the purchase by Madge and
Agatha, for £800, of a cottage on Dartmoor, where they installed
their brother and an elderly, placid and unconventional housekeeper, a doctor's widow, who calmed Monty down and looked
after him happily. Thus, after much wear and tear, one problem
was sorted out.

The other proved less straightforward. In early 1923 the City
had lost the buoyancy and confidence of the immediate post-War
years and Archie, at thirty-four, found it difficult to find a niche.
Anxious and depressed, he fended off Agatha's attempts to
soothe him. She wanted to be helpful but could think of nothing
appropriate to say or do. Untrained, she could not expect to find
anything remunerative for herself, while work for which little
training was necessary was in short supply. Not that she made
any serious attempts to find a job; that would have made Archie
feel even more inadequate. He suggested that she go with Rosalind to Clara or Madge; Agatha, however, was determined to
stay. She made herself useful by cooking and cleaning – they now
had no maid – and the rough patch passed. A firm in the City,
thought to be slightly shady, took Archie on, and within a year
an old friend, Clive Baillieu, returned from Australia and offered
Archie the post he had long wanted.

Agatha's own view of life from 1923 to 1925 is a wry, good-tempered picture of marking time, expending quantities of energy, intellegence and ingenuity in entertaining a small child, keeping the flat in order, cooking, cleaning and tidying, and at the same time trying to write. Of the series of nurses she engaged to help look after Rosalind, two out of three were hopeless, being well-intentioned but lacking imagination and authority. Agatha was constantly distracted by the importunate lamentations of the first of these, 'Cuckoo', a well-meaning but exasperatingly incompetent woman, who survived only because Rosalind swiftly took her in hand. Cuckoo's successor, Miss White ('Site') was a success. Only seventeen, she was capable, dignified, masterful and young enough to enjoy Rosalind's games. When Site left to take a post abroad, she was succeeded by a Swiss nursery governess, recommended by Madge. Marcelle was shy, nervous and ineffectual and Rosalind, unchecked, became rebellious and naughty. Marcelle did not last.

Rosalind was bright, affectionate, beautiful and terrifyingly direct. Archie adored her; Agatha, too, loved her child but felt a certain distance. As she wrote in her *Autobiography*, after describing her fun as she watched Rosalind's development:

> There is nothing more thrilling in this world, I think, than having a child that is yours and yet is mysteriously a stranger. You are the gate through which it came into the world, and you will be allowed to have charge of it for a period of years, and after that it will leave you and blossom out into its own free life, and there it is for you to watch living its life in freedom – it is like a strange plant which you have brought home, planted, and can hardly wait to see how it will turn out.

It was not that Agatha was uninterested in her daughter. She cared about her, worrying and celebrating on her behalf. But Agatha did not live vicariously; Rosalind had her inclinations, opportunities and disappointments, and Agatha hers, as she had indicated when, leaving Rosalind with Clara and Madge, she had accompanied Archie on the Empire Tour. Elsewhere in her autobiography she makes the doubtful generalisation that, as in cats and kittens, so in human mothers and their babies the maternal instinct is appeased by the act of bearing children, whom the mothers, anxious but satisfied, leave to go their own way. Two of her detective stories, *Ordeal by Innocence* and *They Do It With Mirrors*, describe the consequence of woman's overwhelming affection for an adopted child, and in other books – *A Daughter's A Daughter*, and *Absent in the Spring*, for example – she wrote of the unhappiness caused by possessive love. It would be a waste of time to discuss whether Agatha's fiction simply reflected or sought to rationalise her own preference for emotional independence and her feeling that close relationships can become dangerously exclusive. The process of creating fiction is more complicated than that. It is also foolish to try to fit Agatha into some general category – even of her own making – of a type of mother. What we can say, however, is that her attitude to her daughter was warm and loving but, ultimately, detached.

Again, it would be an oversimplification to suggest that Agatha was not wrapped up in her child because she was absorbed by her writing. Her attention was certainly not fixed on her books or her mind obsessed with the details of her transactions with John Lane. She did speculate on plots and wander over possible combinations of character and relationship; she had always had that habit and, as she said herself, it is while doing routine domestic chores that an imaginative mind runs loose. But neither is it correct to conclude from her *Autobiography* that she considered her writing to be only casual jotting, squeezed in between Cuckoo's plaintive entreaties, the cooking and cleaning Agatha shared with Site, and the reprimands which Marcelle's uselessness obliged her to administer to Rosalind. Agatha took her writing seriously. She was beginning to see her books as a body of work – past accomplishments, present preoccupations and future possibilities – rather than a series of happy accidents.

In late 1922 Agatha had in fact sent a letter from Canada in which she discussed the tally of further manuscripts submitted to John Lane. *The Secret Adversary* had been followed by *The Murder on the Links*, which was published in 1923. From the Expedition Agatha sent home a collection of short stories about Hercule Poirot, provisionally entitled *Poirot Investigates*, which John Lane rechristened 'The Grey Cells of Monsieur Poirot', before restoring the original title. These had been published separately as a series for the *Sketch* and with them Agatha sent to John Lane the long fantasy, 'Vision', she had written years before. She joyfully reported his reaction to Clara: 'He has advised against publication of latter (as I thought he would) so that counts as a book, so the next I write will be the *5th*!' It was to take some time, however, before The Bodley Head would agree with Agatha's calculations.

The 'next book' was *The Man in the Brown Suit*, originally called 'The Mystery of the Mill House', a title created to pacify Belcher, who wanted a detective story about his own house and himself. He prevailed against Agatha's not unnatural wish to make him the victim, and much of his swaggering nature can be seen in her creation of Sir Eustace Pedler. ('Give him a title,' suggested Archie. 'I think he'd like that.') *The Man in the Brown Suit* was a thriller – its description of a minor revolution owed everything to Agatha's adventures in Pretoria – and it elaborated two themes which she first touched on in *The Secret Adversary* and to which she often returned. One was the notion of there being a hidden but vigorous international conspiracy, whose operations, whether traffic in arms, drugs, jewels, works of art or human skills, whether intended to promote a single ideology, none, or several, whether fostered via youthful zealots, naïve disciples or cynical experts, were all ultimately fuelled by money – money that could be manipulated in discreet, mysterious ways, that moved through strange, secret channels, that exerted invisible, intangible power, and, by being made immediately available or as suddenly withdrawn, caused devastation, predictable only to those who managed its flow and explicable only by them or by those to whom they answered. Money, as the Millers had found when their fortunes had been so bafflingly undermined, was not a neutral means of exchange. It was a force to be reckoned with.

Close to home, too, was Agatha's other theme: that of a thoughtful, spirited young woman, adventurous but frustrated, constrained less by convention, sex, or youth than by lack of ready cash. Tuppence, in *The Secret Adversary* had no job; Anne, in *The Man in the Brown Suit*, had been left with only debts on the death of her father. In some of Agatha's books these young women were to start as gawky geese and turn into graceful swans; in others they would be recognisable, if shabby, swans from the beginning. Brave, shrewd, resourceful and endowed with remarkable stamina, they would be precipitated by fate or their own restless natures into the adventures for which they sighed. Once immersed, they generally found themselves acting as helpmeet or confederate to the sort of male companion who begins by generously condescending to allow the heroine to join the fun and ends by gratefully acknowledging that she is indispensable.

The Bodley Head received the typescript of *The Man in the Brown Suit* in late 1923. It was at this point that they began to discover that Agatha Christie was becoming a less tractable author. Her relationship with John Lane had moved into a new and predictable phase. During November and December the tone of Agatha's letters to The Bodley Head became increasingly assured. They dealt with three matters: the arrangements for the publication of *Poirot Investigates*, her publishers' plans for *The Man in the Brown Suit*, and her long-term contract. Where *Poirot Investigates* was concerned, she was no longer content to take whatever advance her publisher had in mind. Her letter of November 1st asked, rather, what terms they proposed. Mr Willett, John Lane's colleague, also found himself confronted with a series of suspiciously detailed inquiries and stipulations: in her letter of November 4th, Agatha told him that, in the agreement for 'The Grey Cells of Monseiur Poirot', she did not want to include cinema, dramatic or foreign rights, adding waspishly, 'Do your agreements always count 13 as 12?' Five days later she asked for certain specific amendments to be made to the draft agreement – the deletion of clauses or portions of clauses – and inquired whether ten per cent was the maximum royalty they could pay on a cheap edition. By December 4th her tone was completely confident, as she announced the reception of an offer for Indian serial rights – 'I presume you do not want to raise any objection to this, but in accordance with the request in your letter of the 12th November, I am consulting you before accepting the offer' – and in mid-December she politely backed her own judgment: 'The only things I should like to query are the altering of Insurance Company to *Ass*urance Company, which seems quite unnecessary, and the striking out of the italics on page 52. They make it so much clearer which is question and which is answer ... 'I really prefer my own original title *Poirot Investigates*, and you say you like it also, so why not settle upon that?' This correspondence did not peter out until May 1926, when Agatha was obliged to write to Mr Willett regarding an error – ten per cent instead of twenty per cent – in an account sent her for the sale of twelve copies of the 7/6d edition. For all their mystique, publishers were tradesmen, whose bills should always be checked.

Argument about *The Man in the Brown Suit* was concentrated on the subject of the wrapper, which, Agatha told Mr Willett in June 1924, 'looks to me like a highway robbery and murder in mediaeval times – nothing like a tube station and not in the least striking. I had in mind,' she continued, 'something much more clear, definite and modern. From the finished wrapper it would appear that this is the artist's normal style, and so I do not suppose he could ever alter it to make it like what I wanted.' Mr Willett protested, and a fortnight later Agatha wrote again: 'I do not think I am asking for what you call a "cut out" wrapper. I felt that the one you sent me would never be anything but sombre, and would never look like a "Tube" station. I think if the background was of really white glossy tiles it would improve it greatly.' She was always to have strong views about the presentation of her books, as her new publishers, Collins, were to discover.

For, at least since the autumn of 1922, Agatha had been contemplating a move. The letter she sent to Clara, just before embarking on the homeward journey from Canada, showed how eagerly she was awaiting the moment when she should have submitted the last book, after 'Styles', of those pledged to The Bodley Head. It was no surprise that they should reject the expanded version of 'Vision'; indeed, Agatha not only expected it to be returned but told her mother she had sent it only in order to make a third in the sequence. *Poirot Investigates* was to be the fourth and, acording to this plan, *The Man in the Brown Suit*, being the fifth, would have heralded her release. The Bodley Head, however, proved stubborn. They were not only unwilling to count 'Vision' as a book but also declined to include *Poirot Investigates* in the total for which Agatha was contracted, for the curious reason that these stories had previously been serialised in a newspaper. Agatha was tenacious – and cunning, since she realised that The Bodley Head were on weak ground here and used this as a bargaining point in her own unsteady argument about the status of 'Vision'. Mr Willett stuck to his guns and Agatha stuck to hers:

> I really do not see why you should have thought that this was not submitted as one of the works provided for in the main agreement. Whether it would have been advisable to publish it or not is another matter. Perhaps you were quite right in considering that it would have affected the sales of my detective novels .... I certainly do not feel inclined to sign the agreement relating to the short stories, in which you have stipulated that these are not to count as a book under the terms of the main agreement, without getting this point about *Vision* cleared up first.

She won the point about *Poirot Investigates* but lost on 'Vision'.
The Bodley Head now needed Agatha more than she needed

them. Popular middle-class taste was increasingly for the sort of work with which she was experimenting – novels with a simple shape, a small cast of characters, short chapters and no long, convoluted sentences, with an emphasis on the facts and mechanics of situations and considerable importance given to psychology. Agatha's thrillers and detective stories were stylistically unpretentious but intellectually interesting. She was not, and never became, a writer whose work could intimidate a nervous reader but nonetheless she made welcome demands on her public's attention and perceptiveness. The weekly, fortnightly and monthly magazines – *Grand Magazine, Sovereign Magazine, Blue Book Magazine, Royal Magazine, Novel Magazine* and *The Story-Teller* – wanted her work and their interest quickened that of her publisher. The Bodley Head began to murmur about the terms of her next contract.

Agatha, however, had recognised the strength of her position. Not only were newspaper and magazine editors ready to print her work but even the Inland Revenue was expressing an interest. An Inspector from the tax office called to inquire about the size of her earnings as an author, to her astonishment, since she had regarded any fees as a negligible and occasional supplement to the family's income, keeping no records and submitting no statements, as the amounts fell below the sums then allowed as 'casual profit'. On reflection she decided to become more business-like and to put her affairs in the hands of a professional adviser. This, together with the information she had acquired from the publications of the Society of Authors, which she had discovered on her return from the Expedition, propelled her once more in the direction of Hughes Massie, the literary agency to which Eden Philpotts had recommended her years before.

The fearsome Hughes Massie was now dead and Agatha was received by his successor, Edmund Cork, a tall, elegant young man, with a charming, conspiratorial smile like a benign but artful cat. Mr Cork's manner was not patronising nor intimidating, nor suffused with irritating genialities. He had exactly the right mixture of courtly attentiveness and considered wisdom, and the fact that he had a stammer made Agatha immediately anxious to put him at his ease. She was, in fact, rather the older of the two and by no means a naïve or unpublished author. She lost any remaining nervousness and confided in Cork, who, for the next sixty years was to help realise her hopes and assuage her doubts. He was the most valuable of professional advisers, someone to whom Agatha could trust the complex and sensitive details of her life; he dealt with solicitors, tax inspectors and lawyers, steered her through entanglements with film and theatrical moguls, fended off importunate correspondents and shielded her from much that would otherwise have been demoralising and difficult. She could trust him not simply because he was discreet and sensible but also because he did not intrude. For Edmund Cork had been well schooled by Hughes Massie, who as a young man had been summoned for an interview with his client ... Elinor Glyn, popularly believed to compose her books while reclining, loosely draped, upon a tiger-skin rug. Though it is not clear what actually transpired during this encounter, it certainly led Hughes Massie to emphasise the wisdom of keeping a careful distance between client and literary agent; this, Edmund Cork always observed, was the most useful piece of advice Hughes Massie bequeathed him.

Cork was appropriately appalled by the terms of Agatha's existing contract and by her minuscule royalty. This was gratifying. It was also exciting to hear him speak of film and theatrical rights, first and second serial rights, foreign translations and so on, and, although Agatha regarded all this as rather unlikely speculation, she took it sufficiently seriously to adopt the new tone that was apparent in her correspondence with Mr Willett. The spirit of Cork, perhaps even the hand of Cork, was evident in the no-nonsense letters that established the standing of 'Vision' and the terms for *The Man in the Brown Suit*.

There were other reasons for Agatha's new confidence. One had to do as much with her sister's success as with her own, for at the end of 1923 Madge seemed likely to make an astonishing hit with a piece of writing for the stage. The subject of Madge's play was, as one would have expected, a celebrated case of impersonation; that of Sir Charles Doughty Tichborne, tried in 1873-4 over his claim to a baronetcy, a family mansion and a rent roll of £25,000 a year. Madge's play, *The Claimant*, was a mixture of all the goings-on she adored: dressing-up, disguise, imposture, a party and suspense. To her family's amazement, and even more to her own, Basil Dean agreed to produce the play at St Martin's Theatre in the West End in the autumn of 1924.

The plot was complicated; the cast talented but anarchic. It quickly became clear that Madge was needed to supply and approve changes in the production and the script and to act as adviser and ally to various coalitions among factions of the cast and the management. She therefore moved to rooms in Brown's Hotel off Piccadilly, spending the weekends with Archie and Agatha. Agatha thus heard every detail of the back-stage frenzy from 'Punkie' herself and, judging by the raciness of Madge's breathless letters to Cheadle, these enthusiastic accounts of theatrical life must have been riveting. There was one character in particular for whom both sisters had a special affection, 'Charles', the Claimant's extortionate accomplice, into whom Madge had put much of their infuriating, beloved brother. 'In some occult way,' Madge wrote, 'Basil Dean could evoke Monty exactly, particularly when he demonstrated how "Charles" should pick up 6/8d from the table, but leaving the eightpence behind because, as Monty might have said, "Don't care about copper. Never did."'

Agatha, as Madge put it, was 'mad to see a rehearsal'. The morning they chose turned out to be that on which Madge was told about arrangements for press photographs, and Agatha heard the leading actress observe, 'When they photograph me they always make me look drunk. And when one never touches anything, it's hard. Don't you think so, Mrs Watts?' Agatha liked this remark, since both she and Madge, neither of whom 'touched anything', were now irredeemably unphotogenic. The picture of the two sisters is an attractive one: Madge, excited, busy, the centre of attention, the wife of a respectable Mancunian but herself eccentric and a trifle manic, and Agatha, quiet, shy, amused and noticing everything. Yet it was Agatha who was the better known. As Madge generously reminded her husband and son: 'The head of the Press Bureau approached me for an interview and I said I didn't *want* to be known. He said they'd been very good ..., but after the show he did want to boom me and my writing. All I told him was that I was Mrs Agatha Christie's sister. And he simply *revels* in *Styles* and has read all her books. So perhaps,' Madge added, in an unlikely comparison to a pair of famous dancers of the Charleston, 'we'll have to be the Dolly Sisters after all!'

The Claimant opened on September 11th and, although it did not run for long, its preparation had been the best entertainment. Agatha, especially, enjoyed Madge's brief but heady success. It was not notoriety which was fun – the sisters were too well-mannered and, in Agatha's case, too shy to have taken pleasure in that. The public and the press were irrelevant; Madge and Agatha were writing for their own pleasure in the challenge, as much as a market. Just as Agatha sent inscribed copies of her books, and dedicated them, to her family and close acquaintance, so Madge took boxes and stalls for them at the St Martin's Theatre. They saw themselves as untrained adventurers, whose work was now, to their astonishment, taken in earnest. They were also adult, middle-class women, whose writing took second place, in their own eyes and certainly in their husbands', to the management of their houses and the care of their children. (After describing how masterful she had become, '"Cut those lines, please, Mr Quartermain!" *And* he *did*, at once!!!', Madge appeased James and her own conscience by adding: 'I shall be unbearable at home. The only remedy will be to have Constance a good deal who will keep on telling me how badly I've brought up my son and that the lettuce is wet.') They were simultaneously gratified and disconcerted to find themselves holding their own in the overwhelmingly masculine world of theatrical management and publishing. The fact that Mrs Agatha Christie, the writer, was her sister fortified Madge, and the fact that Mrs Watts, author of *The Claimant*, was *her* sister boosted Agatha's confidence in turn.

Agatha was now thirty-four, at an age when her health and strength, looks and temper were at their most resilient, when it is easy to feel sure of one's own nature and capacities. Greater financial security helped too. As soon as Archie secured the promised job with his friend Clive Baillieu, he and Agatha set about realising their wish to find a cottage in the country, not least because Archie had enthusiastically taken to golf. After a long search, they settled not on a cottage but on a large flat in a house, Scotswood, at Sunningdale, about thirty miles from London. In the nineteen-twenties Sunningdale was embryo 'stockbroker country', prosperous, easy and dull. Agatha had no circle of old friends and familiars, as she had in Torquay, nor the theatres and museums of London to distract her. On the other hand, there was a garden for Rosalind and it was convenient for both the railway to the City and for a celebrated golf course. A further advantage of Scotswood was that another of the four flats was also vacant. Here, for a time, Agatha installed Clara, still lively but with fragile health. In other respects, also, Agatha's domestic arrangements were happy and convenient. After her difficulties with Marcelle, she had searched for someone who would be both a kindly supervisor for Rosalind and, in the mornings while Rosalind was at school, a secretary and typist. Feeling that the Scots tended to be good disciplinarians, who were not bullied by their charges, she added to her advertisement the words 'Scottish preferred'.

Among the replies was one from Miss Charlotte Fisher, a tall, slender, brown-haired girl in her early twenties, quiet, direct and humorous, a capable and well-educated daughter of the manse. (Her father was one of the chaplains to the King in Edinburgh.) Miss Fisher, or 'Carlo', as the family quickly came to call her, immediately took Rosalind in hand and 'the raging demon' left behind by the ineffectual Marcelle became a polite and pleasant child again. The secretarial part of Carlo's duties did not, however, evolve exactly as Agatha and she had envisaged. Agatha was even more nervous when it came to dictating her stories than Carlo was about taking them down in shorthand, and it was soon apparent that Agatha composed much more fluently and naturally when left to herself and her old Corona. Instead, Carlo dealt with letters and accounts and kept Agatha's papers, not in any case untidy, in meticulous order. Most important, she became a steady friend, confidante and watchdog.

The crowning feature of this happy time was Agatha's acquisition of her own car. The *Evening News* had offered £500 for serial rights to *The Man in the Brown Suit*, with which Agatha, thrilled, had thought she might realise such touchingly mundane longings as the purchase of 'a new evening dress, gold or silver evening shoes instead of black, something rather ambitious like a new fairy cycle for Rosalind ....' Buying a car was Archie's suggestion; it was not a stream-lined monster but a small Morris Cowley, upright and with a snub nose. To Agatha it was one of the greatest pleasures of her life. This was not simply because, as she put it in her *Autobiography*, possessing a car 'widened your horizons, it increased your territory', magnificent though that feeling was, particularly in the days when it was a pleasure still confined to a few. This was certainly part of Agatha's joy but it also sprang from the freedom it gave her. There was something peculiarly satisfying in being transported by a machine that went where it was instructed to go, at a pace it was directed to take, at the time when it was required to do so – in short, by a machine that was under her own control. A car meant liberation. Doubly so, since it had been acquired with money she had earned herself. To her surprise, she had achieved independence.

It is interesting that it was her husband who suggested the purchase and who taught Agatha to drive. He was, in an important way, paying his wife a compliment. Archie, who had ecstatically, if a trifle nervously, taken the controls of a rickety aeroplane in 1910, knew the sense of freedom and possibility that came from mastering a machine that moved easily and quickly away. He recognised that Agatha would appreciate this and that she was ready for it. His suggestion perhaps indicated something more. When Agatha recalled Archie's rudimentary driving lessons, she remembered how he asserted that, if she wished to do something, she could do it. Did he also feel, unconsciously, that she would do it, would assert her independence and that he would not restrain her? Fanciful, maybe, but plausible, particularly in the light of the decision Archie and Agatha made when, a couple of years later, they again found themselves rather better-off than they had expected. Agatha proposed that they should have another child, Archie that they buy a fast and smart Delage. Agatha felt Archie had been excited by their neighbour's Bentley, but perhaps the choice signified more than that. The Christies were moving on, not consolidating; choosing independence, not more responsibility; going, if they wished, their separate ways.

Agatha's feeling of security, in herself as a writer and in their joint finances, is demonstrated by her decision to publish her collected poems. In 1924 *The Road of Dreams* appeared, at her own expense, under the imprint of Geoffrey Bles, and it produced a kind letter from Eden Philpotts, who particularly admired the sequence 'A Masque from Italy', the poems about Harlequin and Columbine written ten years before. 'You have great lyric gifts,' wrote Philpotts, 'and I hope you will find time to develop them.' He went on to warn her that, much as he hoped that *The Road of Dreams* would be a success, 'Alas! People don't buy poetry.' He was right – in the nineteen-sixties Agatha's literary agents had to write to ask her what she wanted done with the remaining unsold, unbound copies.

Cork, meanwhile, had been busy on Agatha's behalf. He had discussed her work and her sales with Godfrey Collins, who indicated that his house would pay £200 as an advance on each of her next three books, with a generous royalty. When Cork mentioned this to John Lane, he was told grumpily that anyone who would pay that much was welcome to Agatha's work. A three-book contract was accordingly signed with Collins in January 1924, although Agatha was still pledged to deliver one last book to The Bodley Head. This was *The Secret of Chimneys*, a racy thriller in which she used memories and reflections that are easily

recognisable: there is a glimpse of Bulawayo; 'Chimneys', where
the bulk of the novel is set, is an even grander version of Abney;
Superintendent Battle – appearing for the first time – resembles
Inspector Bucket in *Bleak House*; and elements of the plot not
only echo *The Prisoner of Zenda* and some of the novels of John
Buchan, where sinewy and resourceful second sons return from
the colonies to plunge themselves into desperate tangles, but also
suggest that Agatha had not forgotten a royalist conspiracy
which had excited the visitors to Cauterets when she had stayed
there as a child. In her *Autobiography* she wrote that these events
were 'only very dimly apprehended' by her at the time, but, however vague, those apprehensions had seeped into the silt of her
subconscious.

The summer before *Chimneys* appeared, Agatha had in fact
visited Cauterets, to show Archie the hotel where she had had
such fun. Not unusually, they were disappointed at first ('did not
like the look of the place,' Archie wrote tersely in their joint
typewritten letter to Clara) but they wisely ascribed their disenchantment to the after-effects of an uncomfortable journey – to
economise they had travelled second-class all the way from Victoria, with their reserved seats occupied by interlopers, who upset
cherries all over the carriage, and their neighbours 'two young
Spaniards who hugged one another without ceasing'. Walks and
picnics in the Pyrenees soon improved their tempers; they climbed
mountains by a zig-zag path through the hay fields to eat crêpes
flavoured with anisette in the café at the top and after dinner they
watched Grand Guignol. They drank from the sulphur springs
and 'did *la douche nasale*', played boules and 'perfected the
knockout shot at Billard Japonais', and made a couple of expeditions in a charabanc, about whose occupants Archie was scathing. (The first pages of *The Secret of Chimneys* describe this
form of sightseeing.) The photograph of this vehicle in their
scrap-book shows Agatha looking enthusiastic, but Archie serious and detached, with his hand over his face, as if he is trying
not to be there. From Cauterets they went on to San Sebastian for
more bathing and evenings at the Kursaal, with music and cards.
Archie, who liked to go to bed early, found the Spanish hours
trying – the 'music hall show' started at ten-fifteen – and he would
retire at the first interval. By the end of their stay they were sufficiently relaxed to abandon economy and travel home first class.

It was wise for Agatha and Archie to go away by themselves.
Agatha had been missing the easy companionship of earlier times,

the weekends when they had gone by bus or train to explore the countryside. She now found Saturday and Sunday 'the dullest time, really, for me', as Archie was so engrossed in his golf that she began to appreciate what was meant by being 'a golf widow'. Most of her own friends were married, so she could not ask a wife to stay without the husband, and the only couple she could invite without a qualm was Nan and Nan's second husband, who as a good golfer himself would not bore Archie. The Baillieus, Archie's friends, were neighbours and Agatha was fond of Ruby, Clive Baillieu's wife, but otherwise Sunningdale society was disappointing – 'either,' Agatha wrote, 'the middle-aged who were passionately fond of gardens and talked of practically nothing else, or the gay sporting rich kind who drank a good deal, had cocktail parties, and who were not really my type or indeed, for that matter, Archie's type either.' In comparison with London, or comfortable Torquay, Sunningdale was, as Charlotte Fisher agreed, a dreadful place, complacent, tidy and boring.

Agatha later painted in *Unfinished Portrait* a reproduction of her frustrations at this stage in her marriage. Her description is exaggerated – in the evenings Dermot sits at home 'reading books on financial subjects' – but in essence her picture of Celia's boredom and loneliness resembles her own state for an annoyingly large part of the time. Agatha's difficulty was not that she did not know how to amuse herself; she had always found plenty to occupy herself when she was free to choose how to do so. The problem was that she was no longer on her own. She was part of a couple, in a society and a neighbourhood where people were invited and entertained others as couples, but with a husband who, for the time being at any rate, preferred to relax with his golf clubs on his own or, at best, with an equally fanatical golfing partner. Agatha was thus tied, without the advantages of companionship and collaboration that went with being tied. It is easy to point to the benefits of her position; she enjoyed the status and security of a married woman; she had an intelligent and beautiful child, a large and attractively furnished place to live, in peaceful surroundings that were neither dirty and noisy, like London, nor dank and desolate, as the real country can be; she owned a motor car, was assured of an adequate income, and had a good mind. There are hundreds of women in those circumstances who, because they not only possess keen minds and adventurous dispositions but are also loyal and unrebellious, nonetheless become gently frustrated within their pretty houses and trim gardens.

They pick quarrels, dispute their grocers' bills, long to move house, and resent their own apparently inexplicable behaviour. They are restless.

Agatha, however, had her writing to distract her. Rather than bothering Archie with emotional and intellectual speculation, she could indulge her curiosity and play games with her characters. She could not secure her husband's attention but she could amuse, challenge and tease another audience, her readers. With her next book, *The Murder of Roger Ackroyd*, written in late 1925 and early 1926, she settled down to do so.

'I got hold of a very good formula there,' Agatha later declared, 'and I must confess that I owe it to my brother-in-law, James Watts.' Her autobiography itself says that James Watts's suggestion was that 'A Watson', that is, the narrator, should 'turn out to be the criminal', so there is no need to talk too cryptically here. Indeed, maddening though it was for many readers and to professional critics and writers of detective stories that Agatha should so cleverly mislead them, the notion that the narrator should also be the perpetrator of the crime was not wholly astounding; it is, after all, an obvious variation in a type of story, set in closed worlds with a limited number of victims and suspects, where the number of variations is finite.

One of those to whom the thought had also occurred was Lord Louis Mountbatten, who had written to Agatha on March 28th 1924, sending the letter to the *Sketch* for forwarding. He had read the Poirot stories in that newspaper and now presented his compliments and begged to offer (the letter is written in the third person) a suggestion for another Poirot story. The chief features of his outline were that the narrator of the story should himself be the criminal, that his alibi should be that of 'being with the greatest living detective at a moment when the crime is committed' and that the detective should himself be accused of the crime. Mountbatten attached to his letter a lengthy draft of a plot, whose details unfold in a series of letters betwen Poirot, Hastings and the man who is eventually revealed as the murderer. 'In conclusion,' Mountbatten wrote, 'Lord Louis would ask to be forgiven for having written to a person unknown to him and naturally does not expect Mrs Christie to use this plot unless it appeals to her. He himself is unlikely ever to wish to use such a plot, having no time, as a naval officer, for writing, beyond a few short stories to magazines (under a *nom-de-plume*) for which the enclosed material is quite unsuitable.' Nearly half a century later, in November 1969, Lord Mountbatten was to write again. After congratulating Agatha on the excitement and mystery of her play *The Mousetrap*, which he had just revisited, he went on to mention his earlier letter. Agatha's reply was frank and generous.

> For a number of years I have been haunted, from time to time, by a kind of guilt complex – 'Did I ever acknowledge a letter I received from you?' And an uneasy feeling that I had started to write a letter – but had possibly forgotten to post it. It is a real relief to know that I *did* post it.
>   ... The 'Dr Watson did it' idea came to me from two sources. One a mere remark by my brother-in-law who said, 'someday it ought to be Dr Watson who's the murderer', and I demurred and said, 'that would be terribly difficult technically'. I do not think that I thought much more about it then, but shortly afterwards came your letter, which, if I remember rightly, outlined a most interesting plot ....
>   I thought it a most attractive idea – one which had never been done – but I had great doubts if *I* could ever do it. But it was a great challenge! It stayed at the back of my mind and I gnawed at it – rather like a dog with a bone.

Here was a letter to gladden Lord Mountbatten's spirits. He immediately whisked off a reply, congratulating Agatha on 'the most wonderful job of using my idea in *The Murder of Roger Ackroyd* which I personally think is about the best detective story that has ever been written.' He thanked Agatha for offering to send him her latest book, asking that she should inscribe it 'and possibly mention our original contact forty-five years ago over *The Murder of Roger Ackroyd*', which, obligingly, Agatha did. So everyone was happy, even, one hopes, the self-effacing shade of kindly James Watts.

In the late spring of 1926 *The Murder of Roger Ackroyd* was published in England by Collins and in America by Dodd, Mead, who had acquired John Lane and Co. in 1922. The ingenuity of Agatha's presentation of the case is always said to have caused general astonishment. The detective stories of the nineteen-twenties formed part of the staple diet of the reading public and they were expected to conform to certain strict conventions, eventually encapsulated in the rules of the Detection Club, forbidding the use by an author of Divine Revelation, Feminine Intuition, Acts of God, and the like, as means for the detection of crime. Any sensation aroused by *The Murder of Roger Ackroyd* seems, however, to have been on the small side. Some critics fulminated –

the *News Chronicle* wrote of the book as being 'a tasteless and unfortunate let-down by a writer we had grown to admire' – and a reader wrote a letter of complaint to *The Times*. Agatha's sales certainly increased and the publication of this book was the turning point in her career. The trick she played in *The Murder of Roger Ackroyd* was, however, more of a talking point than a *cause célèbre*. People who were in their twenties and thirties when the book appeared later remembered discussing whether the author had fairly placed every clue before the reader (she had), but their recollections were invariably mixed with memories of a greater public disturbance Agatha was to cause later that same year. Popular memory is curious, and so are myths about popular memory. From a prim letter to *The Times*, a sentence here and there in the newspapers, idle chat in middle and upper-middle-class circles, arose a vague impression that Mrs Christie was interesting, clever and manipulative. These casual opinions affected the public's view of the puzzling events in Agatha's private life, as they were reported and discussed, and, in turn, helped to exaggerate memories of the magnitude of the reaction to *Roger Ackroyd*. More than fifty years on, it is difficult, where *Roger Ackroyd* is concerned, to see what all the fuss was about or, indeed, how much fuss there was at all.

10

'... I do not think she knows who she is ...'

It was a different matter with Agatha's disappearance. It may be hard to explain why she behaved as she did and what exactly took place on that occasion but it is not at all difficult to understand why there was a fuss, on a memorably large scale. To unravel that affair, it is necessary to examine not simply Agatha's actions but also the reactions to them then and ever since. The story is instructive less, perhaps, for what it reveals about Agatha's character and state of mind than for what it shows about the wisdom and professionalism of those who took it up. It is undoubtedly, a remarkable tale, a mixture of the wryly amusing and deeply painful, an affair that, though intensely private, somehow or other – and to Agatha's continuing distress – achieved the status of a popular legend. More than half a century later, it provided the basis of a tasteless piece of fiction *Agatha*, subsequently filmed. The episode was, and has remained, the subject of constant speculation, amateur and professional theorising, and insatiable curiosity. The nature of that 'somehow or other' is as interesting as the facts of the matter themselves.

By the end of 1924 Agatha was unsettled and lonely and the impulse to move house became irresistible. She produced some familiar rationalisations: 'Comfortable though we were in Scotswood, it had a few disadvantages. The management were not particularly reliable. The wiring of the electricity gave us trouble; the advertised constant hot water was neither constant nor hot; the place suffered from a general lack of maintenance ....' (In the first draft of her *Autobiography* this appears as 'suffered from too many cars'.) Men grow bored and restless too, and in this case it seems to have been Archie's idea that they leave Scotswood, not, however, for somewhere other than Sunningdale but to buy a house of their own. Sunningdale, said Archie, had everything they wanted: 'It's the right distance from London and now they're opening Wentworth golf course as well.'

Agatha did not demur. Perhaps the prospect of buying a house – indeed, designing one, since the Wentworth estate had been acquired by a builder – was sufficiently interesting to make her set aside her doubts. Moreover, she was as usual ready to fall in with Archie's plans. Her acquiescence may also have been connected with the fact that her 'golfing ambitions got a sudden booster'. In the finals of the Ladies' Tournament at Sunningdale she had encountered an opponent with the same handicap and the same degree of nervousness as herself and, having utterly despaired of beating her, she relaxed and captured the silver trophy. Mrs Christie in 1926 was not very different from Agatha Miller some fifteen years before, who had persuaded herself that she shared Wilfred Pirie's obsessions. Even when she and Archie decided that they could neither afford nor, even at what seemed to be 'a colossal price', bring themselves to like the sort of house the builder could offer them, they nonetheless bought Agatha a debenture share of £100 in the Wentworth development, which, she touchingly observed, 'would entitle me to play on Saturdays and Sundays on the links there, as a kind of stake for the future. After all,' she added bravely, 'since there would be two courses there, one would be able to play on one at least of them without feeling too much of a rabbit, and until Wentworth had worked itself up to the status of Sunningdale, I should probably be able to play with other rabbits of my acquaintanceship.'

The house on which they eventually settled, after a year or so of looking, appealed to Archie chiefly because of its proximity to the station and to Agatha because of the beauty of its garden. The price was reasonable, though still rather more than they could afford, since the property had been on the market for some time. Agatha found the house itself unnatural and depressing; 'It was,' she wrote, 'a sort of millionaire-style Savoy suite transferred to the country,' decorated regardless of expense with panelling, gilt and 'quantities of bathrooms, basins in bedrooms and everything'. She consoled herself with the thought that, when their finances were in better shape (Archie's income was assured, but her own fluctuating, and they had no capital), they might redesign and redecorate the interior. Waiting to do so was difficult for Agatha, who liked to put her own stamp on her surroundings straightaway. The garden provided some compensation. Long and narrow, it had a lawn bordered by a shallow stream, thick with water plants, in which it was safe for Rosalind and Judy, Nan's daughter, to play. A wild garden, with azaleas and rhododendrons, gave on to a kitchen garden, and beyond that was a tangle of gorse bushes.

The house had a local reputation for being unlucky; Agatha heard that, of the three couples who had lived there, the first had lost their money, the second owner had lost his wife, and the third couple had separated and departed. Agatha and Archie started afresh by renaming the house. Archie proposed that they call it 'Styles', after 'the first book which had begun to bring me a stake in life'. This choice, presumably intended as a joking compliment to Agatha, nonetheless strikes the outsider as odd, for the events that took place in *The Mysterious Affair at Styles* were hardly the sort with whose memory a newly-acquired house should be blessed. Archie's idea, moreover, has an off-hand ring, as if he were implying that the house was Agatha's, not a joint enterprise, while Agatha's agreement suggests that she accepted that they could not invent a new name together. On one wall they hung the painting The Bodley Head had commissioned for the jacket of Agatha's book. It cannot have been a comfortable picture to live with, not only because it is contrived and slapdash, but also because it is extremely sinister. It showed a background of black and sea-green draperies, against which a hollow-eyed figure in a scarlet dressing-gown looked aghast at some unseen horror. The flame from his candle revealed a murky personage busily crouched over a table and the haughty figure of a woman, clutching diaphanous veils round her polished shoulders, with a flock of ghostly shapes, newly roused from sleep, crowding in behind.

The Christies tried to make the best of Styles. They bought new carpets and curtains and, with some difficulty, found a married couple to look after them – the wife an excellent cook, the husband an idle fellow – and a cheerful if languid maid. Setting up the new establishment did not, however, prove the answer to their unease. In fact, it made it worse, as they began to worry about the expense of maintaining the house, two cars and three servants, and of living on an altogether more ample scale. Whether there was real need to worry is beside the point. Agatha, certainly, was insecure: 'Our bank account seemed to be melting in a most extraordinary way.' Madge took her away for a fortnight's holiday to Corsica; Agatha enjoyed being removed from domestic cares but photographs show her looking heavy and strained, although her appearance is not flattered by the clumsy felt cloche hats that were then fashionable.

A month or so after Agatha's return, Clara fell ill with bronchitis. She had stayed for several months at Scotswood, in the flat opposite Archie and Agatha's, taking great pleasure in playing with Rosalind, on whom she practised what the fascinated Miss Fisher, who found Clara 'intelligent but decidedly eccentric', described as 'great ideas of child education'. There was little else to interest Clara in Sunningdale, and eventually Archie and Agatha had arranged for her to take rooms with some friends in London, where she could, if she wished, keep entirely to herself, or join her hosts when she wanted company. Ashfield had not been sold. It remained an important part of Agatha's life, a refuge and a draw. Clara repaired to Torquay from time to time; when Archie and Agatha were in the Pyrenees she looked after Rosalind there. The house was difficult to keep up but its memories were of recuperation and reunions. Clara was at Ashfield when she became ill and Agatha went down to be with her. She was then replaced by Madge, who eventually telegraphed to say that she was moving Clara to Abney, where it would be easier to look after her, and for a time Agatha joined her mother there. Although Clara seemed to mend, she moved little from her room. She was now seventy-two and weakened by illness. Agatha returned to Sunningdale but a week or so later she was urgently summoned back to Abney. In the train to Manchester she had a premonition – 'a feeling, I think, of coldness, as though I was invaded all over' – that her mother was dead.

However many deaths one has seen (and, as Agatha reminded herself in her *Autobiography*, in the hospital she had seen many people die), that of someone close gives a special shock. 'It is only the shell that remains there,' she wrote. 'All my mother's eager, warm, impulsive personality was far away somewhere.' Agatha and Clara had depended upon each other, not just because Clara was Agatha's mother but also because, since Frederick's death, Agatha had to some extent mothered Clara. The fact that Agatha had not been with Clara when she died, may have increased natural feelings of misery and guilt. Archie was unable to reasssure her. At the time of Clara's death and her funeral he was away in Spain on business, and in any case he found unhappiness and inadequacy embarrassing. His own feelings for Clara were mixed; some of their friends suspected he was jealous of Agatha's devotion. At any rate, on Archie's return to his grief-stricken wife he was puzzled and uncomfortable. Rather than proposing, however impracticable it might have been, that he might defer his business to be at home with Agatha and Rosalind, he clumsily suggested that Agatha return with him to Spain. He meant well, for he thought it might distract her. Agatha afterwards blamed herself for preferring to stay at home. 'I see now,' she wrote, 'that that was where I was wrong. My life with Archie lay ahead of me. We were happy together, absolutely assured of each other, and neither of us at that moment would have dreamed that we could ever part, or that anything could come between us.' These brave words are not wholly convincing, for Agatha and Archie's life together seemed already to have lost its momentum. Archie certainly appears to have been thoughtless. He may not have used the exact words that Agatha ascribed to him when she recalled him saying, later, that he had wished her to be 'the same as usual, and full of jokes and fun', but it is significant that she brooded over some such remark. Difficult though it is to share another person's grief, it is nevertheless possible to nurse them through it, blundering, perhaps, by supporting them, rather than for the time being expecting the usual support for oneself. Archie does not appear to have realised this.

Death, moreover, brought in its train not just emotional turmoil but hard physical and intellectual work. There was the estate to settle and clearing up to be done, and this fell on Agatha's shoulders. Clara had left Ashfield to her, together with the immediate responsibility for rescuing it from the disrepair into which it had fallen. Hard physical work was in some respects therapeutic: sorting and ordering helped to soothe shock, ruthless tidying and throwing out assuaged the anger accompanying grief. Agatha attacked the debris and dilapidation, the accumulated treasures and rubbish of years. There had been no money for repairs, the roof was falling in and the walls leaking. All but two of the rooms had been abandoned. From top to bottom the place was crammed with possessions, those brought by Margaret added to Clara's own, all in various stages of decay. Auntie-Grannie's removal from Ealing, and the destruction, waste and chaos it involved, had disturbed Agatha severely when she was younger and more resilient. Now she was miserable, tired and despairing. Her description is of monstrous, pointless objects, like the large wreath of wax flowers, under a glass dome, that was her grandfather's memorial: 'It was all right for Granny – it was her husband's, but I had never even known him. What does one do with a thing of that kind?'

She worked like a demon, assisted by one maid in the morning and another in the afternoon, searching, discarding, carting stuff down flights of stairs. Nor was she clear as to her actual purpose: the first draft of her autobiography speaks of the prospect of 'rehabilitating Ashfield, or, at any rate, if necessary, getting ready to sell it'. Undermining her, too, were further worries about money. The Christies were overdrawn at the bank and, as people often will when they are in a frenzied state, in their efforts to escape that complication they devised another. The scheme was to let Styles for the summer at a good rent. Agatha and Rosalind would stay at Ashfield, while Agatha continued sorting out and stripping down, with Archie staying at his club, making golfing expeditions at weekends. By August, when Madge would be free to leave Abney, the bulk of the work at Ashfield would be done, so that Agatha could leave with a clear conscience and, entrusting Rosalind to Madge, go abroad with Archie for a holiday. They settled on Alassio in Italy; Agatha, writing later in her life, could not remember why, but it may have been related to the serene and sunny associations of Elgar's music 'In the South'. It was a prospect to which she clung during the six weeks' clearing and trudging at Ashfield.

The holiday promised escape, rest and companionship, for Agatha now found herself with no adult in whom she could confide. Archie had retired to business and golf, declining to come to Ashfield at weekends on grounds of inconvenience and expense, and Carlo too had gone. Her father was believed to be in the last stages of cancer and she had returned to Edinburgh. Hating to leave Agatha, she departed. It is not clear exactly when Carlo went away nor when she returned. Agatha describes it as being at the time of 'all this confusion, work and unhappiness', while Carlo herself, in a letter she wrote to Rosalind describing the events of this perplexing and miserable time, spoke of Agatha's sending for her from Scotland and telling her that Clara had died. What is plain, however, is that Agatha's only friend and confidante was absent during these sad summer months.

It is understandable that Agatha's chronology is confused. She was sleeping badly and eating insubstantial and erratic meals, and from time to time would momentarily forget who or where she was. Some believe that Agatha's autobiographical description of her state is a mixture of truth and self-deception and that, although she was undoubtedly ill and upset, she later took pains to establish that she was bewildered and forgetful, the better to sustain the public explanation of the events that followed. Her account is, however, convincing in small, apparently unimportant ways. She speaks, for instance, of hesitating as she signed a cheque, and of doubtfully putting 'Blanche Amory' as her signature. In the second draft of her autobiography this passage was abbreviated; but the first draft was persuasive: 'I still had the feeling that it was not quite right. Was it Blanche, or some other name? Was Amory spelt with an E or with an O?' And, later in that paragraph: 'It had something faintly familiar about it, and in the end I remembered, or at any rate thought I remembered, it was a character apparently in one of Thackeray's novels – *Pendennis*, I thought. I still did not know why I had bagged it for myself: *Pendennis* was not a novel I was particularly fond of though I remembered Thackeray was Father's favourite. But I was not fond of any Thackeray; Dickens was my love – so why Blanche Amory? I put it aside.' This sort of despairing muddle over unimportant detail – 'O' or 'E', the fact that she did not like *Pendennis* – rings true.

August came and with it Rosalind's birthday, Punkie's arrival, Archie and the Italian holiday. Archie, however, seemed unlike himself, edgy and evasive, so much a stranger that Agatha recalled her old nightmare of the Gun Man, in which a familiar, loved and hitherto loving person was suddenly transformed into someone hostile and unreachable. Worried that something might be wrong at the office, even, wildly, that Archie might have, if not embezzled, 'embarked,' as she put it, 'on some transaction for which he had not proper authority', she pressed him to explain. During the next few days he admitted, first, that he had made no arrangements for their holiday, and eventually, that he had fallen in love with someone else, Miss Nancy Neele, with whom he had played golf. Agatha learnt this news at Ashfield, where Rosalind had been born, at the time of Rosalind's birthday.

There are moments in people's lives on which it is unwise, as well as impertinent, for an outsider to speculate, since it is impossible to be certain about what actually took place or how the participants felt about it. Often, indeed, the people most closely concerned cannot themselves explain how they reacted and why. In her *Autobiography* Agatha has given her own account of her reaction to Archie's confession that he no longer loved her and that he wanted a divorce. Her description is entirely plausible and intelligible: bewilderment gave way to shock, shock to guilt and anger. At first she did not understand what Archie was talking about. Then she could not believe his mood would last: 'I thought it was something that would pass.' She looked for reasons, blaming her own preoccupied and miserable state: 'If I'd been cleverer, if I had known more about my husband, had troubled to know more about him, instead of being content to idealise him and to consider him more or less perfect .... If I had not gone to Ashfield ... if I had stayed in London ... I must in some way have not been adequate in filling Archie's life ....' From feeling guilty she turned, increasingly exasperated, to explanations rooted in Archie's character and stratagems for survival: 'He must have been ripe for falling in love with someone else, though he didn't know it himself .... Or was it just this particular girl? Was it just fate with him, falling in love with her quite suddenly? He had certainly not been in love with her on the few occasions we had met her previously. He had even objected to my asking her down .... He said it would spoil his golf. Yet when he did fall in love with her, he fell in love with a suddenness with which he had fallen in love with me, so perhaps it was bound to be ....' There is no reason to disbelieve Agatha's account. She is not manipulating characters in a book – her mother's death and Archie's defection had painfully shown that in real life events were uncontrollable and human beings perverse – but describing an experience of her own, in troubled and untidy phrases.

She now appealed to Carlo to return, other doctors having discovered that her father's illness was not in fact severe. Carlo was horrified at Agatha's condition. She found her unable to eat or sleep, all the day in tears. Of Archie's state we know less, though friends with whom he had stayed during the early part of the summer, while Agatha dismantled Ashfield, thought him subdued and lonely. Agatha herself found him impatient, as much with himself, it appears, as with her, but she later took trouble to try to explain his behaviour. She was frank about Archie's selfishness: 'He said, "I did tell you once, long ago, that I hate it when people are ill or unhappy – it sort of spoils everything for me." Again and again,' she recalled, 'he would say to me: "I can't stand not having what I want and I can't stand not being happy. Everybody can't be happy – somebody has got to be unhappy."' These are childish words, spoken by someone thoroughly miserable. Archie found Agatha increasingly irritating, not least because he was annoyed with himself and with the intractability of their situation. He could not stand tears and depression, Carlo recalled, in a letter to Rosalind later. Agatha spoke of Archie's 'continued unkindness': 'he was unhappy', she wrote, 'because he was, I think, deep down fond of me, and he did really hate to hurt me, but he had to make out for himself that this was not hurting me, that it would be much better for me in the end; that I should have a happy life, that I should travel, that I had got my writing, after all, to console me. But because his conscience really troubled him he could not help behaving with a certain ruthlessness. My mother had always said he was ruthless – she had appreciated that trait in him which I did not; I had always seen so clearly his many acts of kindness, his good nature ... .' Even so, she admitted, 'I had admired his ruthlessness. Now,' she observed, 'I saw the other side of it.'

How our mothers' warnings come back to haunt us. Clara had always emphasised to Agatha that men needed unremitting encouragement and companionship, advice that, later, Agatha herself never failed to give her younger women friends when their husbands' work took them abroad. Now Agatha had lost both Archie and her mother. She had Rosalind but she was a child and should be spared such troubles. She had the perceptive and compassionate Carlo but it would have been disloyal as well as untypical for Agatha to share even with her all her grief and grievances. She felt herself entirely alone. All her love and comfort, she believed, came from a dog, Peter, a wire-haired terrier Rosalind had been given when they moved to Sunningdale. Years later, when Peter died, Agatha told her second husband that, though her sorrow might appear foolish, it would not seem so to someone who understood what it was like to have a dog as the sole source of companionship and consolation.

When Agatha and Rosalind returned to Styles from Ashfield, it at first seemed best for Archie to return to his club in London. It was then that Carlo came back to Styles. After a couple of weeks, however, Archie returned home. He said that 'perhaps he had been wrong,' Agatha wrote. 'Perhaps it was the wrong thing to do.' Moreover, Archie and Rosalind, now aged seven, were devoted to one another and for that reason he tried to stay. Unbearably difficult though he was then, Agatha sought to hold him. She did not want a divorce, for a mixture of reasons. A divorce would be like death, the disappearance of a person with whom, however uncomfortably and disagreeably, an intensely close relationship had been contrived and sustained. Like death, too, it would be complicated materially as well as emotionally: property would have to be apportioned and possessions re-allocated. Divorce, though, is, unlike death, a choice. Rather than inflict pain and inconvenience on all concerned, it is tempting to struggle on or at least to defer the moment of irrevocable decision. Where there are children, the temptation is even greater. In 1926 – and for many years afterwards – there were other pressures, too, against lightly accepting divorce as the means of resolving an emotional dilemma. Obtaining a divorce was difficult and shaming; the only admissible ground was adultery, which had to be proved, generally by various standard, sordid procedures.

Agatha may not have thought this far ahead. It is sufficient to explain her refusal to contemplate a divorce as deriving from her conviction that her marriage to Archie was fundamentally happy and sound. 'There had never been any suspicion of anything of that kind in our lives – we'd been happy together and harmonious. We had never quarrelled and he'd never been the type who looked much at other women.' 'This happens with lots of husbands,' her relations told her. Archie, they said, would return. Agatha, too, believed this but, when Archie remained obdurate, she recognised that his return to Sunningdale had only increased his desire to leave her. He moved back to his club.

Archie was not living with Miss Neele, nor she with him. Conscientious and orderly, steady and reliable, he would not wish to jeopardise his standing with his colleagues in the City – in the late nineteen-twenties a small and conventional society – by behaving recklessly. Moreover, he liked his domestic arrangements to be as well-planned and regular as his business affairs; each morning his breakfast was the same, his day unfolded according to a careful routine, at half-past ten he retired for the night. When it became impossible for him to remain at Styles, he inevitably removed to his club. Any other arrangement would have been even more disruptive, as well as being complicated, expensive and compromising to all concerned. The woman with whom Archie had fallen in love was not a thoughtless girl, but an intelligent and considerate woman, some ten years younger than Archie. She came from a large family – there were twin brothers and another brother and sister besides – and her father had an administrative post with one of the railway boards. When her schooling was finished, Nancy decided to take a course in shorthand and typewriting at one of the secretarial schools for young women recently established in London, choosing Miss Jenkins's Typewriting and Secretarial School, the Triangle, in South

Molton Street, next to Bond Street. When Nancy finished her year at this establishment, famous for its respectability, she joined a City firm called the Imperial Continental Gas Association. At first she was the only woman employed there – male clerks were still the rule – but after a year she was joined by another graduate of the Triangle, and it was this friend who introduced her to Archie.

Madge James and her husband, Sam, lived at Hurtmore in Surrey. Nancy was still living with her family, at Croxley Green, and from time to time she would come to stay with them. Nancy, gregarious and likeable, enjoyed parties and was a pleasant guest. Sam James was a colleague of Archie's in the City and, thinking he looked tired and unhappy, asked him down for a weekend. Madge, who had inquired whether Archie was married and would like to bring his wife, understood from her husband that all was not well between the Christies and that Archie would probably prefer to be invited alone. Nancy, as Madge's friend, was among the other guests. It emerged that Nancy was as keen on golf as Archie and, since Sam did not play, they made a pair. As people will during long weekends in other people's houses, they began to confide in one another.

Agatha and Nancy also knew each other. Indeed, Nancy had been invited by Agatha to stay at Styles and on at least one occasion, when a neighbour had given a dance to which the Christies had taken their guests, Agatha, as a married woman, had chaperoned Nancy, whose family would otherwise not have wished her to be going about so freely. Agatha, writing years later, remembered Archie telling her that since he had been alone in London he had seen a good deal of Nancy, to which she had replied, 'Well, why shouldn't you?' In her *Autobiography* Agatha spoke of Archie's referring to Nancy as 'Belcher's secretary', but either Archie or Agatha was being inaccurate, since Nancy still had her job at the Imperial Continental Gas Association. Major Belcher, now married to an Australian girl who had helped type some of his correspondence on the Empire Tour, certainly knew Nancy, for in 1925 she had stayed with the Belchers on holiday in France. Her acquaintance with Agatha was, however, slight.

By the winter of 1926 these three troubled people were in a state of considerable distress. Archie remained at his club, seeing Nancy at weekends in the company of friends, so that no one's reputation should be injured by gossip. Mrs James in particular sought to arrange matters so that Archie and Nancy could be together at her house with absolute propriety; she was not only anxious not to embarrass her servants by indiscreet behaviour nor to induce her formidable mother to scold her for turning a blind eye to an indecorous courtship but she was also concerned to protect her friend's reputation and happiness. Agatha was in the most unfortunate position. Unlike Archie or Nancy, she had no office to which to take herself each day, no one from whom to draw comfort and love. She was trying to write her next book for Collins and finding it impossible; at night she wandered about. Carlo was frightened by Agatha's distressed state. She sent for the doctor, who suggested that she sleep in the same room. 'I tried to keep the house running smoothly for your sake,' she later wrote to Rosalind, but it cannot have been easy even for such a sensible young woman.

Agatha was in despair but it would be wrong to imagine that she ever seriously contemplated suicide. Had she wished to kill herself, her pharmaceutical knowledge would have made it easy, but that would have been wholly contrary to her strong religious beliefs. She was deeply distraught and undoubtedly ill, in a profoundly unhappy state where no one, not even her own child, could provide consolation or hope. She was sleeping badly, working haphazardly, eating too little. Her appearance deteriorated, she punished herself and everyone around her. Reeling and lurching, her purpose was not fixed.

I I

'A ghastly ten days . . .'

December came, and the approach of Christmas. Agatha told Carlo she should have a day to herself, especially since a friend was urging her to dine and dance with him in London. Reluctantly, because she was uneasy about Agatha, Carlo agreed to go. This was on the evening of Friday, December 3rd. After dinner Carlo telephoned Styles to make sure that Agatha was all right. She was reassured when she came to the telephone, sounding just as usual, and encouraged her to go and dance and to return by the late train.

When Carlo reached Styles, which was within easy walking distance of the station, she found the garage doors wide open and the maids in the kitchen looking scared. They told her that at about eleven o'clock Mrs Christie had come downstairs, got into her car and driven off, without saying where she was going. Carlo, frightened now, calmed the maids and sent them to bed. She herself sat up to wait. In the letter she later sent Rosalind, describing these events, Carlo recalled that, at about six o'clock the following morning, Saturday, a policeman arrived at Styles, with the news that a Morris motor car had been found abandoned some distance away, at a place called Newlands Corner, just beyond Guildford in Surrey. Even on twisting roads, late at night and in bad weather, a driver in a small car would have taken no more than an hour to reach Newlands Corner from Sunningdale. Why Agatha had set off and what her car was still doing there was a mystery.

What follows is, inevitably, after sixty years, a vague and muddled story. Carlo's recollection must be imprecise, since the report of the Superintendent of the Surrey Police records that he did not hear about the car until eleven o'clock that morning. A witness later reported having helped a lady re-start the vehicle at about 6.20 a.m. It must then have taken some time for the Surrey Constabulary to notify the Berkshire Constabulary, in whose district Styles fell, and for the owner of the Morris to be traced.

There is another discrepancy. Carlo's letter states that the policeman informed her that the car had been found upside-down. The Police Superintendent's report states that the car 'was found in such a position as to indicate that some unusual proceeding had taken place, the car being found half-way down a grassy slope well off the main road with its bonnet buried in some bushes ....' It is, however, not surprising that Carlo should have misheard, or misremembered, what the officer told her when he arrived with his frightening news.

Carlo told the policeman that Mrs Christie had not been well and that her family had been worried. Statements in the newspapers subsequently reported that Agatha had left a letter for Carlo, asking her to cancel her arrangements to spend that weekend at a hotel in Yorkshire, and that on the Saturday afternoon Miss Fisher had telegraphed to an hotel in Beverley cancelling Agatha's booking.

Her immediate duty was to let Archie know what had happened. He was staying for the weekend at Hurtmore, with Mr and Mrs James. Nancy was also there. Carlo's telephone call came in the middle of the morning and, almost immediately afterwards, a policeman arrived at the house. On hearing about Agatha's car, Archie straightway left with the policeman to join Carlo at Styles.

By the time Archie returned, the press had got on to the story. She and Archie were taken to examine the car, now surrounded by crowds of people, with vans selling hot drinks and ice-cream. 'A ghastly ten days ensued,' Carlo wrote later. The house was besieged by newspapermen and Rosalind was escorted to school by policemen, who stationed themselves at the front and back doors and by the telephone. Although Styles was in the Berkshire police district, the boundary of the Surrey district began only a few yards away, on the other side of the road, so poor Carlo had two teams of police to deal with. Every morning they interviewed her again. At Archie's suggestion, Carlo sent for her sister Mary, who provided some company and moral support. Archie himself soon showed his annoyance with the press and police, which Carlo thought a mistake. Each day, she remembered, she gave an interview to the *Daily Mail*, Agatha's favourite newspaper.

In 1926, as much as in later years, the *Mail*'s editor, correspondents and managers were engaged in a vigorous battle with rival newspapers for circulation and advertising. To the press, the story of Agatha's disappearance was a gift. The *Daily Mail* and the *Evening News*, its stable-mate, made the running, with articles on the progress of the search for Agatha and the latest speculation as to what might have become of her. Reporters from the *News of the World* and the *Daily News* were also hot on the scent. Careful scrutiny of the sequence of newspaper reports that appeared during the next week or so indicates that it was not only the press who allowed their fervour to go to their heads. Superintendent Goddard, of the Berkshire Constabulary, seems to have said little to the press, but Superintendent Kenward, of Surrey, was constantly cited as having made this or that confident, if sometimes enigmatic, statement. He appears to have enjoyed every minute of his finest hour. A day or so after Agatha's car had been found, he apparently told the *Evening News*, 'I may even have aeroplanes out again,' but in his report for the Home Office he later stated explicitly that: 'The aeroplanes which are said to have taken part in the search are nothing to do with the police.' This example suggests that he may have allowed the attentions of the press to go rather to his head.

On one point, however, it is easy to agree with him. 'There is no doubt,' he wrote, 'that a good deal of press matter circulated in connection with the case was without foundation.' This was, evidently, partly his own fault but it also owed much to the enthusiasm with which the newspapers pursued the story, conjuring witnesses from one unlikely quarter after another, frenziedly reporting far-flung sightings of their quarry, mixing up Agatha's disappearance with those of other persons who had gone missing at the same time, and hiring clairvoyants and experts to propound their own theories as to what might have happened. Reading even a few of those newspaper accounts in sequence shows how easily myths are made and sustained. The correspondents who wrote them were deferential and circumspect to an extent that seems curious today but they nonetheless asked questions. That they did so in a polite and unhectoring tone of voice did not make their suspicions any less insidious or their suggestions less persuasive, as Archie found when, to his amazement, he realised that he was popularly suspected of doing away with his wife, or as Agatha discovered when she subsequently learnt that she had been variously believed to have disappeared as a 'publicity stunt', to join a lover, to cast suspicion on her husband, or for other reasons too lunatic to explore here.

In discovering what happened to Agatha and understanding why, the press is as much of a hindrance as a help. Furthermore,

Superintendent Kenward's report to the Home Office is vague
and defensive, and all other police records have been destroyed
with the passage of time. Taken together, such sources represent
a mixture of speculation, pure fancy and intermittently verifiable
fact that not only confused the interested public at the time but
has misled them ever since.

According to Superintendent Kenward, he spent the afternoon
of Saturday, December 4th and all day on the Sunday and the
Monday, together with seven or eight regular members of the
Surrey Force and 'a good muster of Special Constables (unpaid)
and voluntary civilian helpers', searching the Downs around
Newlands Corner. On the Monday the newspapers reported that
a farm worker, Mr Ernest Cross, had said that on his way to
work on the Saturday morning he had come upon 'a woman in
a frenzied condition standing by a motor car near the top of
Newlands Corner Hill, a few yards from the Newlands Corner
Hotel'. According to Mr Cross, the woman was moaning and
holding her hands to her head. Her teeth were chattering with the
cold, which was not surprising since, he reported, 'she was wearing only a thin frock and a thin pair of shoes, and I think she
was without a hat.' The lights of the car, he went on to say, were
full on and she had stumbled towards him, remarking that it was
very late and begging him to try to start the engine for her. He
had wound up the engine, 'which was quite hot' and, as the
woman had climbed back into the car, he noticed that it was
running smoothly. In later accounts this witness was named as
Mr Edward McAllister; he was also to be quoted as saying that
the radiator was in fact 'quite cold'. He described the woman he
met so accurately, however, that Superintendent Kenward
apparently had little doubt it was Agatha he had seen. The
Superintendent now decided that he needed more help with the
search and, he told his superiors, he 'accordingly gathered
approximately three dozen regular police, drawn from all parts
of the county ... together with innumerable Special Constables.
...' With considerable reinforcements of civilian helpers, a thorough search was made of that portion of the Downs. All that
was found, however, was a woman's black shoe covered with
mud and a woman's brown glove lined with fur.

The newspapers had by now published Agatha's description;
this produced new witnesses and helpful bystanders. One was a
Mrs de Silvo, a neighbour of the Christies, who told the *Mail*'s
correspondent 'the story of a charming and beautiful woman of

whom everyone speaks in the highest terms, of a devoted husband, and of a brilliant brain taxed apparently to its limit to
satisfy a never-ending demand of the public for the fancies it
could weave.' All the information Mrs de Silvo could furnish,
however, was that Agatha had recently been ill, distressed by the
death of her mother, but that her condition had sufficiently improved for her to discuss a plan to take a furnished house in
town, 'so that she could be more with her husband, and of letting
Styles furnished'. On Wednesday, December 1st, she had driven
with Agatha to London, to do some shopping, and they had
discussed plans for going together to Portugal in the New Year.
Agatha proposed to spend that night at her club in town and
when she and Mrs de Silvo parted on Wednesday afternoon this
was the last her neighbour had seen of her.

Three days after Agatha disappeared, Archie visited Scotland
Yard to ask for help. He was told that the Yard could not inter-
vene until asked to do so by the Surrey or the Berkshire Police.
The official view was that Agatha had crashed her car, stumbled
away from it and lost her path in the woods. During the course
of Tuesday, December 7th, according to the *Evening News*, some
five hundred men arrived in charabancs, to search the undergrowth. Dragging parties were detailed to each pond and stream;
a local beauty spot, the Silent Pool, was assailed with a pump
and large grappling irons to tear through its weeds. At Albury
Mill Pond nets were placed across the sluice and the gates then
opened. Nothing was found.

During the course of the week more witnesses came forward.
A Mrs Kitchings reported that at midday on the Saturday she
had encountered a woman wearing 'a toque and a coat and skirt',
who had come up close and peered into her face. 'At first I
thought she was going to speak to me, as she stopped right in
front of me, but then she turned back and walked away in the
opposite direction.' A Mr Frederick Dore claimed to have found
the abandoned Morris as he was going to work on the Saturday
morning and to have noticed 'a quite young girl' walking away
from it, who told him that at about midnight she had heard the
car coming along the track on the top of the Downs. Mr Dore
was tester for a firm of motor car manufacturers and his examination of the vehicle and its path suggested to him that it had
been given a push at the top of the hill and sent down deliberately. A couple who kept the hotel at Newlands Corner claimed
that Agatha had spent the Friday night there, and a Mr Ralph

Brown of Battersea claimed he had met her while he was driving near Newlands Corner at about eleven-fifteen on the Saturday morning. 'She seemed to be in the kind of mood when she did not care what happened,' he reported. 'I offered to give her a lift, but she said, "I am going nowhere in particular; thanks for the offer, but I would rather stay where I am."' A cow-man from Shere declared that on Saturday at 4 a.m. he had seen the car being driven towards Newlands Corner, while a Mr Richards, an accountant who owned a nearby shoot, reported that on the Saturday afternoon he had seen a woman resembling Agatha with a 'well-dressed man of about thirty-two, who wore a grey soft-felt hat with the brim turned down', sitting in a car parked in his lane. According to Mr Richards, this car had been seen in the same lane late on the Friday night, together with a car resembling Mrs Christie's Morris. This account was partly corroborated by a Mr Faulds, the son of a neighbouring farmer. He too claimed to have seen the two cars on the Friday night and on Saturday afternoon, saying that 'twice during the day I saw the woman outside the car, but each time she saw me she went back to it and shut herself up inside so as not to be seen.' 'This struck me,' he declared, 'as being very peculiar.'

Such reports suggested to the press that Agatha might have gone into hiding with a companion. This theory was enhanced by the discovery, in a deserted hut in the woods near Newlands Corner, of a postcard, some letters and a box of face-powder (together with a dead owl in the fireplace). A local woodman excitedly told the press how he had been asked by the police to watch the hut, over whose threshold a conscientious officer sprinkled some of the powder, in the hope of taking footprints.

Meanwhile the *Daily Sketch* crime reporter, who had obtained a powder-puff of Agatha's, showed it to a clairvoyant, who described how the missing woman's body might be found in a log-house. Ritchie Calder, then a young reporter on the *Daily News*, writing in the *New Statesman* fifty years later, described how he and a colleague from the *Westminster Gazette* found such a house in the woods. Closed up for the winter, it had nevertheless recently been occupied and the reporters claimed to find a bottle of opium there. 'Actually,' Ritchie Calder later admitted, 'it was ipecacuanha and opium, in discreet proportions, used in the treatment of chronic diarrhoea. Accepting our wild goose chase, we went back to Guildford and told our colleagues, as an amusing story, about our adventures. They immediately swarmed off to

that clearing. One picture-paper reporter took the barmaid of a
Guildford hotel with him. He scattered face-powder on the doorstep, and got her to step in it. Next day the shoe-print appeared
with the caption "Is this Mrs Christie's?" '

On Wednesday, December 8th, five days after Agatha left
Styles, the newspapers reported that Archie's brother Campbell
had received a letter from her postmarked London SW, 9.45,
December 4. It had been addressed to him at the Royal Military
Academy, Woolwich, and he had found it on his desk there on
Sunday morning. After reading the letter, he had put it on one
side and later, when he learnt of his sister-in-law's disappearance,
could not find it. The envelope had, however, survived and he
had immediately telephoned Archie and sent him the envelope.
Some newspapers stated that in the letter Agatha spoke of being
ill and of intending to go to a Yorkshire spa to stay with friends
and recuperate. According to *The Times*, the Surrey Police had
'communicated with certain centres in Yorkshire, and as a result
are satisfied, it is understood, that Mrs Christie is not in that
county.'

The *Mail* offered an ingenious explanation as to how Agatha
might have contrived to post a letter to her brother-in-law in time
for it to be franked with that date, while at the same time she
was either standing helplessly by her abandoned car, wandering
on the Downs or in the woods, or roaming about the lanes of
Surrey in such a way as to encounter Mrs Kitchings at midday
or Mr Brown at eleven-fifteen. This explanation the newspaper
christened 'SUB-CONSCIOUS PLOT THEORY'. The police, reported the *Mail*, 'are not unmindful of the fact that it is known
that Mrs Christie spent Wednesday night at her club in the
south-western district of London and may then have made
arrangements for posting the letter at a later date.' The *Mail*'s
explanation of what Agatha might have been doing since her
disappearance was a subtle mixture of the notion that she might
have lost her memory and the idea that her skill as a detective
novelist might have something to do with the puzzling nature of
her disappearance. 'It is suggested in some quarters,' the *Mail*
declared, 'that Mrs Christie may be suffering from what psychol-
ogists term a temporary breakdown with loss of identity. In such
a state her sub-conscious mind, controlling all her actions, might
plan an ingenious disappearance similar to that which her trained
and creative brain, under normal conditions, has so often devised
for her works of fiction.' The *Evening News* further muddied the

waters by producing a tailor, Mr Daniels, who lived in Plumstead, about a mile away from Campbell's house in Woolwich. According to Mr Daniels, shortly before 11 p.m. on the night of Monday, December 6th his front door had been suddenly pushed open by an agitated woman who had come into his front hall. The intruder had thrust out her hand, in which she held a one-pound note, and demanded change. When told there was none, she had left the house. Captain Christie, the *Evening News* reported, felt it highly improbable that Agatha had gone anywhere near Woolwich.

In the early days of this saga the newspaper correspondents' sympathies had been as much with Archie as with Agatha. 'Both she and her husband,' the *Mail* had written, 'are extremely popular in the district, and anxiety as to the fate of a brilliant woman is only equalled by the sympathy evoked by the pitiful figure of Colonel Christie, who, driven to distraction by the mystery, finds comfort in the presence of his little daughter Rosalind.' By the middle of the week, however, the press had discovered that all was not well between the Christies. Mrs Hemsley had told the *Mail* of Agatha's recent depression, saying that for some days following her mother's death Agatha had 'seemed at a loss to account for her actions'. Mrs Hemsley had illustrated Agatha's 'frenzied condition' by describing her state when Peter, Rosalind's dog, had been knocked down and taken for dead. She also told the *Mail* that, on the Friday afternoon preceding her disappearance, Agatha had visited her in Dorking for tea. 'When she left me,' Mrs Hemsley added, 'she seemed a little brighter, but sat deep in thought for a few seconds in her car before starting away.'

The press had also made enquiries at Hurtmore, where, they now revealed, Archie had been staying on the night Agatha disappeared. Mrs James's cook and parlourmaid had left her service, whether dismissed for gossiping or because they disapproved of this notoriety the newspapers did not say. Asked about his whereabouts on that evening, Archie told the *Evening News* that he was not prepared to confide in their correspondent. He was becoming increasingly exasperated: 'I have told the police. I do not want my friends to be dragged into this. It is my business alone. I have been badgered and pestered like a criminal, and all I want is to be left alone.' Archie was clearly having a difficult time: 'My telephone is constantly ringing. All manner of people are asking about my wife. Why, I even get clairvoyants ringing up and telling me the only hope I have of finding her is by holding a séance.' He would not explain why she had left home, 'save that her nerves have completely gone, and that she went away for no real purpose whatever'.

Nonetheless, on Sunday, December 10th, a week after Agatha had vanished, Archie gave an interview to the *Mail*. It began with a remark which was afterwards to be quoted over and over again. 'It is quite true,' Archie was reported as saying, 'that my wife had discussed the possibility of disappearing at will. Some time ago she told her sister, "I could disappear if I wished and set about it carefully." They were discussing something that appeared in the papers, I think. That shows that the possibility of engineering a disappearance had been running through her mind, probably for the purpose of her work. Personally, I feel that is what happened. At any rate, I am buoying myself up with that belief.' Archie next gave his own explanation; 'You see, there are three possible explanations of her disappearance: Voluntary, Loss of Memory, and Suicide. I am inclined to the first, although, of course, it may be loss of memory as a result of her highly nervous state.' Archie now developed this train of thought, unwisely in the circumstances: 'I do not believe this is a case of suicide. She never threatened suicide, but if she did contemplate that, I am sure her mind would turn to poison. I do not mean that she has ever discussed the question of taking poison, but that she used poison very largely in her stories. I have remonstrated with her in regard to this form of death, but her mind always turned to it. If she wanted to get poison, I am sure she could have done so. She was very clever at getting anything she wanted.' Archie ended, however, on a common-sense note:

> But against the theory of suicide you have to remember this: if a person intends to end his life he does not take the trouble to go miles away and then remove a heavy coat and walk off into the blue before doing it. That is one reason why I do not think my wife has taken her life. She removed her fur coat and put it into the back of the car before she left it, and then I think she probably walked down the hill and off – God knows where. I suggest she walked down the hill because she always hated walking uphill.

The text of this interview should be treated with caution. In parts it reads naturally: the passage about Agatha's removing her coat and walking off into the blue and the reference to her distaste for walking uphill sound fluent and down-to-earth. Other sequences are, however, more stilted, with the false note that comes when direct speech is turned into indirect speech and remarks strung together to make connected prose. Certainly Archie was not at ease with the press. He was harassed and anxious, guilty at being away from home when Agatha was clearly very ill, and, in any case, unused to giving this sort of interview. The *Mail* correspondent was a skilful journalist, whose account reflected Archie's tense and suspicious state: but was Archie suspecting or suspected? The *Mail*'s correspondent, moreover, 'directed Colonel Christie's attention to certain rumours which have gained currency in Sunningdale and elsewhere'. Archie replied: 'It is absolutely untrue to suggest there was anything in the nature of a row or tiff between my wife and myself on Friday morning. She was perfectly well – that is to say, as well as she had been for months past. She knew I was going away for the weekend; she knew who were going to be the members of the little party at the house at which I was going to stay, and neither then nor at any time did she raise the slightest objection. I strongly deprecate introducing any tittle-tattle into this matter. That will not help me to find my wife; that is what I want to do. My wife has never made the slightest objection to any of my friends, all of whom she knew.' A further puzzle was how Agatha might be living since, Archie told the *Mail*, neither of her bank accounts – one at Sunningdale for household expenses, and the other at Dorking for private purposes – had been drawn upon since she had disappeared. Indeed, she had left both her cheque books behind. Archie believed that when Agatha left Sunningdale she might have had £5 or £10 in her possession; her clothes and fur coat had remained in the Morris. The *Mail* correspondent's report concluded: 'Friends of Mrs Christie have told me to-day that recently she has been particularly depressed, and that on one occasion she said, "If I do not leave Sunningdale, Sunningdale will be the end of me."' The implications of this remark were, in the context of this report, extremely sinister. Knowing what Agatha thought of Sunningdale, however, we can well believe that she might easily, and not altogether flippantly, have said something on those lines.

Agatha's flight and fate were now a matter of intense popular interest. On December 12th the police (including Miss Dorothy Sayers) joined in what the *Evening News* described as the 'Great Sunday Hunt for Mrs Christie'. The police advised civilians to 'wear old clothes and be prepared for a stiff task'; the *News* recommended 'Anyone who may have bloodhounds ... to bring them along.' Men, it warned, should wear thick boots; women would find Russian boots and tweed skirts an advantage. A farmer loaned tractors to explore the bracken, squads of people slashed the undergrowth, and an aeroplane circled overhead. The Silent Pool was dragged again, and, as well as the police dogs, alsatians, collies and terriers were brought. No body was found, and Superintendent Kenward made another plan. The whole area was mapped into sections; heath, quarries, pools and streams. A firm of divers offered its services and eighty members of the Aldershot Motor Cycling Club also came forward to help.

Newspapers were now offering a reward for anyone who could find 'the missing novelist', an invitation which naturally produced reports that she had been spotted simultaneously in places hundreds of miles apart. The work of the police was also complicated by the fact that other cases of missing persons were now attracting the attention of the press. Even when no direct connections were drawn, the placing of the latest reports on the search for Agatha Christie next to those announcing the disappearance of other unfortunate young women doubtless produced the intended effect of linking these events in the public mind.

By this time the press was producing its own expert theorists. One, writing in the *Mail*, was ex-Chief Inspector Gough, veteran of a murder case at Wokingham, who offered some observations on human nature in particular and in general: 'One great difficulty is that the search is for a woman with certain attributes that are not common to the ordinary individual. She is talented. She is a woman who by the very nature of her work would have an exceptionally elastic brain. Consequently one would expect her, consciously or subconsciously, to do something extraordinary.' Edgar Wallace was also wheeled in and made a number of confident assertions. 'The disappearance,' he wrote, 'seems to be a typical case of "mental reprisal" on somebody who has hurt her. To put it vulgarly, her first intention seems to have been to "spite" an unknown person who would be distressed by her disappearance.' He suggested that Agatha had 'deliberately created an atmosphere of suicide' and that, 'In an emotional moment she decided to spend the night in the open.... She would have gone to an hotel to sleep after her night's adventure and might not have heard the commotion her disappearance had caused until Sunday.' His 'reconstruction' ended with the confident statement, printed in heavy type, that: 'If Agatha Christie is not dead of shock and exposure within a limited radius of the place where her car was found, she must be alive and in full possession of her faculties, probably in London.' 'It is impossible,' he declared, 'to lose your memory and find your way to a pre-determined destination.' This last sentence sank gently into the minds of reporters and thence into the public consciousness.

The investigators were now thoroughly confused. The Berkshire Police, led by Superintendent Goddard, had asked that the search be extended to parts of England more distant from Sunningdale. Superintendent Goddard's remarks were brief and direct: 'I do not accept the theory that Mrs Christie committed suicide at Newlands Corner. There is no evidence that I can find to support that theory, nor do I see any special reason to assume that she is dead.' Archie shared this opinion. Superintendent Kenward, however, 'reiterated his view that Mrs Christie is dead, and that her body is somewhere near Newlands Corner.' He based his view, mysteriously, on 'documents in his possession', a letter which Carlo had entrusted to the police.

It was the methodical Superintendent Goddard, rather than his more excitable colleague, who was proved right. On the evening of Tuesday, December 14th, Archie was reunited with Agatha at the Hydropathic Hotel in Harrogate, North Yorkshire. The story ran at enormous length in the following day's newspapers, though not, ironically, in the weekly *Harrogate Herald*, which appeared each Wednesday, since its correspondents had been so preoccupied with telephoning details of the story to the metropolitan newspapers, for which they acted as 'stringers', that they had overlooked their own.

In the week and a half Agatha had spent at the Hydro, where she was said to have been staying under an assumed name (variously reported in the *Mail* as being 'Mrs Theresa Neele' and, presumably based on a reporter's distorted remarks on the telephone, 'Mrs Trazeneil'), she had 'seemed normal and happy' and 'sang, danced, played billiards, read the newspaper reports of the disappearance, chatted with her fellow-guests, and went for walks'. This lively picture derived from the findings of the *Mail*'s special correspondent in Harrogate, whisked from Sunningdale by the fast train to interview the more loquacious of the hotel's staff and guests, and Mr and Mrs Taylor, who managed the Hydro. Neither of the Taylors had seen Agatha when she had arrived on December 4th but Mr Taylor understood that 'without hesitation', she had taken 'a good room on the first floor, fitted with hot and cold water', at the price of seven guineas a week. Mrs Taylor had for some time thought that their guest resembled Agatha's press photographs and so, she told the *Mail*, had some of her staff. 'I told them to say nothing,' she declared but, 'someone outside the hotel informed the police.'

Superintendent McDowell of the Yorkshire Police had alerted the Surrey Police, who telephoned Carlo at Sunningdale. Since she could not leave Rosalind, she telephoned Archie at his office and he took the afternoon train to Harrogate. According to the press, Archie and Superintendent McDowell, and possibly other police officers, had stationed themselves in an alcove by the lift, so that Archie could identify Agatha as she came down the stairs to dinner. As she took up an evening paper, containing the story of the search for herself, with her photograph, Archie made his way towards her. 'She only seemed to regard him as an acquaintance,' Mr Taylor said, 'whose identity she could not quite fix. It was sufficient, however, to permit of her accompanying her husband to the dining-room. . . .'

In a statement to the press, Archie said: 'There is no question about the identity. It is my wife. She has suffered from the most complete loss of memory and I do not think she knows who she is. She does not know me and she does not know where she is. I am hoping that rest and quiet will restore her. I am hoping to take her to London to-morrow to see a doctor and specialist.' Archie, the newspaper stated, then expressed his thanks to the police.

On the following day, December 15th, Agatha and Archie left the hotel, not for London but, temporarily, for Cheadle. That short journey was difficult enough. They were driven to Harrogate Station and, mobbed by the press, transferred to a reserved first-class carriage. At Leeds, where they had to change, they were chased along the platform but managed to find their reserved compartment. Agatha and Archie were met at the end of their journey by James and Madge, whose car took them to Abney. There the gates were shut.

12

'... an unquestionably genuine loss of memory'

There were those who did not talk, or did not tell all they knew, to the press: Carlo, who set down her recollections in the letter to Rosalind; Mrs James, Archie's and Nancy's friend; Albert Whiteley, who played the banjo in the band at the Hydro, and Mrs Schofield, the pianist's wife; Raymond Ross and Stanley Hickes, two young local reporters, and Dick Ledbetter, a local press photographer; Sally Potts, the chambermaid who looked after Agatha's room, and another maid, Rosie Asher. From what they said later, and from Rosalind herself, whose reunion with her mother was sufficiently strange to impress itself on a seven-year-old's memory, we can build up a picture of what befell Agatha after she left Styles on December 3rd.

At first Agatha herself could not recall what had happened between that time and the moment when she was greeted by Archie at Harrogate. The two doctors who were called to Abney to examine her – Dr Henry Wilson, Madge's own doctor at Cheadle, and Dr Donald Core, a distinguished neurologist at the University of Manchester – published a joint announcement that she was suffering from 'an unquestionably genuine loss of memory'. They recommended that she see a psychiatrist. Agatha was unhappy at this suggestion – psychiatry can be painful as well as time-consuming – but Madge insisted. She had reproached Agatha for not telling her how ill and unhappy she had been during the summer and autumn. Agatha, who not unnaturally felt guilty at causing so much worry and unwelcome attention, agreed to see a man in Harley Street. With Carlo and Rosalind, she took a flat in Kensington High Street, from which she went to Harley Street for therapy.

With the psychiatrist's help, Agatha recovered her memory of much that had occurred. She could not recall leaving Styles, nor driving about, nor what had happened to the Morris; according to Carlo, the psychiatrist believed that the blank period was due to concussion. Agatha had apparently caught a milk train from Guildford to Waterloo Station. The walk from Newlands Corner to Guildford would have been strenuous – it is three or four miles at least – although there was in 1926 a penny bus which came over the ridge at breakfast time, to take people into the town to work. We do not know how Agatha made that journey but she did remember that, on arriving at Waterloo, she had a cup of coffee in the buffet. She also recalled that, though she had blood on her face and was dressed only in a skirt and cardigan, no one seemed to notice. At Waterloo she saw a poster advertising the spa at Harrogate. Her arm was hurting and she therefore concluded that she must be on her way to Harrogate for treatment. This was a reasonable deduction. Posters promoting Harrogate's therapeutic attractions were prominently displayed in the London railway termini in the 1920s.

Agatha recalled taking a taxi to Whiteleys, where she bought a coat, a small case and some night things. She not only had money from the small cheque which Carlo had cashed for her earlier in the week but also several hundred pounds in a money belt concealed around her waist. In her anxious state she had evidently been taking to extremes her grandmother's advice that she should always have a hidden supply of ready cash for emergencies.

Agatha had then taken a train to Harrogate, either the Pullman leaving King's Cross at 11.15 a.m. or the 11.45 a.m. from St Pancras. In the nineteen-twenties Harrogate was a fashionable spa. It was frequented not only by people who had made or enlarged fortunes in the provinces and who wished simultaneously to spend their money, pamper their health and be smart, but also by those who were smart already – the local nobility, the occasional foreign duke or duchess and the regular royal relation. The names of visitors, together with the amusements that were available, were published weekly in the *Herald*, which included in the lists published on December 5th and December 15th 'Mrs Neele of Cape Town'. Harrogate, in fact, resembled the spa in which Archie and Agatha had stayed at the end of their holiday in the Pyrenees. Indeed, it was not unlike Torquay, transplanted to the north.

At Harrogate station there were not only cabs available but the larger hotels, of which the Hydro was one, sent their own motors to meet the London trains. The Hydropathic Hotel, from its name alone, would attract someone who obviously needed restoration. It was one of Harrogate's biggest and grandest hotels, set in ornamental gardens near the centre of the town, just above the Pump Room. Smart though it might be, the Hydro was nonetheless most respectable. For one thing, it was practically teetotal. 'Table wine' was available in the evenings for consumption with dinner but the therapeutic purpose of the hotel was emphasised by the fact that in the entrance hall, by the stairs, was an apparatus dispensing health-giving Harrogate water, of which glasses were brought to the bedrooms by a page. A resident nurse arranged courses of treatment – the Turkish Bath, cold douche, Vichy Bath, and so on – at the Royal Baths or in the hotel itself. The Hydro was comfortable but not racy. The maids were strictly disciplined; they lived in a dormitory, dressed soberly and worked long hours. In the public rooms the guests were entertained by Harry Codd's band, which played in the Palm Court at tea-time and after dinner in the evening, excepting Sundays. The dance music was up-to-date – the repertoire included the Charleston, along with more sedate dances – and at the end of the evening guests could waltz to 'The Blue Danube'. In charge of these proceedings was 'a lady entertainer', a combined chaperone, host and guide. She would arrange parties for bridge, encourage visitors to dance (very decorously; a pair of unaccompanied women might be persuaded to take part in the Lancers) and pass on particular requests to the band. She herself also sang and played the piano while Harry Codd and his men ate their sandwiches and surreptitiously stole off for a bottle of beer.

Agatha arrived at the Hydro just before the Christmas season began. There were few guests in addition to the permanent residents and she had no trouble in obtaining a room. She was put in number five, a small room, with a basin and one easy chair. Agatha had arrived with only a dressing-case. She was a reserved and unobtrusive guest, breakfasting quietly in her room on half a grapefruit and 'split toast' (Melba toast), then the latest diet for those who wished not to gain weight. When her breakfast was brought, Agatha was to be found reclining against the pillows, her hands covering her face and chin, as if to hide herself or conceal a bruise. After two or three days the maid who brought Agatha's breakfast asked her how she felt, saying she had been looking rather tired. Agatha had replied that she was tired and that she had some trouble 'but I'll have to sort it out.' Her reticent nature would have prevented her from chattering to the maid, who had only one glimpse of her private affairs, when she was asked to pass a handkerchief from Agatha's dressing-case. Beside the handkerchief was a photograph. Agatha told the maid that this was her 'little girl', but no more.

As a result of her sessions in Harley Street, Agatha remembered playing bridge with her fellow-guests and discussing the disappearance of the missing novelist. After some time she began to worry that her money would not last indefinitely and that there were no letters. She placed an advertisement in *The Times*, which appeared on Saturday, December 11th, asking that: 'Friends and relatives of Theresa Neele, late of South Africa, please communicate,' and giving a box number. Agatha could not produce a reason for calling herself Theresa Neele, except that Theresa was the name of a woman she knew who lived in Torquay and Neele was the name of the woman Archie loved. The newspapers had also reported that Harrods, in Knightsbridge, had received a letter from a Mrs Christie asking that a diamond ring, left for repair, should be posted to Yorkshire. The letter was not kept and Agatha did not speak of it.

Those who observed Agatha during her stay at the Hydro were struck by her reserved and inconspicuous behaviour. Reg Schofield, who as pianist to the band sat sideways, had a different view of the hotel drawing-rooms and he could see Agatha sitting quietly in a corner in the afternoons, doing crosswords, and in the evening retiring to the shadowy part of the conservatory. Contrary to later newspaper reports, she on no occasion played the piano or sang in public. In the afternoon there was no singing in the Palm Court; in the evening the 'lady entertainer' did not encourage guests to usurp her own role.

The *Mail* had published a photograph of 'the missing novelist', and one of the chambermaids, noting the similarity between 'Mrs Neele's' handbag and that in the picture, pointed out the resemblance to Mrs Taylor, the manageress, who felt that an hotel's staff should be discreet and advised them to say nothing. Bob Tappin, the drummer, and Bob Leeming, who played the saxophone, decided that the quiet lady's likeness to Mrs Christie was too close to be ignored. Harry Codd, the band's only professional member, refused to pass on possibly ill-founded suspicions to the police; he had to safeguard his own and the hotel's reputation. Mrs Tappin and Mrs Leeming were next consulted, coming to the hotel to see what they thought. Their husbands did not take their suspicions to the newspapers (thereby forgoing a reward of £100) but to the police, who refused to commit themselves until Colonel Christie had succeeded, or not, in identifying his wife.

According to the bandsmen, who later received silver pencils as a token of Archie's thanks for their discretion, the reunion was 'subdued' and undramatic. The first public announcement of Agatha's discovery came in the *Yorkshire Post*, which had two lines under Stop Press. During the course of the evening, from eight o'clock onwards, the press descended on the Hydro, commandeering the telephones and filling the public rooms. Mr and Mrs Taylor, appalled at the invasion, tried to protect the Christies. The staff were instructed to be wary – the chambermaids parried questions by saying they had only just come on duty – and great care was taken in accepting bookings for rooms. Archie had been installed in number ten, on the opposite side of the staircase to Agatha, but the press was encouraged to believe that Mr and Mrs Christie had taken a suite together. The Northern Editor of the *Mail* managed to book a room on the first floor, in which he sat up all night 'in case they should escape'. The *Mail* also ordered a special train to stand by at Harrogate station. It was thought by younger and more innocent reporters that this was to transport copy to the South as quickly as possible; they were soon told that it was actually intended to carry Agatha to London, should she agree to give the newspaper an 'exclusive' account of her experiences. Nothing could have been less likely. At midnight the stationmaster telephoned to ask what should be done with the train, which, he said, was 'huffing and puffing black smoke in a siding'. The *Mail* reporter consulted his editor in London. 'Cancel it,' he was ordered.

Archie was disinclined to talk to the press and no reporter spoke to Agatha at any point, although at least one claimed to have done so. One journalist, taxed by his colleagues with writing a story based on a fictitious conversation, is said to have declared ingeniously that, even if Agatha denied having spoken to him, no one would believe her, since 'she's lost her memory, hasn't she?' Again, contrary to some press reports, Archie did not give a press conference. What happened was that Superintendent McDowell, a firm but sensible officer who got on well with the press, was asked by the frustrated reporters whether he could persuade Colonel Christie to speak to one of their number, whom they would delegate as their common representative. Archie reluctantly agreed and Kenyon, 'the doyen of the *Yorkshire Post*', was nominated. Archie came to the George Hotel, where Kenyon was quartered, but gave him only the prepared statement that Agatha was suffering from loss of memory. Any reports of other interviews were fabricated.

By morning the journalists were desperate for more detail. Dick Ledbetter and a young assistant enterprisingly took themselves to the Hydro's reception desk and photographed Agatha's signature in the register. At half past nine a landaulette drew up outside the entrance. Reporters flung themselves towards it. Some were draped over the bonnet; eight or nine photographers, including two from the *Sketch*, clustered on its enormous wings. The *Mail's* photographers were more canny. One stayed with the car, while the other hung about the back of the hotel, until a second car pulled up at the goods and staff entrance. Agatha and Archie were bundled inside – and the *Mail* thus obtained 'the scoop picture'.

Pursued to the station, the Christies boarded the train as the journalists followed, running across the tracks. At Leeds they were dogged by more reporters and photographers. The pictures showed Agatha in a 'tubular dress and skirt and a cloche hat'; one reporter remembered her as shielding her face and as having remarkably attractive legs. Archie, he recalled, wore a Norfolk jacket and plus fours, 'rather like Harold Macmillan; it struck me as quite a good outfit.' Agatha was looking thin and pale. At Manchester the pursuers appeared again, to be shaken off only at the gates of Abney. The *Mail* succeeded in obtaining the 'best' photographs. They show Agatha looking hunted and afraid and, years later, when Rosalind was to see newspaper pictures of other bewildered women, their private unhappiness exposed to public view, she was to remember how her mother looked when they were reunited. Agatha did not recognise Rosalind. She was kind but somehow absent, not like a mother embracing a daughter. Something strange had obviously happened.

Gaps remain in the story. No one knows why Agatha fled from Styles late on the night of December 3rd. We can only suppose that, utterly distraught, she felt she must get away. Nor do we know how she spent the time between leaving home at about 11 p.m. and being helped with her car at six-twenty the next morning. She might have gone in search of Carlo, or started for Beverley, forgetting that she had cancelled the booking and frantic to be on her way. She might have driven to London and back, or meandered wildly around the countryside. Perhaps she drove towards Dorking because she had been that way earlier in the day. We do not know why Agatha took with her the few things she packed into the dressing-case. The arbitrariness of the assortment – a nightgown, some clothes and shoes, an out-of-date driving licence – has suggested to some that these were carefully assembled 'red herrings', with the driving licence added as a means of identification. But these bits and pieces might equally well indicate that, in a dazed and irrational state, Agatha had vaguely stuffed into a case the sort of things people do take when they suddenly leave a house, the bizarre and random accumulation of a nightmare. Nor do we know what Agatha's intentions were. There are those who believe she wished to kill herself and who point to the driving licence as the identifying clue she would leave behind. On the other hand, it is odd that someone with that intention should also pack a nightgown. We simply do not know what Agatha planned to do, if indeed she had any plans at all.

Then there is the matter of the car. If the lady Mr McAllister helped was Agatha, the car was obviously behaving erratically. Until comparatively recently motor cars had works that were temperamental, cumbersome and precarious. It was not unusual, particularly in cold weather, to have to start the engine by cranking a handle. Reports of Mr McAllister's story differ as to whether the engine was hot or cold when he restarted it. The car was later found further down the hill, its headlamps still burning, according to Superintendent Kenward's report, or its headlamps extinguished, because the battery had run down, according to the newspapers. Press accounts also described the car as, variously, covered all over with frost, or partly covered with frost, and there were at least three different reports of its position. There is no hope of reconciling or clarifying these contradictions.

Careful examination of the spot at Newlands Corner suggests the following explanation. Coming from the direction of Guildford, the Morris climbed to the top of a steep, winding hill. The weather was cold, the car's engine unhappy. At the top of the hill, where the ground levels out, it stalled. Agatha tried vainly to crank the engine, perhaps taking off her coat, since it was hot and awkward work. Mr McAllister came to her rescue and Agatha then drove over the crest of the hill and down the other side, where the road is, if anything, even more steeply inclined and bending. The Morris was equipped with a 'crash gear box' – to change gear the driver would have to gauge the exact moment when the engine revolutions were at the appropriate speed for the gears to mesh. Agatha, taught to drive at a time when no official tests were necessary, notoriously unmechanical, cold, despairing and exhausted, might easily have missed the gear. The car, out of control, could have started to slide and, either deliberately guided by Agatha or carried by its own weight and momentum, skidded away. On the left-hand side of the hill, about half-way down, there is a small quarry, now greatly overgrown. Although the landscape has changed as the road has been widened, the ground is so steeply embanked that this seems to have been the only spot where a car might have run off the road into the side. The mishap could perfectly well be explained in this way.

Carlo later told Rosalind that the psychiatrist believed Agatha had concussed herself and Agatha, as we have learnt, remembered having blood on her face. The chambermaid recalled that 'Mrs Neele' had shielded her forehead when she was disturbed in the morning before her hair had been dressed. Agatha may well have banged her head during the accident; in any case she would have been shocked and chilled.

There is also the question of the 'trail' of letters Agatha is said to have left. One, which did exist, was the letter to Carlo, asking her to cancel the booking at the hotel in Beverley. This was the letter Carlo gave the police, which was returned, after Agatha was found. Carlo refused to discuss its contents with the press, saying only that 'There were moments when I did not know what to believe.... That letter gave us no idea where she might have gone. ...it was a personal letter, and only told us that she felt she must leave this house.'

Years later Carlo gave this letter to Rosalind, who showed it to her husband. It was exceedingly distraught, saying that in the circumstances Agatha did not believe she could go to Yorkshire, that she was going away and would let Carlo know where she was. Its underlying theme was that Agatha had been treated unjustly; the letter ended 'It just isn't fair.' It was not, it seems, the sort of letter that would be left behind by someone intending to kill herself but, rather, something written by a person who felt that, though she had been badly treated, she was still in control of her own fate, as long as – and this Agatha stressed in the letter – she could 'get away from here'. This was the 'disquieting information' that led to Superintendent Kenward's gloomy conclusion that Mrs Christie must be dead.

There was also the letter Agatha posted to her brother-in-law. How and when it was sent we do not know. Agatha may have left it at her club, earlier in the week. Carlo may have posted it but she does not say so. Agatha may have posted it as she made her purchases at Whiteley's on Saturday morning. If she had it in her handbag, which she took with her from the car, she might well have done so. In that case, it might be asked why the name and address on the envelope did not jolt her memory. We will consider this when we look at the various manifestations amnesia can take.

According to the newspapers, another letter, for Archie, was also left by Agatha, saying that she intended to go to a Yorkshire spa to recover her health. Archie did not mention this to the police but, in any case, it would not have been surprising if Agatha had left such a letter for her husband, as well as sending word of her plans to Campbell Christie. We know she had intended to go to Yorkshire; indeed, she had mentioned it to her publisher, who, when she disappeared, mentioned it to someone else, who, decades later, recalled that he had been told that Agatha had deliberately disappeared to Harrogate; such is the way in which explanations of Agatha's disappearance have been distorted with hindsight. The reasons for Agatha's flight have been more seriously misreported in another account, *The Mystery of Agatha Christie*, by Miss Gwen Robyns. This author declares that Superintendent Kenward's daughter, the late Mrs Dobson, revealed to her, when pressed, that there was 'a fourth letter' addressed to her father, marked 'private and confidential' and posted on the Friday night on which Agatha left home. 'He received it in the 10 a.m. mail on Saturday and brought it to our home nearby to show me before going over immediately to inform the Sunningdale Police Station and begin investigations.' Miss Robyns adds, in a sequence implying that she also learnt this from Mrs Dobson: 'the letter was from a woman who told how she feared for her life and that she was frightened what might happen to her. She was appealing for help. The signature on that letter was Agatha Christie.'

There is little we can do with such unsupported statements, save to ask why Superintendent Kenward failed to refer to this letter in his confidential Home Office report, why he would have behaved so unprofessionally as to show it to his daughter, why Agatha would have written to the police when she hesitated to confide even in her sister, and why she would have sent it to a policeman in the Surrey Force, when she lived in Berkshire. No theories may be based on this fragile tissue.

There are, after all, puzzles enough. Inaccuracy, wishful thinking, zealous speculation and irrelevance dog the whole of this unhappy story, and persist in the various theories which have been and will doubtless continue to be advanced to explain Agatha's behaviour. One view, extraordinary though it may be to those who knew her and knew the events that preceded her flight, is that Agatha was not alone when she ran away; another that she fled to Harrogate in order to join an accomplice or companion. We know enough to dismiss this theory.

A further view is that Agatha fled in order to spite Archie. This opinion derived initially from Edgar Wallace's diagnosis of the case and has been bolstered by loose interpretations of professional psychiatrists' writings on hysterical behaviour. Agatha did feel deeply resentful towards Archie; even so, her actions were hardly well thought out. The Morris was left by the chalk pit and Agatha brought to Harrogate more by a series of accidents than by design.

Others believe that Agatha was experimenting with a plot for one of her own books. This theory gained currency as a result of Archie's unwise remarks and Superintendent Kenward's incautious speculation. It not only sits uneasily with the fact that Agatha's flight and the events that befell her were hardly a course anyone would choose to follow, in mid-winter, let alone anyone as reluctant as Agatha to draw attention to herself. It also sounds highly implausible to anyone who knows how Agatha devised and developed her plots. That was essentially an intellectual process; she did not go about practising or even, in the modern fashion, deliberately 'doing research for a book'.

Related to this theory is another: that Agatha disappeared in order to attract public attention. From what we know of her character, nothing could have been further from her mind. Sam James, Madge James's husband, is partly to blame for this notion. From the lack of other motive – and never having met Agatha – he seemingly formed this theory, in order, one suspects, to protect his friend Archie, who, after all, was suspected or felt himself to be suspected of murder. Sam James was not the only one to seize on this explanation. It seemed obvious to those who were themselves fascinated by the power of the press to generate interest in an individual – that is, to the press themselves. Those whose lives are spent in manufacturing 'publicity' find it difficult, if not impossible, to appreciate that to many people self-advertisement is anathema. A tremendous shout went up from the press when Agatha disappeared. A major press story is a glorious thing but it is like a snowball, rolling along, increasing in size, picking up speed, gathering bits and pieces of clutter along the way, looking more impressive by the minute, until it suddenly melts into a trickle. The newspapers were carried away. The simple and natural explanation – 'she lost her memory' – left them disappointed. They had to find something more complicated, or all the fuss was unnecessary. A 'stunt', too, fitted in with other preconceptions. Much had been made of Agatha's skill as a writer of detective fiction, of the trick she had played on her readers in *The Murder of Roger Ackroyd*. She had been presented as a woman of devilish ingenuity and the press had to believe that they had been outwitted. It flattered their vanity to conclude that Agatha should want so to use them.

Amnesia is, moreover, hard to understand. There are many ways of forgetting, as much as remembering, and even the most up-to-date research has produced more questions than answers in the attempt to understand how memory works. People may lose their memory wholly or partly, they may jumble recollections, make or fail to make connections and associations, put themselves on automatic pilot when they are tired and distracted. Physical pain can be entirely forgotten and, similarly, emotionally painful memories be blotted out. It can take careful psychotherapy – in Agatha's case, hypnosis – to restore them even partially. A rarer and more complex manifestation of this anaesthesising process is the sudden loss of memory known as an 'hysterical fugue', in which a person experiencing great stress flees from intolerable strain by utterly forgetting his or her own identity. Some psychiatric experts believe this probably happened in Agatha's case. Her experience is also illuminated by recent work in which psychiatrists and neuropsychiatrists have explored the nature of 'somnambules', people who are extremely susceptible to hypnosis and who act, or appear to act, rationally in their sleep. It appears that there is a type of person who can induce independently experiences of the kind produced by hypnosis: hallucinating, amnesia, and so on. Hitherto only women have been examined in this research; all to whom such findings apply have a strong propensity to fantasize. They can recall their childhood in detail and as adults claim to spend much of their everyday lives in the world of the imagination, even when their normal daily tasks require concentration.

This suggests a useful line of thought for those who are interested in Agatha's case. A prolific and ingenious fantasist, she was also a person for whom the border between the real and the dreamt was thin. Agatha dreamt vividly, remembered and talked of her dreams, relished them – dreams of flying and even the terrible Gun Man dream. By way of her dreams she perceived the world; some of her most persuasive writing is of the boundary between sleeping and waking: *The Stuff of Dreams*, for example, *The Hound of Death*, *Sleeping Murder* and the opening passages of *The Body in the Library*. Agatha was, too, exceptionally sensitive to what was happening about her. She did not give the impression Clara conveyed of being able to read people's thoughts but there are many examples of her awareness, though nothing had been said, of her friends' need for comfort and help. She herself described her apprehension of Clara's death. Some call this quality 'psychic'; others describe it as an instinct for noticing and putting together information from many sources. Agatha depicted it in *Unfinished Portrait*, when Larraby the painter intuitively recognises Celia's intentions. It is what Hercule Poirot does when he studies 'the psychology of a criminal', or Miss Marple when she matches new problems with remembered experience. Imaginative, shy, intuitive, Agatha had all the characteristics of those who are capable of hypnotising themselves at will. It was perfectly possible for her to have lost her identity and yet to have gone about the business of catching trains, shopping, and the like. Under unreasonable strain, deeply unhappy with herself, she might have induced a loss of memory. Rather than 'making up her mind' to disappear, it might have been that she 'unmade' it.

For many years Agatha was worried by her failure completely to reconstruct the events of that dreadful time. After the War she visited the Regius Professor of Pastoral Theology at Oxford, a well-known psychoanalyst, who did not practise professionally but regarded it as part of his University duties to help people who approached him voluntarily. He is said to have told Agatha that her experience had been extremely serious and, though he was unable to help her replace those missing hours, he tried to help her overcome her self-reproach.

In the half-century since Agatha's disappearance the idea that she disappeared as 'a stunt' has persisted, particularly since it was revived by Lord Ritchie-Calder (as he became) at the time of her death, in an article in the *New Statesman*. Ritchie-Calder has frequently been misreported as declaring that, just before she was recognised by Archie, he encountered Agatha at the Hydro and challenged her, and that to his question, 'You are Agatha Christie?', she replied, 'Yes, but I'm suffering from amnesia.' Ritchie-Calder made no such statement. He did not say that he himself asked Agatha this question, nor that she spoke to him. He only says he 'met' her; at its mildest, this would refer to his seeing Agatha from across the room and, at its strongest, to his approaching her and making his challenge. Miss Robyns cites Ritchie-Calder's story, whether as quotation from the *New Statesman* article or directly from Ritchie-Calder's lips is impossible to tell, since she does not distinguish between reported speech, quotation from published sources, and her own theorising. Ritchie-Calder's own memoirs (as yet unpublished) do not describe a meeting with Agatha but only, oddly, quote Miss Robyns's account. One of two conclusions may be drawn. Ritchie-Calder may be allowing us to infer more than actually happened, or, on the other hand, he might have spoken to Agatha but decided at the time to keep the matter to himself (curious, for a journalist with his reputation to make). Even if he did address Agatha as Mrs Christie and she did respond as he said, that does not take us very far. Agatha may have remembered by that time who she was. She may have been puzzled. She was, as he described her, 'self-possessed', when confronted with people behaving in an embarrassing fashion. 'Self-possession' does not imply 'deception'. In his *New Statesman* piece, Ritchie-Calder wrote: 'Emotionally disturbed, yes. Amnesia, no.' This is impertinent and silly, for on such a slight encounter, if there was an encounter, it was not for him – and is perhaps not for us – to establish where the distinction may be drawn.

The story as it developed and was sustained in the press gives us a neat case-history of the way in which an event becomes an issue, a private matter public property. The real story, as it can be pieced together from actual witnesses, brings home the degree to which, after her discovery, Agatha was harried at a time when she could least bear it. It also shows that there were people who behaved discreetly and with dignity and that there was much indignation at the hounding of an unhappy woman and the revelation of her private affairs.

Some maintained that, by entangling so many people in the search for herself, Agatha forfeited respect for her privacy. There were, indeed, questions in Parliament and in the press as to the costs of the investigation, reported as nearing £12,000 and as having incurred substantial increases for Surrey and Berkshire ratepayers. The episode was described, by Members who had been carried away by what they had read in the papers and by, in some cases, dim remembrance of the trick in *The Murder of Roger Ackroyd*, as 'this cruel hoax'. The Home Secretary told the House that the cost of the search was, 'so far as I can ascertain, about £12.10s.', mostly, his officials had discovered, for cups of tea for the police. Privately, Superintendent Kenward was asked for an explanation, the Home Office view being that, though the cost of the search had been exaggerated, 'there must have been a very considerable diversion of the police force from their ordinary and proper duties to prosecute a search whose justification was somewhat problematical.' Superintendent Kenward, not Agatha Christie, was to answer for that – more charitably, the Superintendent as he had been egged on by the press, for in that heady atmosphere even the most phlegmatic officer might have been carried away.

In summary, then, the press was greedy, sensational and importunate. Superintendent Kenward was unwise. Mrs James, as she later admitted, should not have encouraged Archie to see so much of Miss Neele without knowing more about Agatha and the state of the Christies' marriage. Mrs James was, however, punished enough by the reproaches of her formidable mother, aghast at what she read in the newspapers. Miss Neele herself might have been more circumspect but it is hard to see what she could have done. She promptly departed on a voyage round the world, while the Christies sorted themselves out. Carlo behaved well throughout. She had been in a difficult position, entrusted with too much knowledge and forbidden to pass it on to Madge Watts. She never ceased to reproach herself for going to London on that Friday night; thereafter she devoted herself to Agatha and Rosalind. Archie had been inconsiderate, impetuous and naïve. But he was not a wicked man, nor a philanderer, nor brutal to his wife. Agatha had been stubborn and, in a way, cowardly, too proud to look for help, allowing herself to become more and more troubled and ill until she cracked. The price Archie and Agatha paid for what was, after all is said and done, fairly usual naïvety and folly, was to have their lives and characters become the object of widespread, intense and lasting public interest. It was not easy to bear. Archie surmounted it in the course of a happy marriage to Nancy Neele. Though the shock was deep and lasting, Agatha reassembled her life.

13

'London – Paris – Lausanne
– Milan – Venice . . .'

From this moment it is as if Agatha gradually became two people. One, Agatha Christie, was regarded by the press and to some degree the public as their property, someone in whom there would be continuing interest, about whom there would always be talk, a popular author who every year would apparently without difficulty produce at least one detective story and several shorter pieces. The merits of her work, its technique and fairness would be constantly dissected. There would be unceasing speculation as to her nature and, in particular, about her actions and motives during that time of her life when she had been at her most vulnerable. This Agatha Christie, the subject of public admiration and curiosity, would nonetheless manage to remain extremely private, neither courting publicity nor feeling it necessary to explain herself. That reticence and restraint would only quicken public attention and serve to enhance her mystique. The more she eluded her devotees, the more firmly they appropriated her. The less she said about herself, the more they claimed to know. Agatha Christie was to become a public institution; 'an Agatha Christie' the term, immediately intelligible all over the world, for one of her detective stories.

The other person was Agatha, natural, domestic, an ordinary human being rather than a myth, the person whose development she would herself eventually chart in her autobiography. This woman did not wear a single label, 'Agatha Christie', a guarantee of certain unvarying characteristics. She assumed, rather, a succession of guises at varying moments in her life: 'Agatha-Pagatha, my black hen', trussed up by her grandmother; Agatha Miller, a thoughtful and interested child; 'Mac Miller' and 'Nathaniel Miller', 'Martin West' and 'Mostyn Grey', the pseudonyms under which she first wrote; Mrs Christie, Archie's 'Angel'; and Theresa Neele, who lost herself. There was 'Mary Westmacott', the novelist; 'Miss Agatha Christie', as the detective story writer was often erroneously called; Mrs Mallowan, after her remarriage, and, later, Lady Mallowan, 'Nima' to her grandson and great-grandchildren, and 'Ange', as Punkie and her nephew Jack first called her; and, finally, Dame Agatha, whom the Post Office unhesitatingly recognised as the person to whom they should deliver a letter addressed simply to 'Greatest Novelist, Berkshire'. The public read Agatha Christie's books and saw her plays; it was the other, complex Agatha who wrote them.

Nor was their composition effortless, particularly after the turmoil of 1926. The beginning of the following year found Agatha undergoing treatment in Harley Street, still not knowing what would become of her marriage, where she would live and what the effects of these upheavals would be on Rosalind. Agatha owed her publishers a book and she needed money but, completely unable to write, she could resolve neither of these problems. Fifteen years later, when she asked her agent to hold a manuscript in reserve, she remembered that time. 'I have been, once, in a position where I *wanted* to write just for the sake of money coming in,' she told him, 'and when I felt I *couldn't* – it is a nerve-racking feeling. If I had had one MS then 'up my sleeve' it would have made a big difference. That was the time I had to produce that rotten book *The Big Four* and had to force myself in *The Mystery of the Blue Train*'.

The Big Four was a stopgap, a compilation of the last twelve Poirot stories, published in the *Sketch*. Agatha put them together at Campbell's suggestion and with his help. The book sold well but Agatha was not proud of it. She and Rosalind spent the summer in Devon, calmly with old friends, and in the autumn Agatha tried again to finish the book with which she had been struggling at the time of Clara's death. She attempted to dictate it to Carlo, now living with Agatha and Rosalind in Chelsea. Rosalind went to a small private day school, where she shone – Agatha kept all her reports – but she missed her father, though Archie used regularly to take her out. She wrote to him on Sunday evenings; other girls, Rosalind said regretfully, had only one letter to write. Agatha still hoped her marriage might revive. Archie, however, was convinced that only marriage to Nancy would make him happy. With great reluctance Agatha agreed to divorce him. She was deeply troubled by this decision, partly because she loved and missed her husband, partly because divorce was at that time regarded as something of a disgrace. Agatha's distress was the greater because she felt that she had somehow betrayed Rosalind and, wise though she became about the nature of marriage and the problems people have in sustaining that complicated and demanding tie, she was always to feel a small ache of guilt, in her own eyes and before God. After her divorce, she did not take Communion in Church, fearing that now she might be refused. At this difficult time Agatha greatly depended on two people, her brother-in-law James, who helped her recognise that Archie really had made up his mind and that she should now try to concentrate on her own work and life, and Carlo, who had from the first believed that, once gone, Archie would not return. Encouraged by these two staunch allies, Agatha left England in February 1928, taking Rosalind and Carlo to the Canary Islands, to make a final attack on *The Mystery of the Blue Train*. They moved around in search of good bathing, finding it eventually at Las Palmas, where there was a beach for surfing. Agatha's photographs show her sitting in the sun and paddling among the rocks with Rosalind but she looks drawn around the eyes and her shoulders are tense.

Painfully, the book was finished. A notebook she took with her shows how hard a task it was: beside the heading for each laboriously completed chapter she has written the accumulated total of words. The narrative has strikingly bright patches, as if the sparkling sea, strong sunlight and stripey shadows of the Canaries helped Agatha, and Carlo, with the description of that part of the French Riviera where much of the story occurs. The heroine, Katherine Grey, is one of the humorous, self-sufficient, independent young women Agatha took pleasure in drawing. Like Agatha, she was in her thirties – there are a number of references to her reconciling herself to a single life – but, unlike Agatha, she has just been left a fortune, with which she proceeds to dress and equip herself in a way which makes the most of her natural beauty, hitherto obscured. *The Mystery of the Blue Train* was not well written – it is full of well-worn expressions and soulful sentiment – but as well as being an exciting story it is somehow touching, and not simply for the brooding references in the early chapters to the fading of love and the practicality of divorce. Agatha is trying hard to be spirited and adventurous and there is a good deal of wishful thinking in her picture of Katherine Grey determinedly setting off for the Riviera. The last lines of the book are particularly interesting when we know Agatha's state of mind, and their self-consciousness is perhaps one reason why she always thought of this book with embarrassment. Hercule Poirot is discussing the Blue Train, that runs between London and the Riviera, with a young, lovelorn American girl, who has observed how relentless a thing is a train: 'People are murdered and die, but [trains] go on just the same.' Poirot, reflective and paternal, replies that, in that sense, life is like a train which will at last reach its journey's end. 'Trust the train, Mademoiselle,' he murmurs, 'for it is *le bon Dieu* who drives it.' Agatha is reassuring herself. Not surprisingly, however, her wounds were still raw. *The Mystery of the Blue Train* is dedicated to the two companions to whom, in the difficult days at Styles, she had confided her troubles – Carlo and Peter. The inscription at the front of the book – To the two distinguished members of the OFD, Carlotta and Peter – refers to the 'acid test' Agatha and Carlo applied to their friends and acquaintance, putting the loyal into the honourable Order of the Faithful Dogs. Agatha still felt that Archie had betrayed her. Into a writing-case, with his letters and various mementos, she put a cutting from a copy of Psalm 55, verses 12, 13 and 14:

For it is not an open enemy, that hath done me this dishonour: for then I could have borne it.
Neither was it mine adversary, that did magnify himself against me: for then peradventure I would have hid myself from him.
But it was even thou, my companion: my guide, and mine own familiar friend.

In April 1928 Agatha was given her divorce. In her *Autobiography* she says little about the year that followed, except for a short account of her search for a school for Rosalind, who wanted to go to somewhere large, 'the biggest there was'. After much hunting, Agatha chose a preparatory school at Bexhill, 'Caledonia', whose staff, pupils and routine were later successfully blended with those of her next school, Benenden, to provide the background for Agatha's story *Cat Among the Pigeons*. It is interesting that in her search for a preparatory school Agatha turned to her old friend and colleague, Eileen Morris. True, Eileen's brother John was the headmaster of a boys' preparatory school, so that she might be well placed to assist in the search. But it is also the case that at certain difficult moments in her life, when her resolution needed strengthening, Agatha looked to Eileen for moral reinforcement. It had been Eileen, strong-minded, self-assured, who had encouraged Agatha to write and to send her work to magazines, who had brought her into the dispensary, and who now helped her into her new and independent life as if there were nothing unusual about it. A photograph of the two, taken then, shows Eileen striding out in a smart overcoat, forthright and slightly grim, while Agatha, more slight and soft, is catching up. It is obvious that Eileen would be an unshakeable and confident ally in an emergency.

At this time Agatha was doubtless lonely. She had Carlo, of course, and a circle of married friends in London but, having been used to having a husband, it was not the same to go about alone or even with another woman. As she had always done in such troughs, Agatha worked. In late 1928 and 1929 she produced a number of short stories which she sold to magazines. These, and her next two books, *The Seven Dials Mystery* and *Partners in Crime*, paid the bills.

Agatha's first notes for *The Seven Dials Mystery* were made in a small black notebook Archie had left behind. Its first few pages are taken up with jottings for other stories ('The Stain on the Pavement: Drops on a Tube train? Umbrella that has rested on blood ...'). Agatha habitually took up any handy notebook – including Rosalind's old school exercise books, half-completed account books, out-of-date diaries partly occupied by recipes and lists of bulbs, things to be packed, and inventories – and scribbled her ideas for stories on whatever pages happened to be blank. She wrote fast and illegibly, in pencil or ink, approaching her task in a workmanlike fashion: 'New Book' heads the page on which she started to concoct *Seven Dials*. She was not at first sure of the title (*The Secret Six* was an alternative) nor of the plot, for her initial try begins: 'Bundle and her father. She drives up to London – runs over man – or rather swerves to avoid him – but finds she has killed him – not quite dead – says Secret Six. Tell Jimmy Thesiger – doctor is got – says man has been *shot....*' A page later, however, her notes settle into the story as it eventually appeared. *Seven Dials* is firmly written at the top of the page and her draft goes steadily on: 'Country House Party – at Chequers? – One man can't get up in the morning. Everyone gets up a joke – They buy alarum clocks – and hide them round his room. In the morning man does not appear. He is dead. One clock has disappeared. 7 left....'

Although she experimented before settling on the names of the rest of the cast in *Seven Dials*, Agatha decided from the beginning that she would revive the energetic and aristocratic 'Bundle', who had first appeared in *The Secret of Chimneys*. Her other novel of that year, *Partners in Crime*, also reintroduced a previous invention, Tommy and Tuppence Beresford, now married, slightly older and, perhaps for that reason, even more irritatingly perky. Albert, the assistant porter in *The Secret Adversary*, has become their factotum. Both *Seven Dials* and *Partners in Crime* are cheerful books, with sprightly conversation and deftly-worked plots. Indeed, in *Partners in Crime* some of the mysteries are so delicately fashioned as to be like fragile puddings, delicious but wholly unmemorable, as Agatha herself admitted nearly fifty years later in a letter to Edmund Cork. To show Tommy and Tuppence parodying the speech and mannerisms of characters created by other detective story writers - Freeman Wills Croft's 'Inspector French', for instance, or G.K. Chesterton's 'Father Brown' - seemed, she wrote, 'an amusing idea at the time but doesn't really come off now'. The only story she felt people still remembered was 'The Man Who Was No. 16', in which she was actually making a joke at the expense of her own Hercule Poirot. The fact that Agatha was sufficiently confident to make jokes at all, let alone a pastiche of other crime novelists' creations, indicates that she was regaining her self-esteem and that she was happier. Rather than turning miserable memories over in her mind, in idle moments she spun parodies for herself, as she had done during the companionable days in the dispensary, and was later to do on birthdays and holidays in Devon and the desert, celebrating with verse in the style of Edward Lear, Hilaire Belloc or Lewis Carroll. Agatha was also now less anxious about money. Her books sold well, newspapers and magazines were ready to serialise them, and she had rediscovered her zest for writing. She was fertile with ideas, happy with her new publisher and secure in the hands of an able and understanding agent.

Agatha's state of mind in late 1928 is particularly evident from the fact that at this moment she chose to undertake an experiment, the writing of a long novel, 'straight' only in the sense that it was not a detective story, for its plot was complicated and its theme ambitious. This was *Giant's Bread*, published in 1930 but delivered to Collins in January 1929. She wrote it under the pseudonym of 'Mary Westmacott'; some jottings show that she first tried 'Nathaniel Westmacott', a development of her old disguise of 'Nathaniel West', after her grandfather. It is possible that she chose to write under another name partly because, as she later put it, she felt 'guilty at departing from the usual type of story'; detective fiction was her profession and this something of

an indulgence. This novel is, moreover, very revealing, more dis-
cursive and speculative than a detective story, without the formal
conventions and disciplined construction which in crime fiction
distract the reader's attention. *Giant's Bread* takes in many
themes, too many, written with an immediacy that betrays their
closeness to the author's own experience. The hero's recollection
of his childhood is rooted in Agatha's own memories and other
moments, like the retort the small boy hopes to make on meeting
God, derive from her observations of her nephew Jack. The experience of the hero's wife, Nell Deyre, as she works as a ward
maid during the First World War, echoes Agatha's own and the
picture of Jane, a singer who eventually overstrains her voice,
having her breathing, endurance and aptitude tested by the composer, Radmaager, suggests Agatha's own ordeal as an aspiring
opera singer.

   More disturbing, in that they seem to expose too much of
Agatha's own feelings, are those themes and passages in *Giant's
Bread* which describe how her characters face impossible choices,
how greatly they *mind* about things, how much they hurt themselves thereby. The novel explores painful subjects: frustrated
longing for a particular place (in this case 'Abbots Puissants', the
home of the hero and his ancestors); appeals for love, affection
and vindication; the desire for recognition and for anonymity.
The plot is, on reflection, daft, but – as in her crime fiction –
Agatha convinces, in part because the pace of events leaves little
time for consideration, in part because, however sketchily they
are shown, her characters' appearance, remarks and emotions are
as they should be. Agatha ensures that the detail is right. Just as
poisons, topography and legal niceties are correctly and unobtru-
sively described in her crime novels, so in *Giant's Bread* she exactly depicts the cultural setting of her story, in the years before
and immediately after the First World War. Her references to the
ballet are right, her descriptions of popular reaction to contemporary music appropriate, she conveys perfectly the state of the
theatre, the ambitions of the Futurists and Vorticists, the hope
that was placed in post-Revolutionary Soviet art, and, particularly, the nature and objectives of contemporary musical composition. She was interested in new theories and *Giant's Bread* is
most thoughtful when it examines changing attitudes to new
forms of artistic expression. Agatha had mulled over the difficulties of the composer's struggle with experimental forms while
watching the efforts of Roger Coke, whose mother was a friend

of Madge Watts. Coke offered a stimulus and a sounding-board for Agatha's description of Vernon Deyre but her ideas for Deyre's opera *The Giant* were very much her own. The final form of that opera almost exactly resembles her first notes.

Agatha's portrait of Vernon Deyre, obliged to compose despite himself, is not autobiographical, save for one moment at which Vernon's adult experience comes uncomfortably close. His friends persuade him to see a hypnotist, who tries to restore the memories he has suppressed. The doctor, 'a tall, thin man with eyes that seemed to see right into the centre of you and to read there things that you didn't even know about yourself ...' made you 'see all the things you didn't want to see'. That passage is certainly an allusion to Agatha's treatment in 1927. So is the novel's preoccupation with the idea of personal identity and with the nature of fear, for Vernon Deyre's terror of the 'Beast' resembles Agatha's horror of 'the Gun Man' and, as Vernon faces his nightmare, Agatha, by writing this book, confronts her own. Between the first and second pages of her notes is pressed a four-leaf clover. No one knows when it was put there, or by whom, but it is a fitting symbol.

No longer clinging to what she had known but comfortable with what she had become, a successful, independent, professional woman, Agatha was ready to explore further. In the autumn of 1928, while Rosalind was at school, with, as Agatha airily wrote in her *Autobiography*, 'Carlo and Punkie to visit her', she decided to look for sunshine in the West Indies. Two days before her departure, she dined with friends and met a naval couple who had just returned from Baghdad, a city that had entranced them. Agatha was fascinated by their description and her enthusiasm increased when she learnt that Baghdad could be reached not just by sea but by the Orient Express. She was in large part intoxicated by a heady mixture of vague memories of fairy stories (Baghdad, and the Near East generally, was associated with Aladdin and Sinbad, oil lamps, sultans and genies), of mysterious tales, like those told by Scheherezade, and of the magic of curious names, especially when they are displayed on the side of that equally romantic phenomenon, a train, here the Simplon-Orient Express: London – Paris – Lausanne – Milan – Venice – Trieste – Zagreb – Belgrade – Sofia – Stamboul, and on, as the Taunus Express, to Aleppo and Beirut.

To Agatha, like thousands before and since, a train was marvellously evocative. The engines she knew were steam engines, rearing high above the platform, overwhelming the onlooker with their noise and appearance. Promising the freedom, by the simple act of purchasing a ticket, of anonymous travel towards the horizon, the train was at the same time the most orderly of conveyances, from the regular beat of its pistons and the rhythm of its wheels to the discipline of its timetables and the strictness of its track. The train, as much as the countries through which it passed, was a different world, of travellers accidentally brought together, each with his own intentions, for the time being allied. But, however random a collection, its passengers followed certain conventions. The very geography of their conveyance, self-contained, compartmentalised, with formally arranged seating, dining car and sleeping arrangements, obliged them to do so. Each traveller, too, quickly categorised his fellows, not just by class of ticket but also by manners and appearance, nationality and age. What happened on a railways journey was, in fact, both predictable and unexpected, dangerous and safe. An ideal place for exchanging confidences with strangers, an enclosure whose occupants will disperse, it was, as Agatha had already discerned, a perfect setting for a crime. Many of her most successful murders were to occur and be resolved in a carefully bounded environment and in circumstances where a certain formality prevailed. A railway journey, embracing the familiar and the extraordinary, constructing for the travelling public a private world, was a device she often employed in her stories. It suited her plots and her own experience: a life running along conventional tracks but suddenly taking her into surprising, even frightening territory; an ordered, logical way of proceeding, interrupted by occasional glimpses of the irrationality of human beings and the randomness of events. It was a motif that suited the time at which she began to be successful: a recurring theme of British art and literature in the nineteen-thirties was the crossing of boundaries, the indistinct nature of moral, emotional and political, as well as geographical, frontiers. The train was the raw stuff of fantasy; the Orient Express the most fantastic of all. Agatha hastened to Thomas Cook's and changed her tickets.

Five days later she set off for Baghdad, the longest journey she had taken alone. Her autobiography describes how it was to travel independently, to pass from Europe into Asia ('I felt cut off, but far more interested in what I was doing and where I was going'), to find herself admired by various courtly gentlemen and – Agatha immediately recognised how relentlessly the world befriends those who travel alone – fending off insistently helpful strangers. Until she arrived at Ur, her account of her journey was less about the countries through which she passed than about the people: the Cook's man, a French commercial traveller, a beaming Turkish lady anxious for Agatha to increase her family. She wrote, too, of the artefacts: the terrifying steam bath in the Orient Palace Hotel in Damascus; the handsome brass and silver plates, intricately designed, for sale in the bazaar in Baalbek; the rickety bus in which she crossed the desert to Baghdad. Her descriptions of other memories are, though economical, moving and effective: the first view of the Cilician Gates in the setting sun, at the entrance of the long gorge that leads to Turkey and Syria, or her breakfast in the early morning, the desert's 'sharp-toned air . . . the silence, the absence even of birds, the sand that ran through one's fingers, the rising sun, and the taste of sausages and tea. What else could one ask of life?'

Once in Baghdad, Agatha found herself trapped by a zealously hospitable memsahib whom she had met on the train, eluded in Trieste, but who ominously embraced her on the bus across the desert. Agatha had wished to leave England behind but she now found herself transplanted to a colony of English expatriates with decidedly English habits. She was determined to escape. A further attraction of Baghdad, was its proximity to the ancient city of Ur, near the Persian Gulf. Its name was familiar to those who, like Agatha, knew their Bible, for the city of Ur was the birthplace of Sumerian civilisation, the land of Sumer being an early name for Babylonia. Here the wedge-shaped system of writing, cuneiform script, had been invented, the forerunner of the alphabet. Energetic traders and engineers, the Sumerians built a network of canals and waterways to connect their towns and cities, of which Ur, just below the confluence of two great rivers, the Tigris and the Euphrates, was among the most important. In 1922 excavations had begun there under the direction of Leonard Woolley, a gifted archaeologist who had worked before the First World War with T.E. Lawrence in Syria and, later, in Egypt. His work enabled scholars to trace the history of Ur from its earliest beginnings, in *c.* 4000 BC, to its final days in the fourth century BC.

Although as a girl Agatha had shown no interest in the finds displayed in the Cairo Museum or in the Egyptian monuments, she had been fascinated by the exhibitions she later visited on the Empire Tour, writing home excitedly about African skulls and Tasmanian fossils. It was in the *Illustrated London News* that she had read of Leonard Woolley's discoveries. Partly because he wished to believe it and partly because it made an exciting story, Woolley had become convinced that in the ruins of Ur he had discovered traces of the Great Flood, recorded in the Epic of Gilgamesh and later, as 'Noah's Flood', in the Book of Genesis. At the bottom of a deep shaft, he had come across a band of alluvial clay, mingled with windblown sand. Here he found pre-historic graves, containing, he believed, the remains of the flood's victims, and, below these, traces of the reed huts built by Ur's first inhabitants. Woolley's deductions were in fact incorrect, for the flood deposits he identified derived from a much earlier in-undation, some 1100 years before the Great Flood itself. He nonetheless made the most of the associations his discovery pro-duced in the public mind. By 1928 everyone had heard of Ur and of the Sumerian treasure found in the two thousand graves in the Royal Cemetery, particularly the gold dagger, in its sheath of lapis lazuli and gold, brought out in 1926. The well-informed English public was familiar with the drawings of the ziggurat, as striking in appearance as in its curious name, a three-stage temple-tower, dominating the plain, with its red brickwork and triple staircase, 'standing up', as Agatha described it, 'faintly sha-dowed', in 'a wide sea of sand, with its lovely pale colours of apricot, rose, blue and mauve, changing every minute'.

Eager, as Clara had always been, to see for herself what was new while she had the opportunity, Agatha set off to Ur. Though visitors to the Woolleys' dig were not encouraged, she was warmly received. Their hospitality owed less to the fact that she came with a letter of introduction than to the happy chance that Katharine, Leonard's wife, had recently read and vastly admired *The Murder of Roger Ackroyd*. This was fortunate, since Kathar-ine Woolley was not a woman to whom other women found it easy to appeal. She was one of those females, both infuriatingly self-centred and capable of bewitching grace, who preferred to find herself in a circle of men, whom she expected to submit to her caprices and who for the most part did. She was a competent though unconfident sculptor, depending for encouragement on Leonard. He was her second husband; the first had shot himself, not long after their honeymoon, at the foot of the Great Pyramid, and the shock had made Katharine's temperament even more unpredictable and her health precarious. She was beautiful and, according to Gertrude Bell, the great Arabian traveller and scho-lar, dangerous. Agatha, who felt a fascination composed half of liking and half annoyance, called her an *'allumeuse'*, a woman who inevitably, almost deliberately, lit a sexual bonfire, a type who was to appear from time to time in future detective stories.

It was not unusual for the wife of the Director of an archaeological team to be difficult – there are a number of tales of the combustible atmosphere in the camps of the inter-war years to which forceful ladies like Mrs Garstang and Lady Petrie accompanied their husbands. For a woman who enjoyed exercising emotional power, a camp offered a satisfying court, its labourers and servants exclusively male, the assistants, often impressionable young men fresh from university, ready to be awed by displays of temperament and anxious to show their devotion to their Director by extending it, if need be, to his wife. Other women, as wives of the Director's colleagues were to find, were unwelcome.

Agatha, however, was pressed to extend her visit. When she explained that she must go back to England for Christmas and Rosalind's holidays, she was invited to return the following spring. Why Katharine Woolley took to Agatha is interesting. It may have been because her guest was reserved and modest and, rather than being a threat, showed herself admiring and anxious to learn. Agatha, quiet, observant and shrewd, let others impress themselves on her attention, rather than seeking to make a mark herself, and this provided a receptive audience for an egoist. On the other hand, Katharine, doubting her own ability as an artist, could respect Agatha for her undeniable success as an author; Agatha was not just any curious visitor but one to celebrate. Agatha, what is more, came alone, not as one of a happy, easy couple, who might set Katharine to jealousy and self-reproach, nor as a young, unmarried woman who might constitute a challenge. Nearly forty, she was interesting, interested and independent, neither pining for her former husband nor looking for another, simply enjoying herself and having a holiday. Agatha, as well as Katharine, was to be greatly surprised by what happened later.

Passing through Baghdad on her way home, Agatha encountered traces of her brother Monty, in the not inappropriate setting of the Tigris Palace Hotel. Here she met a Colonel Dwyer, of the King's African Rifles, and they talked affectionately of 'Puffing Billy Miller' – 'mad as a hatter' – and of Monty's extraordinary capacity for charming women. As it turned out, this skill sustained him until the end of his life. He was to die in the autumn of 1929 in Marseilles (Agatha's chronology slips in her own recollections of these events). The cottage on Dartmoor eventually proved too damp and cold for Monty and his housekeeper, so Madge and Agatha arranged rooms for them in a small *pension* in the South of France. Agatha saw them off on the Blue Train, but on the journey Mrs Taylor caught a chill which turned to pneumonia, and died shortly after. Monty, bereft, was taken into the hospital at Marseilles and Madge dispatched to see him. After only a week or so of the usual worry, the problem was resolved in the customary way. Monty's nurse, Charlotte, took him home to her apartment and made herself responsible. With her, to everyone's satisfaction, he remained until he suddenly died of a cerebral haemorrhage in a cafe on the sea-front. His talent for attracting devoted service persisted even then. A kindly retired Sergeant Major, William Archer, now the commissionaire at the branch bank of Lloyd's in Marseilles, arranged to tend his grave at the Military Cemetery, for they had served together in the East Surreys in South Africa. Seven years later, when Mr Archer was transferred to Monte Carlo, Monty's welfare was again entrusted to a woman's hands: Mr Archer's daughter, who had married a Frenchman, promised to look after his grave, decorating it from time to time with a few flowers, placing poppies there on Armistice Day.

Agatha was reinvigorated by her travels and that year, 1929, was a busy one. She bought 22 Cresswell Place in Chelsea, a small mews house which, with the help of a builder, she re-arranged to give a large downstairs room and garage, a maid's room, and upstairs two bedrooms, one doubling as a dining-room, and a handsome bathroom, with green porcelain bath and the walls painted with green dolphins. The kitchen was minute, the stairs dark and awkwardly narrow; everyone who stayed or borrowed Cresswell Place (Agatha was always generous with her houses) wondered how she managed to manoeuvre, for, always tall, she had become heavy. From that tiny kitchen she produced meals so delicious that her friends remembered them for years: impromptu breakfasts of bacon and eggs for surprise visitors; Circassian chicken for those who came with longer notice; salads, omelettes and anchovy toast, as prepared by her more dashing heroines. The other disadvantages of Cresswell Place were that damp seeped into the interior, while from part of the house the view was only of a blank wall – not that this bothered Agatha, who told one visitor that it allowed her to speculate as to what went on at the other side.

Agatha bought and furnished houses when she was happy. She was also now more financially secure. In mid-1928 Edmund Cork had arranged a new contract with Collins for her next six novels, with an advance of £750 for each and a royalty of twenty per cent for the first 8000 copies, rising thereafter to twenty-five per cent. Earlier that year, he also concluded a new agreement with Dodd, Mead. That contract, for *The Mystery of the Blue Train* and the two succeeding novels, gave Agatha an advance of $2500 for each work, with a royalty of fifteen per cent on the first 25000 copies and twenty per cent after that. Her work was by now being regularly published abroad. Collins looked after the Canadian market; countries where other publishers sold translations of her books included Austria and Hungary – and Finland, which paid £15 for the right to publish a first edition of 4000 copies of *The Murder of Roger Ackroyd*.

At this time Agatha was working steadily; she was so prolific that it is difficult to establish the order in which she produced the play, short stories and books which were to appear in 1930. Her early correspondence with Edmund Cork and Collins has disappeared, destroyed or lost during the Second World War and in moves between offices. Some of her work in 1928–29 was for magazines, which took the 'Mr Quin' stories Agatha liked to write from time to time. Like some of her early poems and songs, they were based on the figure of Harlequin, of whom Agatha was fond, because he was both ever-present and elusive. Harlequin has a special care for the difficulties of lovers; an evanescent, multi-coloured apparition, he comes and goes as he pleases. Mr Quin is as mysterious, manifesting himself to the kindly, quiet and rather snobbish Mr Satterthwaite, an elderly gentleman who believes himself a mere bystander but who, when inspired by Mr Quin, finds himself capable of solving problems. Agatha did not write these stories as a series but one collection was published in 1930, as *The Mysterious Mr Quin*.

This was also the year in which another of her favourite creations made the first of [what was to be] many appearances.: Miss Marple. Agatha's notebooks suggest a connection between Mr Quin and Miss Marple, a clue that supports her own recollection of the origins of Miss Marple's name. An outline survives of the ninth story in *The Mysterious Mr Quin*, the tale of 'The Dead Harlequin', which concerns Mr Satterthwaite's purchase of a strange picture. The painting shows Harlequin's body spread upon a black and white marble floor, behind it a window through which appears a figure of the same man, looking in. Mr Satterthwaite recognises the scene of the picture, the Terrace Room at Charnley, and, with the help of the artist (and of Mr Quin) proceeds to solve the mystery of the apparent suicide of its owner. Agatha's preliminary notes, however, refer not to 'Charnley' but to 'Marple Hall' and 'the lady of Marple'.

Marple Hall, now replaced by a housing development, was in Cheshire and Agatha knew it from her visits to Abney. It was a striking-looking house, built of red sandstone on a terrace from which there was a sharp drop to the river valley. The terrace was said to have been haunted by the ghost of King Charles I, carrying his head, and by that of a daughter of the house, weeping for the lover whom she watched from the terrace as he drowned in a nearby mere. In 1968 Agatha told a descendant of the Marple family, who had owned parts of the estate in the sixteenth century, that she had indeed taken Miss Marple's name from this beautiful and unhappy place. Agatha described how Madge had taken her to a sale at the Manor, 'a very *good* sale with fine old Elizabethan and Jacobean furniture, and at it I bought 2 Jacobean oak chairs which I still have – wanting a name for my "old maid" character, I called her Jane Marple.'

Miss Marple's character, however, owed something to Agatha's earlier creation, Miss Caroline Sheppard, of *The Murder of Roger Ackroyd*, another shrewd and observant maiden lady, whose mildly-expressed omniscience is both infuriating and wonderful to her circle of patronising men. She was, as Agatha put it in her autobiography, 'the complete detective service in the home'. St Mary Mead, where Miss Marple was said to live and Agatha now set *The Murder at the Vicarage*, had features of villages in which Agatha had stayed as a girl, while Miss Marple herself possessed many of the characteristics of the old ladies who called to gossip with Agatha's Ealing grandmother. Although Agatha did not model her creation directly on 'Auntie-Grannie' ('she was far more fussy and spinsterish than my grandmother ever was'), in one respect they were alike: 'though a cheerful person, she always expected the worst of everyone and everything and was, with almost frightening accuracy, usually proved right.' Furthermore, in successive appearances, Miss Marple showed that she shared other habits of Agatha's grandmother, such as her fondness for shopping at the Army and Navy Stores, and her liking for an expedition to the sales to augment her stock of table-napkins and bath towels. Miss Marple was also prettier, more humorous and more gentle than Miss Sheppard; 'I chiefly associate her with fluffy wool,' Agatha later told an admirer.

In 1929 Agatha also worked at her first play, *Black Coffee*, which concerned the murder of an eminent scientist and the theft of a formula for making dangerous weapons – exactly the sort of theme to strike the popular imagination. She had been disappointed in the portrayal of Hercule Poirot in the play *Alibi* that Michael Morton had adapted from *The Murder of Roger Ackroyd*, although it had enjoyed a good run in London in 1928. She had been equally unhappy with a film, made in the same year, based on 'The Coming of Mr Quin'. More satisfying was another film, *Die Abenteuer GmbH*, (Adventure Inc.), made by a German company from *The Secret Adversary*, but Agatha's displeasure with the way her novels had generally been adapted for performance decided her to make a start herself. She had always been good at writing plausible dialogue, and had prepared herself for fashioning stage directions by her experience at plotting detective stories, where careful attention had to be given to placing and timing. *Black Coffee* was a success. It was produced at the end of 1930, a year in which she was to make an even greater departure.

14

'... an idea I've never ever considered ...'

In the summer of 1929 Agatha lent the house in Cresswell Place to Leonard and Katharine Woolley, who then proposed that the following spring she should return to Ur, a week before the end of the 1929–30 digging season, and travel back to England with them through Syria and Greece, including Delphi, which Agatha particularly wanted to see. The autumn and winter were difficult. Monty died in September and, after Christmas at Abney, Rosalind caught measles from a friend in London. Agatha took her to Ashfield for the remainder of the holiday, an excruciatingly painful drive, as she had just been vaccinated in the thigh, with what she always maintained was a double-strength batch of vaccine. After a day or two she was taken, delirious, to a nursing home. Rosalind, meanwhile, was nursed by Madge until her mother returned home for their joint convalescence. In mid-February Agatha at last departed for Italy and then by boat to Beirut.

When she arrived at Ur she found the Woolleys' household augmented by another young archaeologist, Max Mallowan, twenty-five years old, who had been away with appendicitis the previous season. Max had first joined Woolley's team in 1925, after reading Greats at New College, Oxford. He had been attracted to archaeology by hearing one of his professors lecture on Greek sculpture, which led him to reflect on the moment at which the Temple at Olympia had been rediscovered. Immediately after taking his final examinations, Mallowan applied for a job to the Keeper of the Ashmolean Museum in Oxford, who, by happy accident, had that morning received a letter from Woolley asking for an assistant at Ur. Mallowan was engaged straight away. He taught himself Arabic, picking up archaeology as they went along. His duties included acting as medical officer to the workforce of 200–250 Arabs, as chief packer and escort of the cargo of antiquities which were carefully stowed at the end of each season in forty or fifty crates, and assistant in making up the pay-book, 'no light task,' he wrote in his *Memoirs*, 'considering the large number of men that we employed and also the fact that we paid in rupees and annas which were extremely difficult to add up.' Mallowan turned out to be good at keeping the accounts, for he was efficient and conscientious, particularly where money was concerned. Among the papers remaining from his own archaeological expeditions in the late nineteen-thirties and forties are all his account books, recording every item of expenditure, from the labourers' wages to payment for half-gallons of petrol.

Mallowan learnt quickly and soon became invaluable. He also managed to please Katharine, for, as Agatha quickly observed, he was tactful and managed both the Woolleys deftly. Agatha did not yet know, however, quite how dutiful Mallowan was expected to be – how, for example, he was required to brush Katharine's hair and administer the massage and application of leeches with which she fought recurrent headache. His diplomatic performance, together with the fact that his absence had made him once more something of a novelty, meant he was Katharine's favourite, a role he was uncomfortably occupying when Agatha arrived in March.

Another of Mallowan's duties was to show the site to visitors, some of whom were, to the Woolleys' gratification, extremely distinguished. (The younger members of the team never forgot Leonard's mortification when the King of the Belgians came to call and the Arabs serving dinner forgot to take away the soup, as they stood, transfixed, at the sight of a king.) With customary imperiousness, Katharine declared that Mallowan's responsibilities would now extend to escorting Agatha on a tour of local sights on the way to Baghdad, where the whole party would be reunited. Agatha thought it a fearful imposition that 'a young man, who had worked hard on an arduous dig and was about to be released for rest and a good time', should be obliged to take about 'a strange woman, a good many years older than him, who knew little about archaeology'. She confided her fears to Archie Whitburn, the expedition's architect and Mallowan's near contemporary and friend, whom she knew from her earlier visit. Whitburn assured her that, if Katharine had made up her mind, everything was as good as settled.

Agatha was therefore rather nervous as she and her guide set off on their expedition. Mallowan was a calm and grave young man; he later wrote: 'I found her immediately a most agreeable

person and the prospect pleasing.' They were not in fact such an
incongruous pair as Agatha had initially feared. Max was a
specialist, ready to explain the origins and associations of the
places they saw, and his command of Arabic added to his authority. The women he had known had all been somewhat out of the
ordinary: his Parisian mother, a Christian Scientist who wrote
lyric poetry ('some of which had, I believe, merit'), who lectured
on the arts and painted enormous, swirling canvases; Lady
Howard, wife of the British Ambassador to Madrid and, later,
Washington, the mother of Max's best friend at Oxford, Esmé;
Gertrude Bell, then in her late fifties, who as Director of Antiquities in Iraq would come to Ur to wrestle with Woolley over
the disposition of the finds; and Katharine herself. Mallowan was
therefore unflustered by the companionship of a successful,
well-known woman, who was in any event now dependent upon
him. Agatha was, for her part, enthusiastic and interested, with
a wry and appealing sense of humour. After the disciplined and
claustrophobic atmosphere of the camp, where all trod carefully
to avoid provoking Katharine, the journey on which Agatha and
Max set out must have seemed a companionable release.

They have both described what happened next, Max in his
Memoirs and Agatha in her *Autobiography*. There was the ziggurat at Nippur, one of Sumer's most ancient sites, and an uncomfortable night at Diwaniyah with a venomously offensive political officer, his sociable wife and two scared missionaries. On
they went to the walled town of Nejeif and then to the castle of
Ukhaidir, where Max handed Agatha round the dizzy parapets.
At this point in their recollections one or the other, or the pair of
them, understandably becomes confused. When did they visit
Kerbela? Before or after their impromptu bathe in a sparkling
salt lake, Agatha demurely clad in a pink silk vest and double
pair of knickers, Max in shorts and a vest? Was it on the way to
Kerbela or on the way to Baghdad that the car stuck inextricably
in the desert and Agatha sensibly lay down in its shadow and
took a nap? Was it five minutes after their Bedouin strode off to
find help, leaving what water he had ('we of the Desert Camel
Corps do not need to drink in emergency,' Agatha, with some
foreboding, heard him say), or an hour later, that a Model T
Ford miraculously arrived, with the Bedouin, to hoist them from
the sand? Did the hospitable policeman at the station in Kerbela,
where they spent the night in neighbouring cells, recite 'Ode to a
Skylark' in English (Agatha's recollection) or 'Twinkle, Twinkle,

Little Star' in Arabic (according to Max)? It doesn't really matter; the point was that each acquired respect for the other and that they began to have fun.

Max and Agatha arrived late, firmly allied, in Baghdad. Katharine was annoyed. Agatha's old friend, Colonel Dwyer, who came to the station to see off the curious party, warned Agatha that for the rest of the journey she would have to stand up for herself. She resolved to do so after several demonstrations of Katharine's insidiously proprietorial behaviour – she managed always to secure the largest room, driest bed, brightest lamp – and after witnessing the automatic capitulation of the men. (The sorest moment was when Agatha discovered that Max had allowed Katharine, because 'she wanted it', the hot bath he had drawn for Agatha.)

With occasional sorties and retreats by one party and then another, they reached Mosul, Aleppo, and next proceeded by boat to Greece. Here Max was to leave the others to make his way to the Temple of Bassae, while the Woolleys took Agatha to Delphi, a visit she eagerly anticipated, despite the risks of being left alone with this unstable pair. But at Athens a pile of accumulated telegrams waited at the hotel: Rosalind had caught pneumonia, was very ill, had been moved to Abney, was in a serious state, was slightly better. There were no air services from Athens to London; the fastest journey home was by train, which took four days. While the men hurried off to the travel agent, Agatha wandered about in a daze, stumbled in the street and sprained her ankle. It was Max who, without fuss, produced bandages and sticking-plaster and announced that he had changed his plans and would travel with Agatha to fetch and carry for her.

They left the next evening and, as people will, talked on the train about themselves, Max distracting Agatha by telling her his history. Years later, when Max seemed to some the model of an Englishman in his appointments (Fellow of All Souls College, a Trustee of the British Museum), appearance (tweeds, pipe and soft hat) and habits (pottering between his club and his Institute, fond of his cellar, a good dinner and cricket), his younger colleagues would remark amusedly that 'he hadn't a drop of English blood in him.' Max's family was indeed cosmopolitan. His grandfather, an Austrian, had lived in Vienna, where he owned a steam-powered flour mill which was so successful that it won many important prizes, including a gold medal struck by the

Emperor Franz Josef. The mill, which was not insured, was eventually burnt to the ground and this disaster left the family impoverished and inspired Max's father, Frederick, to leave Austria for England, where he spent the rest of his life.

In London Frederick found a post with a firm of merchants and after a time established his own business, trading in fats, oils and copra. He was accounted such an expert as to be appointed an official Examiner of Raw Materials for what became the Ministry of Food. After the First World War he acted as chief quality arbitrator to the firm of Unilever; Max delighted in telling the story of how Frederick, appearing before the court in a case concerning alleged food-poisoning, offered to eat on the spot some margarine that was said to be tainted. This tale illustrated how firm Frederick's convictions were. It is an echo of an episode in the eighteen-nineties when, leading his squadron on mid-summer manoeuvres in Bosnia-Herzegovina, he defied instructions to take his troops home in the mid-day sun and, by moving them at night, ensured that they arrived immaculate and unravaged by heatstroke. This successful challenge to authority, which earned him a decoration, was one of the incidents which led Agatha to remark that Frederick reminded her of Monty. In some respects Frederick was a difficult man, caring very much for order and exactitude, testy when his point of view was questioned. This, Max admitted, made for a quarrelsome marriage. Frederick, kind but egocentric, had married an enchanting but restless woman, equally uncompromising: Marguerite Duvivier born in Paris in 1876, the daughter of an engineer and an opera singer. She inherited her mother's recklessness and gaiety, rapturous embrace of artistic things, preference for town life and appetite for society. Max, the eldest boy of three, was born in 1904.

In his *Memoirs* he described what he could recall of his childhood, an account considerably briefer than Agatha's. Unlike her, he was not always happy; unlike her, too, he had an orthodox education. From his preparatory school, where he learned to love Greek, he went to Lancing, the High Church Anglican public school in Sussex, which he found particularly irksome. One problem was chapel, where the boys were expected to worship twice daily and five times on Sunday. Max was so sated with this regime that, to his Headmaster's astonishment, when the time came to be confirmed he refused to take part and thus to become eligible to take Communion. The other irritation was the requirement that a good many hours be devoted to military training and parades. This was all very well while the War lasted; Max himself, from a military family, admitted to being keen for the day when he would go off to fight. But when the War was over it was different. The boys in Max's house, led by the principal rebel, Evelyn Waugh, were passionately anti-militaristic but still they were required to drill.

Max left Lancing early, just after his seventeenth birthday, after only a year in the Sixth Form. He already had a place at New College, Oxford, and the argument with his Headmaster over the confirmation question persuaded him that it was best to leave immediately, since he would plainly be given none of the usual privileges or authority in his last year of school. Frederick agreed, not because he was himself an agnostic (Max did not tell him what had happened) but because Lancing was so obviously inferior to his own thorough Continental education. It is significant that Max took such a strong stand on this point about religion. He did not do so lightly and, indeed, he was to continue to agonise over it. His account of the episode was particularly interesting to Agatha, who was herself quietly devout and, as we have seen, anxious about the religious implications of her divorce from Archie. Max's spiritual troubles were renewed towards the end of his time at Oxford and in the year immediately following it. His friend Esmé Howard was found to be suffering from a wasting disease and was sent to a clinic in Switzerland. On his way to Beirut Max visited the clinic, where Esmé begged him to become a Catholic and take Communion (the Howards were a deeply Catholic family), saying he had suffered for Max's religious doubts. In the diary he kept from 1922 to 1926 Max described how he made and kept that promise, realising, when he thought the question over, that in fact his conviction was sincere.

Esmé died the following year. His illness and death had a profound effect on Max, the more because their friendship had developed at Oxford, which Max had adored. After Lancing, he said, Oxford was 'a step from purgatory to Paradise'; here feelings could be expressed more freely than had been thought appropriate at school. He was not glued to his books, despite the efforts he made in the summer term of his third year, when his diary begins promisingly with a list of his hours of rising (8.45 a.m. on good days) and retiring (between midnight and 3 a.m.) and an account of his vacation reading (some of Plato's *Republic*, all of Keats, Descartes' *Discourse on Method* and, more frivolous, *The New Arabian Nights* and some Robert Louis Stevenson). The most important thing he learnt, Max always said, was how to drink wine with his friends. He was twenty-one and, though he knew what he wanted to do, he was in some ways still immature when he joined Woolley's dig.

Four years at Ur had toughened him; he learnt to give orders and to manage the men – indeed, even to manage Katharine Woolley. He knew some of his own skills and strengths: that he could rough it, that he had great facility for learning languages and that he possessed the intuition, as well as the knowledge, an archaeologist requires. There had been time to reflect on his parents' marriage, on the deaths of Esmé and of other friends, on his colleagues' various and complex relationships. But, when he and Agatha met, Max was in other ways inexperienced. He was not as reckless as Archie had been at the same age but he was as sensitive – easily hurt and, away from the secure ground of his own subject, unconfident. Like Archie, too, he had little money. And, again like Archie, until this encounter he had never been, as one of his oldest friends put it, so 'thoroughly bowled over'. Agatha liked this scholarly and attentive young man and, for all her new-found independence, it was a relief to have an entertaining and discreetly helpful companion on the long journey from Athens, especially with her injured ankle and worries about Rosalind.

There was one more adventure before they reached London. At Milan they left the train to buy oranges and, while they were away, it departed, with their baggage. There was nothing for it but to hire a powerful and expensive car and race the train through the mountains to Domodossola, where they caught up – just – and were assisted into their coach by excited fellow-passengers. As a result of this mishap, neither Max nor Agatha had any money for the last leg of the journey, so that Agatha's first meeting with his mother, who was waiting for Max in Paris, consisted of greeting her briefly and then borrowing all she had. Thus provided for, Agatha went on to London alone.

Rosalind, though unusually listless, was recovering quickly and after a few days Agatha took her back from Abney to Ashfield. Max was now working at the British Museum and had asked Agatha to let him know if she were coming to London. At first there was no prospect of this, until Collins asked her to a party at the Savoy to meet her American publishers. She arranged to travel up on the night train and invited Max to Cresswell Place, 'the only person I've ever asked to breakfast', she wrote to him later. After the rush of confidences at a first encounter and before the comfortable reminiscing of a third, the second meeting was awkward. Initially tongue-tied, they were soon sufficiently relaxed for Agatha to ask Max to come to stay at Ashfield. One weekend in April he left his scholar's sanctuary at the British Museum, travelled with Agatha on the midnight train from Paddington, met Rosalind and Peter at Torquay, and was led off for picnics and strenuous walks on Dartmoor in the rain. On the last night of his visit, after Agatha had retired, Max knocked on her door, came in, sat down on the end of her bed and asked her to marry him.

Agatha was astonished. Then, and for some weeks, she produced all the arguments against such a marriage: Max was fifteen years younger, he was a Catholic, and so on. Max insisted. In any case, as Agatha admitted in her letters to him, the real reason for her hesitation was fear: 'I'm an awful coward and dreadfully afraid of being hurt.' Her *Autobiography* reveals this when she writes of the way in which this 'easy happy relationship' had imperceptibly overtaken them: 'If I had considered Max as a possible husband when I first met him, then I should have been on my guard.'

Agatha did not take as long to accept Max's proposal as it seems from her *Autobiography*, which describes her changes of mind, to-ings and fro-ings, and innumerable conversations with Rosalind, Punkie and James, and the Woolleys. As always, when she is recalling the most important moments in her life, Agatha's chronology goes haywire. It is impossible to establish exactly when she finally succumbed to Max's gentle pressure, since few of the flurry of letters she sent him have any sort of date and none of the postmarked envelopes has survived. But one letter dated with more than the day of the week was written on May 21st. It was not only a perfectly confident and passionate letter to the man she was about to marry but it also dismissed her earlier doubts. Max had asked whether Agatha would mind spending her future with someone whose profession was 'digging up the dead'; she replied, 'I *adore* corpses and stiffs.' As for the religious difference, she wrote: 'I can be converted on my deathbed and die an R.C. . . . where shall we be buried?' As it turned out, because the Catholic Church would not recognise his marriage, Max, infuriated, left his faith.

It is true that James and Punkie warned Agatha to be prudent, her sister being particularly vehement. When Max took Agatha to a summer ball to meet some of his Oxford friends and she realised that he and her nephew Jack had been contemporaries at New College, stunned, she began to argue again that she was too old to marry him. Punkie's opposition was particularly upsetting when Max was not there to sustain Agatha with his calm, reasonable logic. 'I always have a kind of panic after you've gone,' she wrote. 'When you're there I feel everything is all right – I feel just quiet and safe and happy – dear Max – I've felt that with you almost from the beginning. And then a wave of reality comes over me and I say to myself "Idiot – haven't you any sense? What would you say to someone else who was doing this?" I felt so secure in my distrust of life and people – you mustn't be angry with me, Max – I am really *very* slow indeed and it takes me a *long* time to take a thing in – I've got to adjust myself to an idea I've never ever considered....' Their decision not to marry until September, she added, did 'give one time to be sure'. But she was sure enough to promise Max that she would practise 'being tidy tomorrow and punctual the day after', if he would reciprocate; 'are you always going to catch trains by *that* narrow margin all through our married life?!'

To avoid the attention of the press, which so terrified Agatha, they kept their engagement a secret. There is an echo of the small girl who disliked parting with information in Agatha's letter to Max about 'secret happenings'. 'I think,' she wrote, 'one has that instinct – to hide it ... probably it's a wise instinct – the spectacle of other people's happiness doesn't seem able to be borne with equanimity – too many potential Iagos about! Possibly Desdemona and Othello had looked glooey in public so that everyone could have said (with satisfaction) "Not turning out well – poor things – but what can one expect?"'

Rosalind, whom Agatha had consulted in a roundabout way, knew their secret at the beginning of August. 'Darling Max,' Agatha announced, 'Rosie has GUESSED. She will give her consent if you send her by return 2 dozen toffee lollipops from Selfridges (none others genuine).' Agatha thought Rosalind had received the news as 'a *huge joke*' but Max was more serious, glad that Rosalind had taken it in her stride. When Agatha suggested that he bring a small present for Rosalind, possibly a book, 'on the DAY', it was Max who thought of finding her a brooch, to commemorate the marriage and help her feel part of it.

At the end of August Agatha and Rosalind went with Carlo

and her sister Mary to Broadford in Skye, where the banns could
be called. In such an out-of-the-way place the press might fail to
notice – and there were other attractions too. In Carlo and Mary,
Agatha had two friends who thoroughly supported her decision
and with whom Rosalind also felt safe. A month spent far away,
on an island, living quietly and simply in the clear summer air,
gave Agatha an important interval between her old life and her
new. In some ways Skye was like the world in which she had first
met Max, an ancient, empty place, removed from everyday life.
At the same time it allowed her to withdraw from him, as if this
period of seclusion, shared only with her daughter and two
women, cleansed and refreshed her before her wedding. Not that
she was totally removed from Max; they wrote to each other
daily. Agatha's letters were reflective and still slightly anxious,
Max's firm and encouraging. It is as if he were the older one, as
he reported on his work and his arrangements for their passports.
He assured Agatha that it was only to be expected that she should
feel nervous before their 'great enterprise' and promised that she
need not fear his being 'too highbrow', though he had already
started giving her demanding reading lists. Nor would he curb
her freedom; she might see herself as a faithful dog, likely to be
taken off on adventures, but she would not be 'a dog *on a lead*'.
Max and Agatha also seemed to have arrived already at a sensible
understanding regarding money. Agatha earned far more than
Max (and owned two houses, with a flat about to be added). The
arrangement appears to have been that they should not be shy of
discussing how their joint income should be disbursed nor of
regarding some expenditure as more appropriate for one than the
other. Thus Max wrote to Agatha that she should let him know
'the Registrar's fees because it's right that I should pay for all
that'.

By the end of August they were ready. Max had a white blazer
made for their honeymoon in Venice, to be followed by five weeks
on the Dalmatian coast. He was due at Ur in October and at this
point still hoped Agatha would be able to come with him as far
as Baghdad. Katharine Woolley had not been as outraged at the
news of Max and Agatha's intentions as they had at first feared.
After much deliberation, Agatha had written to Katharine, who
had only observed that Max ought to be obliged to wait two
years at least, 'a good long apprenticeship'. 'It's no good,' Agatha
wrote to Max, 'I shall never have the proper K-like Olympian
attitude to the male sex. . . .' Katharine had obviously realised by

late August that Max and Agatha were determined not to wait
and that she had lost her acolyte, for Max happily reported that
she had set out to buy an electric massage machine.

The wedding took place in St Columba's Church in Edinburgh
on September 11th. Rosalind remained there with Carlo at the
Roxburghe Hotel; Max and Agatha, with her new passport (for
which Agatha had *slightly* decreased her age) set off to Italy,
equipped, as Max had instructed, with rugs, pillows and a hot-
water bottle.

The account of their honeymoon in Max's *Memoirs* occupies
four paragraphs and in Agatha's *Autobiography* four pages.
Max's description is circumspect, Agatha's more racy, full of chat
about meals and strange people. She was always a more impressionistic writer than Max, less exact but more vivid and immediate. The difference was also revealed by their handwriting, as
their joint diary shows. Max's words are neatly incised, small and
even, written with a fine-nibbed fountain pen, whereas Agatha's
swoop over the page in huge flourishes, often barely legible, the
ink fading where she rushes on, forgetting to press. Max's sentences are complete; Agatha's substitute dashes for verbs, and are
punctuated by exclamations, stressed with capitals and underlin-
ing. Max conveys facts, Agatha moods.

They travelled first to Venice. Max noted buildings and the
light; he was especially pleased when 'an archaeological Ange'
noticed the carving of a cross in an ancient plaque. Agatha was
more down to earth: 'Sad descent from romance - *bitten by bugs*
- my special kind - in train!!!' She particularly liked their visit to
the Lido: 'Amusing conversation of a lady (tri-lingual) who had
lost her wardrobe in an overturned gondola. "Mais, c'est la fin
de saison!"' On they went to Split (Max: 'Al fresco meals under
the shadow of Diocletian's Peristyle'; Agatha: 'Definite beginning
of positive nausea owing to a surfeit of Venetian Gothic! The
cheese there is dear! ... A really *good* bathing place. Intrusion of
two shy whites amongst mahogany Yugo Slavs.') Max was now
teaching Agatha the Greek alphabet; she persuaded him to bathe
in the sea at every opportunity. At Dubrovnik they bathed by day
and by night. (Agatha: 'Oh! The bathing!! ... Did torch betray
our guilty secret?') They managed to shake off other English
visitors and, by taking first a ferry and then hiring a car, drove
to the old capital of Montenegro in the mountains and then to
Kotor to catch their boat to Greece, the unpronounceable *Sbrin*.

This was a little cargo boat, with a thoughtful captain and

excellent chef. After the first stop Max and Agatha were the only passengers and at every port they wandered off until the ship hooted. They were radiantly happy. 'Glorious walks through olive woods,' Max wrote. 'Feeling of Theocritus and that Ange was my Amaryllis.' Agatha recorded it as 'one of those rare moments of happiness – very still and exquisite – a kind of quivering inner light – the SBRIN HOOTS – but only for fun apparently'.

Max, who had planned the journey as a surprise for Agatha, had arranged at its end a visit to the places each had missed the previous year, Delphi for Agatha and the Temple of Bassae for himself. Their first day in Greece was misery: 'Patras,' Agatha wrote, 'A low hole! ... Noxious insects fed on Ange's legs – Too trusting alas! We have not used Chrysanthemum Powder at the moment when most needed.' She had what she described as 'a hair wash out *à la Grecque* (very queer and plastered down!)' Max recorded: 'My moustache shaved and Ange wanted it back ... constantly saying that I looked different.' The next day was agonising. Agatha wondered if her legs, swollen, despite 'a healing primitive bathe in the Alphaeus', would go into skiing trousers, but she and Max survived the trip in a flea-ridden bus to Olympia. Max's final diary entry has a scholarly fling. (Agatha hopefully left alternate pages blank but he wrote no more, perhaps feeling that this humdrum record was too flippant for Greek temples.) 'One can identify almost every building,' he wrote raptly, 'thanks to that indefatigable pedant Pausanias and to the persevering Curtius who disencumbered Olympia from the thick belt of sand deposited by the wayward Alphaeus in medieval times.' Agatha was in her own way as lyrical: 'Now at last one understands the meaning of a Sacred Grove....' They spent the afternoon there on the hill reading *The Testament of Beauty*, before hobbling home in the moonlight.

The next day was a worse test – a fourteen-hour mule trek to Andritsena, up and down ravines, fording a river (Agatha: 'this appeared to be dangerous from the point of view of the guides to whom ravines – where we blanch – are a matter of course. Rain then began ...'). On and on, and up and up stony paths. 'Acute feeling of misery and indeed regret that I had ever married Max – He's too young for me!! Arrived nearer dead than alive – Max ministered to me so well that I am glad I married him after all. But he mustn't do it again!!' Bassae, Tripolis, Nauplia, Epidaurus – Agatha delighted by temples but most particularly by the bathing – and at last they came to Athens, which 'felt very queer. We no longer seem the same people. A *suite à deux lits* with bath makes us feel all shy and civilised. Gone are the happy lunatics of the last fortnight....' Letters were waiting – with Max's luggage for Ur and Agatha's for the journey home – and this time their correspondence was reassuring. But disaster soon struck, as Agatha told in almost the last entry in the diary: 'Joyful eating of Crevettes and Langoustes.... Retribution for Crevettes and Langoustes'. To the doctor's inquiry – *'Mangez-vous jamais du poisson, Madame?'*, Agatha, who adored fish – especially crustaceans, felt the only reply was 'Best described by dots.....'

They could not establish exactly which fishy meal had poisoned her but she was very ill indeed. Max was obliged to leave, having been firmly instructed by Woolley to meet him and Katharine in Baghdad by October 15th. Just before the marriage it had been made plain to Agatha that wives were regarded as an encumbrance at Ur and Leonard, prompted, Agatha was sure, by Katharine, had even attempted to suggest that she should not accompany Max as far as Baghdad: 'The Trustees would think it odd.' Though Agatha and Max had already arranged to part in Athens, Agatha did not say so, emphasising to Woolley that where she chose to travel with her husband was nothing to do with the dig. Her point was taken but Leonard had stressed that Max must arrive punctually in Baghdad to receive instructions on his first duty of the season – supervising the building of various extensions to the expedition house. Now, with Agatha still extremely weak, Max was reluctant to leave. Agatha insisted, since she knew that if he tarried Katharine would ascribe the blame to her. This was, with luck, the last season Max would spend with Woolley. When he learnt that there was room for only one woman at Ur, he had decided to look elsewhere, so that Agatha could be with him and he could acquire new experience. Dr Campbell Thompson had already sounded him out about coming to Nineveh and, though nothing was settled yet, this seemed the answer. Knowing this was the last six months for which they would have to be apart, Agatha urged Max to keep his promise to Woolley.

Max left, to the astonishment of Agatha's doctor. 'Had Monsieur gone for many days?' Agatha described him as asking, in her first letter to Max. 'I said for 5 months. He asked if I was staying here all that time – evidently regarding ladies as like chessmen – only to be moved from square to square without their own volition!' Two days later she tottered on to the train for London. Max, meanwhile, had arrived in Baghdad to find the Woolleys were not expected for another week. Furious, he took the foreman, Hamoudi, straight to Ur, hired a hundred workmen and ordered them to complete the buildings as quickly as possible to his own specification. The living-room was spacious, with a fireplace modelled on the one at Cresswell Place, and a chimney like that in the room he and Agatha had in Venice. Katharine's bathroom he made as cramped as possible. It had to be torn down and rebuilt – that was Max's revenge. Agatha's wrath burned slower and more lambent. She waited until 1935 to make a literary joke of Max's – albeit unwilling – defection; it can be found in *Death in the Clouds*, where a young archaeologist tells the story of an Englishman, 'who left his wife and went on so as to be "on duty" in time. And both he and his wife thought that quite natural; they thought him noble, unselfish. But the doctor, who was not English, thought him a barbarian.'

Once home, Agatha too had to start work. Though she still felt fragile and Max was not there to cheer her up, she was hopeful and serene. 'Do you know, Max,' she wrote from the Paddington Hotel, 'it is the first time for several years that I have arrived in England without a feeling of sick misery – I always had it – as though I'd escaped from things by going abroad to sunshine – and then came back to them – to memories shadowed and all the things I wanted to forget. But this time – no – Just "Oh, London rainy as usual – but rather a nice funny old place."' Max had, she realised, lifted from her shoulders 'so much that I didn't even know was there'. She could feel the wounds healing over: 'They are still there – and very little would open them again – but they will heal once more.'

15

'... corpses and stiffs ...'

Writing books is more difficult than writing letters and settling to writing books even harder when there is every excuse to correspond with a distant husband. Agatha was quick at thinking of enticing titles and complicated plots, but that did not make it any easier to sit down at her typewriter and begin what she thought of as the 'chore' of starting a book. She was not short of other occupations. She and Max had now acquired another house, made out of 47 and 48 Campden Street and, since it was nearer the Underground line for the British Museum and had a roof garden Agatha liked, she intended to let Cresswell Place. Her letters to Max in the late autumn and winter of 1930 are full of details of purchases at sales – 'a walnut chest all oyster shell', a Worcester tea service – which gave her quite as much fun as her father had enjoyed on his daily expeditions in Torquay.

There was also a spell of anxiety over Rosalind's dog, who had developed a growth in his shoulder. Agatha poured out her despair in a long letter to Max; even he, she felt, would never really understand how deeply attached she was to Peter: 'You've never been through a *really* bad time with nothing but a dog to hold on to.' Max seems to have learned to become fond of Agatha's dogs because they were hers and part of the household, but he did not share that sympathy for animals which some people have from their earliest childhood and which it is difficult for others to fully comprehend. Agatha had always regarded her birds and animals as close friends, each with a character as individual as that of human beings. Her picture of her childhood in the *Autobiography* and the fictional accounts based upon it in some of 'Mary Westmacott's' novels speak at length of the nature and doings of the goldfinch and the dogs, their companionship and the woe caused by their – usually temporary – disappearance. Agatha's closeness to her animals was not due simply to the fact that she spent a great deal of time alone with them, playing with them, talking to them, looking after them, regarding them as an intrinsic part of her life – as people do when there are few, or no, other contemporaries about – but also because in important ways she identified with them. Animals knew things, though they did not speak; they felt pain and affection, though they could not express it in words.

As a child Agatha had felt much the same. Thoughtful, diffident, comfortable with those she knew but embarrassed by effusive strangers, she wanted to convey feelings which she could not frame in speech. One of the most memorable and significant stories in her autobiography is of the occasion when a mountain guide, taking Frederick and his daughters on an excursion in the Pyrenees, caught a butterfly and pinned it, still alive, in Agatha's hat, where, to her horror, it flapped and fluttered until at last it died. The point of the story, as Agatha emphasises, is not so much her misery at the butterfly's condition as her desperate inability either to express her tangled feelings – distress at seeming to spurn the guide's effort to be kind, sorrow at the butterfly's fate, disgust at the beastly flapping noise – or to find anyone who would intuitively understand. Only Clara saw the cause of her tears, as Agatha looked at her in 'that long bondage of silence'. Her mother was a friend to whom Agatha did not need to explain. This basic, instinctive understanding Agatha shared with Peter, who, she felt, had recognised that she was ill and unhappy in the bleak days at Styles and had unquestioningly welcomed her back when that time was over. A 'Faithful Dog' was Agatha's term for a loyal human being; her trust in Max rested on her belief that he, too, understood her silent feelings and needs – she was, as she put it, his 'Dog to be taken for Walks'.

Peter recovered and Agatha resumed her other distractions. She had taken up drawing, though she told Max that 'competent young women ... drawing from life', 'red-haired young women in paint-stained overalls', gave her an inferiority complex. However, having lost nearly a stone after her illness in Athens ('Married life has reduced me'), she at least felt she was 'elegantly thin still – or thin for *me*'. She also tried clay modelling, not very successfully, sending Max pictures of 'a super pot, side elevation, from the NE, the SW etc'. He forwarded reading lists from Ur (Herodotus was the latest addition) and Agatha had her own programme. She was interested in scientific and mathematical theory – the reference to Sir Claude Amory's studies of the disintegration of the atom in *Black Coffee* shows she kept up-to-

date – and especially in current hypotheses regarding notions of
time and the nature of identity.

On her first trip to the Near East an acquaintance had introduced Agatha to a book that had some influence at the end of
the nineteen-twenties, J.W. Dunne's *Experiment with Time*.
Agatha had been profoundly affected by it: 'Somehow,' she wrote
in her *Autobiography*, 'I saw things more in proportion; myself as
less large; as only one facet of a whole, in a vast world with
hundreds of interconnections.' Now, in November 1930, she had
been equally moved by Sir James Jeans's book, *The Mysterious
Universe*. 'I understand very little of it but it fills me with nebulous ideas,' she wrote to Max.

> 'How queer it would be if *God* were in the future – something we
> never created or imagined but who is not yet – supposing him to be
> not *Cause* but *Effect*. The creation of God is what we are moving to
> – is one goal – the aim and purpose of all evolution – all our beliefs
> of God creating the world (on a very wasteful and cruel plan) and
> allowing pain etc – are all *wrong*. But all pain and all waste wouldn't
> matter – the mere cost of production so to speak. I am very incoherent
> – but you can see what I mean. . . . It's fun to play with ideas – That
> God has made the world as it is and is pleased with it seems certainly
> not so. Originally man starved to death and froze to death (on top of
> coal in the ground) and every plague and pestilence caused by Man's
> stupidity was put down to 'God's Will'. If life on this planet is an
> accident, quite unforeseen, and against all the principles of the solar
> system – how amazingly interesting – and when may it end? In some
> complete and marvellous Consciousness. . . ?

There were at this time plenty of new theories for Agatha to
struggle with and attempt to square with familiar teaching: 'If
time *is* infinite it would be the same thing – we could move
through it either way. But I like my idea of God being in the
future and our working every day and hour nearer to Him. In
every cell of matter (even in a jelly fish!!) every potentiality of
Man is present – only latent – so supposing God is latent in
Man?' (Agatha had less faith in new inventions than in new ideas.
This letter to Max continued: 'Your p.c. to Carlo arrived today
– so Air Mail is quicker by far – or at least it is when it happens.
I suppose having killed those people last week, they are flying a
bit carefully this week'.) With relief, she turned, 'somewhat
addled', from *The Mysterious Universe* to 'the Scarab Murder
Case . . . very soothing after too much Relativity'.

Agatha was prevented from much procrastination by immediate professional demands. The most pressing was a request from Dorothy Sayers to help five other crime novelists compose a serial for the BBC, to be broadcast only a few weeks ahead in January 1931. This was the second enterprise of its kind, its predecessor being a six-part serial, broadcast in June and July 1930, just before Agatha left for Skye. The contributors to the first serial were Hugh Walpole, Dorothy L. Sayers, Anthony Berkeley, E.C. Bentley, Ronald Knox and Agatha, who had written the second episode of the story, whose overall title was *Behind the Screen*. The idea for the series had come from J.R. Ackerley, then an Assistant Producer in the BBC's Talks Department, and the contributors' task was complex, since each episode had to be dovetailed into the others. Each writer, nonetheless, sought to make matters difficult for those whose turn came later. Furthermore, despite the producer's efforts to make the story cohesive and coherent, each author succeeded in colouring the episode in question with his or her own idiosyncratic style (Agatha's introduced several false clues, a number of details as to timing and a great deal of conversation), and in giving it a special flavour by the way in which he or she read it aloud. The huge BBC microphones behaved unpredictably and practising an address to the nation was complicated. Three days before Agatha's broadcast on June 21st she was given a voice test, and, after she had read her instalment, the audience was invited to send the Editor of the *Listener* the answers to various complicated questions as to the motives for the crime and its solution.

That earlier venture was sufficiently successful for the BBC to try it again and early in November Dorothy Sayers told Agatha that, 'Feeling their own organisation last time was a trifle rocky', they had now asked her to take the matter in hand and approach the contributors. The other writers, the BBC hoped, would be Anthony Berkeley, E.C. Bentley, Clemence Dane and Freeman Wills Crofts, 'Six *eminent* detective story writers', Max learnt in a letter from Agatha. This time the serial was to have twelve instalments and at the preliminary meeting on December 5th it was agreed that Agatha should write the second and fourth episodes of the story, called *The Scoop*. The team's method was together to make a rough outline of the plot, after which each author sketched his own episode, consulting the others on points of detail. The BBC producers were wise to leave the task of organising these proceedings to Miss Sayers, for the whole undertaking proved extremely complicated.

The plot of *The Scoop* (which was republished by Gollancz, with *Behind the Screen*, in 1933) concerns the killing of a newspaper reporter who has been covering a murder case. The intricacies of the story and the clutter of victims, suspects, weaponry and motivations reflect the compromises that had to be made to accommodate every author's whim. As Dorothy Sayers told Agatha, there was also 'great trouble with the BBC, who ring up every other day to demand that the story shall be simple, with very few characters, no time-table and no complications or suspects to speak of.' Little did the BBC know how mystery stories are created. Matters were made more difficult by the fact that, early in the planning stages, the contributors dispersed for Christmas. Dorothy Sayers found Agatha particularly hard to track down, as she moved between Campden Street, Cresswell Place and Abney. They had many frenzied conversations on the telephone and letters passed busily between them, with embellishments for already ornate bits of plotting. One of Miss Sayers's memoranda to Agatha began with a paragraph of compliments for *The Murder at the Vicarage*: 'Dear old Tabbies,' she observed, 'are the only possible right kind of female detective and Miss M is lovely.... I think this is the best you have done – almost – though I am very fond of *Roger Ackroyd*. But I like this better because it hasn't got a dictaphone in it; I have an anti-dicta-gramophone complex.' Miss Sayers's current concern, however, was with holding together her team for *The Scoop*: 'Mr Crofts has just rung me up (on a wire which, I should say, the GPO must have been hanging out washing, for it was full of strange bangings and flappings) to say that something has gone wrong with the alibi and that the 9.48 may have to get in late. I hope not, because this will upset my newspaper office scene rather badly....'

The BBC, unaware of these ramifications, had meanwhile sent each contributor a solemn warning: 'Very difficult complications such as the significance of minutes or seconds of time should be avoided.... Dialogue should be written in such a way that the listener is never in any doubt as to who is speaking.... The characters in the story should be kept to a minimum....' Miss Sayers gave them short shrift, saying breezily to Agatha that 'Ackerley tells me he has sent you one of his silly letters. I shouldn't give any heed to him. If he keeps on bothering us, I suggest we write as one man, to tell him that he apparently doesn't want a detective story, but a simple love-tale or something.'

Ackerley was oblivious of the mire in which his contributors struggled. Desperate, Dorothy Sayers arranged for them all to meet for lunch – but even that was confused: 'The line was rather noisy, but I *thought* it was Monday you said.' Early in the New Year Agatha, driven almost frantic by this correspondence, meetings at the BBC and the rehearsals for *Black Coffee*, escaped to Switzerland with Rosalind. 'We will never never come to one of these places together,' she wrote to Max. 'I already know two women who have lost husbands to beautiful Amazonian girls who come leaping down mountain sides on skis.' Agatha's disappearance threw Ackerley into a turmoil; 'There are already about fifteen characters in these two instalments ...', he wrote to Agatha, and, made treacherous to his listeners by his desperation, he emphasised, 'it has to be written almost as if for children.'

The second half of the serial was still unwritten when the broadcasts began. Miss Sayers read the first instalment on January 10th and Agatha broadcast hers the following week, having persuaded the BBC to allow her to do so 'from a station in Devonshire'. The BBC had sent a last-minute letter, threatening dreadful repercussions if she should overrun her time. She had more important anxieties – whether, for instance, Max would be able to find a radio with a sufficiently strong signal to hear her in Iraq. He managed to do so by galloping over the desert (riding a horse for the first time in his life) to Major Berry, the Political Officer at Nasiryeh, who had 'a very fine wireless set – he gets London regularly'. Max's admiring letter to 'my EMINENT Ange' did not arrive until several weeks after the serial was finished; he added, 'I wish you could work in a cryptic message!' The idea had also occurred to Agatha, whose letter crossed with his: 'I had a frightful cold and when I broadcasted on Saturday I could *not* think of a suitable plug to put in for you. Also the BBC question every single sentence as being 'relevant or not'. Shall have better wits on the 31st perhaps – I will say something about the East!'

The Scoop involved a great deal of work but for Agatha the tangible reward was relatively small: a fee of fifty guineas, to include the writing and broadcasting of the two instalments and first serial publication in the *Listener*. By now her fee for a short story in a magazine was at least £100. Agatha participated in only one more collaborative venture, *The Floating Admiral*, published in 1931, in which her own chapter was 'Mainly Conversation'. As she lamented to Max, though it was amusing to be regarded as one of the 'eminent' mystery novelists, 'It takes *hours* and I can't get any fun out of it.' In February 1931 she did send Dorothy Sayers a short tale, 'The Adventure of the Clapham Cook', for a collection later in the year. 'A most intriguing little problem for Hercule!' Miss Sayers observed. 'My last volume was much the poorer by his absence.' But Agatha, and her agent, did not find such exercises a useful expenditure of time and energy. 'I have an awful feeling,' wrote Miss Sayers, 'that Hughes Massie wanted an awful (too awfuls) lot of money. I'm not really supposed to offer more than about £7.7.0 for the British rights.' Agatha was now sufficiently professional to put an intelligent price on her work and her agent discouraged her from lowering its market valuation. She preferred to sell her writing for a realistic fee and give the money away than to underprice herself. Sometimes this attitude was difficult for potential purchasers to understand. In September 1932, for instance, she heard again from J.R. Ackerley, proposing that she compose another serial: 'Your idea of giving certain problems to a number of different people to discuss together would be really just what we wanted.' He wondered whether she would write some as 'little plays ... conversation only and the text and descriptive parts omitted', 'with Mrs Marple [sic] coming out on top'. After some to-ing and fro-ing, Agatha wrote him a brief but firm letter: 'The truth of the matter is I hate writing short things and they really are *not* profitable. I don't mind an odd one now and again, but the energy to devise a series is much better employed in writing a couple of books. So there it is! With apologies.'

Ackerley did not see the point at all. People who work as salaried employees in large organisations, however creative themselves, can find it extraordinarily difficult to grasp that freelance contributors have their livings to earn and, indeed, their overheads to carry. Such obtuseness is particularly irritating when it is coupled with the assumption, often conveyed in unconsciously patronising language, that it is the organisation which is granting the contributor a favour. Producers – not, fortunately, all of them – who condescended to Agatha in this way damaged the BBC in her eyes more than the Corporation ever knew. Ackerley's temper had, perhaps, been soured by the glorious complications of *The Scoop*. Asked for his recollections in 1938, he told his successor:

> So far as I recall Agatha Christie, she was surprisingly good-looking and extremely tiresome. She was always late sending in her stuff, very

difficult to pin down to any engagements and invariably late for them. I recall these memories with pain, for she is my favourite detective story writer. Her success as a broadcaster has made less impression upon me. I believe she was quite adequate but nothing more; a little on the feeble side, if I recollect aright, but then anyone in that series would have seemed feeble against the terrific vitality, bullying and bounce of that dreadful woman Dorothy L. Sayers.

His judgements were unjust to both of them but he was obviously still shell-shocked.

Apart from these bits and pieces Agatha published only one full-length book in 1931, *The Sittaford Mystery*, set in a snow-bound village on Dartmoor. It begins with a séance, whose parti-cipants are informed that Captain Trevelyan, living six miles dis-tant, has been murdered. The story is clever and slightly bizarre; it reflects one side of Agatha's attitude to the occult and to those who, half-guiltily, entertained mediums, hunched over ouija boards and marvelled at ectoplasmic manifestations. There was a good deal of such dotty indulgence in the 'thirties and to some extent Agatha regarded it with tolerant scepticism. On the other hand, some of the stories she was writing for magazines, which appeared in the collection *The Hound of Death* in 1933, show a serious interest in hypothetical phenomena like telepathy, extra-sensory perception, and so on. Her early story, 'The Call of Wings', reprinted in this volume, was a reminder that the theme of the power and purpose of art, the significance of emotion and dreams, had intrigued her from adolescence. Like *The Sittaford Mystery*, these are clever stories, appealing both to sceptics and the gullible.

In the spring of 1931, Agatha travelled to Ur to join Max for the last few days of the dig. His moustache had grown again (Katharine had been the only one to comment on its absence) and was to stay, as Agatha could not bear him without it. Tactful letters to Katharine and a copy of *The Murder at the Vicarage* (sent at Max's suggestion: 'Don't forget PROTHEROE,' he kept urging her, remembering only the victim's name) had smoothed Agatha's path and she was graciously received. The Mallowans came home by way of Persia, which Agatha had begged to see; she had been 'simply wild with excitement' after seeing the Per-sian Exhibition in London in January. Agatha's *Autobiography* gives a rapt account of their visit to Shiraz and Isfahan and tells the entertaining tale of their journey home through the Soviet Union. One of Agatha's chief memories of that trip was their consumption of large amounts of delicious and very cheap caviare, a dish she continued to love all her life. (A not untypical surprise invitation Agatha sent a friend in 1961 read: 'Damn and blast your telephone! ... How would it appeal to you to come about 8.30 and eat a *Great Deal* of Caviare? NB There won't be anything else but coffee. But possibly if we eat enough Caviare we shan't want anything more. Anyway there's always Ham.') Its grainy grey appearance also gave Agatha a vague idea for a plot; she scrawled in a notebook: 'Arsenic ... looks like Caviare – plum pudding – passion fruit'.

That summer Agatha worked at two books, *Peril at End House* and *Thirteen Problems*, a collection of stories featuring Miss Marple. *Peril at End House* seems to have been a straightforward exercise. Agatha thought of the plot and, in a tiny black notebook hitherto used only for noting the railway connections between Stockport and Torquay, listed the characters and sketched every chapter in telegraphese: 'The Crofts. Miss Buckley is dead. Terrific agitation. Then – Apparently some relief.... At Nursing Home. P says – you have not told me everything?' A notebook of Rosalind's appropriated by Agatha, who has written 'Ideas 1931' at the top of the first page, gives the origins of *The Thirteen Problems*, which brings together the stories told by Miss Marple and a group of friends, meeting each Tuesday evening. Agatha's initial scheme was for the gathering to consist of some of her collaborators of the winter and spring: 'Mr Wills Crofts and wife, Mr Bentley, Miss Sayers and husband ...' but she thought better of it. Miss Marple is the member who tranquilly perceives the solution to each problem, with her analogies and what her creator describes as her 'special knowledge'. This book was dedicated to the Woolleys.

The first working title for *The Thirteen Problems* was 'Thirteen at Dinner'. Discarded there, this became the title of the American edition of Agatha's next book, *Lord Edgware Dies*. Most of this story was written in Rhodes, to which Agatha took herself for a few weeks in the autumn of 1931 before joining Max at Nineveh, where he was now working with Campbell Thompson. Agatha, who was missing Max, sent him long, chatty letters from the Grand Hôtel des Roses. Her routine was simple:

Breakfast at 8 (now I haven't got you); Meditation 'till 9. Violent hitting of typewriter 'till 11.30 (or the end of the chapter – sometimes if it is a lovely day I cheat to make it a short one!) then to the beach and plunge into the sea – then lie on the beach with a bare back as far as possible. 1.30 lunch – then a wander round the town – or else a chat on the terrace. After tea some more work (sometimes no work but a sleep) 8.30 dinner – and afterwards work if I've slept – or if I have been industrious, intellectual conversation ... punctuated by mosquito slapping. Then to bed inside my mosquito net all alone.

As with all Agatha's detective stories, *Lord Edgware Dies* was meticulously plotted before she began to write. Her central idea for the plot came from watching the American entertainer, Ruth Draper, who had been performing dramatic monologues in London since the nineteen-twenties, transform herself with slight but subtle disguises into one person after another. Having outlined her plot, Agatha's next step was to assemble the characters. She wrote to Max from Rhodes: 'Lord Edgware is getting on nicely. He is dead – Carlotta Adams (Ruth Draper) is dead – and the nephew who succeeds to the property is just talking to Poirot about his beautiful alibi! There is also a film actor with a face like a "Greek God" – but he's looking a bit haggard at present. In fact a very popular mixture, I think. Just a bit cheap, perhaps.' The novel was finished at Nineveh at a table bought for £3 according to Max, £10 according to Agatha, and in either case, according to the notoriously economical Campbell Thompson, an extravagance.

Just before Christmas 1931 Agatha left Max and travelled back by herself on the Orient Express. It was a catastrophic journey, in retrospect hilarious. As soon as she got into Campden Street, at six o'clock in the morning, she sent him an account of her adventures. A long letter, it is nonetheless worth giving in full, not just because it shows how swiftly and entertainingly she could tell a story but also because it gave her the setting – and some elements of the characters – for a novel she wrote in 1933, *Murder on the Orient Express.*

My darling, What a journey! Started out from Stamboul in a violent thunder storm. We went very slowly during the night and about 3 AM stopped altogether. I thought we were at a frontier at about eight o'clock. It seemed to me that even for a Lower Nation the frontier halt was excessive – so I got up, discovered we were in the middle of nowhere and perturbed officials hurrying up and down the train who said the line has flooded further along, *'C'est une inondation, Madame – mais nous ne savons rien – mais rien!'*

A chatty breakfast in the dining car ensued. 'All boys together' spirit! There was an elderly American lady who was catching the

Acquitania [sic] at Cherbourg on 16th – a funny little Englishman from Smyrna – a little fussy man but very interested in archaeology – an old gentleman of 85 with a *most* amusing wife of 70 with a hideous but very attractive face – I think they were Greek but they were some of the richest people in Istanbul and the old boy was going to attend a conference at Buda Pesth. Sitting with them was a Hungarian Minister and his wife and they all four talked very entertaining diplomatic scandal in French. There were also two Danish lady missionaries who never seemed to be there because they had scant food and only came to breakfast. There was also, most fortunately, a director of the Wagons Lits Company. But for his presence I think we should be there still! He was in the same coach as I was and everyone would come to report to him – so I was always in the position of having inside information. I used to creep to the door and listen. *'Oui, M. le Directeur. Non, M. le D. On répond qu'on ne sait rien.'*

It got awfully cold after breakfast and the engineer was sent off to bring back water and *'chaudron pour le chauffage'*. We spent the morning wrapped up in rugs and the conductor fetched my *hot* water bottle and said that last time they had stayed in that particular place three weeks!! He said that of course the passengers had got tired of it at last and had gone back to Stamboul. He said it was all very difficult because the line was washed away in three places – two of them in Greek territory and one in Turkish – and the question of who was to mend what was very complicated. He added *'C'est un sâle pays. Ces gens là ne feront rien.'*

Mrs Hilton, the American lady, was by now full of USA bewilderment. 'But why aren't they *doing* anything? Why, in the States they'd have motored some automobiles along right away – why, they'd have brought aeroplanes. . . .'

However the rumour went round that there was only going to be twelve hours delay and the chauffage was restored and we had lunch on our 'lunch in Yugoslavia' coupon and everyone was more cheerful and then a rumour got about that we were going on a little way by train and then by car – so everyone packed up and put on warm things.

We went on with great éclat to the next station, Pythiou, where Greek officers came aboard and with great politeness begged us not to worry about visas but to all sit and enjoy ourselves fully. As it was then *pouring* down in this slushy snow and at a station and those decrepit huts seemed to be all there was of Pythiou we stayed put! We had 'dinner in Yugoslavia'. In the middle of the night the next Orient Express arrived behind us and five passengers were transferred to us – a large jocose Italian, a little German with a bald head, a Bulgarian lady, a thin and a *terrible* man from Chicago – a Turk by extraction dressed in an orange suit, lots of gold chains and things and a royal blue satin tie with horse shoes on it. He too was going to catch the *Acquitania* and he was devastatingly friendly!!! Sunday was a beautiful day – a lot of snow had fallen in the night but it was all sunny. After 'breakfast in Italy' we all decided to do some telegraphing in spite of my gloomy conductor who warned us, *'Ça n'arrivera jamais.'*

We went in a body to the office where a very unshaven Greek clerk received us with a courtly bow. Some telegrams were then written out – to America, to England, to Berlin, to Smyrna, to Paris, to Buda Pesth!

Then, of course, he wanted to be paid in Drachmas and no one had any. The dining cars had everything else! The polite Greek officers came to the rescue by producing a newspaper some days old and working out exchanges so that we paid in dollars and francs and Marks. It was the cheapest telegram ever sent – mine cost a dollar (and it got there in an hour, what is more!!).

In the afternoon things really happened. We were all taken into one coach and the rest of the train was to go back to Stamboul. As the old gentleman had missed his conference his wife wanted to go back but the old boy was slightly gaga and full of spirit. He'd started for Buda Pesth and he was going to Buda Pesth, flood or no floods!! He extracted rusks and offered them to me in a gracious manner. *'Mais mangez donc, Madame.* You – do – not – know – when – you – will – eat – next.'

We all felt very excited at starting off – the engine went behind and pushed – (so, I suppose, that *we* should bear the brunt!) Nothing happened at first because they'd left the brakes on but all the dining car men got out and undid the brakes by hand – and then we *did* actually start ... and got over the Greek bit safely and then we came to the place where the water had come down from the mountain and hooshed the whole thing away. Then we got out and walked – on planks laid over the chasm (you know how I *hate* walking on planks!) A scene of great confusion – because on the far side was a coach of the *other* train and everyone coming across from *it* to *us*. And the workmen stopped mending the line and carried suitcases with great zeal, so much so that they brought back the ones others had taken and began to return them to the same train and everyone was shouting and trying to keep an eye on all their things at once – and there were the Grandes Bagages and the Mails.

It was *very* beautiful because the moon [?] had risen ... with Adrianople on the far side of it with all its minarets looking too beautiful in the setting sun.

However the poetic feeling didn't last long! In our new coach all had been laid bare. There was nothing to eat – no water in the wash basins – and no water to drink. We all filled in somehow. The American lady discovered she'd lost her sleeping car and the prospect of being shut up with the *very* talkative Bulgarian lady for the night was too much for her and she wept bitterly. 'My daughter said I'd have no trouble at all – no trouble at all. I've never travelled in Europe before and I'll never travel in it again.' We all consoled her, the Danish missionaries made her tea with the scrapings of everybody's water bottle and I produced biscuits and chocolate and the Terrible Chicago Man produced oranges and cheese – and the Bulgarian lady ate everything within sight!

At last everybody got calm and settled and disentangled their luggage which was all mixed up. The chauffage was on (which is all that really matters to me!) and the marvellous little conductor from Ostend made my bed and the Danish ladies' for us, I think because we hadn't been as cross as the others.

A peaceful night except for the Turk who was next door to me and was continuously trying to open the door between our compartments – not, let us hope, for the worst reasons but I think because he thought it was the wash place!!

In the middle of the night we started towards Sofia – got there about six a.m. and were put on to a siding about a mile from the station. Three feet of snow by then – so we all woke up rather hungry and cold about eight and found ourselves marooned. At 10.30 – we were attached once more to a train and became the usual Orient Express – only two days late! And how we enjoyed some hot Coffee!!

At Belgrade we acquired the King and Queen who looked very well and gave charming looks – immediately the train swarmed with detectives looking exactly like they do on Cinemas and in plays. They spent most of the time leaning so firmly against the lavatory doors that you could hardly dislodge them.

On Wednesday instead of Monday I arrived. . . .

16

'... a nice parallel track'

Max was now anxious to lead an expedition of his own and set about raising funds. Agatha shared this goal; indeed, in a Christmas letter to him in 1932 she had joyfully announced that she had been approached by some 'film people who want to engage a few well-known authors' and that, although suggestions she might 'make £200,000 out of it' were obviously ludicrous, it might bring 'a nice little sum and with it we'd raze a mound to the ground!' Nothing came of these advances, though she perhaps had them in mind as she drafted a dramatised version, never performed, of *The Secret of Chimneys*.

Agatha was writing prolifically and well. She was now just in her forties, happy and creative. There had been one sad moment, for the baby she was expecting the year before had miscarried and it was felt that she and Max should not now try to have another child. She was at Abney when this happened. Punkie was concerned and Rosalind alarmed at seeing her mother looking frail and ill, until Agatha assured her that, though shocked, she would be perfectly all right. This sorrow, too, was known to only a few friends, including, later, two or three young archaeologists at the time of their own pregnancies. Despite Agatha's belief that a wife should always go with her husband on his travels, she would advise these women friends to stay at home for their confinement, avoiding the unsteady journeys to the desert. Her marriage to Max was a success and Rosalind got on well with her step-father, who was a natural teacher. He even succeeded with her where he had failed with Agatha, interesting Rosalind in philosophy and drinking wine. She had adjusted well to the new situation, and saw Archie regularly – though he and Agatha did not meet again after the divorce. Rosalind enjoyed her father's games and teasing and managed to remain staunchly loyal to both her parents.

In the spring of 1933 Max eventually managed to attract as sponsors the Trustees of the British Museum and the British

School of Archaeology in Iraq. The mound he chose was at Arpachiyah, some miles north-east of Nineveh, and, after some anxious weeks, he proved to have chosen well, as considerable quantities of beautifully decorated pottery and figures came to the surface. Max's whole expedition, including publication of the results, cost only £2000. The staff was small; apart from the cook, houseboy, labourers, and Gallaher, an Irishman who drove the lorry, it consisted of only three persons: Max, his friend John Rose the architect, and Agatha. Agatha was by no means a passenger. Her duties included keeping a written record and helping to arrange and reassemble pottery fragments. She had continued her lessons in drawing to scale, and, though not the most confident draughtsman, did her best. She also continued her practice, begun at Nineveh, of writing a chapter or two in quiet moments; two detective stories, two collections of short stories and a novel written under the name of Mary Westmacott were all completed in 1933.

One of the full-length detective novels was *Murder on the Orient Express*, which she dedicated to 'M.E.M. Arpachiyah 1933'. The other took its title from a sentence Agatha had noted in her list of ideas for 1931, *Why Didn't They Ask Evans?*, there part of the outline of a complex plot in which Poirot pursued a poisoner ('the poison that makes everything *yellow* ... poison applied to dress – very misleading as another girl had yellow dress'). Like Evans in the story itself, 'Evans' in the notebook is a maid, and, confusingly, also the gardener and baker. 'Why didn't they ask Evans?' is an odd and memorable phrase, just the sort of question which, overheard, would stimulate Agatha to spin a story.

The two collections of short stories she wrote in 1933 were *Parker Pyne Investigates* and *The Listerdale Mystery*. One of the tales in *The Listerdale Mystery*. 'Philomel Cottage' was later adapted for the theatre, as *Love From a Stranger*, and subsequently filmed. Another, 'Accident', almost enjoyed a more interesting fate, for in 1957 Alfred Hitchcock expressed an interest in using the plot for a film, a suggestion, however, that eventually came to nothing. The first working title of the other collection was *The Reminiscences of Mr Parker Pyne*. Some of these stories describe the clients who reply to the advertisement placed in *The Times* by this retired civil servant: 'Are you happy? If not, consult Mr Parker Pyne, 17 Richmond Street.' Others show how Mr Parker Pyne is able to help distressed people whom he meets on his travels (In 'The House at Shiraz' and 'The Oracle at Delphi' Agatha remembered some of the places and people she and Max had seen together.) They are charming stories, particularly because they are a wise and generous mixture of Mr Parker Pyne's own observations about human nature – a statistician, he has concluded that there is a limited number of identifiable ways in which people can be unhappy – and Agatha's own observations and preoccupations – her knowledge of the desire for adventure, her interest in marital jealousy, her understanding (as in 'The Case of the Rich Woman') of the glorious freedom loss of memory affords. Agatha was fond of Parker Pyne, whom she saw as a more realistic figure than, say, Poirot: 'Much more suitable for an American radio series,' she was to tell her agent in 1947. (The larger than life creation of Poirot nonetheless smothered Parker Pyne and the series appeared as 'Starring Hercule Poirot' instead.)

The last book Agatha wrote in 1933 was *Unfinished Portrait*, the novel in which two of the principal characters, Celia and Dermot, derive from Agatha herself and from Archie. Agatha was now sufficiently secure to be able to reflect more calmly on her first marriage; in 1930, on what had until now been a sad anniversary, she had written a thoughtful letter to Max, thanking him for all he had restored to her. Not that she discussed even with her closest friends the end of her first marriage, her illness and recovery. The shock had gone too deep. In any case, it was a private matter and talking about it would have been invading Archie's confidence as much as her own. Moreover, such matters were probably best not dissected in chat; Agatha was one of a generation that knew the value of discreet silence. It is interesting that she did allude to and analyse her private experience in her books, as if there she could not keep from returning to something so important. By building her recollections of that terrible time into other characters and other stories, she avoided exposing herself, except on her own terms. 'Mary Westmacott' was further protection; indeed, her contract with Collins for this and two other novels, drawn up in early 1934, provided yet another disguise, for it is between her publisher and 'Nathaniel Miller', amended before signature to 'Daniel Miller'.

The excavations at Arpachiyah were the last that Max was to conduct in Iraq for many years. There was an increasingly nationalistic mood in the country, whose manifestations had included worrying disputes and delays over the division of the finds between the Iraqi Government and the expedition. Max thought it prudent to move on. He and Agatha accordingly spent the last two months of 1934 in Syria, with the blessing of the British School of Archaeology in Iraq, surveying the Habur Valley and examining a number of mounds, or 'tells', which might be suitable for excavation. They were assisted by a young architect called Robin Macartney, shy and silent but conscientious. As well as being a skilled draughtsman, he was a clever painter. Two of his water-colours of the desert, its sinuous curves painted with firm lines and delicate colours, hung in Agatha's house to the end of her life. She was always entranced by the desert's clear air and cool colours and when she returned to wintry London one year she asked Marion Mackintosh, one of her more artistic friends, to make her a pair of lounging pyjamas, the trousers apricot and the jacket blue, as a reminder of the desert sand and sky. (The effort was not wholly successful, since crêpe de chine tended to slither off Agatha's sloping shoulders.)

Max and Agatha spent several weeks in Beirut, preparing for the expedition. During that time and later, when they had established their base camp, Agatha drafted and typed her books, three in 1934. One was *Death in the Clouds*, in which she used another 'closed circle' by having a passenger murdered during a flight from Le Bourget to Croydon. Agatha's joke about dutiful Englishmen who abandon sick wives was not the only entertainment she and Max had from this book, for it also reflects a private joke they shared about the deficiencies of the airline services that were just being established. Agatha herself had felt little confidence in them since a first lamentable encounter with Imperial Airways in 1930. 'I suppose all airlines are amateurish,' she wrote resignedly to Max, 'they've not had time to become professional yet.' She herself made a rare slip in this book for, as a reader pointed out, the blowpipe featured in the plot was too long to fit into an aeroplane of the type she described, let alone be used. The two other novels Agatha wrote that year, for publication in 1935, were *Three Act Tragedy*, in which Mr Satterthwaite reappeared, and *The ABC Murders*, where Hercule Poirot investigated a series of crimes in which a copy of the 'ABC' railway timetable was prominently displayed. This was an ingenious novel, cleverly misleading. It was later made into a film, retitled *The Alphabet Murders* so that the public would not shun the chain of ABC cinemas that showed it.

As well as writing and helping Max, Agatha busied herself with friends and houses. Another acquisition was 48 Sheffield Terrace, a house of large, well-proportioned rooms, on Campden Hill. There was enough space for Max to have a library, with a large table on which he could spread bits of pottery, and for Agatha to enjoy for the first and last time in her life a room of her own for working and retiring. Here she had 'a large firm table', an upright chair for typing, an armchair and sofa, a Steinway grand piano, and nothing else. In December 1934 she had also bought a house in the country, for Ashfield was now chiefly used during Rosalind's holidays, Torquay being too far from London to be reached easily at weekends. As Max was particularly fond of Oxford, he and Agatha searched that part of the Thames Valley, looking for a small country cottage but eventually finding Winterbrook House at Wallingford. It was a Queen Anne house, close to the road – then much quieter than today – but shielded from it by slightly sinister holly trees. The back of the house was the most attractive part, for the drawing-room window looked out on to the garden and a meadow and down to the river bank. In the middle of a field, soon reclaimed as part of the lawn, was a large cedar, beneath which Agatha immediately decided they would take their tea on summer afternoons. In fact, so naturally did the house give on to the garden that Agatha and her visitors tended always to drift outside after meals on fine days, carrying their cups. Winterbrook House was large, with three bedrooms and three good sitting-rooms. Agatha decorated the drawing-room in her favourite pale mauve, with white woodwork and curtains, the furniture covered in white quilted chintz. The triumph of the house was Max's library, a room he enlarged to double its original length, from which he could look down the river. A walled kitchen garden was Agatha's paradise; she occasionally lent the house to friends but *never* in the soft fruit season.

The Thames Valley is cold and damp in winter, particularly in January and February, but these were the months when the Mallowans were in the East. In 1935 they began to dig at Chagar Bazar, a relatively convenient site, since only forty kilometres to the north was a town with shops, a bank and a post office. At first they rented a spacious mud-brick house, overrun by mice, which Agatha loathed, until they acquired an intelligent cat. They then moved to a house built at the site itself. During that first season their staff consisted of Robin Macartney and Richard Barnett, with 140 or so labourers, mostly Arabs and Kurds, and, as Max described them, 'a sprinkling of Yezidis, the mild devil-worshippers from the Jebel Sinjar, and a few odd Christians'. Some of the best workers were Turks, who had smuggled themselves across the frontier into this unruly part of Syria, controlled at that time by French military officers. Agatha and Max spent the 1935 and 1936 seasons at Chagar Bazar. Agatha found camp life agreeable. She liked its simplicity, the open air, the expedition's intimacy. Not that the Mallowans' camps were without comforts. Agatha organised the supply of much of the furniture and provisions, making sure that fresh local produce (including cream from water buffalo) was used wherever possible, augmented by tinned and dried goods brought from England. The workmen regarded her as a mother and a queen, and she and the cook shared their mysteries. By now Agatha had also learned a good deal of archaeology. Her particular, and gentle, contribution was to remove the dirt and dust from fragments of pottery with her favourite tools, orange sticks and face-cream.

Max's reputation was growing. He was efficient in publishing his reports and had a reputation for hard work and the archaeologist's necessary lucky instinct. He continued to gain confidence and talked entertainingly about his work. This was partly because he was older – he was now in his early thirties – and partly, as their friends remarked, because of Agatha's influence. She liked the fact that her husband was an archaeologist, half-scientist, half-historian, in a profession both practical and scholarly. (What she did not like, and never said, was that one of the pleasures of being married to an archaeologist was that, the older you became, the more interesting you were to him. It was a quip which first appeared in the *Gothenburg Trade and Shipping Journal*, and followed Agatha ever after.)

The Mallowans' camps were known to be among the most serene in the Near East. Agatha was no Katharine but she had not forgotten her. In 1935, egged on by her old friend Archie Whitburn, Woolley's architect, she drew up the outline of a detective story in which a Katharine-like figure was to feature, *Murder in Mesopotamia*. The first three names on the list in her draft are old acquaintances: 'Woolleys, C.T.s, Father Burrows' (the Campbell Thompsons and the epigraphist at Ur). She developed two or three possible plots for *Murder in Mesopotamia*, clarifying her thoughts with a sketch map of the expedition house and a timetable of its occupants' movements, and thinking aloud about various devices: 'Can we work in the window idea?' she asked herself. The expedition house resembled their quarters at Chagar

Bazar but the mood was that of Ur. Her notes began: 'The wife
– very queer – (? Is she being doped against her own knowledge)
– atmosphere gradually develops in intensity – a bomb may ex-
plode any minute. . . .' Agatha mischievously dedicated the novel
to 'my many archaeological friends in Iraq and Syria'; one or
two were annoyed, whether because they believed they figured in
its pages or because they did not was never entirely clear. Robin
Macartney designed a splendid cover for the Crime Club edition,
with a bearded sage on horseback gazing into a deep pit cut into
land curving alongside the river, and labourers hacking and sifting the soil from an excavation like a tomb.

In her second book of 1935, *Cards on the Table*, Agatha enjoyed a joke against herself in her role of crime novelist. Mrs
Ariadne Oliver, who had first appeared in an earlier short story
as an assistant to Mr Parker Pyne, shared some of Agatha's own
characteristics and habits, in particular her taste for eating apples
in the bath. *Cards on the Table* is about a murder during a bridge
party, a game of bridge being a typical nineteen-thirties pastime,
friendly with a touch of daring (rather like a séance), riveting for
those who were engaged in it and dull for those who were not,
apt to degenerate into a quarrel. Agatha herself often played
bridge after dinner. She enjoyed cards and, when alone with Max,
played Poker Patience with him. The bridge game provided her
with another 'closed circle' within which a crime might be committed and investigated, the very setting to which Agatha had
referred in Chapter Three of *The ABC Murders*. It was a circle in
another sense, too, for into *Cards on the Table* Agatha brought
four familiar characters. As well as Mrs Oliver and Poirot, there
was Superintendent Battle (from *Chimneys* and *Seven Dials*) and
Colonel Race (from *The Man in the Brown Suit*). There were four
suspects only; as Agatha explained in a preface, any of them,
given the right circumstances, might have committed the crime.

In one of the books Agatha wrote during the following year,
1936, was a portrait even more firmly drawn from life – of Peter,
who appeared in *Dumb Witness* as Bob, Miss Arundell's wire-
haired terrier. There is something, too, of Wallingford about
Market Basing, a location Agatha found so evocative that she
considered using it for another plot. Set, however, not in a small
market town but in 'No. 14 Bardsley Gardens Mews', that draft
became the title story in the collection *Murder in the Mews*, also
finished in 1936. 'A case of death, apparently murder', ran her
notes; 'pistol in *right* hand (or taken away) windows shut but the

smell of smoke in room'. The Crime Club edition of this book again carried one of Macartney's striking covers, an arch framing the Mews, all the windows dark but one, and the headlamps of a black saloon, with curving mudguards and bumpers, approaching over the cobbles.

Agatha's other novel for 1936 was *Death on the Nile*. Its origins were complicated. In 1933 she had journeyed up the river with Max and Rosalind and the following year had published in the Parker Pyne collection a short story, 'Death on the Nile', describing a poisoning aboard a Nile steamer. During their own voyage, Agatha and Rosalind had speculated about their fellow-passengers, particularly one, a sadistic, domineering woman, on whom Agatha based the character of 'Mrs Boynton', a former prison wardress. These thoughts Agatha first used in a play, *Moon of the Nile*, which she then put aside in favour of a detective novel, also called *Death on the Nile* but different from the earlier short story. The first out-line of this book introduced 'Mrs Boynton' and her cowed but resentful family but Agatha soon dismissed them. She did, however, draw on recollections of her own journey, particularly of the arrangement of the boat. The topography of the *S.S. Karnak* is crucial to the plot; indeed, when a film was made in 1978, the producer had difficulty in finding a steamer of the requisite size and lay-out. *Death on the Nile* was a success and the cover, too, (illustrated opposite pp. 204/205) one of Macartney's best.

Agatha was at this time deeply interested in Egypt and its history. In the ancient Egyptian religion she found something sinister – a strange mixture of human and animal in the deities, an emphasis on death and the ritual surrounding it – but also reassuring, the 'comfortable structure', as she called it, of the 'old gods'. She had also been thinking about parallels between the past and present, the similarity of relations between old and young, male and female, the conflict between good and evil that might be found anywhere at any time. She enjoyed playing with 'nebulous ideas': the manner in which new intellectual and aesthetic fashions took root, the tension between 'warmongers', seeking to defend the fabric of the state, and 'appeasers', believing there were other routes to peace and security, the differences between those who saw the value of system and hierarchy and those who emphasised the importance of change and idiosyncrasy. Agatha was not a rigorous thinker; she argued about these questions with Max but her ideas really surfaced only in her books, as themes and in talk between her characters. She was inclined to laugh at ideologues who merely discussed the path to progress: *Death on the Nile* is only one of her books in which the exponent of some fashionable creed is gently ridiculed.

She nonetheless admired idealists and tried to put some of their beliefs into practice. In a three-act play she wrote in 1937, *Akhnaton*, she made Akhnaton, King Amenhotep IV, a sympathetic figure, whose fall is inevitable but tragic. In his story it was the characters who first attracted Agatha's attention – the king himself; Horenheb, the faithful soldier who betrays his master for a higher cause; Queen Tyi, Akhnaton's mother; his Queen, Nefertiti; Tutankhaton, who promises to restore the old gods and take the throne from Akhnaton; and the High Priest. Agatha was clear about the dramatic side of things – 'Act I, Scene I: Amenhotep the Magnificent is near death. The King of Mitanni sends the image of Ishtar of Nineveh to Egypt (second time such a procedure had happened)' but shaky on the historical side: 'when was first time?' she scribbled in the margin. She was pleased with the play, though it was too difficult and expensive to stage.

In the spring of 1937 Agatha and Max began excavating Tell Brak, a great mound he had resolved to explore when he had first seen it years before. It was some twenty miles from Chagar Bazar, where there was still much digging to do. The Mallowans divided their efforts between the two sites, assisted by their foreman Hamoudi, a defector from Woolley's team, and a group of industrious young people: Guilford Bell, nephew of Agatha's Australian friend Aileen; an ex-Colonel from the Indian Army, Colonel Burn; Louis Osman, known by the name with which he had once wonderingly referred to the Tells, 'Bumps'; and Rosalind, on her first expedition. She took over some of the drawing, as Agatha's artistry had finally been acknowledged to be abysmal. Rosalind was deeply impressed by Max's organisation of the dig. She had not known that he was capable of rising so early and working so rigorously out of doors, and she admired his firm but paternal handling of the labourers. The young men were excellent company for Rosalind; Agatha, too, was interested and encouraging at an important time in their careers. She later gave an affectionate picture of this group in *Come, Tell Me How You Live* and always spoke proudly of their subsequent success, for Louis Osman was to distinguish himself as a craftsman in gold and silver, Guilford as the architect of many original houses, Macartney as a painter, John Rose, another of the Mallowans' architects in Syria, for rebuilding Castries in St Lucia, and Ian Threlfall, a gifted archaeologist, as a leading barrister. All became and remained friends, regularly visiting Greenway and Winterbrook (where 'Bumps' built Agatha a squash court). John Rose entertained Agatha and Max in Barbados, while Guilford made regular pilgrimages from Australia.

Agatha did not neglect her writing while she was in Syria. As usual, she took with her an old exercise book or two, and in one, feelingly labelled, 'Hôtel de l'Expédition, Chagar Bazar', outlined various ideas for that season's writing. The second idea on her list quickly developed into a book, a thought that began with a title, 'Rose Red Murder', or 'Rose Red Death'.

This became *Appointment with Death*, a mystery that unfolded at Petra, which Agatha and Max had visited on one of their journeys home. From the first Agatha had conceived the central figure, and victim, as a greedy, tyrannical matriarch; the location of the crime and the fact that the victim, Mrs Boyton, was the former prison wardress dropped from the first draft of *Death on the Nile* were the two points from which she began. They were naturally associated, for Agatha had retained from her visit not just the memory of Petra's rose-red walls but of the city's confinement within the narrow gorge. Agatha also wanted for her story a forceful woman Member of Parliament, 'given to good works etc'. This was 'Lady Copeman', then 'Lady Bridgeman' and, eventually, 'Lady Westholme', modelled not, as some have suggested, on Lady Astor MP, but on the 'excessively fierce-looking Miss Wilbraham', whom Agatha had encountered leading a party of Anglo-Catholic ladies to Iraq in the spring of 1930.

Lady Westholme's companion, Miss Pierce, bore some resemblance to Miss Wilbraham's second-in-command. Agatha had been particularly struck by Miss Wilbraham's enormous topee, a memory which invaded the early planning of 'the Petra Murder'. Agatha's notes explore two ideas simultaneously: one that the murderer should wear a distinctive hat, and the other that the death should be induced by means of an injection. Ever-fertile, she proceeded to play with variations on these themes. The injection idea split into two more: 'sodium citrate injected in blood before death. Blood keeps liquid'; 'Diabetes gives p.m. [post mortem] stiffening at once. (Clue, sugar in pocket).' The hat idea produced complex ramifications: ' "Same man, different hat", in this case, "Different man, same hat" '; 'Y suddenly sees dead man. ... It's Mr X.... Meets Z.... Kills him and lays him down.

... Conceal's X's body in cave. ... *Hats*, Y wears topee. ... Z wears felt hat.... X wears topee. ... Who are Y, X and Z? Is Z plastic surgeon? Is Y former patient? *Is X just a man of the requisite size?* Topee may be important thing in this kind of country?' At this point Agatha discarded the entire topee idea and started again with a substantially different plot: 'Method of death. Camera? Husband guilty. He is clever with faking things. Arranges a Brownie camera – takes it out – at right moment substitutes it for Mrs P.'s. She lies dead. They rush to her. He drops her camera – picks up his. *Later*, child's camera is missing OR,' Agatha wrote, pulling herself together, 'insulin idea.' Mrs Boynton was eventually killed with a hypodermic syringe – but Miss Wilbraham's topee was not completely discarded. The X, Y, Z plot appeared three years later in *Evil Under the Sun*, amalgamated with some thoughts inspired by Punkie's wig.

Nor was the idea that a murderer might use sodium citrate entirely set aside. In another notebook (beginning with a list of things to bring to London: 'Flower pictures. ... Clothes for Collins'), Agatha headed a page with another working title, 'Who Would Have Thought?', the words of Lady Macbeth: 'Who would have thought the old man to have so much blood in him?' The swift notes that follow constituted an outline for *Hercule Poirot's Christmas*. It was not just with murderous devices that Agatha was economical, taking a left-over fragment of a possible plot from one setting for use elsewhere. Her sketch for this latest book shows how resourceful she had grown at drawing on moods and scenes stored in her memory. Gorston Hall is a little like Abney, even if the family reunion is less festive than Agatha's Christmases in Cheshire; the cerulean skies, blue convolvulus and hedges of plumbago for which Stephen Farr is homesick are taken from Agatha's recollections of South Africa. In planning the shape of her books, too, she was learning stylistic tricks from past experience. Her suggestions to herself for this book began with the notion of 'Short Bits like Death on the Nile?'

A similar scene of a traveller returning to London from the tropics opened *Murder is Easy*, on which Agatha worked in the following year, 1938, while the expedition finished its work at Chagar Bazar and Tell Brak. In the autumn, anticipating trouble from some local Sheikhs determined to persuade the Mallowans' workmen to strike, they moved a hundred miles west to the marshy country of the Balikh Valley, where, with the help of John Rose, they quickly examined five mounds before the winter rains

began. Max had continued to spend the months between digging
seasons writing his account of their procedures and discoveries;
Agatha now decided that she might tell the story of the expedition
from her own perspective. In July 1938 she suggested this to
Edmund Cork, proposing a book that would 'Roughly ... deal
with life on the dig. Not at all serious or archaeological.' Though
Cork encouraged Agatha to start, she did not in fact begin until
the nineteen-forties. But already she was keeping voluminous
notes to draw upon – occasional anecdotes, a long account of
what she learned of devil-worship, sections of diary:

> ... Dinner with the Hudsons – they had *real* plumbing. Most enjoy-
> able. Accounts by the Hudsons why the French differ utterly – as to
> weather – malaria – and drinking water. Started the ABC Murders
> .... 'Le camping' – rose at dawn. Cold sausages but hot tea.... Got
> back in the lorry – very perilous as none of the doors are reliable.

It was nearly ten years since Agatha had made her first visit to
a dig and five since she had begun to come out on expeditions
with Max. This had been a happy time, a regular annual cycle of
summers at Ashfield with Rosalind, Christmas at Abney, the late
autumn and spring in the desert and the rest of the year in
London and Wallingford. As a rule she had produced two or
three books a year, Edmund Cork managing the complicated
details of contracts, serial rights, translations and so on, and
Harold Ober, his American associate, looking after her interests
in the United States. They were smooth and even years, one book
appearing after another in a flow that, as far as anyone could
tell, would continue uninterrupted. (As Max once instructed a
younger colleague, 'There are two sorts of people in the world,
ladies and gentlemen, and both work till they drop.') It was
therefore appropriate that in mid-1938 Agatha, now in her late
forties, should wish to draw these years together by writing about
her expeditions with Max in the Near East.

   In some ways Agatha seemed to be drifting on a warm and
comfortable tide, but there were signs of change in the familiar
pattern of her life. For one thing, Rosalind was now grown up.
Caledonia had been stimulating – like Archie, she was head of
the school – but at Benenden she was bored. Though she did not
want to go on to university, her headmistress insisted that she
take her School Certificate, in which she did well, before leaving
just before her seventeenth birthday. After an exhaustive search
she was installed in Switzerland at a *pension* in Gstaad, which she

disliked intensely. Rescued, she went to a *pension* at Château d'Oex at which she learnt no French. Agatha then sent her to a family in Paris, who spoke no English, so that Rosalind was obliged to learn the French language, habits and history, much as her mother had done, by experience. This was followed by several months with another family near Munich, before she came home to be launched officially into the world with a London 'season'. Agatha was fortunately spared the demands of organising her daughter's attendance at luncheons, tea parties, dinners and dances, managing her wardrobe and scrutinising her friends, for Rosalind shared her season with another debutante, Susan North, whose mother supervised them both. Agatha did, however, scribble an idea in her notebook: 'Debutante teas etc. Mothers killed off in rapid succession.' Agatha had not herself been presented as a girl, her own season being spent quietly in Cairo, and now, having been divorced, she could not present her daughter at Court. Rosalind, in ostrich feathers and train, was therefore taken to the Palace by their friends the Mackintoshes. Ernest Mackintosh, who had been a companion of Monty's and had danced with Madge at balls in Torquay, was now Director of the Science Museum in London and the families saw a great deal of each other. Agatha and Marion Mackintosh would go to matinees, without the men, who, according to Max, found many of the plays 'unsettling'.

Mrs North also became a good friend, with whom Agatha went to exhibitions, opera and the ballet. Allen Lane was another. Agatha had first met him when she called at The Bodley Head to protest to his uncle, John Lane, about the jacket for *Murder on the Links*. In 1935, when Allen, now chairman of the firm, started a series of sixpenny paperbacks, Agatha was among the first to offer her own work to Penguin Books, despite her break with The Bodley Head, and Max edited the archaeological series. Allen Lane's venture was successful – indeed, he was able to wind up his uncle's firm – and he thanked Agatha for her support by giving financial help, as well as an annual Stilton, to Max's expeditions.

Rosalind's season was a success. She was tall, good-looking and forthright. It was difficult to settle on what she and Susan would now do with themselves. Their first idea was, as they put it, 'to take up photography'. When Agatha realised that they meant that their pictures should be taken, in bathing dresses, for advertisements, she was horrified, persuading them instead to take photography classes. As she enquired about courses, however, she became so interested that she booked for herself instead, assiduously practising taking pictures of buckets and spades, flower-pots and balls of string, for she thought her new skills would be useful on the dig. Artistically placed shadows were the vogue but, when Agatha showed her efforts to Max, he thoroughly disapproved. He wanted objects shown clearly, with a scale rod in each picture to indicate their size. Agatha revised her technique for archaeological purposes but her experiments with camera angles and coloured filters provided ideas for her plotting books.

Meanwhile the question of Rosalind's future was settled, for the time being. Mrs North offered to take her and Susan to South Africa, to visit her son, who was at Simonstown with the Navy; Rosalind's photograph album did, after all, display fetching pictures of the two women in bathing dresses, sunning themselves on the ship's deck, but for private enjoyment only.

Agatha had never felt herself constrained by Rosalind, leaving her with Clara during the Empire tour and afterwards regularly consigning her to Punkie's and Carlo's care. Agatha loved her daughter and was proud of her but it was not the demanding close relationship she had had with Clara. Those who knew Agatha and her daughter offered various explanations, some believing that Agatha's memories of happiness with Archie and the later pain of her first marriage had put a gap between her and Rosalind, others suggesting that Agatha felt guilty for divorcing Archie and placing Rosalind in a position where her loyalties would be torn and her childhood complicated. At any rate, both Agatha and Rosalind were strong characters; each cared for the other, in turn, without smothering her or losing too much independence. So it was not that the late nineteen-thirties brought Agatha freedom from maternal duties, for she had never regarded them as fetters; more, that the shape of her year was now no longer influenced by the timetable of Rosalind's school and holidays.

There had been another break with the past. Ashfield, to which Agatha had so relentlessly clung after her father's death and again after Clara's, was no longer a peaceful retreat. Torquay was spreading, its lanes and fields swallowed by small houses, and the large villas of Agatha's childhood had been broken up, converted into nursing homes or demolished. When she and Max had bought Winterbrook, it was, she said, 'Max's house'; Ashfield she regarded as hers, and, I think, Rosalind's. Agatha thought, too, that Max had never liked Ashfield, as being part of her life before their marriage. Rosalind's childhood was over – and Agatha herself, as much as Ashfield, had greatly changed. Her childhood there had shaped her but so, and more immediately, had her work and marriage to Max. She was free to leave Ashfield behind.

Doing so was easier because she had fallen for a large Georgian house, built in the late seventeen-eighties in thirty acres of woodland on the bank of the Dart, some ten miles from Torquay. This was Greenway House. It looked down the estuary towards Dartmouth.

Agatha bought Greenway in October 1938 for £6000. The purchase was arranged by her solicitor in Torquay, whose father had looked after Clara's and Frederick's affairs; it was not easy to raise the money, even with the sale of Ashfield, but somehow she managed it. Agatha showed the house to Guilford Bell and gave him one of his first major commissions; he boldly recommended that she pull half the existing house to the ground. She did – removing among various unsightly additions a large billiards room. Guilford tidied up the place, bringing back its lovely proportions, added a cloakroom with a round window, and helped Agatha instal several bathrooms. On one side of a wide pillared porch was an airy morning-room, giving on to a drawing-room with a curved window and steps to the garden, on the other the library, light and square, and next to that a rectangular dining-room, with two distinctive curved mahogany doors. A square hall led to the back doors and to kitchens, sculleries and pantries. A narrow hall connected the front porch to the stairs, wide and easy. There were five main rooms on the first floor; one became a study, one a dressing-room for Agatha and another one for Max, for Agatha and the fourth, at the front of the house, the bedroom she shared with Max, her large bed in the middle of the room and his smaller one at the side. There was a fifth bedroom on that floor, the rest being taken up by bathrooms and a room for keeping medicines and arranging flowers. The top floor had a big bedsitting-room for Rosalind, whose windows overlooked the river and the woods, a double room and three smaller rooms with two bathrooms, and various deep cupboards and storage places. At the back of the house, above the kitchen quarters, was a warren of rooms for staff. Agatha was a splendid client, interested but trusting, and not unexpectedly she took special care over the plumbing arrangements. 'I want to come with you, Guilford,' she said, before one expedition to choose basins, baths and lavatories, 'I want a big bath and I need a ledge because I like to eat apples.' To London they went, whereupon Agatha stepped into the showroom window and the bath displayed there, drawing an admiring crowd, for she insisted she could not possibly choose a bath unless she sat in it first.

The choice of paint and fabrics was Agatha's and she planned what was to be done with the garden. It had been at one time extremely beautiful. A house had stood here in the sixteenth century and originally the estate had been parkland almost to the river banks. In the late eighteen-sixties new trees were added and in the early years of the twentieth century another owner continued the planting. A garden magazine for 1899 considered the Liriodendron, or tulip tree, growing near the house, to be one of the finest specimens in the country. Early in the First World War the house passed to Charles Williams and his wife, both from famous West Country gardening families, and for the next twenty years there was much new planting, particularly of rhododendrons, magnolias, rare trees and unusual shrubs. In 1937 the house was sold to the father of a childhood friend of Agatha's, Sir Alfred Goodson. The Goodsons did not live at Greenway and by the time Agatha bought it the gardens were in disarray. She set about planning their replanting; some of her outlines for plots are interrupted by lists of roses and bulbs.

Surprises lay among the tangled paths: a landing-place for boats, with a covered swimming-pool for decent but spooky bathing, inside what now became a boathouse; a battery, with ancient mortars, at the spot where Sir Walter Raleigh was reputed to have landed, bringing the first tobacco and potatoes from the New World. There were extensive kitchen gardens, stables and a grass tennis court. Under a nearby farm ran the tunnel of the main London to Dartmouth railway line.

Devonshire was the scene for the other full-length novel Agatha wrote in 1938, *Ten Little Niggers*, whose setting 'Nigger Island' was modelled on Burgh Island off the coast at Kingsbridge. The form of the story is like Haydn's 'Farewell' Symphony, in which different sections of the orchestra gradually steal away at the end. Agatha took her title from the children's chant – where one by one, each of ten small boys disappears until none is left. The words of the song – which is different in the United States – and its anachronistic idiom were to give Agatha's publishers interminable trouble when the book came to be published in America and in later British editions.

Agatha at the time of her disappearance,
leaving the hotel in Harrogate.

Four jackets from Agatha's detective stories;
the top two are by Robin Macartney
and the bottom right by Tom Adams.

Agatha's artistically photographed shadows.

Agatha's house in Baghdad.

Excavating at Nimrud.

Rosalind, Mathew, Agatha and Oliver Gurney
picnicking on Dartmoor in 1948, with animals
and Agatha's bottle of Pure Water.

Another work Agatha completed in 1938 was set nearer Green-way, the title story in *The Regatta Mystery* (a collection published in the United States in 1939), in which Hercule Poirot discovers the perpetrator of a robbery at 'The Royal George in Dartmouth Harbour'. Parker Pyne appeared again in this volume, too, as did Miss Marple, telling a story whose solution depended as always on her 'special knowledge', in this case what Agatha had noted years before as 'Housemaid Idea': 'One of party dressed as house-maid – so no one ever looks at her. *Or* man has an idea he has seen the housemaid before.' (In another set of notes she described it as 'G.K.C. Idea', for Chesterton's story *The Invisible Man* turns on the fact that no one thinks it worthwhile to mention the postman's visit to the scene of a crime.) Agatha's device has since been stupendously misunderstood, for some critics have alleged that it indicated lamentable arrogance, a disposition to regard servants as automata, not individuals. This misses the point en-tirely. Agatha (and her creation Miss Marple) was thoroughly familiar with the fact that gardeners, cooks and parlourmaids – and Colonels, vicars, doctors and maiden ladies – are each a prey to special obsessions, adopt idiosyncratic habits of speech and dress and follow an eccentric personal routine. She also knew how easily human beings fall into a professional role, performing certain tasks as they have been trained to do, assuming an appro-priate style, speech and demeanour: doctors behaving in a doctor-like manner, fishmongers as fishmongers are expected to do, detectives and policemen – and archaeologists and lady crime novelists – each with their *déformation professionelle*. Uniforms help, encouraging the wearer to behave aptly, evoking certain expectations in onlookers and reinforcing these effects by induc-ing the wearer to conform to them.

This was the trick Agatha's criminals were playing. Dressing up as a housemaid was not a way of being anonymous, but of becoming a housemaid – and, in a later development of this device, Agatha noted the idea that the same trick might be played by a fake policeman. A housemaid is remembered as a house-maid, not as a murderer. But, Agatha's critics complain, why does she believe 'no one ever looks at a housemaid?' The answer is that, unless there is exceptional cause, one doesn't, while the housemaid is carrying out her professional duties. Far from being inconsiderate, it is respectful to allow the housemaid – or the postman, waiter, or any professional person – to continue with whatever service she is performing without intruding into her personal affairs. That is partly why she wears a uniform, as a sign saying 'busy', and why it is so convenient for a criminal to borrow it.

Agatha would have been amazed at the need for an explanation. Her attitude had less to do with the class and background from which she came or with the age in which she lived than with common sense. Further, readers know that she uses such a device in many of her books. Her 'stock' characters – as she sets them out in her lists: 'twittery companion', 'prim, irritable, respectable gentleman', even 'BBC type' – are designed not only to carry the story but to fox the reader, whom she knows will have certain expectations and will thus be more easily deluded into overlooking the clues that eventually reveal the criminal beneath the camouflage.

Agatha also wrote most of another detective story, *Sad Cypress*, in 1938, finishing it in July. Her American publishers were uneasy about the title, feeling that readers might confuse the cypress tree with the island of Cyprus. Agatha suggested as an alternative 'I am Slain', from the same song in *Twelfth Night* that gave her the first title; in the end the Americans kept the original. Agatha later told Francis Wyndham, in an interview for the *Sunday Times* in 1966, that she subsequently realised that *Sad Cypress* was spoilt by having Poirot in it. By the end of the 'thirties she was occasionally irritated because Poirot was such a favourite of her readers and publishers – particularly of the American magazine publishers at *Collier's* and the *Saturday Evening Post*, which took most of her work and paid high prices. 'Poirot is rather insufferable,' she wrote to Cork. 'Most public men are who have lived too long. But none of them like retiring! So I am afraid Poirot won't either – certainly not while he is my chief source of income.' For, surprising though it may seem (in 1938, for instance, her earnings from Collins alone came to nearly £2500), Agatha was again anxious about money. Her worries, moreover, had not come singly.

17

'Things all seem to come at once . . .'

The erosion of Agatha's idyll began in the summer of 1938. Faithful Peter died and, though Cork offered to send her a dog, Agatha felt that for the time being she 'could not bear to have another'. The next intimation of trouble came at almost the same time, in a letter from Cork announcing that the American revenue authorities were asking such detailed questions about her financial affairs that his New York counterpart, Harold Ober, had engaged a prominent tax lawyer, Howard E. Reinheimer, 'who deals with the affairs of many important authors', to handle their inquiries on Agatha's behalf. Mr Reinheimer's work was to occupy him for the next decade. As far as Agatha was concerned, there was nothing she could do but wait – and work. After their last efforts in the Balikh Valley in the autumn of 1938, she and Max did not go abroad again, for by the spring of 1939 the European political situation was so delicate that it was unwise to travel, let alone dig in the Near East territories, each with its web of relations with different European powers. Max also refused an invitation to attend, with Agatha, the Archaeological Congress in Berlin in late August, sensibly, for by September, after months of holding back, Britain was at war with Hitler.

The Mallowans – and Mrs North, who was staying at Greenway – heard the Prime Minister's statement on the wireless in the kitchen. Agatha calmly continued mixing a salad. Even for those who, like her, were uninterested in the intricacies of world politics, the announcement was no surprise, although, as she later wrote in her *Autobiography*, after Chamberlain's reassurances, 'we had thought ... "Peace in our time" ... might be the truth.' War does not, in any case, make domestic tasks less pressing, as Agatha knew, for her perspective was essentially mundane. As she had struggled through the First World War, so she would battle in the Second. She worried about the danger for people she loved, celebrated and lamented national victories and defeats, made her own contribution in her hospital work, but her pre-occupations and horizons were limited. She simply carried on.

Max and Agatha had both spent the summer in Devon, he writing up his latest work and she busy with *Sad Cypress*, a collection of short stories and another book. The short stories were the twelve *Labours of Hercules*, delivered to Cork at intervals during 1939 for publication in the *Strand* magazine. They were funny, clever stories (Poirot's exploration of a nightclub called 'Hell', whose stairs are paved with good intentions, is especially comic) and she seems to have had little trouble with them – until, that is, they were published as a collection in 1947, when there was a blast to Cork about the cover design Collins proposed for the book: 'I cannot describe to you the rough for the wrapper ...', she wrote. 'It suggests Poirot going naked to the bath!!! All sorts of obscene suggestions are being made by my family. I have, I hope, been tactful but firm. Put statuary on the cover but make it clear it IS statuary – not Poirot gone peculiar in Hyde Park!!!'

Over the years Collins became accustomed to such explosions. Another came at the end of the summer of 1939 when Agatha learnt that an item in the forthcoming *Crime Club News* was about to summarise the entire plot of *Ten Little Niggers*. Billy Collins reinforced his apologies with small gifts; on this occasion he sent Agatha copies of G.D.H. and Margaret Cole's latest detective story, the new Rex Stout, and an advance copy of the Book Society Choice *Love in the Sun*, promising, too, some of Collins's 'good Autumn books'.

So sustained and mollified, Agatha and Max stayed on for the winter at Greenway. 'Dear W.A.R.', as Agatha called Billy Collins in her happier letters, was always attentive, offering theatre tickets, seats for Wimbledon, lunches and dinners, more books from Collins's lists. 'May I be greedy?' Agatha replied. 'It's rather like a desert island here. We don't drive in the blackout and so the evenings are lonely.' Those she asked for in November 1939 were *Paderewski*, *Gardens of England*, *Brief Return*, *The Dark Star*, *Pamela* and *Dismembered Masterpieces*, all but the last two, not yet published, sent within the week.

As well as the stories in the *The Labours of Hercules* and *Sad Cypress*, in 1939 Agatha also completed *One, Two, Buckle My Shoe*, (published in America as *The Patriotic Murders*). This began with Hercule Poirot's paying a visit to a dentist, who later that day appeared to have shot himself. She had been tinkering with 'Dentist ideas' for some time; the thought had surfaced, for instance, when she was considering the outline of *The ABC Murders* and her notes briefly veered off into thinking about a crime committed by 'legless man – sometimes tall, sometimes short. Ditto – with *teeth* projecting and discoloured, or white and even.' In 1939 she asked Carlo and Mary Smith for an introduction to their dentist in Welbeck Street (where her own dentist also practised). She did not need treatment, she said, but Carlo explained to her dentist that Miss Christie wished to pay him 'a normal fee', ask a few questions and examine his surgery. The receptionist never forgot the sight of her employer showing Agatha the poison cabinet, as she inquired about methods and types of injection. And in the next draft Agatha was off ... 'HP in dentist's chair – latter talks while drilling – Points (i) Never forget a face ...'

As soon as war was declared, Max had applied to join the services. This proved difficult. Unsoldierly men of thirty-five were not then being recruited and the authorities also regarded Max's father's Austrian birth as an obstacle. Nor could he obtain a post in Whitehall, which was at first so disorganised that no use could be found for a qualified Arabist. He therefore did the best he could by joining the Brixham Home Guard, sharing two rifles among ten men. In mid-1940, he found more demanding work. The town of Ercincan in Eastern Turkey had been devastated by an earthquake and British relief was swiftly organised, both for humanitarian reasons and because Britain depended for steel-making on Turkish supplies of chrome. An Anglo-Turkish Relief Committee was formed by Professor Garstang, founder of the British School of Archaeology in Ankara and a friend as well as colleague of Max, who was invited to be the Secretary. He set about organising an appeal and the distribution of relief, duties which preoccupied him until early 1941. Rosalind, meanwhile, looked for work as a land girl on a neighbouring farm in Devon and filled in forms for the Women's Auxiliary Air Force. She made herself useful as best she could and filled in more forms, this time for the ATS. At midsummer, she told Agatha she was going to be married in a few days' time to Hubert Prichard, a regular soldier in the Royal Welch Fusiliers, temporarily attached to Jack Watts's regiment in Cheshire. Hubert was often at Abney and had stayed at Greenway. Agatha insisted on coming to Denbigh, where Captain Prichard was stationed, to see her daughter married, with, as Agatha put it, 'the minimum of *fuss*'. 'All very sudden,' Agatha wrote to Billy Collins, '– but a *very* nice man. I do think they will be happy if only he comes through safely.

However, as far as I can see, any one of us may go up in smoke. Bad luck on the young folk.'

Life at Greenway was no longer undisturbed. The Macleods, doctors whom Agatha had first met in Mosul, had brought their children there, away from the east coast where the first raids were expected. Agatha also found her house 'full of soldiers practising what they would do if the Germans landed – they can hardly move they've got so much on!' Eventually the Macleod children were moved to their grandmother in Wales but, shortly after, Greenway was rented by a Mr and Mrs Arbuthnot, who arrived with two nurses and ten evacuees under five. Agatha meanwhile brought her dispensing knowledge up to date. She had lost Carlo to war work ('without Miss Fisher, I lose *everything*!!') and her gardener at Wallingford had joined the RAF. Agatha decided this was the moment to move to London to be with Max, first in a flat in Half Moon Street, the only building to survive in a road that had been bombed, then a service flat in Park Place, off St James's Street, and, at last, when the tenants of 48 Sheffield Terrace decided to leave, in their own house in Kensington. She moved most of the furniture, since there were 'bombs all round us whistling down'. She also took a course in Air Raid Precautions. In October Sheffield Terrace became very unsafe; with the help of their old friend Stephen Glanville, Max and Agatha found a flat at 22 Lawn Road, Hampstead, in the Bauhaus block where Glanville himself lived. An Egyptologist, he had known Max since 1925. He had helped Agatha with *Akhnaton* and had been greatly entertained by *Death on the Nile*. Now, a Squadron-Leader in a branch of the Air Ministry, he vigorously set about getting Max a proper wartime job.

Agatha wrote steadily on, one of her few indications of strain being a furious letter to Cork, complaining about a proposed cover design. Her protests about jackets served another purpose. Agatha's relations with Collins, orchestrated by the tactful Cork, were generally good and she liked Billy Collins, who personally supervised her dealings there. His introduction to Agatha had been surprisingly friendly, for, shortly after joining the firm, he had been sent by the chairman, his uncle Sir Godfrey, to apologise because Collins had betrayed the identity of the murderer in a cover note. Agatha was cross with Sir Godfrey for using the young man as a shield but the tactic worked; Billy disarmed her and they became friends. It was, nonetheless, difficult for Agatha, possessive about her books, to consign them to her publishers' care. Editing and proof-reading by successive hands, including Carlo's and her own, still tended to leave misprints, untidy ends and inconsistencies, noticeable in any book but particularly obvious in works so tightly plotted and so meticulously scrutinised by hawk-eyed readers. Agatha tended to keep her temper as she went through her proofs; she would make certain changes for which her publishers – especially American magazine publishers – asked, once requests had been diplomatically rephrased by Cork. If all this became too much, she exploded, her wrath generally taking the form of complaints about covers. This time is was *Sad Cypress*. 'Can't you use all your influence?' she begged Cork. 'I *do* think they might consult me first.' Cork explained that it was, alas, too late to change, 'not a question only of the artists and the blockmaker taking time but supplies of the particular paper. ... Collins thinks it would be unpatriotic to destroy 15000 copies of a jacket in these times of paper shortage.' He promised that in future all jackets would have Agatha's prior approval.

Otherwise she remained serene. A dramatised version of *Peril at End House* opened in Brighton in April, adapted by Arnold Ridley. Agatha attended some of the rehearsals and much enjoyed the experience, apart from agitation afterwards as to the whereabouts of a Spanish shawl she had lent for the production. Agatha's clothes were at this time a mixture of the well-made and respectable – dresses and suits from Harvey Nichols and Debenham and Freebody – and the joyously theatrical. She was particularly attached to this flamboyant shawl and relieved that it had not gone permanently astray. The production of *Peril at End House* sparked other interest in the theatrical possibilities of Agatha's work. There was an abortive proposal to send the play to New York and – more attractive in the long run – a request from Reginald Simpson to dramatise *Ten Little Niggers*. 'If anyone is going to dramatise it, I'll have a shot at it myself first!' Agatha told Cork, who replied cautiously: 'Generally speaking, I'm all against such valuable professional time as yours being spent on anything so speculative as the drama, but *Ten Little Niggers* is different.'

Agatha did not embark on this project straight away. The first book she delivered in 1940 was *N or M?*, in which Tommy and Tuppence Beresford expose a network of spies operating on the south coast of England. 'T & T', as Agatha's early notes called it – the title of the draft quickly became 'N or M?' or '2nd

Innings' – began with Agatha's thinking about forms of code; her exercise book was full of words made up of displaced letters, dots and dashes, and numbers replacing phrases. Then she hit upon using a nursery rhyme, in this case, 'Goosey goosey gander', as a central device. It was published in 1941.

N or M? was written quickly and confidently. Its fate in the American market infuriated Agatha. After an unusual delay, Cork heard from Harold Ober that it had been 'declined by likely buyers because it deals with the War. This is a little confusing in view of *Collier's* insistence on a war background being put into *One, Two*, but I suppose editors are afraid that such a strongly anti-Nazi story as *N or M?* would upset a substantial section of their readers.' In reply to a horrified letter from Agatha, Cork assured her that 'when the heat of the election has died down, editors might be more reasonable.' (Franklin Roosevelt had just been re-elected President, with a Democratic but strongly isolationist Congress.) It was not until September 1941 that *N or M?* was sold in America and another two months before Harold Ober could write with relief to Cork: 'We are in the War now. I wish we'd gone in before but it takes this country a good while to get started.' Agatha was upset by *Collier's* attitude, not least because *N or M?* was a patriotic gesture of her own, reflecting, too, her recent thinking and experience. Just after the destruction of Sheffield Terrace, for instance, she suggested enthusiastically to Cork: 'I think that I could do a better last chapter – up-to-date – taking place in a shelter when Tommy and Tuppence had just had their flat bombed. ...'

The rejection of *N or M?* by the American magazine market was also worrying from a financial point of view. Until the position was clearer, Agatha was being very careful about money. 'I *expect* I shall need that £1000,' she wrote to Cork, in January 1940, 'but will leave it to you to decide.' By July she was less sanguine: 'Am I going to get some money from America soon? A good deal of red ink in my bank a/c and they don't seem as fond of overdrafts as they used to be.' In August the American authorities stopped any export of her earnings until the tax matter was settled; in October the hearing was postponed. By December it appeared that anything she earned in the United States would actually be withheld to offset part of an eventual settlement. Strict exchange control regulations made this constraint even easier to enforce.

On top of this, Dodd, Mead were now seeking to draw in their horns. There is no surviving copy of Agatha's September 1940 contract with them but her 1939 contract, for *Murder is Easy*, *Ten Little Niggers* and *The Regatta Mystery*, required them to pay an advance of $5000 for each book, against a 15 per cent royalty on the first 10,000 copies, rising to 20 per cent thereafter. The 1940 contract covered three books, of which the last was *Evil Under the Sun*, delivered to Cork in 1940. Harold Ober had received a plaintive letter from Frank Dodd asking whether Agatha would 'consider some relief on the advances which we have been paying'. Her books sold well and steadily but her sales were not yet as impressive as they were later to be. Cork staved off such a blow; indeed, no word of it ever reached Agatha. Cork and Ober protected her when they could from bad news and hurtful criticism, suppressing or toning down what might only upset her. Their correspondence, erratic during the war years but weekly and often twice weekly in the nineteen-fifties and sixties, shows how carefully they conspired to shield their client, with whose requests they occasionally became exasperated but for whom they always felt affection and respect.

Agatha began two other books in 1940. One was about Poirot and eventually appeared, thirty-five years later, as *Curtain*, the single word at the head of her first draft of the plot: 'Poirot invents story of death believed caused by Ricin or Cobra venom – gets suspect down and takes R from him?' The other was about Miss Marple. Its first working title was *Cover Her Face*, part of a quotation from *The Duchess of Malfi*:

> Cover her face, mine eyes dazzle,
> She died young. . . .

Agatha had first written these words in her plotting books in the mid-'thirties and the reference recurred in several of her exercise books, always with allusions to the plot of *The Duchess of Malfi* and sometimes to Tennyson's *Enoch Arden*. The 'Enoch Arden' theme and, indeed, a character using that name appeared after the War in her novel *Taken at the Flood;* the *Duchess of Malfi* thought occurs elsewhere in Agatha's notes, gradually growing into a story about a performance of that play, when a girl in the audience screams and has to be taken out. Agatha later embodied this, too, in the Marple book. She also brought into her wartime novel elements of another draft, originally with Poirot at the centre, of a story about a woman returning to a house she recognises, which turns out to be the place where her young step-mother died.

Another idea which haunted Agatha and which she took into *Cover Her Face* was of a dead child. She had written in her notes on voodoo, first made while she and Max were in Syria among their Yezidi labourers, about the importance of the notion of the dead child and its spirit in religions where the devil and death are central. For some reason this theme became connected in her mind with another that recurred in several plots. This was the macabre thought that a dead child might be buried in a disused fireplace, an allusion incorporated in *Cover Her Face* and, later, in *The Pale Horse* and *By the Pricking of My Thumbs*. 'One in chimney', 'Behind the *Fireplace*' – these notes reappear in Aga-tha's exercise books. We do not know whether they were refer-ences to an overheard remark or to childhood memories, to an idea that occurred to her at Abney or in some other house ('Priest's hole good place to hide body.' she once noted). The thought may have derived from the Venetian fireplace she and Max had admired, or from the blank wall at Cresswell Place ('What is *behind* bricked-up wall.' read another note). The image must have touched her profoundly, for it not only repeatedly occurs but in each of the three books the reference also appears in a deeply disturbing context.

Neither the wartime Poirot book nor the wartime Marple book were to be published straightaway. Agatha was anxious to build what she described to Cork as her 'nest egg', in case she found herself unable to work – if, for instance, anything should happen to Rosalind or Max. Moreover, the Poirot book was written when Agatha was finding her Belgian detective 'insufferable'; in it he dies. As he was Agatha's main source of income, 'Poirot's Last Case' had inevitably to be put into cold storage. Cork ap-proved, though he did not foresee the complications arising from Agatha's decision to assign one copyright to Rosalind and the other to Max, 'in consideration of the natural love and affection which I bear to my husband'. Her original intention was that Max should have the Poirot and Rosalind the Marple book, but by the end of the war she had changed her mind. The Marple story, eventually published as *Sleeping Murder*, was given to Max and *Curtain* to Rosalind.

Copies were sent to New York in accordance with a general principle of dispersal which Hughes Massie was applying to all important material, for the office at 40 Fleet Street had already been bombed. Harold Ober's reaction was that 'Mrs Mallowan must have been in a rather despondent state when she decided to kill off Poirot.' Indeed, Agatha had every reason to be unhappy, as Cork told Ober in a letter written in December 1940, begging for news of the tax matter. She had lost the refuge of her own houses, for Greenway, Winterbrook and Cresswell Place were let and Sheffield Place was unsafe. Rosalind was in Northern Ireland with Hubert, Max was anxious to serve abroad and – the gravest blow – there was no Carlo. Agatha had given her a house in Ladbroke Terrace Mews and saw her from time to time but now Carlo had gone to do war work in a factory. These anxieties overshadowed Agatha's life far more than worry about money but her financial predicament was nonetheless serious. By the end of January 1941, when the tax hearing had again been postponed and the British Revenue authorities were pressing for their own payment, Cork was writing once more to Ober: 'The situation is pretty desperate with no money coming in. ... It is hard to believe that Christie will have to find money for Income Tax on money she has not received. It does not take much imagination to see what a nightmare it has produced for our most valuable client....'

One expedient which occurred to Agatha was to sell Greenway. She and Max were unable to use it while the War lasted and anyhow Max was now firmly settled in London. After interminable appeals to the authorities he had at last secured a proper post. 'It is, I think, high time,' he had written in irritation to the Ministry of Information, who had messed about with a possible appointment in Turkey, 'that bureaucrats took a sane and just view of the services they are willing to extract from a British-born subject.' So desperate was Max to do some useful service that to his already impressive list of references from Squadron Leaders, Colonels and Air Marshals, he added: 'Wife, British subject. Better known as Agatha Christie, has just written an anti-Nazi book.' And, even: 'I have been accepted as a member of the Home Guard.' This correspondence was copied to Stephen Glanville and in February he succeeded in pressing Max's case. Max joined Glanville at the Air Ministry, in what became the Directorate of Allied and Foreign Liaison. With great reluctance Agatha decided to sell Greenway. 'Two sets of people have been looking over the house,' she wrote miserably to Cork, '– both unpleasant in different ways. Still, they seem to have the money.' To which Cork gently replied: 'I am afraid you will find anyone who wants Greenway most unpleasant. I have a feeling that what with the budget and one thing and another there are not going to be so many people who will "have the money" much longer.' No one bought Greenway.

Agatha's only other way out of her troubles was work but, as she told Cork, who spurred her on: 'Do I gather from your letter that you are urging this sausage machine to turn out a couple more of the same old hand? Feel too depressed by my financial plight at the moment. What's the *good* of writing for money if I don't get *anything* out of it?' She nevertheless made a start. 'The next Christie story,' Cork told Ober exactly a month later, 'will be a perfectly sweet poison pen tragedy featuring Miss Marple.' Indeed, Cork wrote, 'as Mrs Christie is writing hard in an effort to catch up with things, it looks as if we might have an accumulation of books on our hands before long. ...'

The poison pen idea was another Agatha had mulled over for years. Once hurt herself by rumour, she considered its destructive power in several stories; one was 'The Augean Stables' in *The Labours of Hercules*, where gossip is used by the wily Poirot against the scandal-mongers. *The Moving Finger* had a fairly easy birth, except that the *Saturday Evening Post* declined it on the grounds that the action began too slowly to make a successful serial. It was nevertheless first published in America. There were also difficulties about its title. Agatha first suggested *The Tangled Web*, which Collins thought too close to a recently published *Spider's Web*. She then proposed *The Moving Finger* but Cork for some reason preferred *Misdirection*. Agatha won. Cork and Ober agreed that this was one of her best books. When she finished it, she felt something of an anti-climax and her worries resurfaced. Cork again attacked the financial issue, begging Ober to push Reinheimer: 'She is being pressed remorselessly by the tax authorities here and the Bank to pay her English taxation, which for the year will be anything up to four times the total income she will receive. ...' He also found an ingenious way of giving Agatha some financial relief. There had been an offer from an American company, Milestone, for the film rights to *N or M?* and, since such rights were 'world-wide in their scope', Cork advised Ober that, 'it would be possible for sums to be payable in this country, where Mrs Mallowan in the first instance, and the Chancellor of the Exchequer in the second, needs the money so desperately.' Some money was also coming in from unexpected sources: *Peril at End House*, for instance, took £514.17.10½ at the Lyceum, Sheffield, in the first week of May.

Further irritation came in June, when Collins proposed new contractual arrangements: an advance of £1150, rather than £1000, for each new book but with royalty rates of 25 per cent to start after 6000 rather than 3000 copies. Collins's grounds were 'a shocking increase in production costs'. Cork did not give way. Collins next provoked what Cork dismissed as 'a spot of bother' over *N or M?*. Their editor's chief objections were that, though 'a pretty exciting spy story', it lacked the 'murder-mystery and detection element', that it was too short and had too many loose ends. Agatha wrote a stiff letter and Billy tried to soothe her. 'He is sorry,' his secretary replied, 'we had to ask you to make it a bit longer, but one of the reasons for our doing this was that, as it stood, the libraries would find people read it all too quickly, and they would not give repeat orders so readily, as their original order would then last them longer than usual.' Agatha was unconvinced by this explanation of publishing economics and proposed a move. Cork delicately dissuaded her, confessing himself, 'very doubtful whether under present publishing conditions Mr Gollancz would do you any better. ... I admire his cleverness as much as anyone, and he has done very well with a number of books I have sold him this year,' but Collins, Cork believed, enjoyed better relationships with booksellers. Agatha stayed and, though 'rather anti-Collins ... such a thick-headed lot', set to work again.

'Things all seem to come at once,' she told Cork in a sad letter in the autumn of 1941. 'How interminable it all is.' As Reinheimer advised, she gave her representatives in America power of attorney to deal with her affairs and even agreed to permit her American publishers to include in the advance publicity for *N or M?* 'any soft soap you like' about her war work. She was now giving several days a week to the dispensary at University College Hospital and there had been reports of this in the American press. 'Hospital still standing, though flattened buildings all around,' she told Cork. 'If they must have some kind of pictures, let them have that.' There were limits to the sort of stories it was sensible to permit – 'No harm in saying Max is in RAFVR but best leave it strictly at that' – not just because of ubiquitous official warnings against disclosing any information, however trivial, that might be of use to the enemy, but also because of her revulsion at being gossiped about. 'I will NOT be a "Mystery Woman",' she wrote irately to Cork, enclosing an 'infuriating' clipping from the *Saturday Evening Post*, discussing her past and

her second marriage. Equally maddening was an effusive letter
sent by a well-meaning American admirer, who asserted that,
'Agatha was a peach with a swell sense of humour with a dia-
bolically sharp wisdom. More power to you.'

By the end of 1941, however, things began to look up. Agatha
had finished another book, *The Body in the Library*, with which
Collins were delighted. It has a splendid opening, with Mrs Bantry gently emerging from sleep to find the maid indeed telling her
there is a body in the library; something simultaneously so apt
but incongruous that it is likely only in a dream – or a detective
story. Another reassuring development was that two American
film companies, RKO and Warner Brothers, were interested in
the rights to *Ten Little Niggers*. (The first production, however,
was eventually made in 1945 by Twentieth Century Fox, as *And
Then There Were None*, directed by René Clair.) Cork and Ober
also managed to arrange for the option on the film rights for *N
or M?* to be paid by Milestone in London; Ober even held out
some hope that, now the United States had entered the War,
there might be changes in the tax regulations applying to payments to non-resident aliens. Collins parted with advances for
The Moving Finger and *The Body in the Library* and, as for the
British Revenue authorities, Cork stoutly advised Agatha to 'take
no notice of this preposterous nominal assessment. ... Everyone
is getting them.' By mid-December Agatha was again able to
report that she was 'writing passionately and in consequence had
paid no bills, answered no letters and am in fact getting into
trouble all round!' A week later she sent Cork the revised proofs
of *The Body in the Library* and the typescript of another novel,
Towards Zero. 'That,' she said triumphantly, 'ought to help the
New Year Depression a bit!'

Agatha asked Cork to 'take a little time' over thinking about
serialising *Towards Zero*. It was in this letter that she spoke of
her misery when she had forced herself to finish *The Big Four*
and *The Mystery of the Blue Train* and of her wish to have at
least 'one book up her sleeve'. *Towards Zero*, she thought, was
'reasonably non-dating'. It is understandable that Agatha felt
insecure. Like all her fellow-countrymen she was living from day
to day. Buildings and streets would be wiped out overnight,
houses that still stood could be requisitioned. No one knew
whether they, their families, friends and acquaintance, would still
be alive the next day. In squirrelling away this book, Agatha was
storing up supplies, as her grandmother had done. (The Mack-

intoshes harboured a small cache of tinned ham and olive oil for her, in case Lawn Road was knocked flat.) Moreover, Agatha was now without Max, or ready news of him. In February he had volunteered as one of two officers to establish a branch of the Directorate in Cairo. He was promoted to Squadron Leader and set off; there, on a terrace at the Continental Hotel in Cairo, he at once spotted his brother Cecil, drinking coffee. Cecil had been interned by the Finns in 1940, evacuated to Sweden, where he worked as a lumberjack, and eventually repatriated to England, via Germany, France and Portugal. He had now been sent by the British Council to direct its Institutes in Egypt and, after this fortunate coincidence, settled down amicably with Max in a house overlooking the Nile.

Agatha, exhausted, missing Max, and, despite his farewell present of a Jaeger dressing-gown, cold, spent most of her evenings and weekends writing. She assured Cork that, even if he took his time over placing *Towards Zero*, 'I am starting on another so the serial market won't be neglected.' This was *Five Little Pigs*, one of Agatha's 'Artist Ideas'. The setting, 'Alderbury', was Greenway, and the plot a 'story of man who has affairs – really loves his wife – his mistress intent on marriage.' It was published in America as *Murder in Retrospect*. Taken together, *Five Little Pigs* and *Towards Zero* show how flexible Agatha's style of plotting and technique was at this time. *Five Little Pigs* is an intimate, fast-moving story, *Towards Zero* a picture of long-drawn-out revenge, a tale so striking that some years later it caught the attention of Claude Chabrol, who talked of making it into a film.

There was still no news from Reinheimer. The best Cork could report was that an American tax return had been filed for 1941: 'I hope,' he wrote, 'this dreadful business is to be settled at last.' Ober, however, no longer sent reassuring messages. Agatha's most urgent desire was to join Max in Cairo and Cork agreed to see what might be done. If he could arrange for a magazine to commission articles, she might be allowed to go. Meanwhile, she was offered 'the exact job I should like in England if I *didn't* get out to Cairo ... dispenser to a doctor in Wendover.' Cork told her she 'should be doing a much more important job' than that, 'but you're the best judge.' It turned out, however, that the *Saturday Evening Post* was interested in Cairo material and Agatha's hopes rose.

Cork squared his brief with Agatha: 'articles about the Middle

East, topical interest for America by describing how the war has affected life' - and arranged to have lunch with 'the all-powerful Quentin Reynolds', the distinguished American journalist whose press and radio reports of Britain's wartime efforts did much to sustain support for the Allies in the United States. Even Reynolds, Cork reported, found it impossible to remove official hurdles. By July Agatha was more resigned to Max's absence. In any case, he might soon be moved, though everything was doubtful, she told Cork. There was also a great deal to do at Greenway, now requisitioned by the Admiralty for eventual use by the officers of an American flotilla. The Arbuthnots departed, leaving Agatha and an elderly gardener to move the furniture into the drawing-room, the only quarters the Admiralty allowed her to set aside. 'I am sick of loading trunks and getting filthy with cobwebs and am generally fed up!' Agatha wrote to Cork in the autumn. He thoughtfully invited her to lunch at the Ecu de France.

'In spite of my sadness about it,' Agatha wrote to Max, 'there might be two consolation prizes. First, I should say it is quite likely that they may bring mains electricity' (they didn't) 'and, second, old man Hannaford' (the gardener) 'might be removed without pain'. (He stayed.) She worried about the trees and shrubs, writing to Charles Williams, the former owner, asking him to keep an eye on things. As M.P. for Torquay, she hoped, 'he might have more influence - naval and political - than I should.' She also reported that there had been an offer for Winterbrook; 'we must decide some time which house we are going to stick to. I don't believe we can keep both.' Winterbrook was not sold but, as it was let to friends of the Goodsons in Torquay, Agatha, with all her houses, stayed at 17 Lawn Road. (She had disposed of 47 Campden Street.) Her hopes for a visit to Cairo had revived with a letter from Ober saying that *Collier's* would definitely send her, but Cork now discovered the full extent of the official obstruction. There was no insuperable objection from the Ministry of Information itself, he reported, but Brendan Bracken, the Minister, had written to say that the War Office was not prepared to accredit women correspondents in the Middle East. Cork tried to put a cheerful face on the news: 'At any rate we know what we're up against - either the War Office must be induced to make an exception, or we must wait until the military situation is retrieved.'

Agatha consoled herself with writing long letters to Max, typed at first (though James, her new dog, disliked the noise of the machine) and later handwritten on flimsy 'aerogrames'. Many of her letters that autumn were descriptions of Greenway and the trees, with Hannaford, 'leaf moulding and ashing before he takes on duties for the Navy'. By the end of October the house was empty.

> I stayed for a little while after the men had gone and then I walked up and sat on the seat overlooking the house and the river and made believe you were sitting beside me. ... It looked very white and lovely – serene and aloof as always. I felt a kind of pang over its beauty. I discovered today that there is no *personal* loss in leaving it – because queerly enough I can't really recall ever being very happy in it – when I think of it I always seem to have felt so tired. ... And then, after that, the War – and then the Turks, so that you couldn't be there that Spring. All my happy memories are of the garden and you planting your magnolias and I making my new path down by the river. And yet the house is not an *un*happy home – and I love it. It is untouched by what the people in it feel and think, but it wanted to be beautiful – I consider I *made* it beautiful, or rather, displayed its beauty. Greenway has been a mistress rather than a wife! 'Too dear for our possessing' but what excitement to possess it! I thought tonight sitting there – it is the loveliest place in the world – it quite takes my breath away.

For her wedding anniversary present from Max, Agatha bought 'two of Mr Arbuthnot's sketches – 'one side view of the house showing the Delavayi and the other an impression from the Battery.' 'Tell me,' she asked, 'is that all right ... or would you rather I got a ring?'

She need not have worried about the house. The Admiralty and the American sailors were solicitous: 'A very nice Commander Kirkwood (real Navy) came and was really very concerned about our beautiful mahogany doors, especially the curved ones. ...' These were promptly removed and, she told Max, 'a "leading shipwright" is coming ... to consult about them and possibly cover them with beaverboard.' Commander Kirkwood was interested in trees and shrubs, telling Agatha, 'They suggested Dittisham for headquarters – but I said this was far and away the best.' 'Like the old song,' Agatha wrote, now homeless, 'No dwelling more, by sea or shore, But only in your heart – And a very nice place to have as a dwelling, and keep me there, darling, till the War ends.'

18

'... only an interruption ...'

Agatha and Max each kept all the letters of their wartime separation. It was an unusual correspondence, more like a sustained conversation, for as well as sending gossip and news Agatha wrote at great length about her theories and ideas, and Max replied with his own comments and a great deal of detailed reporting on local antiquities and unusual geological formations. Agatha's letters are fluent, immediate, less legible and vastly entertaining. In comparison, Max's letters are solemn and painstaking – but it reassured and delighted her that he took such pains and wrote so regularly.

Much of their correspondence in the autumn and winter of 1942 was about Shakespeare. Agatha was full of theories about *Othello*,

> Desdemona was *not* a ninny. She was unconventional, daring, with great strength of character. ... Iago and Emilia are really a couple of common swindlers, confidence tricksters ... plain sexual jealousy the crux of Iago's hatred of the Moor. ... He has suffered through Emilia again and again – not because he cares for her specially, but because of the deep humiliation to him as a man. ...

Then Agatha was puzzled by the character of Ophelia in *Hamlet*:

> All Shakespeare's women are very definitely characterised – he was feminine enough himself to see men through their eyes. ... I feel that in Ophelia he is describing some real character he has met or heard or seen, and that she is correct but that he himself is ignorant of the factor that made her act as she did. Just as in Shylock, he set down the villainous character of a usurer, but put the pathos and the injustice of the treatment accorded to Jews in quite unconsciously, because it was *there*.

Agatha now went to the theatre as often as she could, read a great deal of theatrical criticism, and spent many hours with theatrical friends. 'I don't think, you know,' she wrote to Max, 'that there is anything that takes you so much away from real

things and happenings as the acting world. It *is* a world of its
own and actors never are thinking of anything but themselves
and their lines and their business, and what they are going to
wear!' Her interest was more than casual, for in the autumn and
winter she started to adapt *Ten Little Niggers* for the stage.

In December 1941 Cork had started to seek backers but found
it difficult. Charles Cochran was interested, although he and
Larry Sullivan (who had played Poirot in *Black Coffee* and *Peril
at End House*) were unhappy with the way the story ended. Cork
therefore looked over some of Agatha's earlier work to see what,
dramatised, might find financial backing and a theatre. 'What a
sale there would be for these books if there were only enough
paper available,' he told her. His first idea was for her to adapt
Three Act Tragedy but, on rereading it, he felt it a better idea to
take 'Triangle at Rhodes' from *Murder in the Mews:* 'A perfectly
marvellous dramatic situation and not the later, highly character-
ised Poirot,' he thought.

Agatha had meanwhile begun to think of ways in which the
closing chapter of *Ten Little Niggers* might be changed. The
rhyme on which the story was based had, in fact, an alternative
ending, 'He got married and then there were none,' and, as she
wrote to Max in 1942, she certainly 'contemplated this as a possibility *if* I can do it my way. ...' In September 1942 she made her
proposals to Cork: 'Here is the hashed-up product. ... I don't
think I like these cheap comedy effects and silly to build up love
interest *unless* (quite possible) you end play by Vera and Lombard
turning tables on judge – having been shamming dead to catch
him.' 'Sacrilege,' observed Cork, loyally, 'but it would make easier theatre.' He put the proposal to Bertie Meyer, who had
backed *Alibi*, and 'subject to certain alterations by Agatha', they
thought they could draw up a contract.

Cork remained keen for 'a Poirot play'; Agatha, still 'rather
anti-Poirot', was not. Then Cork reported that Larry Sullivan
was interested in her old script *Moon on the Nile*. Pressed by both
Cork and Sullivan, with Bertie Meyer ready to back a second
play, Agatha agreed to try her hand at this as well. A series of
entertaining luncheons with Cork, Sullivan and Meyer did the
trick; as it was, Agatha was by now thoroughly enamoured of
the theatre. Her letters to Max are full of reports of plays and
extracts from reviews.

Ten Little Niggers proved easy to adapt but Agatha had repeated discussions with Sullivan about *Moon on the Nile*, as they

intended the other play should be called. The difficulty was Poirot, to whom she had taken an intense dislike. In late October, she told Max she had led Sullivan gently to the idea of chopping Poirot: 'suggested instead a retired Barrister – a solicitor – an ex-diplomat – a clergyman – canon or bishop – And suddenly he bit! His eyes half closed – "Oh yes – purple silk front and a *large* cross" – He *saw* it, you see. Not the speaking part – the *appearance*! I bet you whoever played Hamlet argued a good deal as to whether to play it in a hat or not!' Agatha, as it happened, had just read Edith Sitwell's *Bath*: 'Lovely discussions of the time of Beau Nash, various actors – *all* hinging on what they wore – Garrick played Othello in *uniform* – someone else in Arab robes etc.' *Moon on the Nile* was finished in early December. Agatha told Max she thought she had written Larry Sullivan 'quite a good part as Canon Pennefather – a kind of budding Archbishop of Canterbury and Sir William Beveridge rolled into one'. Her enthusiastic remarks – 'Why aren't you here to talk to?' – are a reminder of how these interests interlocked: disguise, uniform, theatricality, codes and conventions, mystery and mystique. In the theatre she lost her shyness. The 'serene girl with a Cockney accent and an intense young man with masses of black hair', with whom she discussed alterations to *Ten Little Niggers*, were not intimidating, for they were raw material. She entered, too, into the spirit of her own part and relaxed: 'I am very theatrical now,' she confessed to Max, 'and call all the most frightful people "Darling".'

As Christmas approached, Agatha missed Max desperately. Rosalind, 'who lives the life of a Wandering Jew', occasionally passed through London and went with her mother to the theatre. She scolded Agatha for 'doing too much knitting – I shall end by being one of those women who knit everything they have on! However my "elephant" knickers are a great success.' There was no going to Greenway; she had sold half the garden tools to the tenant of the kitchen garden, prudently arranging to buy them back after the war, and auctioned unusable china, some of the less comfortable chairs and 'the one Mr Arbuthnot burned a hole in with his cigar', to cover the cost of having the contents valued and insured. As winter set in, she took to wandering round London, looking for Max's Christmas present but 'bookshops are getting very difficult – either old *old* men like *crabs* in them, *very* cross and not wanting to sell you or get you anything – or else superior research girls who only know about economics or town

planning.' As Max's present to her, she bought a square jade
ring, but without him she was miserable. 'I have been sad tonight
and cried a bit.' She had his letters to read over, 'a shade
microscopic', and letter cards which she could 'just manage with
a good light and my spectacles and a magnifying glass handy'.
These reassured her. The fact that he could write so lovingly
'after all the years we have been married ... makes me feel that,
after all, I have not been a failure in life – that I have succeeded
as a wife. What a change now from the unhappy, forlorn person
you met in Baghdad. You have done *everything* for me. ...' Max
had with him a copy of *The Testament of Beauty*, Agatha's farewell present in 1941. Now he told her to look out a poem, Number Eleven, in the *Oxford Book of Sixteenth-Century English
Verse*, and she went down to Winterbrook to do so. 'Is that the
one you meant? – To His Lady. If so, I feel all puffed up with
pride.'

In February Max left Cairo for Tripolitania, making his way
by train to the coast, where he found not the aeroplane he had
been promised but, eventually, a ship carrying war equipment
which gave him a lift. His first assignment was to serve as assistant to the Senior Civil Affairs Officer in the Western Province, a
glorious attachment, for the headquarters of the province were at
Sabratha, an ancient Phoenician city, with Roman ruins, a classical theatre restored by the Italians, a museum 'with its beautiful
peacock mosaic ... and a carpet of mesembryanthemum', and a
well-stocked library of classical literature and books on history
and archaeology. For the first six months Max lived there in an
Italian villa with a courtyard and patio overlooking the sea, dining on fresh caught tunnyfish and olives. It was a striking contrast
to dilapidated London and Agatha's meals of S.P.O. (sausage,
potatoes and onion), snatched from a stall on her way to the
hospital.

Christmas and the New Year over, Agatha's optimism returned. The *Ten Little Niggers* project, which had at one point
seemed near collapse, was revived; Agatha told Max she now
thought of writing 'a wild spy drama' about the WAAF. The
proofs arrived of *Five Little Pigs;* there was no trouble about
these, although Agatha did protest to Collins about recurrent
misprints in lists of her other titles: *Death on the Hill*, for instance,
instead of *Death on the Nile*, which had sent several people in
search of an extra Christie. Billy Collins sent apologies and with
the jacket design for *Five Little Pigs* a book on roses.

Spring was difficult. Max, reminded to send his usual Valentine card to Katharine Woolley, sent another to Agatha: 'You remember how when I married you I told you that we would be like Disraeli and Mary Anne? Well, that is how it has been and I expect we will live to a ripe old age together.' (Mary Anne had been ten years older than Disraeli, when they married in 1859.) At the end of March she looked in on Greenway, 'still only occupied by the guard', the garden 'incredibly beautiful and all the mimosa in flower and doing well after the mild winter'. She could 'hardly bear' to write to Max in his villa by the sea – 'and who likes the sea? *I* do. Oh! the unfairness of life.'

He had been away a year. Unsettled, Agatha moved for a week or two to the Park Place service flat, ostensibly to be nearer rehearsals for *Ten Little Niggers*, then to the Marine Hotel in Salcombe. She spent weekends with friends in the country – Allen and Lettice Lane, Larry and Danae Sullivan – and in London people were kind. There was Dorothy North and Ernest and Marion Mackintosh, and some of Max's archaeological colleagues, like Sidney and Mary Smith. But it was Max Agatha wanted. Though tired, she felt her energy was unused. She tried to organise canteen work but that fizzled out. 'No spring for us together,' Agatha wrote in a letter remembering their parting. She had been reading sonnets: 'What lovely first lines Shakespeare wrote – his "attack" is always more arresting than his climax.' Now she took the opening line of one, 'From thee have I been absent in the spring' for the title of a novel, quickly written, as a present for Max. 'Life owes one a spring – with you!' she wrote.

It is a powerful book. Like everything Agatha wrote as 'Mary Westmacott', it considers the theme of possessive love and its dangers. The central figure, Joan Scudamore, examines her life and, like Agatha's other creations, Miss Marple and Hercule Poirot, comes to realise that there are many ways of seeing the same experience and that she has misinterpreted her own motives and misunderstood those to whom she believed she was closest. What good these reflections do her is another matter. Agatha wrote *Absent in the Spring* in three days, her back aching, and sent Max his copy in July. 'I think it is *good*,' she wrote from Winterbrook, where she had spent a month with Rosalind, 'à la Turgenev', eating an abundance of salmon, unavailable in London but thrust on to every customer by the Wallingford fishmonger, 'rebuffing those who demand a nice bit of skate or hake'.

Rosalind was expecting a baby in September. She had for a while taken a flat at Lawn Road and now, after four weeks at Wallingford, she and Agatha were to go to Abney, 'with the "old School Trunk", full of baby clothes.' Abney had been invaded at ten days' notice in November 1942; Punkie and a valiant former kitchenmaid looked after the officers billeted in that enormous house (Punkie occasionally disguising herself as a maid when she brought their breakfast). Agatha was more nervous about the baby's birth than Rosalind appeared to be. 'I get (all mothers seem alike) so panicky sometimes,' she told Max, 'though I never show it. It's silly, I know, but [Rosalind's] lifeline is broken in both hands – and I think of it sometimes. It's the one thing I want for her happiness. ...' The baby, 'a large boy ... looking so like Hubert to my mind that all he needs is a monocle', was born on September 21st. Agatha had rushed up to Cheshire, where Hubert telephoned repeatedly, asking anxiously about Rosalind, 'Does she *like* it?' She did; Agatha was overjoyed.

At such an emotional time Agatha longed for Max. She dreamed of going to have lunch with him, 'in a large country house full of flowerbeds' and finding him gone. 'I woke up in a panic and had to say over and over. "It's *not* true. ... I've got his letter" and I turned on the light and read it.' During the summer she had tried to calm herself by starting 'a detective story, set in ancient Egypt'. This was Stephen Glanville's suggestion and he had lent her 'some lovely books – so far I have been enjoying them under false pretences ... but soon I shall either have to have a shot at it – or else admit I am *beat*! Cork horrified at the idea which rather spurs me on.' Glanville's 'serpent's tongue' persuaded Agatha and during July she typed the beginning of *Death Comes as the End* in Max's library at Winterbrook, 'lowbrow stuff in your highbrow sanctuary'. One of the books Agatha borrowed discussed the Hekanakhthe Papers, found in a rock tomb near Luxor in the early nineteen-twenties by the Egyptian Expedition of the Metropolitan Museum of Art. These letters from a village landowner, who looked after the tomb, gave her a start. Her notebook was full of quotations and Glanville was pressed with questions. He was glad to help, for this was a difficult time for him. His wife and children were in Canada and, though he fell into one romantic scrape after another, he was lonely. A good friend to the Mallowans, he now kept an eye on Agatha, who had dedicated *Five Little Pigs* to him, celebrating its publication by cooking Stephen a dinner: 'Some pâté (ersatz but

I incorporated some truffles in it to create the right illusion), a lobster – hot – in the shell and Petit Pois – and stewed cherries.' They opened 'a bottle of the remaining wine ... apparently it was very good', she told Max, 'and you were duly toasted in it by Stephen.' (Agatha herself preferred 'Pure Water' to drink, ordering alcohol for herself only once in her adult life, when an exceedingly prim Fundamentalist came to lunch and so preached on the evils of drink that she cheerfully and ostentatiously demanded 'Bottled Beer'.)

At the end of July Agatha finished the first draft of 'my 11th Dynasty Egyptian Detective Story'. She submitted it to Glanville: 'Awkward for him if he thinks it perfectly frightful! How will his well-known tact get over that? I myself,' she told Max, 'felt most despondent about it half way through (but then one always does about that stage). Nearly gave up in despair! In fact wrote furious letter to S saying I couldn't do it and it was all his fault! Then R read it and said she "couldn't see much wrong with it" – High praise from R?! So I went ahead and finished it.' Max wrote anxiously to Agatha and to Glanville, who reassured him: 'No archaeological apparatus was to be imported that was not essential or at least perfectly natural in the telling of the tale. No showing off at all costs. At the same time there had to be enough implicit Egyptian feeling to make it impossible for the layman to feel that this particular story could have happened in Pimlico, and to make the Egyptologist feel that there was no reason why it shouldn't have happened in Thebes. It was an extraordinarily difficult thing to do, and she's brought it off.'

Glanville, Max and Agatha made an interesting trio. Max cared for Glanville and wrote warmly about him to Agatha, glad she was keeping an eye on him and grateful for the companionship he gave. Agatha reported to Max when Stephen was unhappy and consoled Stephen, who confided freely in her. Agatha also begged Stephen to find Max a job that would bring him home or to help her find something in Tripoli, possibilities Stephen discussed in his correspondence with Max, letters which also spoke of the importance of his relationship with Agatha. She was now in her mid-fifties, no longer slim but heavy and awkward. She remained, however, very attractive, for she was sympathetic and a good listener, interested, intelligent, instinctively understanding, and diplomatic. Not surprisingly, Glanville relied much upon his neighbour at Lawn Road worn down as he was feeling by the pressure of his work in Whitehall and the compli-

cations of his private life. He spent many evenings pouring out
his troubles to her and when they were apart he wrote to her
seeking comfort, which she gave, in tactful measure. Agatha
wrote often to Max about Stephen, neither revealing all his confidences nor complaining of the time and emotional energy he
demanded. There seemed to be no jealousy on Max's part,
although his anxiety over *Death Comes as the End* may have
partly sprung from a feeling that Stephen and Agatha were conspiring to produce something of which he would not have himself
approved. But Stephen's enthusiasm reassured Max, as did the
fact that Cork liked the book and Collins took it.

Stephen also helped Agatha with *Moon on the Nile*, though
only to the extent of composing cries for Arab vendors 'off'. That
play was languishing for want of a cast and a theatre. It eventually opened at the Wimbledon Theatre in September and in the
West End in November 1943, to favourable reviews. 'I felt *awful*,
of course,' Agatha wrote to Max when she returned to Lawn
Road after the first night. 'It *is* an agony but Stephen came again
and was very kind and soothing and he and Rosalind pulled me
through. Party at Prunier's afterwards. Smoked salmon and oysters, hot lobster Thermidor and chocolate mousse. We were 9
Little Niggers – the 10th was in Tripolitania (or perhaps Cairo?).'
It was the last party Agatha enjoyed for some time, for the following week she got 'flu. 'Nothing to eat and aspirin has made
me a very elegant shape', she told Max happily. (A six-year-old
god-daughter had recently remarked, 'with devastating frankness.
... "You're *fat*. I remember you as thin!" I told her she had been
remembering wrong. "And I thought you had fair hair. It's quite
grey!" Then, a little later, "I'm getting used to you now".')

Little wonder Agatha fell ill. It had been a long year, with
her hospital work, two plays, a Mary Westmacott novel and a detective story, regular play-going and rehearsals. ('It's all new to
me. Rather like an Arab at the cinema.') Agatha had also been
helping Rosalind look after Mathew. Rosalind and the baby had
been unable to move immediately into Hubert's house at Pwllywrach in Glamorgan, where his mother and sister were solidly installed. For a month they lived in London. Fortunately there was
a nurse for Mathew, who told her family, when they reported
that 'the best thing they'd seen was *Ten Little Niggers*, by Agatha
Christie', "Ee, I know – she's our cook." The mistake was understandable, for Agatha arrived from time to time to help with
meals and shopping. She admitted that she was very tired. She kept

falling down, too: 'Very painful and ruin to stockings (3 coupons!).'

By Christmas Agatha was at Pwllywrach with Rosalind and Mathew. The house, she told Max, was 'lovely but much in the state of Greenway before we got it'. She longed for the days before the War, when, 'plutocratic', she was 'able to keep (I mean spend!) a reasonable whack of the money I earned'. Not a financial dirge, she said, 'just the longing of the "inferior decorator" to do things to Rosalind's house'. Not that Agatha would have had the energy, for she still felt very tired and depressed after the 'flu, 'as though I was dimmed like a headlight on a car'.

Agatha went often to Wales to be with Rosalind and Mathew. She was fond of her grandson but acknowledged that looking after a baby was tiring. Agatha had written Max occasional sentimental letters about infants and small children; one, after a visit to Allen and Lettice Lane, described how Agatha and Allen had 'cooked some of your favourite potatoes and onions and sweetbreads in a kind of creamy sauce' and fed them, with milk pudding and prunes, to Clare, 'quite the most adorable baby I have ever come across'. Max sagely sent a description of a colleague who had been staying with him and had brought a baby: 'My word, it seems to be strenuous work ... getting up to feed it at God knows what hours and examining it for wind or what not and perpetual washing. Lucky [Max] can have Agatha all to himself and no one to be jealous of'.

There was still no firm news from Reinheimer. Some money came in from *Ten Little Niggers*, in addition to royalties on work published in Britain and the Colonies, but in February Agatha reported to Max that '*Ten Little Niggers* is a war casualty (or rather their abode was)'. Collins, too, were completely bombed out; records that remain – copies of letters and fragments of royalty statements typed with blotchy ink on scraps of reprint order sheets – indicate the struggle the office had to keep going. Life was haphazard, unpredictable and hand-to-mouth for everyone; Agatha was determined not to panic about her accumulating debt but she was rueful. She again suggested that Greenway should be sold, writing to Max for advice. He was not helpful, merely assuring her that he supported whatever decision she might take and observing feebly that: 'As you say, it is obvious that we must reconcile ourselves to giving up that lovely place.'

Max was equally pessimistic about his work after the War: 'as you know, my bent and inclinations are all for Archaeology, where I have much to publish and still much to do. But one must be practical. We shall no longer be able to put up the money to indulge in digging and it is an uncertain profession.' He had begun to consider a future as a colonial administrator, the sort of work he now found himself doing in Tripolitania. After a blissful six months at Sabratha, much of which he spent oversee-ing the allocation of grain rations in the Western Province, he had moved to a lonely oasis, Hun, in the Eastern Province. His next posting was to the coastal town of Misurata. 'As magistrate,' he told Agatha, 'I also try cases in the Courts regularly and this type of work is more satisfactory because you are given a definite problem and have to come to a definite solution in accordance with certain well-defined principles. ...' Max was suited to these duties and pressed Glanville to find him something of the sort for the future, especially if no archaeological posts appeared. But his plans were half-hearted at best; in October when he had moved to Tripoli, as Adviser on Arab Affairs, he spent a day in an airy library, and remembered that he had a scholar's training and temperament. His elevation to Deputy Chief Secretary for Arab Affairs, with the rank of Wing Commander, only confirmed his awareness that he was not an administrator at heart, for he found 'the higher echelons' less agreeable than 'administering the prov-inces in a humbler capacity ... in touch with the Nomads, small land owners, peasants and the unsophisticated characters of the countryside'.

One advantage of remaining in North Africa after the War was that at least it would enable Max to show Agatha the places he had visited – Leptis Magna and Zliten and less celebrated sites: 'I think your work sounds interesting and *real*,' she had written. 'I want one day to go to the places where you have been in the war and – as it were – recoup myself.' But she encouraged him to think of these visits as part of a future that would focus on archaeology, a profession ideally suited to both of them: 'A pri-vate concern,' she wrote, 'for [we] are very private people.'

She tried to raise Max's spirits in small ways. One joyful dis-covery was that for two years she had been wasting a quarter of the space on her aerogrames by leaving the first page empty. 'Max, we have been mugs. Always leaving a blank page,' she wrote, having at last worked out how to fold the flimsy paper. And they had each other. Agatha remembered that as she spent a week with Hubert, Rosalind and Mathew in Wales. 'I can just imagine,' she told Max, 'how it would be coming back to London, just a lonely person, thinking of Ros and Hubert and the baby, a unit by themselves and having really no place in their lives. As it is, I am so happy to think of them, and that I can be "sent for" when wanted and feel useful, and yet have a real life of my own.' Hubert's regiment was now stationed in France. Rosalind's occasional letters to Max consisted mainly of accounts of her struggles with an unheated house, recalcitrant livestock and a small baby. Agatha admired Rosalind's spirit but worried privately about Hubert's safety.

Early in 1944 it seemed that Agatha might be able to come out to Africa with an ENSA tour. It would be a way of seeing Max, but the project came to nothing. She practised patience but missed him with 'a sort of corkscrew feeling' – 'Definitely [your] emotion', Max replied, 'with me it is a sort of emptiness, of being unfilled, not unlike being hungry.' Without constant exposure to Agatha's conversation and teasing, his letters became more wooden. She sent him books to take his mind away from bureaucracy and court cases – two volumes of Herodotus in the Greek and in translation, *A Preface to Paradise Lost*, Arthur Waley's translations of Chinese poetry, the latest novels by Monica Dickens and Compton Mackenzie and – a concession to Max's speculations about his professional future – Nigel Balchin's novel about administrative life, *The Small Back Room*.

Agatha worked. Rehearsals for *Hidden Horizon*, as *Moon on the Nile* was now called, began in January in Dundee. She enjoyed these: 'Larry is a Canon and is toying with the idea of being a Bishop in the London production (if there is a London production!!)' Danae Sullivan supplied costumes and properties, 'like a general store'. 'Such a rest and I had such fun', she told Max. For the first night she was 'well hidden away up in the balcony with Danae'. A friend of the Sullivans '(from Cabaret)' did 'Arab noises off at Abu Simbel during the second act and it did give a desert feeling'. The house was full and it was 'so good [that] many people booked again the second night'.

Full of enthusiasm, she dramatised *Appointment with Death*, finishing it in March. *Absent in the Spring* came out and *Towards Zero*, one of her most original books, deferred from the previous year. She had plenty of plots ready to work up into detective stories but there was one 'of those terrible blank pauses when nothing gets through. You feel despairing.' She thought this all part of 'creative work ... a release from the body's hold ...

always followed by withdrawal, an absence of place'. 'It is part of the same thing', she went on, as 'voodoo or levitation'. For Agatha continued to be puzzled by levitation: '*All* children dream of it,' she wrote to Max and, remembering only her own child-hood dreams, 'the flying dreams one has are not bird flights at all – they are always floating off the ground. And one can't dream of something of which one has no racial memory and of which one has never heard.'

'Ideas for June 1944,' Agatha wrote firmly in her exercise book. One was for a play on the Harlequin theme ('R. Helpmann?' she put hopefully beside this, having seen him earlier in the year in *Hamlet*). She considered a ballet, with Harlequin and Columbine dancing with a mortal ('a Pavlova'). It was interesting that Agatha should think of this and odd that no one took it up, for many of her detective stories are intricately choreographed. Movement, time and place were the basis of her plots; her clues were often visual rather than verbal. In 1944 she also explored a familiar idea, domestic murder, a thought to which she had lately returned in her correspondence with Max about Greek drama: 'an inter-esting point,' Agatha noticed, 'was the distinction made between killing a mother and killing a husband.' Another preoccupation was what she called 'Moral issue' – provoked by reading a book of essays on Shakespeare and, in particular, one on Richard III. 'Do evil men ever acknowledge to themselves that they are evil?' she asked, believing herself that 'most "bad" people do *not* think themselves bad. It is all right for them to do the things they do ...'

The plot on which Agatha settled was a loose amalgamation of these two last themes, domestic murder and the nature of evil, in a novel she called *Remembered Death*. It does not seem to have been easy to draft; Agatha began with a list of characters and a play on the names Rosemary and Rue but tried several variants before fixing on who actually was the murderer, and why. Collins reported that booksellers felt uncomfortable with its title: '*Re-membered Death*,' they said, 'may have a particular application that would upset many people at this juncture.' They preferred *Sparkling Cyanide* but Agatha did not: 'a flippant title for a really rather serious book', she told Collins. There was, however, no time to mull over alternatives, though *Remembered Death* was retained as the title of the American edition.

'Our separation is only an interruption,' Agatha had assured Max – and herself – in 1943. It seemed, now, to be dragging on eternally. Agatha continued to write. She finished *The Hollow*, a detective story dedicated to the Sullivans, 'with apologies for using their swimming pool as the scene of the murder', and started to adapt *Towards Zero* for the stage. At Christmas she put together a collection of stories and poems on religious themes, one of which, 'Promotion in the Highest', is very funny. Agatha sent these shyly to Cork in the New Year: 'Any good anywhere? I can hardly believe so.' The volume was put aside for twenty years.

The autumn of 1944 was sorrowful. Hubert had been reported missing and in August Rosalind learnt that he had been killed. Max did not hear until October, so long was mail taking to arrive. Rosalind's letter was brief and matter-of-fact. Agatha wondered at her daughter's directness and courage. She described how bravely Rosalind had broken the news to her and reminded Max, and herself, that they had expected it, but she could not bring herself to write more.

In her mid-fifties, as in her childhood, Agatha grew dumb when she was moved. She confided neither in her family nor her friends; they might sense her emotion, as she often guessed at, and sought to soothe, their pain, but nothing was said. She had always been tongue-tied; successive shocks – Archie's defection, Clara's death, the divorce, her miscarriage, her son-in-law's death – did not unlock speech but deepened her silence. She could convey her feelings only through her work: in the novels she wrote as Mary Westmacott, protected by that pseudonym, in plays and detective stories where convention and form circumscribed her. As a wife, a mother and a friend, she held back, self-protective. As a writer, she gave generously and incessantly, book after book. The bulk of her work was of one type: fiction, in which a mystery was propounded, clues given and connections made, and a problem solved, with a twist at the end. In her books Agatha 'parted with information' but, even there, obliquely, on her own terms.

The feelings and beliefs Agatha revealed through her writing, if only there, were genuine and strongly held. That, as well as the fact that her work dealt with familiar, universal themes, accounts for the success of her books and plays. Their style is not graceful or magical, their characters are stereotypes, the plots often implausible, but her work is sincere and, for all its contrivance, spontaneous. Agatha minded greatly about the way people should treat one another; she had firm views about good and evil, justice and mercy, innocence, cruelty and revenge. She said what she felt in her books and, increasingly as she grew older, her plays. Outwardly passive and undemonstrative, she found herself at ease in the theatre. It was an arena where she could safely experience and express emotion.

By the end of 1944 Agatha had left the dispensary, not so much because she was exhausted, though she was, but because her theatrical fervour frequently took her away from London. 'Am quite worn out with the strain of theatrical life,' she wrote to Cork in January 1945, 'what with flu ... colds, snow, films, matinees and dressmakers ... most of the cast are never there'. *Appointment with Death* was to open in February but Agatha believed that 'it really seems quite impossible that the play *can* be ready for Glasgow! *However*, one has felt like this before. Sullivan seems to have all the dates booked – but no producer or cast or anything settled. What a queer lot they all are!'

The play came to the Piccadilly Theatre in London at the end of March. The critics were harsh. Cork sent a batch of unfavourable press cuttings, with a kindly letter: 'The public seem to like it and figures from Bertie Meyer show it is doing better business than *10 Little Niggers* at the beginning.' The poor reception for *Appointment with Death* added to the difficulties Sullivan had in finding a London theatre for *Hidden Horizon*. There were other problems. An official at the Ministry of Labour objected to the presence in the play of a maid: 'so unreasonable at this stage', Cork remarked, promising to take the matter up with 'the Director-General of Manpower, a neighbour of mine'. This hitch was not overcome until September, when the play opened in Cambridge. Agatha was there to criticise her work and make suggestions: 'How would it be to make Simon in Commandos and have play definitely post-war – possibly 1946 – one or two of Simon's lines would need altering – what do you think?'

For the European War had ended in May and the war in Japan in August. Agatha's life had returned to a sort of normality some months earlier, for in February she had begun to 'struggle into Greenway', filling the front of an exercise book with details of cleaning-up procedures ('Coats and hats (heavy): Hang in Air 24 hours. Send away to steam'), things to do ('Pack: sheets and towels, Hot water bottle, Jam, Honey'), and, optimistically in view of the shortages that prevailed, items that needed replacement ('Dusters, Saucepan cleaner, 63 yds carpet A's bedroom ...'). The tenants had left the house in a better state of repair than she had expected. The mahogany doors were unshrouded and rehung and in the library Agatha decided to retain one reminder of the American sailors' occupation, a long frieze, in blue and white, painted around the cornice, showing the flotilla and the places where its ships had called, with Greenway and the trees, and – at journey's end – the luscious figure of what in her autobiography Agatha aptly called 'a houri'.

She was delighted to have her house and garden again. Even better, Max came home, arriving at Lawn Road unexpectedly one evening in May, via Sicily and Swindon. Agatha had known for two months that he would be coming back to the Air Ministry and she was not unnaturally anxious about the changes in their relationship that their separation might have caused. 'I am so afraid sometimes that we shall grow outwards instead of a nice parallel track,' she had written. Not convergent, but 'parallel', for Agatha was now sufficiently wise, and content, to recognise that in many respects she and Max were unalike. She was also aware that time and increased responsibility and authority, not just separation, might have altered her husband. May 1944, a year before his return, had brought Max's fortieth birthday. 'It makes such a difference to me,' Agatha had written, '... it closes the gap a little.' As Agatha watched Stephen Glanville's troubles, she had wondered whether she and Max were 'idealising each other in absence. It would break my heart.'

Her fears were unfounded. Max found his wife older, wearier, greyer, but everything at home was aged, exhausted and bruised by six years of war. His return recharged Agatha's batteries. *Come, Tell Me How You Live*, which gives her memories of Syria, was finished by the end of June and sent off for comment to various friends and colleagues. Their opinions were mixed. Stephen Glanville, for instance, found it 'delightful', whereas Sidney Smith, Keeper of the Department of Egyptian and Assyrian Antiquities at the British Museum (who had helped Agatha pass the War by teaching her the algebra she had forgotten) felt that, 'while the whole thing is thoroughly enjoyable reading, I am not quite sure that you would be wise to print it all.' Cork also liked the book and Max himself greatly approved of his homecoming present, which Agatha insisted should be published under her married name.

Her standing at Collins was now gratifyingly high. Figures for sales of her books at the end of January 1945 showed that the last three British and Colonial editions had nearly sold out (*Towards Zero* and *The Moving Finger* with a printing of 25,000 copies each and *Five Little Pigs* with 24,000). Despite the diffi-

culty of assembling a run of figures from those records that had
survived the bombing, Agatha's publishers had the impression
that her overall sales were huge and her prospects promising.
Pushed by Cork, who felt that Collins now 'rather took her books
for granted', in mid-1945 they doubled her advance to £2000.
This so woke them up, Cork told Ober, that 'the books are
promoted more intensively and the sales have actually gone up
to three times what they were.' *Sparkling Cyanide* was serialised
by the *Daily Express* in the summer; Agatha, consulted in good
time about the jacket, was even obliged to confess that she had
'no very solid idea ... a Rosemary motif – sprig of same – on a
Restaurant Table set for dinner with bowl of Rosemary in
centre?'

Agatha's finances were generally improving, at least in prospect. In February 1945 the British Revenue Authorities reached
a settlement with her accountant on the amount of additional tax
for which she was liable; in May Harold Ober reported that the
United States was to conclude a double taxation treaty with the
United Kingdom, with all matters in dispute being settled on a
sympathetic basis, 'whatever,' he prudently observed, 'that may
mean'. It was a relief to think that Agatha might be able to
receive her American earnings, which far outstripped even the
total of her income from Collins and from other countries over-
seas. Moreover, René Clair's *Ten Little Niggers* film, *And Then
There Were None*, opened at the Roxy Cinema in New York in
the autumn, 'a really big Twentieth Century Fox success', Cork
told Agatha, which should have an important effect 'on the film
value of your other subjects'. The BBC began to come round too,
requesting Agatha's participation in a 'Quiz Match ... in the
Home Service, for which they would offer a courtesy fee of Five
Guineas', and the Ministry of Information made up for its refusal
to sanction her wartime visit to Cairo by asking Agatha to write
an article 'on the four leading detective writers this century (including yourself, of course) for publication in Russian in a Mos-
cow magazine'. Cork emphasised that the Ministry 'seem to think
that detective stories may even rival football in effecting a mutual
rapprochement'. Agatha found herself unavailable on the date of
the proposed BBC quiz (she loathed such performances) but she
was ready to help the Ministry of Information: 'I am not anta-
gonistic to writing the articles for Russian publication – I think
it very important to "get together" with Russia in any non-pol-
itical way.'

Agatha had slackened speed now Max was home. 'What a bore!' she complained to Cork, when Ober pressed for a reply to the American magazine editor's comments on *The Hollow*. *Collier's* wanted the story to be shortened for serialisation, with the murder brought into the story much earlier – 'a very considerable job of reorganisation and revision', they acknowledged. 'Maddening ...' Agatha said, returning her copy, 'suitably mutilated', adding hopefully, 'Money in the USA to blue someday?' Collins had asked for revisions too, obliging Agatha to spend part of the autumn modifying the book itself. 'I feel most guilty in urging these nasty little jobs on you when you have better things to do,' Cork assured her, consolingly promising that Collins's cheque for £2000 could now be collected at any time. But 'I am afraid there is another chore. ...'

This was the adaptation of *Towards Zero* for the stage. Lee Shubert, the American impresario, had taken it at the end of 1944 but had proposed a number of alterations. 'I hope they only want me to OK them and don't want anything requiring any concentration,' Agatha had written in January 1945, overwhelmed with work on *Appointment with Death*. Shubert's proposal was for the Mallowans to come to the United States in 1946, for Agatha to make the necessary revisions there. She was at first excited but by the end of 1945 she was happily settled at Greenway: 'Trying to restrain my pullets which fly into the kitchen garden ... but they *are* laying eggs!' She was willing to leave Devon only for Christmas at Pwllywrach: 'We're going to Wales. Hard work there – but lovely eats!! Ducks, geese, a turkey, all walking about waiting their doom.' Her letters at the end of 1945 were happy and relaxed, signed simply 'Agatha', those to Cork closing with cheerful admonitions. She was no longer writing compulsively and, indeed, took mischievous delight in being lazy. As Cork explained to Ober, 'Mrs. Mallowan is going through one of those phases when she needs some *psychological* stimulus to write, and I feel you may be able to provide it. ... Some sort of an account is needed – how well her stuff is doing. This weakness,' he added, 'may seem strange to you, but we find it quite usual here for sensitive folk to find themselves more war weary since VE Day than when they were strung up to meet the unknown.'

19

'. . . a certain amount
of fêting . . .'

Looking back, Agatha wrote in her *Autobiography*, she realised
she had produced 'an *incredible* amount of stuff' during the war
years. She believed that this was because there were few social
distractions and because, until 1945, she had not realised that the
expenditure of time and increasingly precious energy was financially pointless, so much of any proceeds going in tax. This explanation was incomplete. As we have seen, Agatha was extremely busy throughout the War, reading a great many new
books as well as old favourites and the works of history and
classical literature prescribed by Max. She went often to the
theatre and the cinema and saw a good deal of her friends. Old
friends – Archie Whitburn was one – whom she met in the street
were carried off for lunch or dinner and to the theatre and, as
Max's colleagues passed through London, she cooked them a
meal. It was as if she wrote *because* she was busy, fully-charged,
anxious about Max and Rosalind, about her lack of a home, and
about money.

Cork was right; after the War people were worn out, as much
by prolonged uncertainty as by sustained living with danger and
other privations. It took time to shake off that deep exhaustion
and return to normal life. In any case, Britain's circumstances
were greatly changed. After the immediate euphoria at the end
of the War, there was a long struggle not only to rebuild the
fabric of the country but to reshape the framework of society.
Though this was exciting, it required people to adjust – to new
systems of education, health and welfare, new plans for running
the transport and energy industries, new arrangements for planning the growth of towns and protecting the countryside. Regulations and restrictions did not fall away when war ended; they
continued in the shape of licences, forms, controls. There were
still queues, and rationing. The rest of the nineteen-forties were
in some ways hopeful and promising; they were also dreary years,

of bread shortages, fuel shortages, drab utility furniture, unexciting clothes. The nervous stimulus of war was lacking now. It was a long, chilly, depressing haul.

Max and Agatha did not rush off to the United States to see what could be done to *Towards Zero*. There had been quite enough travelling. They gradually settled into Greenway, adding to the trees and shrubs and supervising a not very prospersous market garden that had started life during the war. Max spent most of 1946 writing up the account of his pre-war digs and consulting archaeological colleagues about possible academic posts. He and Agatha began to tidy up the house and garden at Winterbrook and to review their London arrangements, leaving Lawn Road and moving back into Cresswell Place. Here too there was plenty of clearing up to do. Life in some ways seemed empty. Carlo, who was now suffering from severe arthritis, eventually moved to Eastbourne to be with her sister Mary. Madge, in her late sixties, came only rarely to London. Her son Jack could, however, be relied upon for entertainment in London and at Greenway. He had a house in Chester Street, from which he would come to Chelsea to amuse his aunt. Their tastes in books and painting were similar, for Jack liked Dickens, Compton Mackenzie and '*All* Primitives', and he too was fond of music, though he preferred Bach to Wagner. Like Agatha, Jack was interested in theology (he never passed a church without visiting it and knew a great deal about different religions) and he shared her pleasure in simple, carefully prepared food. He always carried with him oil, vinegar, fresh pepper and salt for mixing a salad, which he then submitted to his chauffeur for appraisal, a habit that was known to head waiters all over England, from the Savoy (where legend held that he once took his entire regiment) to the railway restaurant car in which he travelled down from Cheshire.

Many of Agatha's older friends lived quietly in the country; some of her contemporaries were dead. Younger people she and Max knew from the pre-war expeditions to Syria were scattered, while friends from the diplomatic community were taking up new posts. It would be some time before the Mallowans' circle came together again, and friends and relations would once more flock regularly to Greenway in summer and autumn. For the time being, Agatha's life was filled less with friends than with books, for her work was as much in demand after the war as during it. Editions multiplied, reprints were issued as fast as paper could be obtained. Agatha herself, however, was war-weary.

She wrote little in 1946. A birthday ode for Rosalind, composed in August, was rueful:

> 'In my youth', said the crone, 'I had elegant legs
> And my eyes were a beautiful blue,
> I could play parlour games and go off with the prize,
> I was far more accomplished than you!'

> 'You are old,' said her child, 'And really I doubt
> Whether all that you say can be true.
> I admit that you still got away with the crimes,
> But come now, what else can you do?'

There was no doubt that Agatha could 'still get away with the crimes'. Since the daring *The Murder of Roger Ackroyd,* all her books had sold well and each new one was keenly expected. It is true that in the nineteen-thirties and forties the public had a particularly ravenous appetite for detective fiction, notably the successful 'classic' detective story, an intellectual puzzle, set by the author for the reader, who was given a series of clues, some of them misleading. The triumphant practitioner of the technique of writing crime novels was the author who could artfully trick the reader. It was a specialised category of fiction; publishers, booksellers and advertisers on the one hand and the public on the other contrived to keep it so, the former by issuing detective stories under distinctive imprints, awarding special trophies (generally in the form of offensive weapons) for spectacular popular successes, and by emphasising their authors' cunning and ingenuity, and the latter by their hunger for new forms of murder and detection and unwearying fondness for certain sleuths. In October 1944 the American critic, Edmund Wilson, wrote a celebrated article in which he sought to unravel the spell of the detective story, a type of fiction which, he confessed, he had outgrown. It had, he believed, 'borne all its finest fruits by the end of the nineteenth century'; ingenious puzzles, like those offered in Agatha's work, did no more than mildly entertain and astonish. Wilson was, in fact, scathing about Agatha's style, which he found so mawkish and banal that it was 'literally impossible to read'. She must have come across this piece, if not in 1944, for she was interested in what critics thought of detective fiction in general and her own in particular, but she did not mention Wilson's views to her family or friends. Any dismay would have been assuaged by her steady sales and her quiet confidence in her own craftsmanship; she might have been consoled, too, by Wilson's admission that he had read only *Death Comes as the End*, which may have disconcerted him.

There are several explanations for the popularity of detective fiction in the 'thirties and 'forties: that, in the pre-war years, a now largely literate public wanted books that were exciting, self-contained and not too demanding; that detective stories sold well from increasingly well-stocked railway bookstalls; that, between the wars, people looked to crime fiction for escape from a time of turmoil and economic depression, or, in a rival theory, that the public turned to the ordered world of the mystery novel to calm their nerves after the 1914–18 war and (assuming foresight) before the 1939–45 war.

In fact, however, Britain in the 'thirties was for many, particularly in London and the South, an agreeable place to live. Real incomes were rising (for those who had a job), more people had motor cars and wirelesses and were buying their own homes. Life was in many ways placid and, if the newspapers reported foreign crises, they told you what to think of them. This climate perhaps explains the detective novel's vogue. The classic mystery story was small-scale, meticulously worked, domestic, an alternative to the smooth tenor of everyday life, yet actually not all that different from it. Insular, parochial, and, apart from the initial drama of the crime itself, reasonable – its nature suited the attitudes of the time. Perhaps the explanation for its popularity was even more simple: every class in every society needs some form of 'soap opera', popular sagas whose central themes – love, death, jealousy, quests, greed, conflict between good and evil – are highly coloured representations of its own preoccupations. As for the 'forties during the War existence was precarious and people wanted distraction from the chaos around them; they looked for cheap, portable, absorbing fiction to read on interminable, tedious journeys and during the long periods of waiting that irregularly punctuate a war. The crime novel provided a haven; some of its characters were old friends. It was trivial enough to be easily picked up and put down, as circumstances required. No intellectual gear-change was needed, for the prose was not difficult and the chief requirement that the reader be alert, a condition in which the majority of the population spent all the wartime years. Plots varied but the moral was predictable: good would triumph and order be restored. Readers might not only lead a variety of other lives vicariously but also hope that these held comforting lessons for their own.

In the 'thirties and 'forties there was a cluster of authors who were especially adept at the technique of the classic detective story. Their work was snatched up and they wrote prolifically. Some, like Agatha, continued to write for decades. Many belonged to that loosely organised group, the Detection Club, founded at Anthony Berkeley's suggestion in the late nineteen-twenties. Agatha was a member, though with her dignity and acute sense of the ridiculous she must have found it hard to keep a straight face as the members went through 'the Ceremonies' Dorothy Sayers had devised – 'Eric the Skull', for instance, borne in on a black cushion, his eyes aglow with batteries. Agatha submitted to her own initiation – she took the oath on Poison – in a spirit of fun, as thirty years later she agreed to be the Club's President, on condition that a Co-President be appointed to make speeches and orchestrate proceedings. Only with an effort did she talk shop with other detective story writers at the Club's occasional dinners, held before the War in restaurants and after it at rooms in Kingly Street, behind Liberty in Regent Street, which Miss Sayers's connection with Church authorities allowed them to use for a token rent. More to Agatha's taste were the spring and summer dinners, at the Garrick Club and the Café Royal, to which members might bring guests and where a speaker – a senior policeman, a judge, and so on – would address these students and exponents of his profession. A succession of Agatha's friends were entertained at these agreeably eccentric parties.

She was, furthermore, insufficiently reverent towards the Detection Club's rules. (They can be found in Ronald Knox's *Detective Decalogue*.) These set out the conventions which the classic detective story should observe: concealing a vital clue from the reader was abhorred, for example, as was immoderate use of such devices as conspiracies, trap-doors, and 'Mysterious Poisons unknown to Science'. The fuss over *The Murder of Roger Ackroyd* indicated that these principles had even taken popular root. After the experience of *Behind the Screen, The Scoop*, and *The Floating Admiral*, Agatha also declined a part in any more collaborative ventures. It was encouraging though, even for someone who was not a joiner or an organiser, to think of herself as one of a recognised school of writers, one of those, like John Dickson Carr, Margery Allingham, Freeman Wills Crofts, Craig Rice, Elizabeth Daley and the Lockridges, in whose fictions Agatha herself became engrossed. In one important respect, however, Agatha's work differed from that of her colleagues. She produced a succession of dazzlingly cunning plots, whose elucidation was the sole purpose of each book. Unlike other detective story writers, she was not stylistically ambitious; her prose is pedestrian but undistracting. She did not seek to capture the reader's sympathy for one character or another, nor to enlist support for views and theories of her own. Her characters, and the places and circumstances in which they find themselves, are sketches only; she does not make a point of displaying familiarity with various types of people and their world. She herself is as inconspicuous as can be. Some see these characteristics as flaws and criticise Agatha's work for the flatness of her writing and its lack of emotional and topographical colour. Her admirers regard this as part of her strength; they defend her work because it appeals to pure reason. Agatha Christie's fascination, as Robert Barnard described it in his useful appreciation, *A Talent to Deceive*, lies not in appeasing the reader's appetite for sensation or emotion but in satisfying curiosity.

Her books do not make the blood run quicker. As Barnard points out, they present not a succession of incidents leading to a climax but an accumulation of evidence from which deductions may eventually be made. Each has a pattern of 'progressive mystification and progressive enlightenment', with each revelation and the complications it apparently causes falling, at the end, into an ordered and convincing whole. This approach underlies the popularity of Agatha's work. Her detective stories exploit universal doubts, hopes and fears, offered as intellectual exercises. It is an addictive mixture. By the mid-'forties Agatha's readers knew they could rely on her to produce it; while her plots were surprising, her instinct was faultless.

Publishers recognised this by offering high prices for her work. In 1945, for instance, an American film producer proposed £5000 for the rights to *Love from a Stranger* and *Good Housekeeping* magazine $15,000 for a 30,000 to 40,000 word short story. *This Week* offered $2000 for 4000 words, while Frederick Dannay, who admittedly paid contributors to *Ellery Queen's Mystery Magazine* rates considerably higher than many similar competing magazines, concluded a contract to reprint Agatha's short stories for the next two years, at $150 a story, paying for twelve in advance. The Mutual Network arranged a radio series in America, starring Hercule Poirot; '£65 a week,' Cork told Agatha, 'but dizzy heights are possible.' At home, ninepenny paperback editions of Agatha's books and cheap editions, at between two-

and-sixpence and four-and-sixpence, moved as steadily after the War as during it, while eight-and-sixpenny editions would sell from 17,000 to 20,000 copies in the first year of publication. Max's mother constantly urged Agatha to turn her hand to something 'serious' (by which her daughter-in-law thought she meant 'the biography of some world-famous figure'). Agatha stuck to her last. She recognised where her skills lay and, as she admitted in preparing her article for Russia, her pre-eminence. In settling on 'the four leading detective-story writers', she told Max, 'the MOI [Ministry of Information] has suggested Dorothy Sayers but I ... think ... she's now an entirely different type of writer – religious plays and so on. ... Rather invidious to single out 4. To set aside modesty – Myself (!!) Margery Allingham? Dickson Carr? And then who? Bentley? Ngaio Marsh? Anthony Berkeley? For Russia you must have someone who is writing *now* – in full spate.'

Though Agatha herself wrote little in the autumn of 1945 and early 1946, her name was everywhere. *Hidden Horizon* opened in Wimbledon in March and in New York, as *Murder on the Nile* for a brief run, in September. *Come, Tell Me How You Live* appeared and *The Hollow*, not without argument about 'blurbs' (Agatha preferred to write her own) and covers: 'I do *not* like a naturalistic jacket of an actual incident or scene from the book and I don't like human figures on a jacket.' Collins capitulated. Billy provided tickets for Wimbledon ('almost like peace, more than anything since the war ...', Agatha wrote ecstatically) and, even harder to obtain, tennis balls, sent by registered post to Devonshire.

Agatha did eventually embark on two new pieces of writing. The 'psychological stimulus' Cork thought she needed came in the spring, ironically from the BBC. Queen Mary, the mother of King George VI, was asked by the Corporation to suggest how her eightieth birthday might be celebrated on the wireless. It appeared that Queen Mary was a particular admirer of Agatha's work and the BBC accordingly sounded out Cork on the telephone and then invited Agatha to write a half-hour radio play to be broadcast on May 26th. As Cork told Agatha in mid-May: '... all the items on the programme have been officially chosen by her.' There was a stately minuet to make arrangements about the fee, which Agatha wished to take the form of a donation to the Southport Infirmary Children's Toys Fund. The Corporation sent a cheque for a hundred guineas to the Fund, Cork refused commission, and everyone was pleased. The play that resulted from these negotiations was *Three Blind Mice*, which Agatha based on an idea she had first formulated in 1945, when she read of the death of a young boy, Daniel O'Neill, placed with his small brother in the care of foster-parents, who had maltreated both children. The tragedy had moved her deeply. *Three Blind Mice* next became a short story, bought by *Cosmopolitan* in the United States after great competition, and the title story in a collection published in America in 1950. It was to enjoy another incarnation, as *The Mousetrap*, two years later.

Agatha's other preoccupation in 1946 was a novel. At the beginning of 1945, when Cork reported that 'Mary Westmacott' was to be published by Rinehart in the United States, she had told him she was eager for 'MW to do some work again – but when?!!' Like *Absent in the Spring*, it germinated not from a list of characters or a plot, but from a quotation. In her exercise book – after a note about the best source (Clermont Faugier, she thought) of Crème de Marrons – Agatha quoted lines from various poems: by Laurence Binyon, Cecil Day Lewis, W.J. Turner and, especially, T.S. Eliot, whose *Four Quartets* suggested a number of possible titles. Her choice fell on *The Rose and the Yew Tree*, from an image in Eliot's 'Little Gidding', a poem she greatly liked. She was interested in the interweaving of religion and philosophy in Eliot's work, its elevation of the ordinary and perception of the spiritual. She also admired his theatrical technique: *Murder in the Cathedral*, she wrote to Max in 1943, was 'a revelation in the effect of human voices, in tone and rhythm, on the musical senses.' Eliot, for his part, was said (in a memoir by W.T. Levy) to have observed that Agatha Christie was his favourite detective-story writer, with 'the best-constructed plots' (He recommended *The Murder of Roger Ackroyd*.) It is appropriate that the character who unravels the mysteries in Eliot's play *The Family Reunion* should have been named 'Agatha'.

Cork liked *The Rose and the Yew Tree*, but it gave him a difficult time. Agatha's story is narrated by a convalescent, disabled not in the War but, to his embarrassment, in a car smash. It is set in the Cornish constituency during the 1945 election campaign, where the local Conservative Committee has chosen as its candidate not 'an old-fashioned chap' but a self-made man, who holds the Victoria Cross and, though 'slick', 'knows all the answers'. Like her narrator, Agatha's understanding of politics was that of a shrewd observer only, and she distilled in this novel what she had learned from Madge and her nephew Jack, later a Conservative M.P. and formerly a Councillor in Manchester. Agatha's editor at Collins found some of her treatment shaky, her description of a Party Whist Drive, for instance, since during an election campaign 'Social activities are suspended.' More woundingly, Billy Collins told Agatha: 'We felt that it was perhaps rather unfortunate having a story round the last General Election with such an undesirable person as a candidate at a time like this.' She replied coldly: 'I don't feel the new Westmacott is quite your cup of tea. Perhaps we'd better stick to crime?' To Cork she was more blunt: '*Do* let M.W. be published by someone else. Collins never have appreciated the lady – and have you ever seen anything more *idiotic* than Billy Collins's letter – missing the whole point of the book. Definitely they shall *not* have my "ewe lamb" so will you try it on someone else – Michael Joseph?' (In the same week Collins had also foolishly sent the proposed wrapper for *The Labours of Hercules*, 'the naked Poirot' adding to Agatha's wrath.) Cork duly sent *The Rose and the Yew Tree* to Michael Joseph, and then to Heinemann, who thought 'Billy is crackers' and took it for publication in 1948. Rinehart and Co. were again the American publishers.

There were other irritations. At the end of 1946 Agatha delivered a new Hercule Poirot story, *Taken at the Flood*. The American magazines were cool, Ober explaining to Cork that they felt Poirot was 'rather dragged in' and detracted from the story's reality. It was, he said, becoming difficult to sell, 'a mystery story solved by one of the stock detectives. This kind of story will continue to sell well in book form, but the Ngaio Marsh type of murder mystery is I think what editors are going to be looking for.' He suggested that serialisation might be possible if Agatha 'felt like rewriting and leaving out Poirot' but 'of course, I want you to use your judgment about mentioning this to Mrs Mallowan.' Cork tactfully refrained from referring to Ngaio Marsh (another of his clients) and persuaded Agatha to change her text. To everyone's fury, however, Ober reported in December that the American editor who had asked to buy the non-Poirot version had now let him down. The *Toronto Star* bought *There is a Tide* (the American title), with Poirot, but Agatha was annoyed: 'Really it was a beast to alter. ...'

To crown her fury, Agatha discovered that, in one of the American reviews of *Absent in the Spring*, Mary Westmacott's identity was revealed. Cork had asked the Library of Congress to catalogue Agatha's work as 'M.W.' under her pseudonym only but 'some journalistic sleuth', he believed, had discovered the secret through the Copyright Registration Office. One embarrassment seemed to follow another, also upsetting Agatha: 'An "interview" in the *News Review*,' she wrote miserably to Cork. 'Quite dreadful – saying I had red hair – my father was an American stockbroker and I was one of the richest women in the world! ... Can they *do* these things?'

Agatha had 'flu in the New Year. She had been in Wales with Rosalind, helping to nurse Mathew through bronchitis. 'How difficult everything is nowadays with no *servants* – it's all the chores and the cooking to be done – I really wonder how Rosalind stands up to it all.' After her own illness Agatha felt 'sunk in listless depression', until suddenly, at the end of January, 'the clouds lifted'. Cork nonetheless wisely encouraged her not to try to work, ordering at her request theatre tickets for *Born Yesterday* and *The Man from the Ministry*, and, in June, *Annie Get Your Gun*. He helped arrange a trip to Switzerland and the South of France in the early spring, Agatha's first foreign expedition since the outbreak of war, five days in Lugano and five in Cannes. (Cap Martin, her preference, had been badly damaged by Italian shelling.) Obtaining foreign exchange was complicated but Cork managed it. He flattered Agatha over the success of a BBC television broadcast of *Three Blind Mice*, arranged for the story called 'Star over Bethlehem' to be printed in an American magazine at Christmas, suggested that Sullivan might be able to take *Alibi* on an American tour. There were frequent delicious lunches and friendly bets on the outcome of the Derby.

Cork and Ober between them also protected Agatha on one particular matter, the objections of many readers to 'anti-Semitic' and 'anti-Catholic' allusions in her work. Sensitive readers were certainly struck by Agatha's blunt and often uncomplimentary references to her Jewish characters. (There are in fact no disparaging allusions to Catholics.) The triviality of these remarks made them no less hurtful. *The Mysterious Mr Quin*, for example, had a passage about 'men of Hebraic extraction, sallow men with hooked noses, wearing flamboyant jewellery', and *Peril at End House* a condescending reference to 'the long-nosed Mr Lazarus', an art dealer whom another character described as 'a Jew, of course, but a frightfully decent one.'. It was only after the war, however, that Agatha's publishers and then just her American publishers, began to receive protesting letters: 'It is a downright

shame,' Dodd, Mead was told, 'to see an institution such as
yours, which could be used in the interests of a permanent peace,
publish such trash.' In 1947 the Anti-Defamation League sent an
official objection to Dodd, Mead, who forwarded it to Ober.
'This letter is typical,' he told Cork, 'of a number that have come
in recently.' He proposed not that Agatha should see the letters
but that Cork might warn her to omit any references to Jews and
Catholics in future books, since 'these are two very delicate subjects over here.' An unidentified reference in *The Hollow* had been
found especially offensive. Cork handled this awkward commission with his usual tact. He did not write to Agatha about it,
though he may have spoken to her, but with Ober ensured that
in subsequent books the offending remarks disappeared. Indeed,
Dodd, Mead was given permission to change such references.
Ober also arranged that Dodd, Mead should cease to forward
correspondence from the public directly to Agatha; he had recently discovered that since 1938 they had continued to send
letters to Ashfield.

Agatha mirrored in her books the attitudes of her class and
generation, 'the usual tedious British anti-Semitism', as the historian Jacques Barzun called it in *A Catalogue of Crime*, prejudices that were also displayed in, for example, the work of John
Buchan and M.R. James. Agatha's unsophisticated general-
isations about Jews and Jewishness are a reminder that she did
not share the inhibitions of a generation sensitised by the suffer-
ings of the Jewish people since 1933, though the picture she gave
of the Levinnes in *Giant's Bread* shows that she could also write
delicately and sympathetically about the prejudices a Jewish
family encountered among upper-class English people. The
phrases with which Agatha offended were painful not because
they were vicious but because they seemed flippant; when she
eventually met truly fanatical anti-Semitism she was, like many
of her compatriots, incredulous. She described in her *Autobiography* her first encounter with National Socialism, in 1933, when
the Director of Antiquities in Baghdad, a fierce Nazi, astounded
her with a passionate outburst: 'his face changed in an extraordinary way that I had never noticed on anyone's face before.'

For there was much that Agatha did not notice, unless it occurred in surroundings and among people she knew. Though she
travelled and was familiar with classical and European art, literature and music, she was insular. If she lived in a place, she could
understand its people and their culture; she could sympathise

with any sort of friends, whatever their race, age, religion, habits
and proclivities. She was at ease with what was basic and local;
she was neither cosmopolitan nor intellectually sophisticated. Her
horizons were limited and her perspective that of an ordinary,
upper-class Edwardian Englishwoman. Yet her understanding
was instinctive and her appeal universal, so that in her work she
transcended her insularity. It is, for example, remarkable that an
amateur adaptation of *Ten Little Niggers* (a story both macabre
and, to some, offensively titled) should have been devised and
performed by a group of prisoners in Buchenwald concentration
camp, who found, as a survivor later told Agatha, that it sustained them. It is, moreover, equally interesting that Agatha,
though touched by this story, found nothing unusual about it.

Max was the scholar and the cosmopolitan. He loved complex-
ity and academic intrigue. Now in his early forties, he was already
greatly respected for his pre-war work in Syria, for his conscientiously written accounts of the excavations and for his encouragement of the young. In the autumn of 1947 his search for a
post bore fruit, when he was appointed to the first Chair of
Western Asiatic Archaeology at the Institute of Archaeology in
the University of London. The Institute had come officially into
being in 1934, eventually moving into a commodious home in
Regent's Park, with, to Max's delight, a rotunda. During the
course of the War it had been eased into the University, which
thereafter took full responsibility for it. Max's new post required
him to lecture and to teach. It also gave him access to a source
of funds to use for travel and his own research, so, after all, the
Mallowans could continue to dig. Agatha immediately began to
think of ways in which she might justifiably return to the Near
East. The amount of sterling British travellers might take abroad
was strictly limited but Cork saw no difficulty in obtaining a
business allowance for her, were she to base a book on her travels.
'After all,' he assured her, 'a book by you with a Mesopota-
mian setting would bring in to the Treasury numbers of dollars!'
As a precaution, Ober sounded out *Collier's* and Dodd, Mead,
who sent letters expressing enthusiasm for *The House in Baghdad*,
as Agatha called her new project.

There were two tasks to perform before the Mallowans left.
One was moving from Cresswell Place, which they let, to 48 Swan
Court, an apartment in a block off the King's Road in Chelsea,
which Mrs North helped Agatha find. The other was Max's in-
augural lecture. Agatha herself put the last touches to a short

story, 'Witness for the Prosecution', and a new detective novel, *Crooked House*. There was a final admonition to Billy about *Taken at the Flood*: 'Do NOT put *any* representation of my poor Hercule on the jacket – confine yourself to a stormy (or sunlit) sea or synthetic ship etc.' Agatha and Max then joyfully departed.

They spent almost five months in Baghdad, negotiating with the authorities as to where Max might resume digging. Living first at the Zia Hotel ('Even the rioting students,' Agatha wrote to Cork, 'conduce to greater laziness') they later moved to a house which, like many of Agatha's houses, overlooked the river. There, in a sumptuous dressing-gown, Agatha sat on the balcony each morning. She read 'thousands of American detective stories .... None of mine about except one very peculiar edition of *And Then There Were None*, with pictures of all the film scenes – Rather Fun.' During her absence Cork, Ober and her financial advisers wrestled with the demands of the American and British Revenue authorities. Reinheimer believed he had reached a settlement on the American side; 'Not one I'm proud of,' Cork had reported, 'but the lawyers seem to think it is the best that can be obtained amicably.' Agatha, it appeared, might at last receive the balance of the income frozen in the United States; the problem would now be with the British tax authorities who, unfamiliar with the details of this history, would see these earnings suddenly arrive. 'It admits,' Cork added, gloomily, 'of many permutations in view of varying rates of tax and exchange during the period. ...'

All Agatha's affairs had been promptly and legally dealt with at the time. The difficulty was that they were extremely complicated, her earnings subject to several different sets of laws and regulations and spread over many years. Furthermore, the more frequently Agatha's advisers were asked to produce information, the more muddled things became, because the sets of accounts and figures, each with different corrections and amendments, multiplied, went astray, contradicted one another and altogether caused confusion. One authority wanted figures presented one way, another differently. Letters and cables crossed. Errors crept in and were perpetuated. Ober, advised by his lawyers, now made it a practice to consult Cork by cable or letter for any offer for any work by Agatha Christie, when he received it from anywhere in the world. 'We have not yet reached finality,' Cork wrote to Agatha. 'Obviously the best thing to do is to put it out of your mind until someone can produce the ultimate figure.'

When Agatha returned from Baghdad she found these matters far from settled, and it was not easy to follow Cork's advice. Her mood in the summer of 1948 varied between anxiety and reckless pleasure in each moment. 'Oh, it is so beautiful, I shall go on enjoying myself and then have a slap-up bankruptcy!!!' Cork feared it might come to that. At the end of September, he was writing to Ober in much the same terms as years before: 'there seems to be little likelihood of Mrs Mallowan avoiding bankruptcy. It seems almost incredible to me that she should be liable for tax on income that arose in a foreign country and which could not be transmitted to her because of the action of the government of that country – but apparently this is how our law stands.' He told her accountant, Dickson, that these uncertainties were affecting her work: 'She has not written one word for over 12 months – a disastrous state of affairs for her, and incidentally pretty serious for us, as she is by far our most remunerative client.' Cork's letter was designed to frighten Dickson into working even more vigorously on Agatha's behalf, but there was some basis for his anxiety.

Agatha had indeed failed to write a word all year, despite a short trip to Paris with Max in the autumn to see her French publisher and boost her spirits. Nor had she been moved to begin another book by flattering letters from Pocket Books in America, announcing the award of a 'Golden Gertrude', 'a replica of our Kangaroo mascot ... the equivalent of an Oscar in the film industry', marking the sale of over five million copies of her work in their editions – an accolade, declared Cork, who cleared 'Gertie' through Customs, of no commercial value but 'for merit, in the same class as a Lonsdale belt'. Fortunately her publisher had two detective stories and *The Rose and the Yew Tree* for 1948, and in America there was the collection, *Witness for the Prosecution*. *The Rose and the Yew Tree* was warmly received and, despite the earlier revelation, Mary Westmacott's identity still baffled reviewers: '... promises extremely well', said *Books of Today*. Agatha's earlier work was also now greatly sought after. Penguin wanted back titles and Cork was obliged to advertise for old editions, as his own stock and Collins's had been destroyed in the Blitz. Ober hunted up file copies and Rosalind was persuaded to lend *Murder at Hazlemoor*, though she emphasised to Cork that he should take the greatest care: 'My mother has always impressed on me not to let my American copies out of the house.'

Requests were made with increasing frequency for permission to adapt Agatha's work for the stage, television and the wireless. The most persistent applicant was an American impresario and actor, who had played Poirot in a radio series and now wanted to televise his exploits. Agatha refused her blessing; he then pressed Ober to write Cork a highly technological letter about the growth of television viewing in the United States, asking whether Mrs Mallowan's hesitation might stem from her wish to wait for the completion of 'the cross-country coaxial cable', which would be hungry for material and would drive up the price – not a likely explanation in Agatha's case. The playwright Ben Hecht inquired whether he might adapt for the stage *Murder on the Calais Coach*, as the American edition of *Murder on the Orient Express* was called, Cork, however, told Ober that Agatha had not abandoned the idea that she might someday adapt this book herself, but: 'not as a conventional "whodunnit",' since she saw it 'starting in New York at the time of the kidnapping'. (Much on the lines of the film that eventually appeared in 1974.) She was more sympathetic to an approach by Barbara Toy and Moie Charles, who ran a small theatre company called Farndale to which Bertie Meyer had brought *Ten Little Niggers* during the War. At the end of 1948 they asked Agatha whether she would dramatise another book for them and, to their surprise, she agreed immediately. They chose *The Murder at the Vicarage*. 'Sex and religion always goes down well,' Miss Toy told Agatha, who completed her stage version in 1949.

In the New Year she started writing prolifically again. In January she and Max left England for Baghdad and at the beginning of February they started to dig at the site he had chosen, Nimrud. Layard had first explored this lovely place exactly a century before – a great green mound, grazed by sheep, full of wild flowers in spring. Two miles to the west, the Tigris flowed quickly between steep banks; northwards was downland; to the south a fertile plain and to the east the mountains of Iran, glowing softly purple. Agatha and Max set about finding a house – 'much nicer than an Hotel', she wrote to Cork, 'a very peaceful and happy life'. They were assisted by Dr Mahmud al Amin from the Iraq Antiquities Department at the University of Baghdad, who kept the records in Arabic, and Robert Hamilton, a surveyor and classicist. All four lived in a wing of a Sheikh's mud-brick house and were fed on their cook's delicious curries, cakes and excellent mayonnaise. Agatha was ready for work. She asked

Cork whether he could find her a decent typewriter but, even before he had arranged for Ober to send the 'very latest noiseless Remington' from the United States, she had equipped herself with a small Swiss machine 'very neat – nothing much has come out of it yet but a few ideas are floating around in my elderly brain!'

The ideas were mostly about Miss Marple. The previous summer Agatha had mentioned to Cork that she was thinking on these lines and he encouraged her, perhaps believing that the way to ease her back into writing might be by means of one of her favourite characters, but definitely not via the 'insufferable Poirot'. '*Short Marples*', she now wrote in her exercise book, listing a string of ideas that included 'Committee Crime (Poisoned glass of *water*?)'; 'Infra-red Photograph', a favourite idea since she had taken up photography; 'Cryptogram in letter' and 'Extra course at dinner. Cream? Shrimps?' There was an old friend: 'Legless man. Tall? Short?' She also noted more of Miss Marple's 'special knowledge': 'Maid's day out – never Monday'; '*Reasons* for "Apple Sauce". Ham and Spinach. ...' A look at *Three Blind Mice*, the collection that appeared in 1950, shows what happened to some of these conceits.

She also began work on a full-length detective story, *A Murder is Announced*. Agatha had already begun to think about the details of the plot the previous autumn and had conducted preliminary research with the help of neighbours at Wallingford, the Severns. 'I want you to act it for me,' she told old Mrs Severn and her two grown-up sons one evening, sending them outside the drawing-room while she moved the furniture, and then instructing them to come in with a torch. 'Now what have you seen?' she asked everyone in the room. The test, in fact, Guy Severn perceived when the book was published, was of what they had *failed* to see.

Cork, meanwhile, was overseeing the arrangements for publication of *Crooked House*, which *John Bull* was to serialise before Collins brought it out in May. The American market was stickier. Ober had to tell Cork that plans to serialise the book on the air had fallen through, since 'the National Broadcasting Company in this country has become very moral.' The network's censorship department had ruled that *Crooked House* was unsuitable for broadcasting into the public's homes on Sunday nights, for in the late 'forties and 'fifties America was passing through one of its periodic righteous phases. 'It seems,' Ober continued, 'that the public has been complaining in droves about the number of murders being committed over the air. ...'

Crooked House was published shortly after Agatha and Max returned to England in May 1949. But there was an immediate distraction, the appraisal of Barbara Toy's work on *The Murder at the Vicarage*. Miss Toy had made few changes but Agatha thought more should be done. On the whole, she told Cork, 'a very good job has been made of it. It still has the rather too cosy novelish atmosphere of "let's sit down and wonder whodunnit" – but I never could see how that could be avoided in this particular book.' She did, however, like the idea of 'a kind of duel' between Miss Marple and Lawrence at the end of the play. 'Excellent,' but, she added, showing confidence that her audience would share her own horticultural and criminological expertise: 'Everyone knows the symptoms of weedkiller far too well – death after hours or days of sickness, vomiting etc. Suggest cyanide. Miss M always has it handy for wasps' nest (right time of year).' Or else 'concentrated solution of nicotine, dilute form of which is used for green fly etc.' On the other hand, she added, knowing the popular affection for villainous old ladies, 'more fun to be got out of Miss M saying it was really Providential she had cyanide so handy! Audience might easily think she was mad and *had* done it.'

Production of *The Murder at the Vicarage* was delayed because Bertie Meyer was busy touring *Ten Little Niggers* for the Army of Occupation in Germany. Rehearsals eventually began in the summer, with Agatha attending to make suggestions, while the director, Irene Hentschel, whipped the play into shape. It opened in October in Northampton. Barbara Toy drove Agatha there from London and helped her up the stairs of the hotel – awkward for Agatha, whose ankles now tended to swell. The play was a success, 'not at all bad,' Cork told Agatha, 'that they should have played to over 1200 in the same week as Bertram Mills circus.' It was a happy time for Agatha, at ease with the cast at the back-stage party, the only person not drinking alcohol but intoxicated, as always, by the theatre.

Agatha was also full of pleasure at Rosalind's remarriage. In October Agatha and Max had received a hurried letter to say the wedding would take place in a day or two's time, in London. Rosalind and her future husband, Anthony Hicks, would come up on the train but there would be no time for lunch, since they had to race back to Pwllywrach to feed the dogs. If Agatha and

Max cared to come, they were welcome, but there was no need. Agatha was vastly amused – and delighted, for she liked Anthony, who had met Rosalind in Somerset. He was a scholarly man, knowledgeable about all sorts of things, trained as a barrister and in Oriental studies, full of curiosity about people and the world, interested in gardens, religions, unusual butterflies, rare postage stamps, fond, like Agatha, of an occasional bet, able to keep his future mother-in-law amused, and, like her, passionately keen on travel.

Agatha's spirits were high. She began to consider dramatising a story she had first published in 1948, 'The Witness for the Prosecution', after an approach from America about the film rights. A *New Yorker* cartoon, published in mid-May, had amused her (Ober sent the engraver's proof) and she had taken in her stride an accident-prone BBC broadcast in August: 'Just as well I *didn't* see 10 Little Niggers on the Television! I hear General MacArthur, after being stabbed, got up and strolled away with his hands in his pockets, quite unaware he was "in view". I should have been *livid*.' She now followed Cork's recommendation to put aside thoughts of her financial anxieties. 'Magnificent letter from Reinheimer,' she told him. 'I don't understand a word of it! Anyway, what the Hell is what I now feel about income tax.' Cork was now dealing with yet another Inspector from the Revenue, the Torquay office having temporarily retreated. This time a letter came from the City, and it appeared that the whole saga would begin again, since this latest raiding party was clearly ignorant of all that had gone before. 'I understand,' the letter ended (although this may have been bureaucratic irony), 'that Agatha Christie is to all intents and purposes a pen name, and it would appear that the tax district of the husband is the one that is required.' Agatha, after eating Billy Collins's Christmas present of pheasant that 'melted in the mouth – quite unlike my butcher's tough productions', escaped with Max to Nimrud.

20

'... digging up the dead ...'

At sixty, Agatha remained energetic and productive; her wits
were sharp, her health was good, and during the next ten years
she produced work that, though lacking the sparkle of her post-
war books, remained interesting and popular. If that decade
followed a routine, it was an unusual one: the creation of at least
one annual detective story, sometimes accompanied by a novel,
a play, a collection of short stories, and a yearly expedition to
Iraq. The Mallowans would leave England in December or January, going first to Baghdad and on to Nimrud, returning in
March after a season's digging. During those expeditions Agatha
would plan and write her books. The simplicity of life in the
desert and her absence from England during the worst of the
winter, added to her strong constitution and remarkable stamina,
account for her physical and intellectual resilience, while Max,
her family and a group of much-loved friends buoyed up her
spirits. At the School of Archaeology in Baghdad or in the camp
in the desert Agatha was serene, busy and at home.

In many respects archaeology was like detection. It required its
practitioners to recognise, match and arrange fragments of clues,
to reconstruct what might have happened from evidence that
remained. Luck and intuition were needed, as well as persistence.
Like detection, too, archaeology had changed since Agatha had
been first enraptured by it in the nineteen-thirties. Even then it
was no longer the preserve of enthusiastic amateurs, supporting
expeditions from a private fortune, using methods that were often
ruthless and slapdash. By the time Max had joined Woolley at
Ur, archaeologists tended to be trained professionals, competing
for posts, staff and funds within the universities, museums and
learned societies. They looked for resources from public institu-
tions; their finds were not all hauled triumphantly home but distributed among their benefactors, including the countries that
had given them permission to dig. Their goals – sifting through
the remnants of a mound rather than unveiling monumental

buildings – were more modest than those of their nineteenth-century forebears and their techniques more sophisticated, for after the First World War significant advances had been made in methods of digging, recording stratification, analysing and cataloguing finds.

During the years Agatha spent in Syria and Iraq, archaeology gradually became even more scientific, as complicated techniques of detection and dating developed in laboratories reduced the part played by instinct and chance in unravelling the past. Fewer of the public were familiar with Biblical and classical literature, but other means of popularising archaeology, including television, sustained attention – and thereby a flow of small and large donations. The past was still accessible, although those who wished to investigate it were finding it more difficult to do so. The authorities in those countries where an excavation was taking place were becoming increasingly sensitive to exploration of their soil, although nationalism and isolationism had not yet grown so fervent that all access by aliens was forbidden.

In temperament and attitude, however, the archaeologists among whom Max and Agatha worked in the nineteen-fifties and sixties resembled their colleagues before the War and, indeed, their Victorian predecessors. Members of a close-knit profession, with fierce rivalries among different schools, often obsessional but capable of extraordinary patience, they were specialists who worked in teams. An expedition brought together many different experts: an architect, surveyor, epigraphist, historian, people who knew about theology, geology, photography, drawing, and so on. Max's expeditions were small and economical, with each member serving more than one role. Agatha was an important member of the team.

The photographic record of the finds was, for instance, still largely her responsibility: In 1951 she asked Cork to arrange for Ober to acquire a special camera, complete with flash equipment. She also took charge of cleaning the pieces of broken ivories, part of the treasure found at Nimrud, spreading the fragments on towels and meticulously sponging them with Innoxa cleansing milk, a method she had hit upon herself. She was equally inventive in her domestic arrangements, inspiring the creation of éclairs with cream from water buffalo and nut or hot chocolate soufflés cooked in a tin box by successive cooks, 'drunk or mad or both', one guest remembered. If a soufflé dropped, one cook would apologise to her with the refrain, 'Squeeze me, madam, squeeze me!' Compared with other expeditions, the Mallowans' team lived, as Max put it, 'like fighting cocks', enjoying Stilton sent by Allen Lane from England, and the airmail copy of *The Times*, delivered to Mosul by special arrangement. Cork forwarded post, which took only four or five days to arrive. At Nimrud, as everywhere else, the Mallowans changed for dinner, Agatha wearing a fur jacket with voluminous sleeves, which tended to knock glasses of water into her neighbour's lap. She dressed in the desert much as at home, in sensible tweed, silk and cashmere, with dresses from Worth for special occasions and a variety of clothes from cheap shops for ordinary days. There is a remarkable photograph of her pottering across the sand, silhouetted against the Mound, like a thoughtful bird, in stockings and laced-up shoes, carrying a handbag. Hats were tied on with scarves to keep them from vanishing in the constant wind. On her return to London each year Agatha, always tidy, rushed immediately to a hairdresser to be rearranged. Like everyone on the dig, she slept in a tent, but at the end of the expedition house had a room of her own for writing. There she was not to be disturbed, even though groups of visitors constantly arrived, not so much to see the excavations, some of Max's colleagues thought, as to try to catch a glimpse of Agatha – at least in the case of Finns and Swedes, among whom her books were now enormously popular.

The camp was sparsely furnished but the British School of Archaeology in Baghdad quickly became a repository for the objects Agatha acquired on frequent shopping expeditions over the seasons. Accompanied by women friends from the British diplomatic community and the School, she descended on the bazaars, buying ornaments, lamps, fabrics and great quantities of rugs. It was not always entirely clear for whom these purchases were intended. Sometimes Agatha's companions, ostensibly recruited to help her buy presents for other people, would find her bestowing the articles on themselves on the way home. Purchases might be packed up for sending to London or taken back to the Institute, where they would remain for a season or two and then suddenly be despatched to England, for Agatha and Max regarded the Institute as in many respects an extension of their home and saw their colleagues, particularly the younger ones, as part of their family. Indeed, a clause of Max's will was to provide for a sum to be set aside to furnish an annual dinner for members of the British School of Archaeology in Persia and Iraq, at which at least one member of the Mallowan – Hicks – Prichard family would try to be present, and where a toast would be drunk in memory of Max and Agatha.

It was, however, an extended family, as people came and went at different stages in their careers, with a core of those who were at Nimrud every year, of whom perhaps the most faithful and indispensable were the foreman, Hamoudi, and the tireless Barbara Parker, who organised the details of the expedition and took the blame when things went wrong. Agatha presided, like an eccentric mother – rather like Clara, in fact – watching with amusement as members of the expedition fell for one another, or infuriated each other, counselling the younger married women on the dangers of miscarrying in the difficult surroundings of Iraq (almost before they themselves knew they were expecting babies) and building up the scraggier young men on a diet of chocolate truffles. Max has described the members of successive expeditions in his *Memoirs*, where he included extracts from some of the 'Cautionary Verses for Archaeologists' with which Agatha commemorated each person. The *Memoirs* also give some of the 'Nimrud Odes'. with which, as at Greenway and Pwllywrach, she marked birthdays and other celebrations. There was a 'Nimrud Book of Dreams', as well, the outcome of Agatha's protesting that Max refused to listen to her recital at breakfast of what she had discovered in sleep the night before. 'Dear Professor Mallowan,' she wrote in the covering letter, 'it has been brought to my notice that you adopt a somewhat unsympathetic attitude towards dreams. You have heard, no doubt, of Napoleon's famous Dream Book. I am submitting for your attention the Nimrud Book of Dreams. This contains certain well authenticated dreams ... both curious and interesting and [which] shed a valuable light on the psychology of the dreamers ... we hope to publish a further series shortly and hope we may enrol you as a regular subscriber ... Yours faithfully, Snore and Moonshine. PP' (for Agatha now tended to nod off) 'A. Snooze.'

Max's team worked hard and by the beginning of 1951 their excavations began to produce interesting finds. As well as the Governor's Palace and the Burnt Palace in the eastern section of the mound, they were by then examining the buildings in the western sector, looking particularly at the northern and southern wings of Ashurnasirpal's North-West Palace. Layard's excavations a century before had concentrated on the State Apartments; Max and his assistants began to look at the domestic wing, where a rich collection of ivories came to light, including a large figure of a bull and what Max's *Memoirs* describe as 'little feminine trinkets', among them a collection of shells, sometimes engraved, containing cosmetics. A grave contained the remains of a princess, wearing a jewelled pendant – 'the Nimrud jewel' – her tunic held by a pin twenty-six-and-a-half centuries old. In the Administrative Wing of the Palace were treasures of a different kind, the royal archives, and, most wonderful, a sandstone monument erected by Ashurnasirpal, inscribed with the record of the completion of the City in 879 BC, which concluded, appropriately, with 'an account of a sumptuous banquet' given on the acropolis over a period of ten days to nearly 7,000 persons. It gave, Max claimed, a living vision of the feasts held in the spring of 879 BC, vast alfresco meals served in the spacious courtyards.

In 1952 Max decided to explore the wells in the Administrative Wing of the Palace, a difficult and perilous operation. Despite the warning from an American oil expert, 'Every well claims a life,' the undertaking was completed without a single loss. In earlier excavations Layard had investigated the wells down as far as the water level. Max's team now looked below, finding in the first shaft the remains of a number of texts, fragments of cuneiform writing on wax, ivory binding and boards, before the bottom of the well collapsed. Max was more prudent in his investigation of the second well, thus missing remarkable discoveries which the Iraq Department of Antiquities were to make forty years later of ivories, ivory heads and bowls, painted and decorated in gold leaf. He made stunning finds, however, in the third shaft. Brick-lined, it was very deep, with a corkscrew bend in the middle. Seventy or eighty feet down, in the sludge beneath the oozing water, digging all day and, by the light of hurricane lamps, all night, they unearthed a cache of treasure: the ivory head of a beauty and, in contrast, of one they christened 'The Ugly Sister'; horses' cheek-pieces decorated with a relief of a female sphinx; a winged cobra emerging from her skirt – all the objects Max subsequently described in *Nimrud and Its Remains*, and which may be seen in the British Museum, the Metropolitan Museum in New York City and the Iraq Museum in Baghdad. Agatha carefully wrapped these objects in damp towels, realising that after two thousand years they needed gently drying out. The most marvellous discovery was a pair of plaques in chryselephantine, one of which remained in Baghdad, the other being flown to London in May. Max described in his *Memoirs* the cruel scene they showed: a man being mauled by a lioness in a thicket of papyrus reeds and lotus flowers, waving in the wind. The colours of the flowers were indicated by touches of lapis lazuli and carnelian and the man's curly hair was of fine ivory capped with gold. The British Museum published a poster displaying this treasure; a copy hung at Winterbrook and hangs at Greenway today.

The hazards of these undertakings were sometimes increased by appalling weather, particularly in the 1953 season: 'Living in constant damp seems to be a cure for rheumatism,' Agatha wrote to Cork, 'I can't think why!!!' The beginning of that year was exceptionally difficult: 'The weather has been awful, roads cut as well as bridges. Snow on the foothills and we have been breaking ice on the water tubs each morning.' Machinery sent by the Iraq Petroleum Company for exploring the second well was delayed when the lorry became bogged down in the mud: 'Thunderstorms, rain, and we all huddle in quantities of jerseys and woolly knickers. Tents keep out the rain all right, but, oh, how clammy to creep into the sheets each night – and clothes like damp fish in the morning.' These were uncomfortable surroundings for a woman of sixty-three but Agatha retained her good humour. Meals were important to keep up the expedition's spirits: 'I wish I could bring home our charming Persian cook,' Agatha wrote. 'He makes lovely walnut soufflés. He has just been discoursing on meat. "You can tell me when you want turkey. I kill. That day, tough very. Next day, tough. Next day, not very tender. Day after that he good tender very nice. Chicken he very good lay eggs. If not good, not lay eggs, him cock."'

Another season – 1955 – also started unpromisingly, when they were assailed by dust storms and thunderstorms alternately. Agatha was a good sport, clambering in and out of trucks with the rest, despite her heavy frame and swollen ankles, enduring bumpy roads and nightmarish fording of rivers. When spring came, however, the desert became beautiful again, with fields of delicate wild flowers in glowing colours, under a clear sky.

After seven years at Nimrud it seemed that Max's work on the acropolis might be done. He began to discuss with Cork his plans for publishing a large, lavishly illustrated book, on Nimrud and its remains. His expedition had by then recovered and distributed an outstanding collection of finds; it appeared, moreover, that the political situation in Iraq was becoming increasingly unstable. The young King Feisal (to whom Agatha had presented one of her books when he came to lay the foundation stone of the new museum in Baghdad) and his Prime Minister, Nuri-es-Said, were being threatened by various subversive factions, some vehemently nationalist. The atmosphere was growing unfriendly and suspicious; even the books Cork sent to Baghdad for Agatha were detained by the Customs, which believed that, because the ends of the parcels were closed, they must contain at worst bombs, at best Communist propaganda.

In March, however, the expedition discovered traces of another palace, Fort Shalmaneser. More of an arsenal, it was enormous, over two hundred rooms spread over some twelve acres. The sides of the Fort were protected by towers, walls and canals, and on the western side were two great mounds of mud-brick. Max's team began to investigate the eastern and higher mound, where they discovered the debris of King Shalmaneser's throne-room, whose massive walls had toppled. After days of digging, they unearthed the huge throne base inscribed with scenes of the King's triumphs. Max's *Memoirs* describe the other discoveries made by his indefatigable team of twelve, including Agatha – and a large force of labourers: beautifully executed murals; a talisman in five colours, showing the King beneath a winged disk and the tree of life, surrounded by foliage and gazelle; superb ivories, some 'burned blue and grey in the avenging fire', found in the rooms Max believed to have been the Queen's apartments and the harem, including an ivory lunette illustrating a winged sphinx with a lion's body, and a winged cobra. Despite the uncertain political climate, he decided to continue these excavations; their completion was to take another three years.

During the decade of Max and Agatha's labours at Nimrud, much extra work fell to Edmund Cork, now more than Agatha's literary agent. She had entrusted him with power of attorney and he knew, as far as anyone could, the intricacies of her financial and literary affairs. He also found himself acting every spring as general factotum, chivvying Agatha's tenant at Cresswell Place, who constantly forgot to pay the rent, dealing with her gas, telephone and electricity bills and forwarding correspondence for collection to the British Consul in Mosul. There were some hiccoughs in these long distance operations: 'By the way, I usually have to pay about 1½d on letters from you,' Agatha wrote to Cork one season. 'It's not the money that worries me! But occasionally if I and the Persian cook (reasonably opulent) are out, there's only the bottle washer who apparently never has more than 2d in his possession and so the postman won't leave it! Also don't want the Consulate in future to have to pay.'

Cork sent Agatha's proofs (*A Pocket Full of Rye*, suspected of being 'Agricultural Propaganda', was detained by Customs), and books: in 1953 she asked for 'recent French novels, not too heavy', in 1957 the list included *The Fountain Overflows*, *The Comforters*, *In Defence of Colonies*, *Maine Architecture*, and *The Life of Marie Antoinette*. Some of Cork's commissions were odd: 'there may be a parcel of Ham from Australia. Better be passed on to Miss Fisher to Eat or Keep . . .' and 'please forward nylon stockings to Mosul, my only hope in life, as nothing here fits me!'

In 1958 there was a revolution in Iraq. Young King Feisal, his uncle and the Prime Minister were murdered. The Mallowans were deeply upset, not simply because, like many in the West, they feared the international consequences of these events, but also because they had known and liked many of those who now suffered at the hands of the revolutionaries. They were not harassed by the new régime but it was time to leave. Nimrud itself was changing. The extension of a rough track, linking the dig to the main road, and the tarring of much of the main road to Mosul had brought a great many visitors in the last three or four years of the expedition's work, more, indeed, than were welcome. 'Latest Holiday Resort', Agatha wrote in 'The Last Days of Nimrud'; 'All Amenities. Highly Mechanised. Visitors Welcomed. Bring the Kiddies. Combine Culture and Amusement. Visitors' Car Park 50 fils. Admission to Mound Quarter Dinar. Ascent of the Ziggurat and view of surrounding country through telescope 100 fils. *Don't* miss *NIMRUD-ON-TIGRIS:*

> A guaranteed Epigraphist
> In Kurdish trousers gay
> For fifty fils will write your name
> In cuneiform on clay.
> A famous Novelist's on view
> For forty fils a peep,
> But if you want a photograph
> It will not be so cheap!

The mound had anyway lost its beauty. Scarred by the archaeologists' bulldozers, it no longer had its innocent simplicity, with the stone heads poking up out of the green grass, studded with spring flowers. The last 'Nursery Rhyme of Nimrud' was not light-hearted:

> Hush a bye, children, the storm's coming fast.
> The roof it is leaking, the House cannot last.
> When the wind rises, the tents too will fall.
> And that is the end, RIP, of you all.

In the early months of 1960 Max and Agatha left Nimrud for the last time. Her straw hat still hangs in the British School of Archaeology.

21

'. . . all the panoply and misdirection of the conjuror's art'

Dramatic change is unusual in people in their sixties. Agatha welcomed new friends, new books, plays and films, she discussed new ideas and visited new places, but her tastes and habits were fixed. Though she accepted and adjusted to change, advancing age reinforced her natural conservatism. This was also true of her work. Throughout the nineteen-fifties she produced a succession of detective stories that in superficial respects changed with the times; as her work of the 'forties had reflected attitudes, circumstances and tricks of speech of the late 'thirties, so the books she wrote between 1950 and 1960 suggested the manners, situation and expectations of English middle-class society in the decade following the war. These changes were, however, so subtle, and her books came so regularly, that they were barely perceptible. Moreover, shifts in her tone of voice were easily overlooked because stylistically she made few experiments. She continued to impress the public by the way in which she manipulated her characters and her readers and by the sleight-of-hand she demonstrated in her plots. She did not wish to try new forms.

This is disappointing if one believes that, had Agatha written fewer books with greater care, she might have polished her style and explored other avenues. That, however, is an unrealistic assumption. Agatha knew what she did well and stuck to it. Writing was not the most important aspect of her life; she drafted her books, as she had always done, in interludes between other occupations – gardening, cooking, outings, helping Max – and she would willingly abandon a chapter for a walk, a conversation or a picnic. She did not talk about her detective stories and her friends knew better than to discuss them with her. Where her writing was concerned, Agatha was self-sufficient. She understood her market, knew how to satisfy it, and was content with that.

It was hard work, 'a chore', she called it. Ideas for plots came easily but she found writing difficult and tedious. It is a mistake to think that because her technique did not vary and her style remained simple in book after book, Agatha took few pains with her work. It was not effortless. She had developed a certain knack which needed constant practice. She was unambitious but industrious.

She was, as she had admitted to Max, unadventurous. If invited, she would go with a guide but her disposition was to wait prudently at home. As a child, she had amused herself privately and in her own time; grown up and growing old, she was reflective, unhurried. She was, however, immensely energetic. In her sixties she walked, gardened, drove and ran errands enthusiastically and, though she ran more slowly on the tennis court, placed the ball as firmly as ever. Her emotions were active, too. There were no displays, for Agatha had never been quarrelsome or complaining, but she cared intensely about the way people behaved towards each other, their behaviour to children and animals, the beauty and misery of the world. She seemed calm but from time to time psoriasis, a sure sign of tension, inflamed her feet, hands and scalp.

Her imagination was unceasingly busy. She dreamt at night and mused during the day, jotting down her ideas for plots and characters on any scrap of paper. These energies fuelled her writing and gave her books their force. They did not change them. Though each plot was a surprise, her technique varied little. Her detective stories continued to follow a pattern of progressive mystification interwoven with progressive enlightenment and there was to be only one more Mary Westmacott. Her style was unaltered, though she still had a sharp ear for colloquial speech, and by this time could invent convincing dialogue. Writing books was demanding but it was routine. Now, rather than producing a different sort of book, she turned increasingly to the theatre. By the end of the decade she had proved herself as much a popular dramatist as a novelist.

There was initially little sign of this. Her first delivery to Cork, before setting off for Nimrud at the beginning of 1950, had been a typescript she had completed at Greenway the previous summer, *They Came to Baghdad*, the book the currency authorities had been told Agatha intended to write when she and Max had first set out again for Iraq after the war. She had been true to her word; as much a thriller as a detective story, the book was set in places where she had stayed, including the Hotel Zia, and her

own house, Karradet Mariam 17. The fourth edition of Bren-
tano's *Baghdad: How To See It*, saved from 1939, also came in
useful. There was something familiar about one of the characters,
too: the figure of Sir Rupert Crofton Lee, with 'curling grey hair
growing down over a muscular red-brown neck', had a strong
suggestion of Max's archaeological colleague, Mortimer Wheeler,
Cork and Ober both liked this book, Ober thinking it in some
ways the best novel she had done recently, though he was bothered by 'a feeling of unreality' towards the end.

Collins's editor was blunt: 'difficult to believe that Mrs Christie
regards this as more than a joke ... Plot and many of the situations far-fetched and puerile to a degree.' He was obliged to
admit, however, that it was 'eminently readable'; as with all Agatha's novels, the reader whose attention has been engaged by the
first page will generally pursue the story to the end, disregarding
the improbability of the plot, the contrivance of the situation, or
even banalities of style. Agatha, who certainly did not regard the
book as a joke, was anxious that it should be published as soon
as possible, since the political situation in the Near East was
precarious and she was afraid the story would date. Collins promised publication in early 1951 and Dodd, Mead's American edition appeared shortly afterwards.

Agatha had arrived in Baghdad in 1950 with a heavy cold. She
felt very ill for a fortnight: 'lay in bed and groaned', she informed
Cork, but 'enforced meditation has given me heaps of brilliant
ideas.' Once at Nimrud, she was cheered by glorious weather and
the hoard they discovered in the Governor's Palace. She began
to work enthusiastically, drafting nearly all the book that became
Mrs McGinty's Dead, thinking about plans for 'Mary Westmacott', and tinkering with older ideas. One typescript she dusted
off was the Marple book she had written during the War. 'As I
seem to be well ahead,' she told Cork, 'I thought I might as well
go over it thoroughly, as a lot of it seems to date very much. I
have removed all political references, etc., or remarks which seem
to echo the trend of the time. The scene of it must remain laid in
that period, as so much of the action depends on servants (plen-
tiful then) and ample meals, etc.!' Rightly, she observed, 'It's
more catchwords and particular phrases that seem to make a
book old-fashioned.' Nevertheless, she concluded, 'On rereading
it, I think it's quite a good one. I am not sure I haven't gone
down the hill since then!'

Agatha also brought herself to look over the dramatised ver-

Greenway.

Winterbrook House, with Max's library on the right.

In the Old Bailey – On the set of *Witness for the Prosecution*.

Agatha with the Queen at the première of
Murder on the Orient Express. Nat Cohen,
the chairman of EMI Film Productions,
stands between them.

Agatha, Peter Saunders and one of *The Mousetrap's*
birthday cakes.

Anthony and Max in the garden at New College, Oxford.

sion of *Towards Zero*, with which Lee Shubert had been vaguely dissatisfied at the end of the War. She, too, felt uncomfortable about this play. As she told Cork, 'the Whodunnit with everyone suspected in turn, and plenty of comic red herrings thrown in, really by now quite sickens me on the stage! And it's not the *kind* of story that *Towards Zero* is!' She went on, 'Lots of my books *are* what I should describe as "light-hearted thrillers" (*10 Little Niggers* was) and, if you want that kind of play, dramatise one of them. Don't twist the kind of book that hasn't the right atmosphere. You might just as well start with an entirely new story.' 'Frankly,' Agatha observed, 'I have never seen *Towards Zero* as good material for a play ... its point is *not* suspicion on everybody – but suspicion and everything pointing toward the incrimination of *one* person – and rescue of that victim at the moment when she seems to be hopelessly doomed. But, if fun and thrills are wanted, go to some other of my fifty offspring!' She concluded, 'It might be better to pass the whole thing up. What do you think?' Cork advised Agatha to wait.

During her absence he took care to keep her fully informed about the progress of *The Murder at the Vicarage*, her play, and *A Muder is Announced*, her novel, now in proof. ('Quite unobjectionable,' he wrote of the jacket, 'no silly hooded figures.') The play was still doing well at the end of January 1950, though Bertie Meyer had been disappointed in his hope of gaining extra publicity by holding a party on the stage 'to say farewell to a famous authoress going off to the Middle East to dig with famous husband'. Cork had been sceptical and Agatha had firmly dished that idea. At the beginning of February, audiences dropped in 'the wettest and most dismal weather on record', Cork reported, and, it was believed, because of the imminent general election. Everyone, including Bertie Meyer, took cuts, hoping for what Cork termed 'an uplift'. Cork also arranged to bring forward the serialisation of *A Murder is Announced* in the *Daily Express*, which might remind readers that *The Murder at the Vicarage* was still playing. In April, however, the play had come, in Cork's words, to 'an ignominious conclusion', but, he assured Agatha, 'it was on long enough to build a fine property for repertory and amateurs.' He now encouraged her to pursue another idea, the dramatisation of *The Hollow*. A contract with Bertie Meyer was signed, Cork's plan being that the play should be 'presented in a de luxe manner in time for the Festival next year'. (The Festival of Britain was to be opened in May 1951 as a celebration, in the

words of the official guide, of 'faith in the Nation's future', after
the difficult struggles of the dreary post-war years). 'I really am
delighted,' Agatha assured Cork. '*Do* hope it goes well when the
time comes (or *if*, of course – it's always "if" in theatrical matters, isn't it?).'

On her return to England, Agatha worked furiously, complet-
ing two typescripts – *Mrs McGinty's Dead* and *They Do It With
Mirrors* – and finishing the adaptation of *The Hollow*. Meanwhile, Dodd, Mead put together a collection of early stories,
including the one about the Clapham Cook Agatha had sent
Dorothy L. Sayers, for publication in America as 'The Under-
dog'. There was more. During the autumn, as she turned out
some old papers, Agatha came across something by Mary Westmacott which she had written at the end of the nineteen-thirties,
a play called *A Daughter's A Daughter*, dealing with the familiar
Westmacott theme of possessiveness. *A Daughter's A Daughter*
has at its centre a widow, still young, who pushes aside a suitor
and another marriage when her nineteen-year-old daughter objects. It is an obvious theme for Agatha to have considered, given
her interest in the nature of maternal love, in independence and
self-assertion. The relationship she described here had nothing to
do with herself or Rosalind, however, though to those who knew
them there were touches of Agatha's old friend from Asney, Nan,
and her daughter, Judith.

It is not clear when this play was written, though Cork had
reported in January 1940 that Basil Dean was interested in it.
Now Agatha sent Cork another copy: 'Any good ...?' He forwarded it to Peter Saunders, a young impresario who had taken
over the rights to *The Hollow* from Meyer and whose enthusiasm
and energy Agatha had admired. Saunders returned the play at
the beginning of December 1950, with suggested alterations,
mostly to small remarks that dated the original: Edith, for example, 'would not ask for six-penn'orth of ice'; 'muffins' would
probably be 'buttered toast'; and, 'I do not think that today one
"falls back on Austrian maids"'. That is pre-War.' Agatha approved these amendments and Saunders sent the play to various
actresses. To Agatha's disappointment none was sufficiently keen.
'Feel sure it is sentimental enough to be a success,' she told Cork,
'if only someone would fancy themselves in it.' In the end the
play, billed as being by Mary Westmacott, was tried out in Bath.
The author's identity was not a secret for long and the theatre
was packed. Saunders, however, did not believe the play would

survive in the West End but Agatha was, for once, uncritical. (He thought she judged *A Daughter's A Daughter* less acutely than her other plays.) Saunders said no more and, in his words, 'Agatha allowed it to slide from her memory.' As a play, that is, but not otherwise, for she turned *A Daughter's A Daughter* into a novel, 'knocked off without a word to anybody', Cork told Harold Ober, who had been enquiring repeatedly on Rinehart's behalf as to when another Mary Westmacott might be expected.

The weather that summer was dreadful. Agatha stayed at Greenway, beautiful even when the garden was sodden and the estuary obscured by drizzle. It was there, at the very end of August, that she heard the news of Madge's death. She hurried north to Abney, and on her return to Devonshire she felt the summer and her holiday had ended. 'Do send some typewriting paper to Greenway,' she begged Cork, for it was impossible to find locally. 'You see, I mean to work.' Her own generation of the family was vanishing but Greenway was not lonely. Rosalind and Anthony brought Mathew in the late spring and summer, colleagues and students came to stay, and Mrs North was a regular visitor. Agatha spent her days tranquilly but she was always ready to join an expedition along the estuary, to the moors and the beach, to bathe in the sea or take a picnic to Dartmoor. She was still, as she had once explained to Max, 'a dog to be taken for walks', amusing herself quietly but taking part in any fun that was proposed.

Mid-September brought her sixtieth birthday. Cork had warned Agatha that a certain amount of fêting was inevitable, to which, she replied, she was quite agreeable, as long as she did not have to make any speeches. Collins celebrated her anniversary and her sixtieth book, *A Murder is Announced*, with a festive party. Agatha had not entirely forgotten recent skirmishes: 'Thank you for asking me to meet Agatha Christie,' she replied to the official invitation. 'If you don't mind, I am bringing my old friend Mary Westmacott with me....' Penguin Books marked the occasion by reprinting a list advertised as the 'Christie Million', which in fact sold two and a half million copies, while Dodd, Mead agreed with the Avon Publishing Company to reprint eight titles in America, starting with *The Mysterious Affair at Styles*.

It was at Greenway, however, that Agatha really celebrated her birthday, enjoying herself robustly: 'Thank goodness,' she told Cork, 'we've got a wonderful temporary cook. Her Vol-au-Vents! Her Soufflés! Though rain pours down, eating is always eating!'

1951 was a successful year. It began with Peter Saunders's production of *The Hollow*, directed by Hubert Gregg, a well-known actor in light comedy but then an inexperienced director. The play opened in Cambridge at the beginning of February. Agatha had been anxious because Peter Saunders wished to produce it as a thriller: 'Don't like this ... "Whodunnit" publicity,' she told Cork. She was also worried about the author's photographs. 'Which one is it of me? ... I won't have them using pictures I have not seen or authorised. Rub it in!' She was unable to attend the first night of the provincial tour, but arranged from Iraq for flowers to be delivered to 'my actresses ... something rather exotic for Jeanne de Casalis' (who played Lady Angkatell) 'and probably tulips of different colours for the others.' She was nervous: 'Oh dear, I *hope* it will be a success. I do think it is a good cast and well produced and I *want* it to be a success. The omens are good since it opens on St Agatha's Day. A candle for St Agatha.'

Peter Saunders cabled Agatha to say that the play was a hit and Cork confirmed this by air-mail, adding, however, that during the first night's performance he had been afraid that 'the drama might be sunk by the comedy', particularly as Jeanne de Casalis had made the most of a part suited to 'a natural droll'. At a six-hour conference afterwards, he, Saunders and Gregg had discussed remedies, with the result, he assured Agatha, that on the following night 'there were no unexpected laughs and it seemed to have already got a nice balance'. 'How maddening that I can't see it,' she replied. 'It's just got to be running in London in May.' Saunders pleased her greatly by sending regular cables reporting the play's progress. It proved difficult to find a suitable West End theatre but he eventually managed to secure the Fortune Theatre, starting in the first week in June. The play was taken off for a few weeks after its provincial tour, slightly recast, and brought back first to the Fortune and then to the Ambassadors. It ran in London for eleven months altogether, so Agatha was able to see it after all.

Saunders was in favour, Bertie Meyer out. Cork, however, now reported that Meyer wished to hold them to the arrangement that 'because of old associations' he should put *Towards Zero* on the stage, if he could adapt it. Meyer had sent the play to Gerald Verner, who supplied something unobjectionable; in fact, Cork ventured, 'we think it is damn good.' Agatha sportingly replied, 'I must hand it to Bertie Meyer for sticking to it!!' Nothing, in fact, happened, nor was to happen for another five years.

Agatha thoroughly approved of Peter Saunders. He was keen and knew she liked to be kept well-informed; he was deferential when suggesting amendments and understood how to flatter. Most important, he seemed to care about Agatha's work as much as she did herself, believing her plays to be highly entertaining, even if he did not see them as vehicles for important statements. Furthermore, Saunders was full of ingenious ideas for attracting publicity. Agatha had always been upset when her work was insufficiently well publicised in bookshops; she liked her publishers and producers to be visibly proud of it and, while she shrank from publicity herself – and had occasional qualms about some of Saunders's more exotic notions – she welcomed his efforts. Disliking self-advertisement, she would nonetheless fall in with his schemes – perhaps because he could cajole her, possibly because somehow the theatre and everything associated with it was in a way unreal.

There was one sadness at the beginning of 1951. A month after Agatha and Max arrived in Baghdad, they had heard from Philip Mallowan, a schoolmaster in Surrey and the younger of Max's two brothers, that Agatha's mother-in-law was not expected to live much longer than a fortnight. Her health had been poor for some time but when the Mallowans had left England they thought she had been suffering only from exhaustion after bronchitis – 'if I'd known I'd have stayed,' Agatha wrote to Cork. Cecil Mallowan was also abroad. In fact, Marguerite had incurable cancer. Moved to a nursing home, she asked to be taken home. Agatha arranged for nurses and for flowers to be sent twice a week. 'I imagine she will be kept under sedatives most of the time,' she wrote to Cork, 'but she *does* love flowers.' Agatha was also very anxious that Mrs Mallowan should have an advance copy of *They Came to Baghdad*; 'If you could get hold of one and have it delivered . . . at once, I think it would be a great pleasure to her. Not that she can read it – but every time I went to see her she asked me for it and said, 'I can't wait. I want it *now*.' Before Marguerite could return home, however, she died quickly and peacefully. It was a great shock to Max. Fortunately there was much to do at Nimrud.

They were so busy that spring that there was hardly time for writing. Agatha had, however, left behind two typescripts: *Mrs McGinty's Dead* and *They Do It With Mirrors*. Hughes Massie sent corrected copies out to Nimrud with Robert Hamilton; 'I still feel a glow of gratitude,' Cork wrote to Agatha, 'for your producing all those manuscripts out of the blue.' 'Mrs McGinty's Dead' was the name of a children's game, unknown in the United States, where the phrase caused some perplexity, but Collins were delighted: 'It's like a breath of fresh air,' they told Agatha, in rather an odd simile, 'to get away from the old blood, murder and death formulas of our title pages.' There was, on the other hand, an argument about the jacket. Mrs McGinty, an old woman apparently done to death by her lodger, was hit on the head 'with something rather in the nature of a meat chopper with a very sharp edge'. The weapon turned out to be a sugar hammer, or, as Agatha called it in her letter to Cork, a sugar cutter, and it was this she wanted on the jacket, photographing her own as a sample.

The ideas in this book are familiar – the complexities of relations between mothers and daughters, the burden the innocent carry until the guilty are identified, and, as in many of Agatha's other stories, the importance of visual clues, in this case provided by old photographs. *Mrs McGinty's Dead* is in some respects a gruesome book, as a later jacket designer, Tom Adams, perceived when he chose to paint a large bluebottle hovering malevolently over what could be discerned, just, as Mrs McGinty's dead body. Even the title was too unappetising for *Woman's Journal*, which was to serialise the book in Britain. They wanted to change it to something more innocuous; Agatha wrote scathingly to Cork, 'I really think WJ shouldn't *take* murder stories if they funk labelling them as such. "Just like Mrs McGinty" doesn't seem to make any sense, as the second murder doesn't take place until halfway through the book. Why not put "Mrs McGinty" or something weak like "A Condemned Man" or "The Paying Guest"?' Agatha dedicated *Mrs McGinty's Dead* to Peter Saunders, 'in gratitude for his kindness to authors'.

They Do It With Mirrors, the second mystery Agatha left for Cork in 1951, also alluded to the theme of maternal love and to the possessiveness which, Agatha believed, was even more strongly felt by women, not themselves mothers, towards children for whom they assumed responsibility. It took up, too, another thought which had always interested her, the nature of reality and illusion. Part of the story deals with preparations for the production of a play (*The Nile at Sunset*) by the various inhabitants of a school for rehabilitating juvenile delinquents. In Agatha's description, not only are some of these children confused about their identity and motivation, but the adults who look after them are for the most part equally muddled, though to themselves their theories and objectives are crystal clear. 'The illusion is in the eye of the beholder,' as one of the characters says. A theatrical designer, his remarks give Miss Marple the clue to solving the mystery. The theatricality of the crime has bemused them all: 'This is a stage scene,' she realises, 'only cardboard and canvas and wood.' Miss Marple sees how illusion is created: 'Bowls of goldfish, yards of coloured ribbon . . . vanishing ladies . . . all the panoply and misdirection of the conjuror's art.' Agatha, so cunning at misleading her readers, constructing a narrative to convey distracting information, spoke here through Miss Marple, and in this novel again revealed her fascination with the suspension of disbelief that can be produced on the stage. 'They do it with mirrors' is an expression used to explain how magicians perform their sleight of hand. It is also an apt phrase to describe Agatha's work; much of it concerned mirrors, looking glasses, window panes, which, like the rivers she loved and by which she lived, refracted as well as reflected. A pity, then, that in America *They Do It With Mirrors* was considered too puzzling a title and *Murder With Mirrors* used instead. It completely missed the point.

Agatha's affection for Peter Saunders was in part for a fellow-illusionist, an ingenious theatrical producer who was also skilled at attracting attention by tricks of publicity – anniversary parties, special performances, press stories about the cast – in which the quickness of the hand deceived the eye. In the summer of 1951 she finished a piece of work which was to give his gift for advertisement its fullest scope, the adaptation for the stage of her story *Three Blind Mice*. The original radio play of 1947, which had been very short, had since been a great success in America, and Agatha had been pursued by American film companies for the rights, though she had not permitted Cork to negotiate. Now she expanded the play, calling it *The Mousetrap*, a title supplied by Rosalind's husband Anthony. On seeing the play, Saunders was delighted. He declared that, if he could find a theatre, it would be produced in 1952. Agatha, pleased, asked Cork to look out another effort, an old play adapted from *The Secret of Chimneys*, which, she reminded him, 'was going to be done at the Embassy' and was 'all about oil concessions'. This had never been produced. Cork, however, put that script aside, pressing rather for another Mary Westmacott. Agatha promised that

something would be coming but, apart from the book based on
A Daughter's A Daughter, there was to be nothing more from
that author for a year or two. Instead, she sent for copies of the
American edition of 'Witness for the Prosecution' and brooded
about dramatising that.

Summer and autumn were happy. American sales of *They
Came to Baghdad* outstripped those of any of Agatha's previous
books. She was chosen by the readers of *Ellery Queen's Mystery
Magazine*, in what Frank Dodd reported to be an international
poll, as one of the 'ten greatest living mystery writers', or, rather,
'ten greatest active mystery writers', the criterion being changed
at the last minute to exclude Dorothy L. Sayers, ostensibly
because she now wrote largely about religion, but actually to
conceal the organisers' embarrassment at disqualifying Dashiell
Hammett, jailed on charges of sympathising with Communism.
It took some months for Agatha to receive her prize, a small
wooden plaque from which was suspended an antique pistol,
which the United States Post Office refused to accept for mailing,
on the grounds that, 'even theoretically', it could be fired. They
did agree to dispatch another item marking Agatha's apotheosis;
'squares of yellow muslin,' she told Cork derisively, 'for me to
sign and send back to be incorporated in a quilt! Object, a Mothers' Milk Bank!!! I *do* think Americans phrase things unfortunately! I long to write back and say I thought it was a most
indelicate idea – and one which I believed was only practised in
Soviet Russia!!' To have been charged with such an un-American
activity would indeed have shocked the matrons proposing it.

In 1952 the Mallowans returned to Iraq, for what was to be,
as Max described it, the expedition's *annus mirabilis*. A month
after they arrived King George VI died in London. Agatha and
Max took part in the memorial service in Baghdad, 'all the Iraqi
Cabinet attending and a procession of Sheikhs signing the book
at the Embassy. All my clothes are unfortunately rather lurid,'
Agatha told Cork, 'and I have to wear my one black dress in all
weathers.' This year there was no difficulty in finding a typewriter,
'they seem to be flowing in Baghdad ... so I have bought myself
a portable Royal which I like very much – and which I hope will
encourage me to be industrious.' In fact she did little writing that
spring, managing only to provide a new ending for *A Daughter's
A Daughter*, 'less sloppy, I think.'

The exploration of Nimrud's wells was not her sole distraction,
for there was an interminable correspondence with Cork about a

crisis at home. Agatha had engaged someone to oversee the gardener and two boys who looked after the struggling market garden at Greenway. In 1952 the new supervisor took up her post and immediately – and ominously – began bombarding Hughes Massie with requests for helpful literature – books about commercial glass house crops, and the like. 'So far, she seems rather zealous,' was all Cork needed to report to Agatha in Iraq. Three weeks later, while on holiday in the South of France, he was summoned home: the supervisor, depressed by her failure to organise the gardeners and, it later turned out, to forecast winning horses, had tried to do away with herself, the police had called Rosalind and Anthony from Wales, while Agatha's butler and housekeeper had decided to emigrate to Australia. Rosalind and Anthony searched for a new gardener, 'preferably married to a treasure'; Cork dealt with a torrent of bills. The crux of the situation, however, was, as he wrote to Agatha, the whole future of the market gardening scheme. This was his first and only visit to Greenway (for he observed to the end Hughes Massie's advice about keeping a distance from his authors) and he was astonished at its extent and expense. 'The freshness and graciousness of everything was a dream,' he assured Agatha, 'but it is a big expensive dream, which increasing costs have made extremely difficult to carry on.' Agatha's staff had as their only object the supply of whatever she liked, rather than growing for the market: 'There is an exceptional crop of peaches and they are almost ecstatic as to how much you will enjoy them – Excuse this digression, but it does illustrate the conflict of viewpoint....' At least mushrooms were showing signs of life and could be sold locally. Heroic efforts by Rosalind, Anthony and Cork, however, saved the garden; a new man was hired; Mr Heaven, the new accountant, managed to put matters on a footing that would satisfy the Revenue; and, by the end of 1952, Agatha was able to tell Cork that 'the garden looks *wonderful*. All bursting with plants and lettuces, etc. It really does look professional at last.'

Agatha wrote little at Nimrud in 1952 and came home full of plans not for books but for plays. She completed a short radio drama for the BBC, *Personal Call*, about a woman who either pushes herself or is was pushed by her husband under a train: 'Any station will do,' Agatha wrote. 'Newton Abbot telephone boxes and station geography would have to be vetted, of course,' and 'more or less fun can be had with trains by the BBC as they choose.' The producer found the play first-rate, 'making full use

of radio techniques and possibilities.' As for the stage, Peter
Saunders had secured Richard Attenborough and his wife Sheila
Sim for the cast of *The Mousetrap*, which he intended to open in
Nottingham in October and bring to the West End in December
in time for Christmas. Auditions began in August and in September Saunders engaged Peter Cotes as producer. (The original plan
to have John Fennell had fallen through.) Bertie Meyer was still
sitting on *Towards Zero* ('I never feel it is properly my child,'
Agatha lamented to Cork) and Lee Shubert, though constantly
making what Cork called 'excited noises', had still done nothing
about the American production of *The Hollow*, though the play
continued to flourish in London, hardly dented by a decline in
theatre attendance after the King's death.

The *Mousetrap* opened in Nottingham in October 1952.
Though the play needed minor adjustments, Peter Saunders was
happy with it, if 'not terribly excited'. Agatha, who was there,
thought it 'quite a nice little play' and forecast a run of six
months or so. There is a myth that she wept and declared it a
disaster; nothing could be less true. Nor was it the case, as some
maintain, that its reception in London was cool. One newspaper,
the *Sunday Dispatch*, disliked the play; other critics were enthusiastic. All seats were full for the first three months and to Saunders's amazement it continued to prosper. Agatha was quietly
amused, keeping an eye on her creation by discreetly dropping
into the theatre from time to time and reporting any lack of
polish. The launching of *The Mousetrap* in fact marked an important moment. Agatha had learnt to apply her knack to the
theatre. Here, too, she instinctively understood what the public
wanted. Like her books, her plays had a strong story, a mixture
of tragedy and comedy, and a swift pace. Her acts and scenes,
like her chapters and paragraphs, closed at exactly the right point,
and, as she stimulated her readers by constantly providing new
information, so she presented her audience with a succession of
characters and possible relationships. Like her books, her plays
were intellectually demanding but safe; violence occurred off-
stage. By now Agatha knew her audience as she knew her readers,
and her producers, like her editors, acknowledged it. She judged
casts and sets as coolly as titles and plots and she was rarely
mistaken. Her theatrical touch was sure.

1952 was a particularly wet summer in the South-West. At
Lynmouth the estuary broke its banks and Agatha donated the
takings from the midweek matinée of *The Hollow*, playing at

Exeter, to the disaster fund. Confined to the house, she made up for lost time by planning two detective stories, *After The Funeral* and *A Pocket Full of Rye*. The first of these mysteries was delivered at the end of August; by November Agatha was tersely writing 'No!!!' against Collins's draft blurb. She was frustrated in her efforts to finish *A Pocket Full of Rye* before the autumn ended, for in September, on her birthday, she fell and broke her wrist, putting an end to typing. Cork produced a dictating machine and, despite her loathing of gadgets, by October she had mastered it sufficiently well to deliver several chapters for transcription. It was not until November, however, that she could send Cork a shakily handwritten note: 'What a pest I must be to you! But oh dear; All this money rolling in and a far more working life than when we had £400 a year and I wheeled a pram to the Park every day!!'

A Pocket Full of Rye was delivered to Collins in February 1953. Agatha's editor liked it, especially the 'exotic element ... lent by the murderer's curious insistence on the paraphernalia of the nursery rhyme "Sing a Song of Sixpence".' This macabre children's rhyme had been the first Agatha ever used as the theme of a detective novel. Her short story with that title had formed part of the collection, *The Listerdale Mystery*, published in 1934, and a story called 'Four and Twenty Blackbirds' had also appeared in 1940. Collins were to publish *A Pocket Full of Rye* in the winter, Dodd, Mead in the spring, the *Daily Express* first serialising it in Britain and the *Chicago Tribune* in America. Ober's only qualm was that the murderer was such an attractive character, though Cork disagreed: 'Patricia was my sweetie.' Rosalind, listening to Agatha reading aloud each chapter on summer evenings at Greenway, guessed the murderer's identity from the start. The royalties from this book were given to the British School of Archaeology in Iraq, part of the benefaction being set aside to support Max's book on Nimrud.

Collins were now more enthusiastic than ever about their best-selling author. Agatha's paperback sales had doubled, sometimes tripled, between 1951 and 1952, returning to 1948 levels, which had been phenomenal. It was decided that for the new Fontana paperback edition she should receive a higher royalty than had been negotiated with other authors: a penny ha'penny a copy for home sales and a penny for export sales. (She had been receiving three-farthings on the one-and-sixpenny White Circles.) In her absence abroad, Collins made arrangements for a new car. Before leaving for Baghdad in 1953 she inspected various models; as she wrote to Cork, the new Humber Imperial 'is very much our cup of tea. Really lashings of *room*. And with the continual transport of Max's books, flowers and vegetables that I bring up from Wallingford, and being able to get seven or eight people down to the beach or for picnics in summer, I think *room* is the thing.' Billy Collins suggested that a Jaguar would be more fun, 'but I think,' said Agatha, 'pure fun is less important to me now than comfort and *space*. You've no idea the amount of things archaeologists take about with them!' So a black seven-seater Humber Imperial was ordered, for Agatha's return in May. Collins could not do enough: 'Do you know,' they asked Cork, 'if Mrs Mallowan wants any extras like radio, heater, loose covers?'

Agatha spent the beginning of 1953 in Baghdad 'sitting on the balcony in the sun recovering from OVERWORK!' She did, however, adjust the end of *Witness for the Prosecution*, which she had now discussed with Peter Saunders, who had initially tried to dramatise it himself. Agatha had explained to him how she wrote a play. It was, she said, as if one were driving a car, knowing the point of departure and the ultimate destination but choosing one of several ways to get there. On reading Saunders's draft of *Witness for the Prosecution*, she had proposed a destination which surprised him. The dénouement she wanted was highly ambitious in terms of staging, since she wished to set the end of the play in a courtroom. It was equally ambitious dramatically, for she proposed a final twist she hoped would leave the audience gasping. Saunders himself gulped but agreed to try. Agatha now tidied up her draft, sending it home 'by one of the Embassy lads'. 'I devoutly hope this won't turn out to be Saunders' Folly,' she told Cork. 'Anyway he seems to be rushing upon his doom!'

Cork replied that Saunders was sure *Witness for the Prosecution* was going to be tremendous. He had concocted a good deal of 'legal fun' and the play had been sent for vetting to the barristers actor Leo Genn and the barrister Humphrey Tilling. It also seemed that, were there ever to be a film, Charles Laughton, who had played Poirot in *Alibi* in 1928, might take the part of the Q.C. who defends the suspected murderer. Saunders's arrangements for bringing *Witness for the Prosecution* to London depended to some extent on whether Bertie Meyer hoped to put on *Towards Zero*; there was more talk but still nothing happened. 'I'm really fed up with Bertie,' Agatha wrote to Cork. 'He's had years.... Peter does *put* my plays on.' Cork and Saunders were, if anything, more exasperated with Lee Shubert over the delay in putting on *The Hollow* in America. Saunders was anxious to buy out the American rights but it proved impossible to prise them away, so the only course was to wait. *The Mousetrap*, however, continued to do well, though business in the theatre was otherwise poor. Advance bookings, too, Cork told Agatha, were exceptionally strong.

Theatrical prospects were exciting – but there was no sign of any new book. Collins had for their winter 1953 list *A Pocket Full of Rye* (dedicated to Bruce Ingram, who had first published Agatha's stories in the *Sketch*) and *After The Funeral*, but they were asking anxiously for a novel for 1954. Agatha brought nothing back from Nimrud and in August cheerfully told Billy Collins, 'I haven't begun another book yet – at least I have – but have got hopelessly stuck. I really don't *want* to do *any* work!! Do you ever feel like that?' It had been too pleasant a summer for work: Coronation summer. The tireless Cork, unfrustrated by successive requests for additional tickets, had procured fifty-guinea seats at 145 Piccadilly for Agatha's large party, 'with a scrumptious lunch in the marquee', he promised, 'and everything'. There was Wimbledon (thanks to Billy Collins), a brief trip to Paris with Max and expeditions to Dartmoor and the beach. Despite Agatha's vow to Billy Collins that 'the old rattle trap' would do for Devon lanes, 'car has been *heavenly*. We went eleven in it the other day to a picnic.' Its only flaw was revealed one day as Max drove Agatha to Greenway from Torquay. The window beside her exploded; 'You nearly lost an author,' she told Collins, 'I thought I was shot.'

When Agatha was stimulated, however, she could work fast. In September 1953 a theatrical agent asked Peter Saunders whether she would write a play for a client of his, Margaret Lockwood, who had hitherto appeared in the West End only in a popular *Peter Pan*. Agatha was introduced to Miss Lockwood over luncheon at the Mirabelle and within a month delivered *Spider's Web*, in which she had not only written, at Miss Lockwood's request, parts for the actress herself and for Wilfrid Hyde White, but also, unsolicited, for Miss Lockwood's fourteen-year-old daughter, Julia.

That script was completed during the last weeks of preparation for *Witness for the Prosecution*, which was fortunate, for it occupied Agatha when she might otherwise have wanted to sit in on final rehearsals. As Cork tactfully explained, this time there was no need for her to be there. The first night of *Witness for the Prosecution* was September 26th at Nottingham. 'It's a very expensive production,' Cork wrote to Ober, 'so it has to click from the word go.' Much of the expense derived from the fact that the play had a cast of thirty, with two sets, one a huge replica of the Old Bailey. It opened in London on October 28th. Saunders had experienced the usual difficulty in securing a theatre and was obliged to take the Winter Garden in Drury Lane, a cavernous place with more than sixteen hundred seats. The production was a sensational success, the only first night Agatha ever enjoyed. She beamed and waved as the company and the audience turned to her box and applauded, something she remembered to the end of her life, together with the words of a woman outside the theatre; 'Best you've written yet, dearie.'

'It is the most successful play Agatha Christie has written,' Cork told Ober in mid-November, 'though I do not suppose it will run more than a few months, as it is such an expensive production.' A fortnight later, he wrote again, 'It was put on at the worst time of year in the worst theatre in the West End, and it is just packing out. We are selling rights of it all over Europe on terms which we had only heard about before!' Lee Shubert dared to bid for the right to produce the play in America but there were no dealings with him this time. Instead, Peter Saunders joined the Dramatists' Guild in the United States and arranged that Gilbert Miller should take over the American production. In London it ran for 468 performances. Bids began to come in from Hollywood – from United Artists, Warner Brothers and Twentieth Century Fox. It was a triumph for Agatha – and a relief for Saunders, for the cost of the production had far outstripped his expectations and before the opening in London he knew his capital was exhausted. It had seemed that the enterprise might indeed turn out to be 'Saunders' Folly', but, as he confessed years later, Agatha's instinct was right.

Christmas was celebrated on a wave of delight. 'A bit bemused by heavy eating', Agatha carried off an immense party to the pantomime at Plymouth and another to *Witness for the Prosecution* in January. At the beginning of February 1954, she invited a hundred guests to the Savoy – Dorothy North, James Watts, Barbara Toy and Moie Charles, Dorothy L. Sayers and Margery Sharp, Humphrey Tilling the barrister, Campbell and Dorothy Christie, whose *Carrington VC* was also a West End hit – all her friends, colleagues and relations. 'You might send me an invitation card to let me see what it looks like!' she wrote joyfully to Cork, who took care of liaison with the Banqueting Manager over such matters as flowers, champagne, extending the licence and provision of 'a little map'. Agatha also celebrated less conspicuously, proposing to Cork that she donate a story to the Fund for the Restoration of Westminster Abbey. This was 'Sanctuary', her first short story for eight years. The only difficulty was – as usual – arranging for the American fee to be paid. 'The Save the Abbey Fund does not pay tax in this country, so the Dean cannot properly sign the Tax Exemption Certificate,' Cork confided to Ober; 'How can we get round *this*?' Somehow they managed.

Collins were becoming increasingly worried by the absence of any new book for 1954. They had considered the idea of publishing a volume of short stories but that had foundered, since difficulties in sorting out copyrights were compounded by the fact that Agatha did not wish 'Three Blind Mice' to be republished while *The Mousetrap* was running. She also felt that to reprint the original 'Witness for the Prosecution' would disappoint her readers, as the 1948 version was so far removed from the present play. There were, nonetheless, no reproaches from Billy Collins who produced instead a gift of 'Hardy Rhododendrons' and a detective story called *The Cretan Counterfeit*, 'which might appeal to Max as well'.

Agatha had in fact been planning a detective story, *Destination Unknown*, promised to Cork in February 1954, she could not complete it until she could work on it at Nimrud, undistracted by the theatre. A thriller, it concerned the search for an international group of scientists and their eventual escape from a remote and extraordinary prison. The story, labelled 'preposterous nonsense' by one American magazine editor, was nevertheless a success within the United States and at home, perhaps because it dealt not only with popular fantasies of conspiracy and escapism but also with a theme – the causes and consequences of defection – that had obsessed the public since the conviction of Klaus Fuchs the nuclear scientist, in 1950.

Agatha brought the finished draft of this novel back from Iraq in May but, again, her chief preoccupation was plays. *Spider's Web* was to open in Nottingham in September, coming to the Savoy Theatre in London in mid-December, while the American production of *Witness for the Prosecution* was being tried out at the same time in New Haven, opening in New York in December. She had drunk her fill of publicity and urged Cork to spare her this time: 'You can give any personal details you can think of or invent. I cannot have any more photographers taking pictures of me, so choke them off!' In the summer, when there were constant applications for a meeting with her at Winterbrook, she wrote adamantly: 'Interviews, yes, *if* you say so. Photos: *no!* Look at poor old Allen Lane in this week's *Sunday Times*, looking a tired old man of *seventy* - was thinking of writing an indignant letter to them!'

New York embraced *Witness for the Prosecution* with rapture. It played for nearly two years on Broadway and was chosen by the New York Drama Critics Circle as the best foreign play of 1954. *Spider's Web*, meanwhile, was an immediate hit at home, running even longer. Agatha, as much as her audience, was enchanted with Margaret Lockwood, who starred in the first fifteen months' performance. She played Clarissa, a diplomat's whimsical but clever wife, who attempts to dispose of a body discovered in her drawing-room. Though Clarissa had Agatha's mother's name and her impulsiveness, she was not modelled on Clara. There was, however, an echo of Agatha's own daydreaming in her heroine's game of 'supposing', but, when Clarissa fantasised about finding a body in the library, it was a joke. For Agatha it was not only fun but, more convincingly than ever, her profession.

22

'I shall go on enjoying myself . . .'

'So much bathing in holiday sunshine I've no time for work,' Agatha wrote to Cork in the summer of 1954. These were languorous months at Greenway, with all the garden blossoming. Agatha's new gardener, Frank Lavin, carried off so many prizes at the Brixham Flower Show that she presented a cup for those who gardened without paid help. There were tiny new vegetables from the kitchen garden, strawberries, peaches, grapes, nectarines and figs, the fruit served on Auntie-Grannie's green-bordered dessert plates, each with a different painted fruit in the centre. Gowler, the mediumistic butler, craftily managed so to distribute the plates that, on raising the finger bowl and lace mat, each member of the family found his favourite plate, once and only once a week. Agatha's was the Fig, Rosalind's the Gooseberry. There was salmon from the Dart, plaice and shellfish from Brixham. Mrs Gowler's dairy bill was phenomenal, though Max and Anthony, whose discussions about wine seemed to Agatha interminable, were in no position to reproach her for her fondness for thick cream. Not all the meals were rich, however, for she liked simple food as much as banquets, especially if it could be eaten out of doors.

Anthony, Rosalind and Mathew spent part of every summer at Greenway. Agatha had great pleasure in watching her grandson growing up. He was at Elstree, a preparatory school in Berkshire, and during term she would drive over from Wallingford to take him out for picnics. She sent him each of her stories as soon as they were published; vetted first by the staff, they were returned to Mathew well-thumbed. Max tried to teach Mathew cuneiform script, and he and Agatha encouraged his liking for cricket. In the summer Gowler spent hours bowling to him at the nets – and doing conjuring tricks, at which he was an expert. (Gowler was not, however, omnicompetent; he invariably failed to take the prize at Brixham for 'A Salad', despite his artistic pipings of mayonnaise, coming second even in the year when his was the only entry.)

Greenway was the model for the setting of the book Agatha wrote that autumn in Wallingford, *Dead Man's Folly*, in which an agitated Mrs Oliver summons Poirot to a local fête, for which she has arranged a 'murder hunt' at which someone is indeed killed. The book has much of Greenway, from the Battery to the boathouse, the long grassy slope leading to the 'top gardens', and a nearby youth hostel like that abutting on to Agatha's own land (from which errant hikers would sometimes wander into the garden, gazing dumbstruck through the tall windows at the family's full-dress Sunday luncheon). Agatha was often asked to lend the garden for fêtes and was inundated with requests, always declined, to open others. She delighted in arranging treasure hunts for Mathew, Cecil's boys – John and Peter – and the children of the diplomatic and archaeological friends who stayed at Greenway. All this was woven into a sprightly story that begins sunnily but ends grimly. Agatha's preoccupation with wigs also has an airing, in the shape of Mrs Oliver's postiche and other people's changes of headgear.

Another novel was drafted at Nimrud in the first months of 1955, *Hickory, Dickory Dock*. It was the last whose title was derived from a nursery rhyme, although Agatha had an exercise book full of other ideas: 'Ding Dong Bell, Pussy's in the Well – An old maid murdered; One, Two, Three, Four, Five, Catching Fishes all Alive – Mrs C has daughter by first husband (bad lot) ... Mary, Mary, Quite Contrary, How does your garden grow? ... Flowers on each body – viola, pansy'. Some of these plots she later used. The story is set in a hostel for students owned by a 'Mrs Nicoletis'; Agatha's picture was sufficiently realistic to provoke a Mr Nicoletis to write when the book was published, alleging that she had libelled his mother, who claimed to remember Agatha as a guest in her own *pension*. 'I *invented* the name,' Agatha expostulated to Cork. 'I'm sure it's all nonsense ... If this is supposed to have happened in France, I've certainly never stayed in a hostel for students of any kind.... When I was with my mother, we always stayed at the Hotel d'Iéna and of later years it's always been Hotels round about the rue de Rivoli, and the dear Bristol.' (Agatha always capitalised 'Hotels', along with 'Bathrooms', 'Bathes', and her favourite food, 'Caviare', 'Ham', 'Vol au Vents', 'Lobster', etc.) Agatha added robustly, 'Mr Nicoletis must just be obsessed by having a disagreeable mother.

It's terrible that if you invent characters they should come out so true to life. Positively uncanny!.'

Agatha gave the royalties from *Hickory, Dickory Dock* to a trust for her nephews, John and Pete, Mallowan, and celebrated its completion by descending on the bazaars and acquiring a silk rug and pictures by Iraqi artists. Otherwise, she admitted, 'this is a place where my immense natural spending powers have little scope.' Max was happy, too, for they were digging a promising spot: 'Boxes and boxes of winged genii and devils to avert evil are coming up,' Agatha told Cork, 'and yesterday a large something of broken ivory and charred wood appeared!' The weather, however, turned stormy and at the end of March she caught a chill so severe that she was taken to hospital at Mosul. She recovered by Easter, apologising for the grumpy letters she had sent and attributing the 'backwash of bad temper' to 'strepto-chloro etc. mycetins killing my amiability'. Her cure had been accelerated by Cork's sending exactly the book to appeal to her, the exposure as a forgery of the 'prehistoric' skull of the so-called 'Piltdown Man': 'What a *wonderful* hoax the whole thing was!' she wrote ecstatically.

Equally stimulating was Cork's telegram to say that the Queen was to attend a special performance of *Witness for the Prosecution* at the Windsor Repertory Theatre. The play continued to flourish and, when Agatha returned to England in May 1955, Cork told her that it had also encouraged a flood of requests for dramatic rights to her other work, applications he continued to decline on her behalf. All Agatha's theatrical ventures were prospering. It began to seem as if Peter Saunders might at last extract *Towards Zero* from Bertie Meyer, while the legal wrangling over the American rights to *The Hollow* had entered a headier realm with the death in November 1954 of their American bugbear, Lee Shubert. Though *The Mousetrap* had begun to flag in February, after Richard Attenborough's engagement ended, Saunders thought it worth keeping on for the thousandth performance, since only fourteen plays in the history of the British theatre had run as long. He primed his press agent, issuing a commemorative silk programme, free of charge, to every member of the audience on that night. Business shot up. Saunders wrote in rapture to Agatha – but the letter went astray: 'Envelope arrived with nothing in it, marked No Contents,' she told Cork. 'Tell him less silk programmes and more licking of envelope flaps!'

Letters poured in from admirers and entrepreneurs. Did Agatha prefer to be called Mrs or Miss Christie? (Mrs Christie.) Would she contribute to a book of favourite dishes of famous people? (No.) Might the BBC take television pictures of Greenway? (No). Would she take part in a BBC programme called *Frankly Speaking*? ('One, I think,' Cork advised, 'you should turn down in person.') The BBC had for some time been hoping to make a programme about Agatha. In 1953 they had invited her to take part in a new programme called *Panorama*, 'to sit in an armchair' and be 'gently interviewed'. Cork had told the producer that: 'I am afraid Mrs Christie feels she would definitely not like to appear on television, under any circumstances whatever, She is, as I told you, very shy, and she hates publicity of any kind, so I fear there is nothing more we can do.' In February 1955, nonetheless, the BBC put out a radio programme *Close-Up*, written by Gale Pedrick, with contributions from a number of Agatha's friends and colleagues. She was not pleased.

Her relations with the BBC were not always prickly. Though Agatha distrusted television, she liked working for the wireless and with one producer in particular, Martyn Webster. At the end of 1955 he produced a play she had written, based on one of her favourite phrases from the Bible, *Butter in a Lordly Dish*. This macabre drama, which lasted an hour, told the story of Sir Luke Enderby, K.C., a distinguished barrister and a womaniser. Sir Luke, it appeared, had persuaded the Court to hang an innocent man, a death horribly avenged, for he was destroyed much as Jael destroyed Sisera, when, having brought him 'butter in a lordly dish', she hammered a nail into his forehead. Luckily Agatha was able to provide only sound effects.

In September 1955 Agatha and Max celebrated their silver wedding. Billy Collins made his first visit to Greenway: 'Black tie for the celebrations and the bathing is still nice and warm,' Agatha told him. Cork could not come but sent a silver candlestick: 'But *no* chopper fortunately to chop off our heads,' said Agatha speculatively. Last-minute problems were turned to advantage: 'Some of the guests had gastric flu and we had domestic help trouble. Result – LOTS of Caviare!!'

Agatha could also celebrate the fact that she was well ahead of her commitments. Not only was *Dead Man's Folly* ready for 1956 but since the spring of 1955 she had been working, 'at an Oriental pace', on a new Mary Westmacott. 'There are a good many tentative Christian names, she told Cork. 'I can't start writing till I can get names that I feel *fit*.' This novel became *The Burden*.

Agatha had settled from the start on its theme: 'Two sisters – Elder loving and possessive, determined that the younger one shall be happy.' She added a maxim which she often cited: 'Take what you want, and pay for it, says God.' As she worked on the novel at Winterbrook in the autumn, Agatha developed this metaphor: 'Sometimes you haven't the right currency. And then someone else has to pay.'

From the beginning Agatha was certain of one of the novel's central notions, the conjunctions between separate lives, the way in which each can be affected by coincidence or deliberate meddling. Her proposed titles at this stage were 'Double Entry' (remembered from her book-keeping lessons), 'Cross Reference', 'Angles of Attack', or 'Point of Interception'. This outline then became entangled with a different plot, taken, interestingly, from *Unfinished Portrait*. It concerned a small girl, Hazel, sent away from home to live with an aunt – rather as Clara had been sent to live with Margaret. 'Witch Hazel' believes (again like Clara) that she has second sight, and her unusual gifts are eventually exploited by an impresario. Though Agatha abandoned that narrative before the dénouement, it provided the basis for the story of the evangelist whose history is, somewhat oddly, entangled with that of the sisters in *The Burden*. 'What shall it profit a man if he gain the whole world and lose his own soul?' Agatha wrote in the middle of her notes for 'General Projects 1955: M.W.'; it provides the key to this idiosyncratic novel.

Agatha was able to leave the typescript of *The Burden* with Cork when she set off for Nimrud at the beginning of 1956. She had become a C.B.E. in the New Year's Honours List: 'One up to the Low-Brows!!' she wrote to Cork from Baghdad, reporting that, 'My social position has risen here a lot. I am asked about exclusively to parties with Ambassadors and Ministers and the Iraq *Times* has promoted me to a Dame!!'

Installed at Nimrud, she completed a detective story she had begun in the autumn. This took up a notion that had often crossed her mind and had crept into an early draft of *The Burden* – of two trains either passing each other in opposite directions or of one train overtaking another. Long ago she had made the note: 'Man sees girl being strangled in train' and now she developed it as a new problem for Miss Marple. 'Train. Coming from London, Reading – passes local – no corridors? ... Now – what really happened? Man strangles woman. Her body thrown out of carriage on to embankment or field. Or tunnel? If tunnel, how far fom London? Embankment or field his own. ...' So Agatha launched into the story, introducing Mrs McGillicuddy and Lucy Eyelesbarrow, 'leg man' for Miss Marple who, like Agatha, found it increasingly difficult to scramble about. (Miss Eyelesbarrow, being exceptionally clever, had recognised that the best-paid posts were to be found in domestic service, thereby illustrating one of Agatha's most heart-felt lamentations.) There are, as well, some lively small boys in the story, rather like Mathew.

The title of Agatha's new mystery had a number of changes. First it was 'The 4.15 from Paddington', then 'The 4.30', next 'The 4.50' and, when Agatha sent her draft to Cork in March 1956, 'The 4.54'. At Nimrud she consulted Peter Hulin, an epigraphist with a passion for railway trains and timetables, and on his advice fixed upon 4.54, since he assured her that no train left Paddington at that time. Otherwise, she informed Cork: 'I thought people might write and say "but the 4.40 (or whatever it was) goes to Weston-Super-Mare."' Collins found this too clumsy, while Dodd, Mead suggested that American readers might not recognise the station. Exasperated, Agatha offered Cork '4.54 from London' adding that, if they feared another Mr Nicoletis, 'possibly refer to the Terminus as Padderloo – in case someone lives in a large house surrounded by railway....' They settled on *The 4.50 from Paddington*. Amid all these adjustments, Agatha overlooked the matter of Miss Marple's age: she now appeared to be ninety. Careful excisions were made and the book was done. 'It's lovely to feel I haven't got to write anything for a good long time!!!' Agatha told Cork blissfully. 'Just knit and read!'

Her next project was the organisation of a visit to America with Max, who had been awarded a gold medal by the University of Pennsylvania. They were to be away for two weeks in May. Cork and Ober satisfied the authorities that Agatha, who had paid thousands of dollars in American tax, would not be a charge on public funds in the United States, while Agatha investigated railway routes – 'I hate the idea of all this flying' – and sought out *quiet* hotels. 'It will all be very expensive,' she confessed, 'but I've got to *go* comfortably at my time of life.' She thought of travelling by train to Los Angeles, where Charles Laughton, Tyrone Power and Marlene Dietrich were filming *Witness for the Prosecution*, but Ober and Cork between them tried to dissuade her from 'this crazy idea of flitting over to Hollywood', and Agatha promised to make 'other plans for *my* week of fun'. She was ready, Cork told Ober, to do whatever was necessary or desirable during her last forty-eight hours in New York, but until then she wanted it to be understood that the star of the occasion was Max and that she was going to Philadelphia as Mrs Mallowan.

Agatha and Max came back from Nimrud earlier than usual in 1957, and after ringing up Cork for what she described as 'the latest dope' and having her nails and hair dealt with 'so as not to alight in New York looking like a savage', they set off, Agatha arriving, Cork learnt from Ober's colleague, Dorothy Olding, 'full of bounce'. After the presentation, Agatha and Max had, according to her postcard, three days' peace at the Grand Canyon: 'Am enjoying myself terrifically. In fact couldn't be enjoying myself more!! Must do this all again!' She did after all go to Los Angeles; photographs of her and Max were sent to Dorothy Olding by the Swanson office, with a note from Agatha, saying that all was going well with *Witness for the Prosecution.* 'We're all enchanted with her,' Dorothy reported, and Agatha was just as delighted with America as she had been on her first visit in the 'twenties.

Greenway was waiting – and work. No interviews, Agatha told Cork, no articles or book reviews: 'It will take all my time and energy to do the yearly book!!' There was one ordeal to be faced before she could settle undisturbed to writing, Peter Saunders's party for *The Mousetrap,* which on September 13th would have run for 1998 performances, becoming, he proudly announced, the longest-running play in the history of the British theatre. Special programmes were again printed, with a photograph of Agatha (approved by her) on the cover. 'Am full of nervous apprehension,' she confided in Cork. 'However it *may* be fun? (Very doubtful.)' With that behind her, Agatha could enjoy Greenway and, towards the end of the autumn, work at a new plot, suggested by Stella Kirwan, who helped Agatha keep her typing and letters in order. She had drawn Agatha's attention to the story of an Antarctic explorer, who had recently been telling the newspapers about the strangeness of returning home after months without news. Agatha brooded and in October sent Cork a note: 'I want to know,' she wrote, 'from one of our barrister or solicitor advisers, what would happen in a case as follows:

Young A is charged with the murder of his stepmother, whom he hits on the head. He is tried, convicted and gets life imprisonment. His defence was an alibi: he had been with a certain person, B, a stranger, at the time of the murder. B however could never be found and the thing sounded clearly like a trumped-up story.

If B reappears and exonerates A, who has by then died in prison, Agatha asked, 'what would be the position legally? Would a "free pardon" be granted posthumously? What steps, if any, would be taken; also would the police be likely to re-open the case? A has left a family, wife, sisters etc. A word as to this as soon as possible would help me to get to work industriously.'

The book was to be *Ordeal by Innocence*, an examination of another of Agatha's preoccupations: the harm that is done by the guilty not only to the victim of a crime but also to the innocent, suspected themselves and suspecting each other until guilt is clearly assigned. Another familiar theme was the emotional and psychological price exacted by maternal love, particularly that of an adoptive mother. The book was submitted to Collins as *The Innocent*. Cork suggested the new title, celebrating with Agatha over lunch at the Caprice. The book, which her publishers thought the best for some years, was dedicated 'with affection and respect' to Billy Collins.

In the middle of her work on *Ordeal by Innocence*, Agatha produced a short story, 'The Dressmaker's Doll'. 'Do tell me what you make of it,' Cork asked Dorothy Olding. 'She was well on with a new mystery novel when she suddenly felt she had to write this little piece.' It may be found in two collections, *Double Sin*, which appeared in America in 1961, and *Miss Marple's Final Cases*, published in the United Kingdom in 1979. It had, in fact, nothing to do with Miss Marple, being more weirdly exotic, the sort of story Agatha had written earlier in her career, like those in *The Hound of Death*. 'The Dressmaker's Doll' is exactly that, a life-sized doll of 'velvet and silk and a lick of paint', lying on the sofa, 'the Puppet Doll, the whim of Rich Women, who lolls beside the telephone, or among the cushions of the divan'. This doll, however, has an uncanny property of moving about when alone. Otherwise it sits, 'with an extraordinary naturalness', looking intelligent, 'as though she knew something we didn't'. So unnerving is the doll's behaviour that eventually the dressmaker throws it from the window, to be claimed by an urchin. Horrified, the dressmaker tries to persuade the child to give up the frightening thing but she carries it away: 'If you didn't hate her you wouldn't have pushed her out of the window. I love her, I tell

you, and that's what she wants.' The story is so odd and powerful
that it may have grown from a fear or a dream, perhaps one of
Agatha's, still reticent, as she had been as a child, but no longer
ignored – or it may just be the story of a puppet animated by
anxiety to be loved.

The book done, Agatha amused herself with books and gardens, opera and theatre, delicious food and travel. She and Max
went to Barbados for the sun and in London she went often to
the theatre, seeing everything from *The Cherry Orchard* to
Mourning Becomes Electra and *The Elder Statesman*, in a stall
well to the front, as she was growing deafer. Her base for such
expeditions was Chelsea, where she kept 48 Swan Court, having
joyfully regained possession of Cresswell Place but almost immediately let it again.

After Christmas (Cork delicately thanked her for a plate 'a
little broken in the post'), Max and Agatha returned to Iraq. The
revolution had taken place the previous July; it was to figure in
the mystery she put together in the spring of 1958, *Cat Among
the Pigeons*, dedicated to Stella and Larry Kirwan. A Poirot
story, with much about disguise and the deceptiveness of appearances, it is set in a girls' school, loosely based on Caledonia and,
to a lesser extent, Benenden. Part of the plot was left over from
some of Agatha's early thoughts for *They Came to Baghdad:*
'Idea,' she had noted then, 'Jewels concealed in plaster cast round
arm.... Could whole thing be jewel robbery, or smuggling?' Or,
Agatha surmised, for she kept in touch (there is mention of 'the
sputnik' in *Ordeal by Innocence*), 'microfilms?'

While Agatha was away, Saunders rehearsed her latest play,
No Fields of Amaranth, in which a student, in love with a
middle-aged refugee professor, kills his crippled wife. Her title
was taken from a line from Walter Savage Landor: 'There are no
fields of amaranth this side of the grave.' It appeared, however,
that it already belonged to another work written for amateur
theatre groups, so the play opened at the Strand on May 22nd as
Verdict. It got a pasting. Agatha believed the change of title had
led the audience to expect a thriller or a play about detection,
whereas this was a more complex drama. 'Critics,' she told Billy
Collins and his wife Pierre, 'are definitely anti-murder without
mystery. One still hopes, as many people did seem to be enjoying
it.' Cork, who did not think it a good play, hoped Agatha's name
would carry it but after a month, and a bad press that wounded
her, it was taken off. Peter Saunders immediately encouraged her

to complete another, *The Unexpected Guest*, which she delivered in July. She had put down some notes for this and now, having finished *After the Funeral*, she took up that early sketch and developed it (on the back of three laundry lists, one made out by Max, and a sonnet for Rosalind's birthday). The key idea was 'FOG' and a voice repeating the words 'you can do it, Jan, you can do it,' either from 'a record or a dictaphone or spoken by a parrot'. There was also complicated play with the theme that the clever might in fact be unbalanced and the apparently half-witted astute. Agatha allowed something of her brother to creep into her portrayal of the murdered man, who, like Monty, had taken a pot-shot at a woman coming up through the garden to the house. Peter Saunders put on *The Unexpected Guest* in Bristol and Agatha wrote cheerfully to Cork: 'You kept your fingers crossed to good purpose. As you will have heard by now, the play went well and I had quite a job being "modest in the dress circle".' It came to London on August 12th. More happily received than *Verdict*, it ran, to everyone's relief, for eighteen months. 'All right,' Agatha said of the notices. 'The Mixture as before and *Verdict* atoned for. ...'

The Mousetrap, meanwhile, celebrated its next anniversary, for on April 13th 1958 it became the 'longest-running production *of any kind* in the history of the British theatre', to the delight of Peter Saunders, who grasped the opportunity to give the play a huge public relations boost. A thousand guests were invited to a party at the Savoy Hotel, which set aside its restaurant for the occasion. There were two rooms for the press, including cinema newsreel and television cameramen. 'See you at "Hell at the Savoy" on Sunday,' Agatha wrote shudderingly to Cork the week before, but she loyally stood with Peter Saunders and received the guests. It is an indication of how dreadful an ordeal this was for Agatha that, arriving early as instructed, she nearly allowed herself to be turned away by an over-zealous porter. That story, too, got into the papers.

Agatha was grateful to Peter; indeed, she asked Cork to try to find her two of the original printed texts of *The Mousetrap*, to have specially bound for him and Anthony (who never received his). She believed, however, that the play's popularity continued because it was clever and well-constructed, which it was. Nonetheless, it was clear even to Agatha that *The Mousetrap* was becoming a theatrical monument. The longer it ran, the longer the run would be sustained if, that is, Saunders continued to act as a super-ingenious barker. It was therefore evident that Agatha, increasingly averse to self-promotion, would be obliged to participate in one set of high jinks after another, as it celebrated successive anniversaries. She swallowed all this – going to Peter's parties, donating the Mousetrap Cup for the handicap steeplechase at Exeter races, which she always attended, being photographed with each new cast – by treating it as a family joke, in which her relations also joined, bestowing on her, and eventually Mathew, who owned the rights to *The Mousetrap*, ornamental mice of one sort or another, china mouse cheese-covers and so forth, even a diamond ring with a tiny mouse climbing over the wearer's finger. This attitude was shared by British critics; as tourists from every country in the world flocked to *The Mousetrap*, their seats booked by travel agencies months in advance, or as productions were exported to Tokyo and beyond, so Agatha's countrymen treated the whole enterprise with tolerant hilarity mixed with pride, keeping their dignity by being gently disparaging about something so energetically marketed. But it would be unfair to imply that Agatha was not proud of *The Mousetrap*. Amazed and amused by its success, she thought it an excellent piece of craftsmanship and cared about the message it conveyed. To the end of her life she carried in her ever-present handbag a tiny silver mouse sent by an admirer and, without being aware of it, in moments of particular anxiety she would stroke it gently.

There was no new book for Collins in 1959 and they were obliged to assemble for 1960 the collection of long stories they had first discussed some years before. The volume was called *The Adventure of the Christmas Pudding*; it contained six stories, five featuring Poirot and one Miss Marple, a collection which had hitherto not appeared in Britain and of which all but one title had been published in book form only in America. It seemed at one point as if even this might not be published. A printing strike, lasting six and a half weeks, took place in the summer of 1959, and when the strike was over, there were further difficulties, since Agatha refused to allow 'Three Blind Mice' to be included in the volume: 'It will spoil somebody's pleasure in the play and masses of people haven't seen it yet!!' She suggested, rather, that she enlarge some of the stories, so that *The Adventure of the Christmas Pudding* was eventually put together in the spring of 1960, after she had returned from her winter travels.

For the conclusion of the annual expedition to Nimrud did not end Max's and Agatha's journeys. Max, who had been made a CBE in the New Year's Honours List, now launched another project that was dear to him, the establishment of British Schools and institutes of archaeology in other countries in the East. In January 1960 he and Agatha set off to India, Pakistan and Persia, going first to Ceylon for a short holiday with Rosalind, Anthony and Mathew. 'Delicious bathing. Nice quantity of ruins for Max and some lovely mountain scenery,' Agatha wrote to Cork. She did not, however, manage to retain her anonymity: 'Two rude photographers attempting to photograph me bathing were (I think) foiled by Rosalind and Mathew rushing between me on either side. I hope successfully, as it was a particularly ungainly attitude I was in at that moment. (Practically a close-up of a big behind.)' The Colombo *Times* described Agatha as a 'warm-hearted woman unspoilt by fame', but, 'thank goodness', she reported to Cork, 'girlishly care-free' from Bombay, 'fame hasn't caught up with me here.' Max was amazed that Agatha survived the trip: 'We travelled about 3000 miles right up to the Khyber Pass,' he told the Kirwans, looking at digs and museums and taking part in festive parties, 'even more stuffed with ideas than with food'. 'Apparently,' he went on, 'Agatha is very widely read in Pakistan for at the most obscure places we had fans jumping on the train and hammering at the cabin doors to get a signature. Everyone incredibly friendly but any possible chance of privacy on our travels seems to have vanished.' In late February they flew from Katmandu to Persia, where Agatha was besieged again; at the Park Hotel in Tehran seven photographers congregated in the passage outside her bedroom door.

She returned in time for the first night of *Go Back for Murder*, her dramatisation of *Five Little Pigs*, which opened at the Duchess Theatre in London on March 23rd. It was panned by 'the most malicious press we have ever had, not even excepting *Verdict*', Cork told Rosalind, who reported that Agatha had been very upset, 'although I know she didn't think some of the actors good enough'. *The Mousetrap* went on regardless. 'What is Peter's amusing idea for the 3000th?,' Agatha asked Cork warily. 'A performance in a plushy aeroplane to Edinburgh?'

The end of the decade was marked by more than the completion of Max's work at Nimrud. In the autumn of 1959 Harold Ober had a heart attack and died in New York. He was seventy-eight. For thirty years he had looked after Agatha's affairs in America; he and Cork between them had been twin pillars supporting their demanding but rewarding client, and the record of their discussions, conducted by letter, cable and memorandum – only rarely in meetings or on the telephone – shows the trust and understanding that had developed between them. The correspondence between Cork and Ober and Cork and Agatha is, in fact, a remarkable archive, illuminating an aspect of an author's life to which attention is rarely drawn – the role of the literary agent as representative, ally and intermediary. Over the years Ober, tutored by Cork, had developed an instinct for what Agatha would or would not accept. It was fortunate that Dorothy Olding had worked closely with Ober during his last years and that she and Cork were good friends, for though Ober's death was a blow, Agatha's affairs remained in strong and familiar hands.

Her mood was happy and serene. In 1954 she had taken out the 'Confessions' and made a new entry. Her favourite occupation she described as 'sitting in the sun doing nothing'; her 'pet aversion', she said, was 'crowds, noise, parties, too much conversation'. At the top of the page she put: '*Tout comprendre, c'est tout pardonner,*' and in that spirit she wrote to Archie, after years of silence, when Nancy died in the summer of 1958, saying that she understood how hard it must be after so much happiness. Archie had now retired, after a successful career as a director of various investment trusts and other companies in the City. He and Nancy had settled in the country, with their son, also called Archie but known as Beau, and they had continued to see a good deal of Sam and Madge James. Indeed, when Sam James suddenly died in his forties, they had been a great comfort to Madge, whose financial affairs Archie had diligently sorted out. Now Madge kept an eye on Archie. He continued to see Rosalind occasionally and in 1962 he heard from Mathew, who wrote from Eton asking if they might meet, for he had never known his grandfather. They arranged to see each other in London but, shortly before the day they had chosen, Archie collapsed. Madge James, who was with him, sent for an ambulance and visited him in hospital, thoughtfully smuggling in a bottle of his favourite whisky to ease his pain. He died, without seeing Mathew, in December.

Agatha was full of gratitude for her own calm, full life. In the mid-1950s, she decided to make what she called her 'thanksgiving' by offering a window to the church at Churston, the parish in which Greenway came. Cork approached the Diocesan authorities at Exeter and with their permission she arranged that a stained glass east window should be installed, to replace one she had always thought dull and uninspiring. There was to be no indication that Agatha was the donor but she did insist that her window would not depict the Crucifixion, as is customary in an east window, but 'the goodness of God'. She emphasised to the designer, Mr James Paterson, the Principal of Bideford School of Art, that she wished it to be 'a happy window ... for a simple country church with a rural population', and that she thought it should inspire the sort of innocent delight people must have derived from medieval Mystery Plays. Mr Paterson's suggestions pleased her but she was anxious that the central figure should not have 'too old and sad a face'. She liked his suggestion of portraying the Wise Men but had reservations about the other ideas: 'I have never been attracted either by the doctrine or by pictures of the Annunciation, as to me the angel arriving with a lily is a kind of ecclesiastical symbol which looks silly. If you have a strong feeling for the angel,' she wrote to Mr Paterson, 'could he not appear to the shepherds instead?' In the spring of 1957 a five-light and tracery east window was installed. By then Mr Paterson had discovered that Mrs Mallowan was also Agatha Christie, but only because his wife had heard it on the wireless.

In September 1960 Agatha was seventy, and still industrious. To a South American journalist who wanted to portray her as an example to encourage Brazilian women to do something more than spend the day on trivialities, she replied ruefully to Cork, 'Brazilian women are jolly lucky.' But with the passage of time she had become more philosophical. When Christianna Brand, a friend from the Detection Club, warned her that Ritchie-Calder intended to mark Agatha's anniversary with a *New Statesman* piece on her disappearance in 1926, she took the news calmly: 'I dare say you have heard of this already,' she told Cork, 'and you may worry about its coming to my ears, but after all it's only what crops up from time to time every few years, and what does it matter after all this time? One of the advantages of being seventy is that you really don't care any longer what anyone says about you. It's a thing that can't be helped – just slightly annoying – and the less notice we take of it the better, don't you agree?' She ignored the piece and concentrated on enjoying her birthday, with *Rheingold* at Covent Garden, plans to see the Passion Play at Oberammergau, a little holiday with Max in

Ireland: 'The Moules Marinière and the Dublin Bay Prawns, hot and cold, simply super!!' On the day itself she dined in state at Greenway, in her special birthday chair, garlanded with flowers. 'Hardly felt my age!!' she declared. '*Rich* hot lobster for dinner.'

23

'. . . an onlooker and an observer'

As Agatha's fame grew, so did her correspondence from admirers. Some asked for advice; others sent plots. She declined to read unsolicited manuscripts (the successful author's bane) and refused well-meant suggestions by saying that she preferred to do her plotting herself.

Agatha was never short of ideas. A train of thought might be prompted by an object, a place, a quotation, some overheard remark or unexpected sight. A paperknife with a curious handle featured in 'Murder on the Links' (she always kept it, dangerously rusty); 'The Bloodstained Pavement' owed something to her seeing Madge's face covered in blood that turned out to be cochineal from nougat at Dartmouth Regatta, and to the gory exudations of the carob tree. 'Why didn't they ask Evans?' was a phrase as thought-provoking as 'She will have to choose between them some time.' Mrs Dane Calthorp, the vicar's wife in *The Murder at the Vicarage*, resembled an imaginative and eccentric friend of the Mallowans, Lady Burnett. Ruth Draper's impressionistic impersonations provided a theme for *Lord Edgware Dies*; a visit to a laboratory produced 'Isotope idea: Carbon 14', never, alas, developed. 'Borodene Mansions' in *Third Girl* had something of Swan Court, where a woman had in fact cast herself from an upper window; 'Market Basing' had features of Wallingford. *The Secret of Chimneys* was partly the product of Agatha's musing on Serbian politics. As she told Cork, half a century later, 'No need to tell the butler that Queen Draga was my murderess!!'

She always described herself as being unobservant, but for people's habits and bearing Agatha had a noticing ear and eye. Katharine Woolley did not escape her scrutiny; the portraits of Nurse Leatheran in *Murder in Mesopotamia* and of Mrs Oliver in later books show that Agatha also looked coolly at herself. Nor was her family immune: 'I turned out an old Gladstone bag,' she told a correspondent, 'and found my Grandmother's motheaten sealskin coat, a purse with two aged but intact five pound

notes, six needle books classified 'for the servants next Christmas'
. . . you see where I get data for Miss Marple's life. . . .' This is not
to say that any of Agatha's characters were drawn exactly from
life. Her companions on the stranded train were no more than
the starting point for *Murder on the Orient Express*, fellow voy-
agers on the Nile steamer no more than a stimulus for *Appointment with Death*. It was behaviour and attitudes to which Agatha
was attuned; in declaring herself unobservant, she meant that she
took in general impressions. Her skill was in discerning 'types':
there was, for instance, the middle-aged diplomat, 'with an idiosyncratic sense of humour, a taste for the bizarre and an intellectual independence' that had prevented him, like some of Max
and Agatha's own friends, from reaching the top of his profession; he became Sir Stafford Nye in *Passenger to Frankfurt*. The
megalomaniac, sadistic mother appeared in that novel, too, as
she had done in *Appointment with Death*. Agatha's fellow guests
at the Grand Hôtel des Roses in 1931 were others whom she
classified in her notebook: 'the kind of woman who never moves
from Mayfair . . . and has complicated diseases; an ass of a
woman but with a real genius for clothes and how to put them
on; a family – or, rather, a collection . . . Italian man . . . two girls,
one dark . . . with foreign accent . . . lovely legs. . . .'

It is difficult to explain how writers work, not least because
their readers, perversely, often wish to recognise themselves in a
story, at the same time resenting the fact that, as they suspect,
the writer may be secretly 'taking notes'. Writers as prone to
fantasise as Agatha cannot help but invent people and situations;
they were her creations, born, as a dream takes shape, from a
mixture of association, inspiration and random recollection, given
form and sequence by the dreamer. This, not just pride, was why
Agatha could not take up offers of plots, why other people's
detective stories were a pleasure but not a guide, and collaborative exercises like *The Scoop* a horror. She had to develop a story
herself; composition was not a procedure but a process. The
plotting books show Agatha's mind at work, taking up an idea,
playing with it, making increasingly elaborate variations, turning
it inside out.

There are more than thirty of these books, of all shapes and
sizes. They cannot be indexed, though Agatha made a brave try
late in life, because the notes for several stories are frequently
intertwined, a single idea being developed in different ways,
dropped and taken up again, or combined with others. By ex-

ploring half a dozen notebooks it is possible to disentangle the origins of each plot, and tempting, for it illuminates the way in which Agatha settled on an idea, proceeding from the first inkling to the concept, itself by association, hypothesis, paradox and logic. This, however, is not the place to explain the genesis of every plot and every story and a single example must do: *One, Two, Buckle My Shoe*, which Agatha drafted at the beginning of the War.

The starting point was the notion that a body might be identified by dental records. It first seemed promising material for a short story; in one exercise book Agatha noted: 'Railway accident – claimant to estate. Much hinges on evidence of *teeth* (Death of dentist?); Dentist murder etc.' In another notebook, she took up the aspect of this thought: 'A Private life *and* a Public life. A blackmailer. What a marvellous chance to do away with a blackmailer, if you had him in the dentist's chair. You can pass yourself off as a dentist,' she went on. 'But then – what to do with the *real* dentist? Bribe him – or kill him?' At the top of this page Agatha set out the six questions the detective story writer has to settle: 'Who? Why? When? How? What? Which? At the bottom she noted a phrase that had struck her (it comes in *Stalky and Co*): ' "A downy fellow" – Dentist?'

A single story in which a dentist identifies a body (or, as in Dorothy Sayers's *In the Teeth of the Evidence*, works on a victim's jaw) was insufficiently subtle for Agatha. In a third exercise book she investigated: 'Sub-idea: Two "friends", Miss B and Miss R. One goes to dentist. *OR* does wife go to a certain dentist? Miss B makes appointment with dentist. Miss R keeps it. Miss R's teeth labelled under Miss B's name. Miss B dies ... attacked by tramp. Idea is that Miss B (rich) leaves money to Miss R (poor). Miss R does in Miss B and hooks it. Search out for Miss R. *Really* Miss B does in Miss R, so hunt is out for Miss R who *is* dead.' Agatha's imagination was now well away: 'Miss B rich woman – opens a/c with bank – stocks, shares, etc., alters investments, enthusiastic about her 'friend' Miss Richards – latter has been in 'mental home' for some years or abroad – in Canada – or governess in Italy. Both Miss B and Miss R go to Mr Morley – car accident. *One* body found – Miss B – identified by teeth....'

Characteristically, Agatha did not stop there. Twelve 'latest Dentist ideas' followed. One concerned a dentist's partner ('unprofessional conduct?'), another the chairman of a board, 'a little snappy - toothache - at board meeting'. An entire paragraph involves Hercule Poirot meeting on the dentist's doorstep a man with 'very white teeth', or, alternatively, a woman, 'husband secret service etc. Her face disfigured - unrecognisable', and another a person with projecting teeth being seen in silhouette. The last two suggestions display signs of exhaustion: 'Two friends go to dentist together. One infected with diphtheria - *or* dentist takes other dentist's place - could inject novocaine - or *something else* - and kill his rival.' An inspection of *One, Two, Buckle my Shoe* shows the plot on which Agatha eventually settled.

No variation was discarded for ever. Agatha was as parsimonious with her plots as Handel was musically and, sometimes decades later, an idea she had failed to use for one story would appear in another. Her imagination was unflagging: *The Girdle of Nippolyta*, she wrote, when preparing *The Labours of Hercules*, 'Headmistress? Oxford don? Precious manuscript?' *Augean Stables*: A sham murder? H.P. gets medical student to produce dead body?' She accumulated lists of ideas like a file of recipes: 'A. Poison Pen. Big hearty girl is it; B. Cricket Story (with terms used). . . . E. Facing Up story . . . going to confess the truth, killed first; F. District Nurse. Somebody run over, in uniform but drives car *well*'. . . . H. Arty Spinster friends 'another couple of old maids'; I. Poor Little Rich Girl (House on hill - luxury gadgets etc - original owner. . .): J. Lady's maid and parlour maid do robbery. . .; K. Stamp Story; Woman/Man withdraws money from bank - Miss M has found nephew's stamp album. Found on love letters from abroad.'

Miss Marple always stimulated Agatha's invention. She need only look about her to see hints for plots; 'takes down shoes; Hundreds and Thousands'. The analogies that occurred to Miss Marple derived from Agatha's own observation of human behaviour, clues, as Miss Marple mused in *They Do It With Mirrors*, drawn from: 'the curious behaviour of Mr Selkirk's delivery van, the absent-minded postman, the gardener who worked on Whit Monday, and that very curious affair of the summer weight combinations.'

For all her verisimilitude, however, Miss Marple was unreal, a composite, created character. Assiduous readers might breathe life into her, and into Hercule Poirot, Parker Pyne, Inspector Japp, Mr Quin, Superintendent Spence and Mrs Oliver, worrying about discrepancies in successive accounts of their habits and situation, pleading for Miss Marple and Poirot to be brought

together in a plot. Agatha herself was more breezy; these were
her creations, members of a repertoire on which she drew, manipulating them when it suited her and her market. 'Hercule Poirot'
and 'Miss Marple' were not old friends for whom Agatha sighed
as she sat in the desert; 'a Poirot', 'a Marple' were 'her children',
but they were inventions, crafted with respect and affection. In
creating Mrs Oliver, Agatha made this very point, portraying a
crime novelist who thinks her own readers absurd for taking her
hero, a Finnish detective, too seriously. It was a good joke of
Agatha's to model Mrs Oliver on herself and to give her as a
sparring partner to Poirot, an egoist who had all too successfully
stolen the limelight.

It was not possessiveness alone which made Agatha resist the
blandishments of those who begged to televise her characters, put
them on the wireless, on stage or on film. She – and Cork –
guarded her creations with an eye as much to business as to
artistry, but Agatha's reason went deeper than either. She preferred her characters to remain nebulous; even the depiction of
Poirot on a book-jacket pained her. Agatha's people, their
appearance and surroundings, were created as archetypes, intelligible anywhere, in any epoch – as Stephen Glanville recognised
when he assured Max that, in *Death Comes as the End*, the Egyptian background was, as he put it, 'psychologically' no more
significant than the Devon setting in *Five Little Pigs*. They remained recognisable, she was sure, only as long as the detail was
left to her readers' imagination. Literature permitted that; other
forms did not. Giving her creations an actual voice was the first
step towards imprisoning them: 'Perish the thought,' she told
Cork in 1949, 'that I should ever have a synthetic Poirot on the
wireless in this country. It's not easy to bear the thought of it in
America.' It is an indication of Agatha's growing dislike of
Poirot, almost as if she were jealous of him, that she gradually
sold the pass where his portrayal was concerned, to the point of
allowing, at the end of her life, his depiction on a Nicaraguan
postage stamp commemorating the centenary of Interpol. 'He
appears,' she exclaimed derisively to Cork, 'to have large quantities of *intestines* coming out of his head. Somebody's idea of
little grey cells, I suppose!' Even so, she remained convinced that
Hercule Poirot was 'utterly unsuited to appear in any detective
play, because a detective must necessarily be an onlooker and an
observer.' In her own adaptations she cut him out.

Agatha maintained that works made for one medium were not

readily translated into material for another. She understood that her books could be adapted for the stage only with great care, preferring to make the necessary amendments herself: ' This *could* be managed,' she had assured Cork in 1942, in the discussions over *Ten Little Niggers*, 'but *I* would have to do it.' To suit the story to the stage, she drastically altered the end, as she did again in her adaptation of *Death on the Nile*: 'Less explanation – more action – I think there was too much *reasoning* before.' The more Agatha wrote for the stage and the radio, watching her plays in rehearsal, the more technically assured she became. She knew, as Peter Saunders admitted when *Witness for the Prosecution* succeeded, how to hold and manipulate her audience. She was also firm about which stories would work as theatre and which not: 'There is a large class of my books,' she explained to Cork, 'which is not full of "thrills" and "humour", such as, for instance, *Towards Zero*, *Sparkling Cyanide*, *Five Little Pigs*, *Sad Cypress*, *The Hollow* etc. And you really can't turn a Class B story into a Class A story.' Major surgery might be needed; 'the method of killing' in *Towards Zero* was, for example, 'not at all suitable, as difficult to explain', and *The Murder at the Vicarage* was as it stood too complicated, 'particularly the clock business, ... utterly confusing to an audience and one of those things which in a book you sit down and puzzle out....' There were nevertheless limits to her willingness to pander to an audience: 'I have become a bit bored with the perennial humorous policeman,' she informed Lee Shubert in 1950, while Barbara Toy was reproached for having Miss Marple faint at the end of the draft script for *The Murder at the Vicarage*: 'It is, it really is *corny*. Just done for the curtain – and absolutely untypical of her. No, that really cannot be.' Agatha's own suggestions were, however, not wholly dispassionate: 'Griselda might express delight at having a real live-in servant – even if it *is* only Mary,' and, 'if it's present day one's little bit of boiled beef is sure to be tough.' Finally: 'tentative, very tentative suggestion from me. Why not, after exit of Inspector etc., a young man enters from window, note book in hand, "Excuse me, I represent the *Daily Blether*. I wonder if you could give me a few... etc." ... All exhibit horror and consternation.'

Agatha had to learn the technique of writing spoken dialogue. Doing so seems to have loosened the conversation in her books and to have made her narrative and descriptive prose less awkward and contrived. She could sometimes write extraordinarily badly, her grammar uncertain and her sentences full of tired metaphors. A reader whose attention is urgently fixed on a story might overlook these deficiencies but critics, lingering on each passage, are appalled. Such sentences can sound even more strikingly stilted and freighted with clichés when read aloud and many actors, forbidden to deviate from her text for fear that artfully placed clues might thereby be lost, have found themselves struggling to make the dialogue in her pre-'fifties work sound natural. Scriptwriting and, later, using a dictaphone, had a noticeably beneficial effect on Agatha's style. She had in any case the advantage of an excellent ear for tricks of speech and unusual phrases. Her dialogue tends to ring true in those books which venture into 'other worlds', whether of students, crazy ideologues, messy adolescents or eleventh Dynasty Egyptians. She read vastly: a wide range of books, including anything that anyone (children, the cook, philosophers) brought into the house, and an assortment of newspapers, including the *Daily Mirror* and the *Telegraph*. She did not like the radio or television but listened closely to other people's conversation, noticing popular catchphrases as soon as they became current. Agatha did not talk much herself, except among her immediate family, and some of those who recall her conversation as brilliant are in fact remembering how fluently they talked themselves, drawn out by an attentive listener, who occasionally prompted them or produced some pithy remark. If there always remained something slightly 'stagey' about the conversation in Agatha's novels, it perhaps derives from that withdrawn personality; the talk in her books was vicarious, planned.

Using a dictaphone did not, however, seriously affect the tightness of Agatha's plotting or the consistency of the details of her narrative. In the nineteen-sixties loose ends appeared more often in her books, and there were slips and omissions, but these owed more to advancing age than to a change in working habits.

She tried to be meticulous, reading proofs twice, once for the sense and once for the spelling. Misprints particularly vexed her but certain things escaped her eye and, especially in her paperback editions, she was not always well served by her publishers. 'I hate silly slips in a book,' she told Billy Collins, and in detective stories, so carefully constructed, it was all the more important to have the details right. Collins, at least, learnt to be vigilant. Year after year Agatha scolded them over the accuracy of the text, quality of the paper, nature of the jackets, their publicity material (on one terrible occasion the plot of *Ten Little Niggers* was nearly revealed in *Crime Club News*) and, with special vehemence, the language of their cover notes. 'No, I don't like the blurb at all!' Agatha wrote crossly to Billy Collins, on receiving their suggestions for *The Body in the Library*. 'I think a blurb ought to be aimed at arousing attention, rather than just recapitulating the opening events of the book. I enclose a suggestion of my own as being more provocative.' Nor did she like sycophancy. To her draft note for *The 4.50 from Paddington*, she appended the comment: 'The publishers can then add their favourite fulsome bit about me! In which, by the way, I would urge moderation. Too much praise I am sure *annoys* readers.'

Collins did take trouble. A particularly successful series of jackets was commissioned for Fontana paperbacks from Tom Adams, whose first cover for *A Murder is Announced* in 1962 was followed by over ninety other designs. Some are grisly – a knife sticks out of Lord Edgware's jacket – and some deceptively serene. All are remarkable and perceptive, identifying Agatha's own obsessions – reflection; refraction; transformation of people, animals, landscape; malevolence insidiously victimising innocence. Agatha, and later her family, found several of these designs disturbing, but acknowledged, rightly, that every cover was interesting, ingenious and apt.

It was inevitable that Agatha would argue about the editing and presentation of her work, as a parent struggles with self-willed infants: 'It is a very old war,' she wrote to Billy Collins during one incident, 'and I seem to have been battling over the years and getting more and more furious ... it is *my* books, *my* children.' To condense her books was to mutilate her offspring: 'I am *totally* opposed to *abridged* versions and Basic English,' she reminded Cork. 'A writer's work *as written* is his or her offering to the world and must *not* be interfered with.' As she wrote to one publisher, 'I know from conversation that it is often difficult for persons who are themselves not imaginative writers to appreciate that writing an abridged version of a book conceived by an imaginative author is equivalent to mutilating his or her brain-child, and this cannot be expected to give an author any satisfaction, no matter how keenly the operation and excision is performed.' She had no objection to her books being put into Braille or 'Large Print' or to their being recorded for the deaf, but simplification was out of the question: 'I am *not* a teacher and have nothing whatever to do with education for foreign students.'

She was particularly irritated by *Thirteen for Luck*, presented by Dodd, Mead in the United States in 1961 as 'a selection of mystery stories for young readers'. 'My books,' she objected 'are written for adults and always have been.... I *hate* this silly teenager business.'

Some of Agatha's critics and admirers are interested less in her methods of composition than in the fact that her thoughts turned almost invariably to one theme. Apart from the books she wrote as Mary Westmacott, her play *Verdict*, her poetry and those stories that were parables or riddles (like the Parker Pyne Series) or concerned psychic phenomena, everything she wrote was about crime and its detection. The explanation is very simple: she could do it, she liked doing it, and it was her life. Quiet and competent, Agatha taught herself the trick of writing detective stories. Their length was one with which she was comfortable; she discovered exactly when to break each paragraph and close each chapter, she had a genius for titles and for plotting, and she was scholarly about checking medical, legal and topographical detail. As a girl she had abandoned a career as a pianist or a singer because she was not sufficiently talented; having found her *metier*, she kept to it. One reason for her refusal to write for television was that she believed producers required more sensational scripts than she could comfortably provide: 'The triumph of Evil,' she explained to one applicant, after seeing a sensational film, 'as in *Rosemary's Baby*, makes one feel sick when seeing it, and recurs like a bad taste.' For herself: 'Hadn't I better stick to my last? You'll find plenty of people – younger people – to give you what you want – and perhaps to speak for the future.'

Her mind returned constantly to plots and their unravelling. Secretive, oblique, clever at solving problems, she instinctively gave a twist to a tale. Agatha was, moreover, a comfortable, sensible, ordinary person, and ordinary people are interested in good and evil, innocence and guilt. 'I am of the same belief as Dorothy Sayers,' she told a correspondent, 'that the detective story is the direct successor of the old Morality Play. It is the triumph of good over evil – the deliverance of the innocent from the aggressor – that is what makes it exciting.' For all her fascination with international conspiracies, Agatha knew, too, that most murder is essentially domestic, a revelation of the passions coursing beneath apparently ordinary lives. In the front of one of her notebooks, like a talisman, she copied a quotation: 'John Lockwood Kipling from Rabbi Hillel: "Nothing worse in the world than yourself – and nothing better." ' She added a note of her own: 'Substantially the R.H. says the worst men and women meet in the world is just men and women and their notions.' It was in a way an epitaph for the Gun Man.

24

'... like a cinema film
run backwards ...'

In August 1961 UNESCO reported that Agatha was now the world's best-selling author writing in the English language, her books being sold in 102 countries (twice as many as the runner-up, Graham Greene). From the letters that flowed unremittingly into the offices of Hughes Massie and Harold Ober Associates, it was easy to believe. Admirers were disappointed at not being received by Agatha, at her failure to sustain a lengthy correspondence, to edit their own manuscripts or send hints on writing. They did not realise not only that she was busy with her own life and work but also that such requests now totalled dozens by the week. An African who had chosen Agatha as his mother proposed to come to claim her, an Italian enquired where one might obtain Lapsang Souchong. A French magazine asked for articles on *'les grands sujets féminins'* ('Nothing I'd hate more!'); there were requests for help in saving the temples of Nubia (she sent a cheque) and with litigation over a sun tan lotion mentioned in *Death in the Air*. 'It was just a joke people made, not a reference to a specific preparation!' she told Cork desperately, begging him to 'Deal with enclosed by saying I am abroad!'

Secluded at Winterbrook, Agatha pressed on with the book Collins were to publish in 1961, the bizarre story in which she commemorated the pharmacist who first gave her practical training. It took its title from the *Book of Revelation*: 'And I looked, and behold a pale horse; and his name that sat upon him was Death, and Hell followed with him.' *The Pale Horse* combined two ideas. One, with the working title of 'The Thallium Mystery', she thought would 'start somehow with a list of names ... all of them dead.' The other reintroduced Agatha's earlier thoughts about 'Voodoo etc., White Cocks, Arsenic? Childish stuff – work on the mind and what can the law do to you? Love Potions and Death Potions – the aphrodisiac and the cup of poison. Nowadays we know better – Suggestion.'

Mrs Oliver appeared in *The Pale Horse*, with Mrs Dane Calthorp and her husband, who had last been seen in *The Moving Finger*. Agatha was now finding it difficult to keep track of her creations. 'Was he a rector or a vicar?' she asked Cork. 'And was there a hyphen?'

The Pale Horse was delivered in January 1961 before Agatha and Max departed once more for Iran. She also left behind the proofs of *Double Sin*, a collection of eight stories for publication in America, including 'The Dressmaker's Doll'. Arrangements were made to reprint the early Mary Westmacott novels in the United States. Agatha was still sad that her cover had been blown – 'it spoilt my fun,' she told Cork – but she now agreed that her American publishers might indicate on the book-jackets that Mary Westmacott and she were the same. Mary Westmacott's name, however, was to be given greater prominence. Collins were enthusiastic about *The Pale Horse*, and seized on its publication as the moment to launch a special campaign, to be related, in Cork's words, to the fact that Agatha was now 'out of the suspense writer class', and could be regarded as 'a considerable novelist exciting world-wide interest'.

Cork wondered whether Agatha would give the theatre a rest. Her passion for the stage, however, was unsated. In the summer of 1961 she drafted the first acts of two different plays. 'Don't much like either of them,' she informed Cork sunnily, 'but hope for better things soon.' These were the beginnings of *The Patient* and *Afternoon at the Seaside*, to which Agatha added *The Rats*, and, after Peter Saunders had read the scripts, a further seventeen pages of dialogue, so that *Rule of Three*, as the combined sequence was entitled, was long enough to fill an evening at the theatre. To keep abreast of current trends, she took herself to see Samuel Beckett's plays, and found them difficult; less earnestly, she went often to the opera. The 'Cork Intelligence Service' was also asked how one might secure a box at Covent Garden and obtain tickets for the Bayreuth Festival, for to delight Agatha had discovered that Mathew, now eighteen, was also a Wagner enthusiast. 'As you will perceive,' she told Cork, 'I am devoting a lot of attention to *enjoying myself*.'

The key to Agatha's work in the nineteen-forties was books and in the 'fifties, plays. In the 'sixties it was visual – films and paintings, though not, as yet, the television she so loathed. Early in 1960 Cork had concluded a contract with Metro-Goldwyn-Mayer for the film rights to some of the Miss Marple stories.

Agatha had given way reluctantly: 'I hope there won't be "broken hearts",' she warned Cork. 'What one loses in cash one may gain in absence of worry. But don't break *your* heart over it, Edmund dear.' In the summer of 1961 the first film was released, an adaptation of *The 4.50 From Paddington*, now called *Murder, She Said*. After a preliminary glimpse Agatha had feared that the story would be 'mixed up' and in September gave Cork her reactions after seeing the film in Torquay. 'My spies (daily helps!) duly tracked it down,' she reported, 'at the Regal at Torquay and we went *en famille* this afternoon. Frankly, it's pretty poor! I thought so that evening in London, but I couldn't say so before Margaret Rutherford. The truth is there's no sustained interest – it's muddling with a lot of brothers turning up in the middle, and *no* kind of suspense, no feeling of things happening.' She had wondered from the start why MGM had chosen that particular book, a difficult one, she thought. Even so, she added, 'I do think it a bad script (*I* could have made it more exciting).' She also thought it badly produced and the photography poor. She went on, 'As my eldest nephew said to me in a sad voice as we left, "It *wasn't* very exciting, was it?" and I really couldn't have agreed with him more. None of us thought much of it.' 'There's no doubt about it,' Agatha concluded, 'I have been spared a good deal by keeping aloof from films etc. *Ten Little Niggers* was bad. *Spider's Web* moderate. Only *Witness* was *good*.' But, she assured Cork in a postscript, 'Don't think I'm upset by *Murder, She Said*. I'm not! It's more or less what I expected all along.'

To Margaret Rutherford Agatha dedicated the novel she planned in the summer of 1961, *The Mirror Crack'd from Side to Side*. Agatha first conceived this as a story of 'Miss M – Unravelling', and her initial working title was 'Development Murder', for she liked to speculate about the tastes and habits of the owners of the new houses 'developed' on the estates she saw on country drives around Oxfordshire and Berkshire. At the centre of the plot was a film star, Marina Gregg, and Agatha's notes for the book show that she saw it first as a series of scenes:

M buys Bantry's old home. Mrs B lives in lodge – rather like le Rougetels' cottage. Good garden.... Heather Beasley (?) – in a 'development' house. Miss M – out walking – falls down – Heather picks her up. Cup of tea. Talk etc. Miss M and Mrs B. Tea at Lodge.... The Do – Grounds graciously opened (for Nurses?) Or house? En-

counter between M & H – husband there.... her eyes ... staring –
over Heather's head – as though she saw something terrible – at what?

The plot was inspired by Agatha's reflections on a mother's
feelings for a child born mentally or physically afflicted. Shortly
before the book was to be published, the attention of Americans
was drawn by the case of Gene Tierney, the actress, to such a
case and a similar tragedy involving the Dutch Royal family had
recently been given a great deal of publicity in Britain. Dorothy
Olding and Collins's editor, who had guessed the key to Agatha's
plot after reading only a chapter or two, recommended that she
alter her draft, out of delicacy as much as the need to keep the
reader guessing. This Agatha neatly did, not without a qualm,
confessing to Cork that this time she felt she was cheating her
readers: '*Not* quite fair – but you were all against me!'

The next novel done, in the autumn of 1961 Agatha went with
Max on a three-month trip to Persia and Kashmir. Max had
recovered from a slight stroke in the summer; Cork told Dorothy
Olding that, though Agatha was playing it down, he looked twice
his age. Max's life was now less strenuous, since in 1962 he had
left the University of London for a Fellowship at All Souls'
College, Oxford, where he was not obliged to teach or to lecture.
There he could concentrate on research and writing, principally
the preparation of *Nimrud and Its Remains*, and on promoting
the interests of his protégés. From Oxford it was still easy for him
to go to London. He had become a Trustee of the British
Museum and of the British Academy and he was a busy and
conspiratorial member of academies and institutes. Rather than
taking the train, he drove himself furiously along the A40 to
London, maintaining that his car was 'much heavier than anything I might barge into'. It was a miracle that he and Agatha
had only a single major accident, skidding on icy roads as they
drove to Wales one winter. Agatha was bruised and shaken; Max
found it 'all actually rather exciting ... wasn't it?' Sometimes
Max's secretaries and research assistants would be persuaded to
drive him but this was almost as terrifying. He urged them to
perform U-turns where it was forbidden and shouted 'Why so
slow?' when they did less than seventy in the thirty-mile-an-hour
zone. The only quarrels he and Agatha ever conducted in the
presence of others were about motoring: what the route should
be, how long it would take and whether Max might drive more
prudently.

While Max worked in college, Agatha wrote, or cultivated the garden at Winterbrook, taking special pride in her white peonies. Max had a good eye for fine things; he and Agatha made a collection of silver, a piece for every year from 1700 to 1800. ('Wrong year,' Max would say regretfully, putting aside a marginally interesting piece brought forward in a shop.) Agatha's days were serene, her companion Treacle, a Manchester terrier obtained from Rosalind. The house was beginning to need a good deal of repair – the plumbing in one bathroom did not connect, but 'it will last my time,' observed Agatha. Mrs Belson ensured that its running was orderly. Winterbrook was managed with pre-war formality but Agatha's nephews and godchildren, however unkempt, were always welcomed to ample meals prepared by the housekeeper, Mrs Belson. Agatha did not, for instance, seem to turn a hair when a godson hitch-hiked up to the door with an equally scruffy-looking friend and bravely asked for luncheon.

Agatha was generous to children – and to adults, for she loved giving: benefactions to her small cluster of charities; unexpected presents (a guitar, a camera, opera glasses, a fishing rod, a thirty-six-piece dinner set for a wedding present, baby clothes – Agatha, like Miss Marple, sensibly sent the *second* size – glass bottles, copies of Pinter's plays and Jane Austen's novels, pieces of Lalique glass produced from a canvas shopping bag). She gave presents to the children around her, imaginative gifts to her relations (a squash court for Mathew), treasures to old friends (spring bulbs, powder puffs, glasses, real sponges). She was lavish with food and drink: a dealer in an Oxford antique shop was asked for the *very* largest Chinese porcelain bowl and, finally satisfying Agatha with a particularly precious piece, was told it was for holding rice. Agatha had, of course, to take care not to give to all who applied to her, for many did. If once she were to depart from her own list of beneficiaries, her disbursements would never end. Cork screened most requests and Agatha herself was sufficiently level-headed to realise that some of the 'long-lost cousins' who wrote to her were self-appointed. (In any case none of her elderly cousins was lost and any needy ones were helped.)

The transfer of Max's work to Oxford did not mean that he and Agatha ceased to go to London. They continued to entertain their friends at the Detection Club and at Boodles, where Agatha liked the veal dishes and Boodles' Orange Fool. There was also theatre and the opera. In 1962 Agatha went further in search of

Wagner. Cork had obtained tickets for the Bayreuth Festival in late August and Thomas Cook made arrangements for Agatha and Max to progress gently through Germany. 'By the way,' Agatha told Cork, 'tourist class by air is quite alright as they are only short hops. It's only if I am going to be all night – or for about 24 hours – that I need enough room for my behind and my elbows.' There they joined forces with Mathew who, Agatha insisted, studied the scores with her each day. A considerate hotel proprietor protected her from hordes of admirers by arranging that each morning, for one hour only, books might be delivered for autograph. 'I got a great ovation in Bayreuth,' Agatha told Cork, with mixed feelings: 'I got a few privileges, anyway, so didn't mind as much as I usually do!'

On her return Agatha began a Hollywood venture of her own. This was not the first time she had dipped a toe into the turbulent waters of work for film studios; in 1956 she had agreed to prepare a screenplay of *Spider's Web*. Her suggestions for its treatment had been guided by the tone and direction of the plot: 'Commence with vast spider's web gradually dissolving into Clarissa studying a spider's web in country house.... Angle could be (A) Shots of antique shop and house – all leading up from that, or: (B) All leading up from Clarissa. Depends on whether sinister aspect or romantic aspect is to be stressed. Personally think B is better.' Her method was the same in 1962 when MGM asked her for a screenplay of *Bleak House*, her favourite Dickens novel. She began, as she had opened *The Unexpected Guest*, with Dickens's description of fog, and with the scene in Chancery, where the origins of the case of Jarndyce v. Jarndyce were now lost in the mists of the past. That case and the people whose lives were shaped by it, she told Cork, represented the essence of the film. Through it, she emphasised, ran 'a thriller or detective streak that Dickens nearly always had'. She found it difficult to reduce his densely worked plot: 'Two thirds of the book I have already thrown out, and have selected for the chuck those people and incidents which, delightful in themselves, might just as well have figured in any other of Dickens' works.... I quite realise,' she told Cork, 'that perhaps a third (or more!) of the present script will have to go.' Her supposition was correct. MGM's only concern was its length, a 270-page draft that would play for four hours. They asked Agatha to boil it down, and she therefore conferred with Larry Bachmann, the MGM producer ultimately responsible for adapting her own work. His team, however, was ruthless and eventually the project was abandoned. In a sad appendix to her notes, added in 1970, she closed the saga: 'Two portions of it were completed and sent – they wished to complete it themselves. I did not like their ideas – I wished to end it as forming a circle to the beginning – Jarndyce v. Jarndyce. End of famous case – and fog coming over London. From my point of view it was a good film.'

Agatha still seemed in the best of health, although in 1962 her back began to give trouble. Her hearing and sight were dimming and walking was more difficult; the gardens at Greenway had several strategically placed wrought-iron and wooden seats. Even now she enjoyed bathing in the sea, and, for a woman of seventy-two, produced a prodigious amount of work. New projects excited her. For example, Mathew brought to Greenway John Wells, a former master at Eton, and Alexis Weissenberg, the pianist, to discuss the adaptation of *Hickory, Dickory Dock* as a musical, with John Dankworth to orchestrate the score, Peter Sellers to play Poirot and Sean Kenny to design the sets. A title was produced by John Wells – *Death Beat* – and some songs written. Though the project came to nothing, Agatha enjoyed these preliminaries. Then there was another idea – for a play she provisionally entitled 'Ten Little Niggers 2', a reunion dinner of those whose lives were touched by the earlier horrors. This proposal, perhaps fortunately, also petered out. One initiative, however, was a triumph. For the first and last time in her life, Agatha made a speech. At the end of 1962 *The Mousetrap* celebrated its tenth anniversary and, at another huge party at the Savoy, Agatha's friend, the actress Dame Sybil Thorndike, presented her with a copy of the original script, bound in gold. 'Don't let anyone ever say to you that nothing exciting ever happens to you when you are old,' Agatha replied, as proud, surprised and shyly determined as a child.

Mathew had now left Eton, after staying an extra year to captain the cricket team. Summers of practice at Greenway had borne fruit, for he was now a considerable cricketer, and in 1961 and 1962 Agatha, who liked the game, had proudly watched him play in the annual match against Harrow at Lord's. In 1962, when he was captain, they celebrated by taking the team to *The Mousetrap*, where she beamed at the way in which her play amused and tantalised even these worldly young men. There was, however, a shadow over that first match, for on that day Jack Watts died. He had never married (to the question 'What are your favourite qualities in woman?' in the *Confessions*, he had answered, half-truthfully, 'Don't know any well enough') and he left Mathew much of his property and Agatha his house in London, with the furniture that had belonged to him and his mother.

Agatha's own generation was vanishing too but Greenway was always full in summer. As well as Mathew's friends, there were John and Peter Mallowan, and the children of neighbours and old friends who came to stay. Agatha presided, saying little but listening benevolently. She was most at ease with small children; more than one guest, missing her at tea time, found her at the top of the house playing Animal Snap and telling stories. Those children who stayed up for supper, however, were expected to take part in conversation, which for some was an ordeal, since the regular cycle of guests who came for a weekend or a week at Greenway included scholars and diplomats who were terrified of children and who therefore needed encouraging with tactful small talk. This lively household, and the books, ideas and anecdotes that filled it, stimulated Agatha not into chat but, as always, into trying new books and plays. There, even at seventy-two, she remained adventurous.

One venture was her play *Rule of Three*, tried out in Aberdeen at the end of 1962. Cork sent bulletins to Persepolis, which Agatha was enjoying with Max ('cool nights, hot sun, glorious ruins ...') Of the plays that made up the trilogy, two had pleased the audience, *Afternoon at the Seaside* being, he reported, 'an absolute riot' and *The Rats* needing only some tightening to convey its 'claustrophobic sense of horror'. *The Patient*, the last of the three, presented more serious difficulties. It concerned the identification of the would-be murderer of a woman, pushed from a balcony and now heavily bandaged, completely paralysed and unable to speak (a sort of 'Dressmaker's Doll'). The play ended with a policeman telling the murderer to emerge from behind a screen and at that point, as the curtain fell, Agatha's recorded voice was heard asking the audience whom they believed the murderer to be. This device was a flop. 'By and large,' Cork informed Agatha: 'it looks as if the customers are there for easy entertainment, and are inclined to resent the riddle ...' Backstage conferences persuaded Peter Saunders to try another version, with a recorded voice directing the audience's attention to two clues and thus the indisputable solution. This, too, failed, and after much cabling Agatha agreed that simplicity was preferable; the murderer appeared.

Agatha came home to poor reviews of *Rule of Three*, which

played in London for only two months, but to the better news that in the early months of 1963 *The Mirror Crack'd* had been a best seller. So stimulated, she told Cork, 'I have written the first chapter of Agatha Christie's next masterpiece.' This was to be *The Clocks*. Her notes drew together two ideas now running strongly in her thoughts, awareness of the passage of time and of events being conveyed through pictures as much as words. Though doubtless stirred by old age and current experience, these perceptions were not new. In 1930, writing to Max about *The Mysterious Universe*, Agatha had wondered whether 'time might be like a cinema film run backwards, so that to us life has no sequence or meaning, because until we see to the beginning we *can't* see. . . .' In other letters she had explored the theory, fashionable in the early 'fifties, that the narrative conventions of the stage and cinema interpreted 'reality' in a way quite different from literary methods.

'Speculation – only,' Agatha now put in her notebook: 'A. Clocks represent a *time* that corresponds to houses in crescent. B. Braille in some way comes into it (Secret Service angle?) Documents taken out . . . photographed during lunch hour etc. Their hiding place is a stippled picture. Dots really are *raised* and can be felt.' Her variants reflected other preoccupations: the way in which simply effected physical transformations can mislead, the ease with which stimulation of one sense distracts attention from signals intended for another. Her notes alluded both to events that touched her directly, like the translation of her work into Braille, and the larger world: there are references to the espionage case concerning William Vassall, convicted the previous autumn. The dedication of *The Clocks*, finished in May 1963, commemorated less serious pursuits; the book was for Mario Galloti, the *patron* at the Caprice, 'with happy memories of delicious food'.

The remainder of 1963 was bedevilled by an argument with MGM. Larry Bachmann had bravely proposed that Agatha complete and adapt for the screen another Dickens novel, *The Mystery of Edwin Drood*, a commission she firmly declined. Next, MGM proposed to make a screenplay of *Murder on the Orient Express*. Agatha vehemently objected. That book, she told Cork, 'took a lot of careful planning and technique and to have it possibly transformed into a rollicking farce with Miss Marple injected into it and probably acting as the engine driver, though great fun, no doubt, would be *somewhat* harmful to *my* reputation!'

Her fears had been increased by MGM's recently released adaptation of *After the Funeral*, in which Poirot had been replaced by Miss Marple, who was then shown joining a riding academy in order to investigate the death of an elderly recluse. Agatha had found *Murder at the Gallop*, as the film was called, 'incredibly silly' and complained to Bachmann about 'these travesties!' Unpalatable though *Murder, She Said* had been, she recognised that MGM had the right to adapt fairly freely, and that the first film had at least 'satisfied basic requirements' as to setting and plot. Margaret Rutherford, while 'not much like Miss Marple', gave an enjoyable performance; 'Whether I liked it or not,' she declared bravely, 'was my headache!' But with *Murder at the Gallop*, she considered that MGM had gone too far. Not only was the book 'a *Poirot* one' and Margaret Rutherford ludicrously unlike Miss Marple, but MGM's alterations had caused great difficulty about acknowledgements to the original story, let alone the publishers' publicity campaign for further editions of *After the Funeral*. Agatha was dreading, she confessed, what MGM would do in *Murder Most Foul*. ('Can you imagine a triter title?') to be adapted from *Mrs McGinty's Dead*, one of her favourite books.

In the meantime Agatha sought refuge in drafting *A Caribbean Mystery*, transporting Miss Marple to the fictitious island of St Honoré. Her island was a composite; some features were remembered from Barbados, where she had noticed an elderly gentleman in a wheelchair, on whom she built the character of Mr Rafiel, who was to figure again in *Nemesis*. A book about the birds and flowers of Tobago provided further ideas, and recollections and people she had seen on another holiday gave the essence of the plot: 'Rhodes, lovely siren – her husband divorced. Dark, cynical. Little brown mouse, nice little woman, wife. Plain. Stupid husband. Dark husband really has liaison with mouse. ... Or a quartet. Friends. One pair appears very devoted. One day wife confides they never speak to each other in private. Husband (to girl) says wonderful life together (which is lying?).' Agatha's notes now had more reminders to herself ('look up datura poisoning. ... And re-read *Cretan Bull*,) and she had begun, as the old do, to remember the distant past more clearly than yesterday. Major Palgrave, for instance, resembled Belcher, and their 'stories ... picked up in the course of travel' were not unalike. Provisionally the book was called *Shadow in Sunlight*; Agatha had tired of the struggle to spell 'Caribbean'.

Max, too, had been writing steadily and in December 1963 *Nimrud and Its Remains* was finished. He had severe 'flu in the winter but Agatha managed to carry him off to Upper Egypt in the New Year, sending Cork a merry letter in February: 'I'm sitting in the sun feeling placid as a sacred cow.' It was a deceptively calm beginning to a difficult year.

1964 began with a thundering row with MGM. *Murder, Most Foul* turned out to be as appalling as Agatha had feared, with Poirot again transformed into Miss Marple, this time a member of a jury. Mrs McGinty, originally a charwoman, had become an actress and a blackmailer. Cork warned Collins, who were considering how Agatha's books might be marketed to take advantage of the associated publicity, that she believed the films a source of great danger 'in imposing their image of Marple and Poirot on a faithful public'. Billy Collins, embarrassed at having first introduced Bachmann to Agatha, agreed not to use any stills on the wrappers of soft cover editions of her books, nor to mention the connection beyond the mere fact that a film had been made. An 'Agatha Christie Fortnight' was planned for early May, when some ten million paperbacks would be put into the shops. Although this would coincide with the release of *Murder, Most Foul*, Collins promised to do their best to ignore the coincidence.

Worse was to come. Agatha learnt of MGM's plans for another film, even now being made. This was *Murder Ahoy!*, in which Miss Marple was to enquire into murder and blackmail on a training ship in the Royal Navy. It was not based on one of Agatha's own plots and, if anything, this outraged her more than the previous distortions. Larry Bachmann tried to mollify her; 'Soft words butter no parsnips,' she answered spiritedly. Rosalind, discouraged and upset, felt the family and Cork had let her mother down by concluding the MGM deal. She wrote a strong letter to Cork. Agatha registered extreme disapproval; she was particularly upset because 'all this *Murder Ahoy* business' had been sprung upon her, having been advanced hitherto only as a suggestion. Next she learnt that shooting would begin in a fortnight. Despite her protests, MGM insisted on proceeding. To Agatha this violated her integrity as an author. She explained that 'to have one's characters incorporated in somebody else's film seems to me monstrous and highly unethical'.

MGM's next plan horrified Agatha – and Rosalind – still more. This was to be an adaptation of *The ABC Murders*, in which, according to advance announcements, it seemed Poirot's character was to be vastly changed. 'Do MGM really think this kind of publicity is good for a film?' Agatha asked Cork. 'They needn't have [Poirot]. I'd far rather they didn't – and if their director hates him and everything about him, why not cut him out and make up one of their own? ... One thing I will *not* have – H.P. turned into some sort of gorilla or private eye – and a lot of violence and brutality. This is a matter of principle with me. I loathe the tough kind of thriller and I think it has done untold harm. Possibly nothing like that is contemplated. But one never knows. They do so adore it in the USA. Anyway, if people have liked Poirot for about forty years as an ego-centric creep they would probably prefer him to go on that way.'

MGM were shaken by Cork's reports. They cancelled a contract with Zero Mostel, whom they had intended to play Poirot, and Agatha was assured that the screenplay would be rewritten. The contract with MGM was terminated. (The Studio maintained that the focus of their interests had changed.) George Pollock, who had directed their three 'Miss Marple' films, did produce *Ten Little Indians* for Seven Arts Films in 1965, but otherwise that was that. In 1967, when other approaches were made, Agatha told Cork emphatically: 'Don't talk to me about film rights!! It always makes my blood boil. ... My own feeling remains the same. I have suffered enough!'

The end of 1964 brought some cheer. Collins asked whether they might publish *Star over Bethlehem* the following Christmas, proposing illustrations and a jacket that, for once, Agatha found 'exactly right'. During the winter and spring she concentrated on her next mystery, an adventure for Miss Marple based on such a skilfully and enjoyably plotted conceit that it suggested that Agatha took great pleasure in it. Her notes for *At Bertram's Hotel* began, not with archetypal characters, but an archetypal place (for anthropologists. 'an Ur-Hotel'): 'Real bit of old England. ... Edwardian comfort. ... "Only get muffins at Bertrams").' It is a marvellous idea, another way of exploring the distinction between real and created worlds. The hotel is a fake, the respectable characters theatrical props. But are they any more artificial than their 'real' fellow-guests? 'Film stars. Pop singers. Rich woman, ran away with Irish groom. Racing driver', and, a stray from a draft made years before, 'Frog-faced old Major'. Only Miss Marple moves easily between the two worlds, noticing discrepancies.

Agatha's device also gently reproached those who criticised her books for being filled with 'stock characters', illustrating more directly than any of its predecessors that people in fact conceive of the world as being full of stock characters and that this can be exploited. So tidily, for instance, did Agatha's portrait of the adolescent Elvira fit the notion of a rebellious, spoilt teenager, that *Good Housekeeping*, which was to serialise the story in America, asked her to amend the text so that the girl seemed 'salvageable'. And so skilfully did Agatha describe the atmosphere and situation of 'Bertram's Hotel' that for years readers believed they could identify it. Charles Osborne, for instance, has declared it 'an open secret' that the model was Brown's Hotel in Mayfair. In fact, in so far as there was a model, it was Fleming's Hotel. Before the book was sent to Collins, Cork and Agatha between them ensured that any similarities were blurred. 'I have altered Crescent Street to Square Street,' Cork told Agatha, and together they changed the name of the manager from Capello, 'too similar to Manetta, who is the real proprietor. . . .'

Putting the book together was not easy, with its intricate juggling between the real and the contrived. Agatha was now skating on the surface of actual memories – Miss Marple at the Army and Navy Stores, the Canon's amnesia, a train slowing in the night, a Morris teetering through the lanes. Like Canon Pennefather, she met herself. 'I have never liked fog,' says Miss Marple, as it comes down over London, obscuring the everyday – or apparently everyday – pattern of things, yet distorting and highlighting people and their surroundings so they are differently perceived. It was a remarkable book for an old lady of seventy-five (the age now given for Miss Marple) and the public immediately took to it. Published on November 15th, *At Bertram's Hotel* had already sold 50,000 copies by the end of December.

Both Max and Agatha were particularly happy that Christmas. *Star over Bethlehem* was well received and Agatha was actually pleased at the number of requests for copies to be autographed. *Nimrud and Its Remains* was ready for publication. They spent the holiday at Pwllywrach, enjoying a pile of books from Billy Collins. 'I am beginning at the Low Brow end,' wrote Agatha, 'which is all I am fit for on my super diet of LOTS of Turkey, Plum Pudding, Preserved Fruits and Marrons Glacés!' She sent Cork an additional Christmas present in 1965: 'I hope you won't blanch too much at what I am unloading upon you! And there will be a further instalment to come, but I feel I must get rid of this now.' It was the dictated draft of part of her memoirs – 'not a finished product, of course. Lots will have to be cut – but I don't feel I have the discrimination at the moment. It is really the available material from which to choose.' When Agatha's auto-biography was eventually published, after her death, the intro-duction explained that she had written it at intervals between 1950 and 1965. In fact the story was more complicated. She certainly kept notes and occasional diaries during that time but, until the beginning of 1962, she had considered using these for nothing more than a short book or books – perhaps something about Nimrud, like *Come, Tell Me How You Live*, or a piece about her childhood. Many people wrote to Agatha asking for permission to write an 'authorised life'; in February 1962, for instance, she asked Cork to answer one applicant by making it clear that: 'I have *no* wish for a biography of myself or anyone else – I write books to be sold and I hope people will enjoy them but I think people should be interested in *books* and not their authors!'

As she aged, her attitude changed – but only slightly. Three years later, in February 1965, she told Cork: 'Someone writes to me every week wanting to write my biography – and I turn them down as I am not dead yet – and none of these people know anything about me personally.' Now, at the end of 1965, she said: 'I am delighted that if I die, everything is ready for me to be first in the field with my own life, cutting the ground from under the feet of others!' For she now recognised that there would be others. In an interview with Francis Wyndham, published in the *Sunday Times* in 1966, an autobiography was mentioned. It is not clear how the interview was pieced together from what was presumably a rambling conversation but Agatha is reported as saying of her own book that: 'If anybody writes about my life in the future, I'd rather they got the facts right.'

The draft Cork received was stronger on impressions and re-miniscence than on facts. 'I have purposely made it informal,' Agatha declared. The chronology followed that of her notes, beginning with 'Ashfield' and 'Father and Mother, happy mar-riage', taking the draft up to the chapter describing her parting from Archie. One notebook had a list of 'questions to ask Cork' and special points were noted: 'Find out date Monty's death,' 'Verify dates of publication – Mary Westmacott etc.,' 'Ask Ed-mund for dates of plays produced.' Other thoughts were grouped under: 'Some Items': 'A. Barter, Soup incident; "not part with information ..."; B. Reading – Henty. Charlotte Yonge ...; C.

Prince of Wales laying Foundation stone of Naval College ...; D. Boer War. Attitude. White Feathers ...; E. Father's Health ...; F. New York ... Ealing, My Grandmother's Sundays. ...'

Once Agatha had the outline, she dictated swiftly, vividly re- calling her childhood and youth. The most difficult part, the events of 1926, came out halting and troubled, so indistinct that her dictation could not be transcribed. The rest, from 'Second Spring' to the end, was easy. It took longer than the week or two Agatha promised Cork, but at the end of 1966 it was ready. She was enthusiastic: 'A suggestion, an appendix, possibly giving a short selection of fan letters, some of the funny ones, some of the touching ones etc. And perhaps the first story I wrote might be of interest.' Now she said: 'I shall break to Rosalind what I have been at! I imagine she has an idea.' Agatha suggested that three copies of the autobiography should be typed, 'one for you, one for Rosalind, one for me. ... Then we could compare notes and see how you both react.'

Agatha may have been stirred into sending Cork her draft by an interview she had given at Swan Court in December 1965 to an American friend of Phelps Platt, the President of Dodd, Mead. Gordon Ramsey, who taught at Worcester Academy in Massa- chusetts, proposed to write not a biography but, according to Phelps Platt, an evaluation of Agatha's work. That, she told Cork, 'I leave to you. I am quite indifferent.' Ramsey was true to his word, confining his remarks about Agatha's own life to one short chapter in *Agatha Christie: Mistress of Mystery*, which Dodd, Mead published in 1967, and Collins in 1972. Agatha cooperated cheerfully at first, seeing Ramsey at Swan Court and Greenway, passing on to Cork innumerable detailed questions about her books. Eventually even she tired. She was particularly unhappy with enquiries about the two unpublished detective stories she had written during the War. 'Why should anyone know in advance anything about a book that belongs to someone else?' she asked, reminding Cork that not even Max or Rosalind knew the plots of the Marple and Poirot books. Ramsey re- spected her wishes by refraining from mentioning 'the final Poirot and final Marple', although Francis Wyndham's article had in fact alluded to them both.

Agatha was testy partly because she was worn out. It had been a bad winter, 'nothing but domestic worries and dashing up and down to Devon in icy weather and all our roof at Wallingford more or less slipping into the back yard. What bliss 3 good servants in a small house would be nowadays. No wonder Pakistanis pity English women so deeply – they *enjoy* Purdah and sit in rich jewels being waited on!' A trip to Paris with Max in January 1966 was not a complete success. Always worried about money, Max had written to Cork complaining about the price of the room at the Ritz – £18 for bed and breakfast – and, compared with the Bristol, its *'mauvais style'*. In March Agatha had greatly enjoyed but had been tired by a party Collins gave to celebrate the completion of *Nimrud*. Now she became unusually difficult over invitations to mark the increasing success of her own books. When her publishers proposed a collected edition of her work, she reminded Cork of her earlier objections to their typeface (particularly *The Clocks*) and of her half-joking remarks to Billy about the superiority of the firm's writing paper to that of their publications. "A distinguished collected edition I consider *most* desirable – but Collins must make print and paper good and definitely high class!!' Though ironical, she was pleased, however, with 'the butter about the literary recognition of my high quality work!!' The overall title for the collection was, after much pondering, to be 'The Greenway Edition'. Agatha disapproved: 'Not as though I'd lived here all my life.' Throughout the spring of 1966 there were discussions about presentation and in April Agatha lunched at Collins to discuss design. There was to be no photograph of her on the jacket but it would carry a small distinguishing device, a sign of three interlinked fish. It resembled a design Agatha had seen in Baalbek, on her expeditions to the bazaars in the 1930s. Some believed it was a scribble Agatha herself made when she was preoccupied but this was not so. Max was the one who drew, always pots, some of which decorate Agatha's plotting books. Her play was with words, trifles of codes and word games, parodies and foolish verses. The person who did idly draw three intertwined fish was a victim in 'The House of Lurking Death', in *Partners in Crime*. Agatha reproduced the device for the Greenway Edition and was pleased when Phelps Platt gave her a silver brooch in that pattern.

During the summer Agatha relaxed. She and Max enjoyed five days in Belgium in June, inspecting a museum named after Hercule Poirot, and in late August they went to Switzerland. Mathew came to stay at Greenway with a group of Oxford friends. He had just graduated, after reading first history and then politics, philosophy and economics at New College, Max's old college, and now intended to try his hand at publishing. Allen Lane had

offered him a job at Penguin. Agatha was reading science fiction.
She kept up with new novels and plays, making an expedition to
London to see *The Prime of Miss Jean Brodie*. After a slow start
she began a new book in the Autumn: 'Back to work as promised!' *Third Girl* was another complicated tissue of ideas. The
underlying theme was, as so often in her work, similarity and
change. At the centre of the story is a flat whose occupants
advertise for a 'third girl' to share accommodation and expenses.
Agatha's notebooks have many drafts of stories about rooms
where the decoration is altered or furniture moved either to make
different places look the same or the same place look different, a
device of particular relevance to blocks of service apartments
which outwardly resemble each other while being distinctive
within. Agatha's recollections of her own nursery wallpaper, and
the plots of 'The Blue Geranium', 'The Third Floor Flat', 'The
Adventure of the Cheap Flat', are instances of her observing how
easy it is to be disoriented by such alterations and thus in some
way deceived.

Into *Third Girl* came, too, the idea of the deceptive picture, a
reminder of Agatha's preoccupation with hidden messages in
paintings, fake ancestral portraits, galleries that are a front for
some racket, pictures as misleading as her own portraits in words.
Again Agatha emphasised how appearances may conceal as well
as reveal: 'Is boyfriend – a Mod? – like a Van Dyck – Brocade
waistcoat – long glossy hair – is he the evil genius?' her notes for
Third Girl enquired. Is 'an Ophelia, devoid of physical attraction',
a well-connected girl, fallen amongst bad company? One of her
characters is skilful with cosmetics: another is interested in psychiatry, for personalities can also be altered. 'Does Norman take
Purple Hearts?' Agatha wondered. Nor are neighbourhoods invariably what they seem. In parts of London where Agatha had
lived for years smart streets now suddenly gave on to extraordinary avenues lined with 'boutiques' and ephemeral restaurants,
thoroughfares crowded with oddly-dressed people, some deliberately scruffy, others ultra-theatrical, all apparently aged about
seventeen. Quiet squares became threatening at night, studios and
alleys sinister. She drew on this as well. Far more terrifying than
any journey Miss Marple makes in the altered London of 'Bertram's Hotel' is Mrs Oliver's fearful exploitation of hallucinatory
Chelsea.

'*You're too old.* Nobody told me you were old,' blurts the child
of the 'sixties who comes to Poirot for help in *Third Girl*. Like

Poirot, Agatha was ageless to her admirers. Like him, she remained professionally competent. She could nonetheless be ruefully funny about her own generation. In the autumn of 1966, on a trip to America with Max, lecturing in various university cities, she encountered a good many gallant octogenarians about whom her letters and diaries were devastatingly objective. One evening at Princeton was especially memorable: 'Everyone seemed *very* rich, evening dress and they put on white gloves to go out to the lecture and all nice but incredibly aged and ailing – the husbands were mostly ill in bed or in hospital and everyone I talked to was either stone deaf or paralytic, or blind, and a dear old lady hung over with deaf-aids, nearly blind and eighty-eight, accompanied us to the lecture and insisted on supporting me in case I fell down. "Of course I can't see anything on the screen," she explained, "only light and dark, and these hearing aids are no good, so I can't hear anything – but I like to be *in* things. You'd better put on your coat again, my dear, or you'll catch a chill."' 'She was most valiant,' Agatha recalled, 'and went home after the reception still as bright and untired as ever – I was half dead by then – with shouting *and* my feet!!'

Dissuaded from lecturing herself to help with expenses, Agatha concentrated on two unshakeable resolutions. One was to visit Nathaniel Frary Miller's grave in Greenwood Cemetery, a private ground, accessible only with a pass. Amazed, she described it to Cork: 'looks like Luxor ... granite monoliths everywhere', her grandfather's grave square black marble, six feet high and topped with an obelisk. Her other goal was more mundane, 'to pick up some outsize knickers', Cork warned Dorothy Olding, who had once located an enormous swimsuit for their favourite client. 'She remembered your prowess and I am awfully afraid, sweetie, you are for it.'

Agatha's obsessions figure in her notes from this trip. She was profoundly impressed by American central heating and the Cleveland Symphony Orchestra, by the paintings and sculpture adorning private houses as well as museums in Washington, and by the variety of people she and Max confronted: 'Supermatriarch – *femme formidable*'; 'an odious man in my opinion', who said, 'we always call you Aggie, you know, so you don't mind if I call you Aggie. Cold look from me'; 'a kind of palsy – rather pathetic – dripping with emotional hero-worship but kind ...'; 'a cultural prototype – a demon for work'; 'a 60-year-old platinum blonde, running him. ...' She adored Vermont in the frosty fall, 'lovely

scenery and the best *real* butter I've tasted for years'. Some deficiencies had compensations: 'a super-stopper train in the last
stages of decrepitude – everyone had long ago given up cleaning
the windows ... and the lunch was practically uneatable. In fact
I now think better of British Railways.' Texas astounded her:
'Austin very civilized as well as rich ... a quite unexpectedly
attractive city – from snow to warmth [they had been in Ohio]
80°F and almost a Near East Baghdad feeling of gardens and
green trees and leisure ... dinner at top of recent well-built sky-
scraper – very good food ... Dallas ... Monied – lectured to a
very select audience. Much too select. Wonderful display of a
loan exhibition of carpets, nobody knew a thing about them – or
was interested – a dull lot.'

After Christmas in Wales, Agatha returned to chilly Winterbrook. There she wrote a book for which she had begun to make
notes in America, *Endless Night*. It was set at Gypsy's Acre, a
strange and beautiful place which Agatha had first seen in Wales
years before, when Nora Prichard, Rosalind's mother-in-law, had
told her the legend attached to it. *Endless Night* had few characters. Collins's editor wondered whether this made the mystery too
easy and Agatha was asked to enlarge the part played by one,
Stanford Lloyd, trustee of a rich American girl who is the victim.
Every character, however, is interesting, particularly Santonix, a
young, dying architect, with a touch of 'Vernon Lee' from *Giant's
Bread* and of Max's friend Esmé Howard. Another is Michael
Rodgers, who dreams of Gypsy's Acre and of the house Santonix
will build there. Into Rodgers Agatha put something of her
feeling about Richard III, described in her wartime letters to
Max: 'An outlaw ...' *Endless Night* had some of the warmest
notices Agatha ever received, with praise from friends whose
discrimination she particularly respected – John Sparrow, for
instance, the Warden of All Souls', and Steven Runciman, the
historian.

Stimulated by success, Agatha told Collins she intended to
continue to produce a book a year and had already thought of
the next one. It was drafted in the spring of 1967, after a trip she
and Max made with Mortimer Wheeler to the British Institute in
Persia. Max had received a knighthood in the New Year's Honours List, so that Agatha's latest change of name was now to
'Lady Mallowan'. It somehow concealed 'Agatha Christie' even
more effectively than 'Mrs Mallowan'; there are many stories of
visitors to Winterbrook or to All Souls' being introduced to Sir

Max's unknown and unassuming wife. (Max knew, however, when Agatha should have the limelight. 'I don't think we've been introduced,' he would say at the Detection Club dinners. I'm Agatha's husband.') Stella Kirwan would now pencil 'A.M.' or 'A.C.' at the foot of letters, to remind Agatha in which capacity she should sign them.

The early months of 1967 were so busy that it was as well that the next book came easily. After Mathew's marriage in May to Angela Maples, whose name had been appearing with increasing frequency in his grandmother's Visitors' Book, Agatha and Max went for a fortnight to Yugoslavia, to recall their own honeymoon and, more prosaically, to spend Agatha's accumulated dinars. 'I don't *really* contemplate any Real Estate purchase,' Agatha teased Cork, but 'Ample funds' means nothing. You must have *some* idea of whether I personally have got £50 or £100 – or £500 – or even (vain hope?) a thousand pounds at my disposal.' They spent the summer at Greenway and part of the autumn in Spain. In July there had been treatment for her intermittent deafness: 'Splendid time with Doctor,' she told Cork, 'Can hear clocks ticking again *and* most telephone voices!!!' Max was less robust; in the autumn he had a second stroke while lecturing in Persia. He made little of it, simply taking a chair and delivering the rest of the lecture from there, but afterwards he was carried off to hospital. Visitors remembered that, though professing not to like detective stories, he loyally displayed Agatha's books by his bedside. Max was flown home in late October. Agatha, who had remained at Wallingford, wrote to Cork: 'I feel pretty awful but do believe it is a good thing he is not flying home in too much of a hurry. But waiting and wondering is Hell.'

She vented her anxiety on Collins in a series of furious letters to Billy about the proofs of her new book, *By the Pricking of My Thumbs*: 'Ordinary post brought me an unmarked lot, five days later a special delivery at 7/6d arrived – typescript and half a marked lot ... then yesterday the other half, also special delivery, at full expense ...' 'Perhaps you would make it clear not to change the spelling of the author unless it is actually misspelt. If I prefer *phantasy* to *fantasy* (both words are in dictionary) I want it left alone. ...' 'I don't want sentences twisted round to be more grammatical when they are part of someone's *spoken* conversation. Otherwise everyone's conversation would sound exactly alike and not like ordinary variable human beings. ...'

By the Pricking of My Thumbs pleased her, however, when it appeared at the end of 1968. The plot was another she had started to think out during the American tour, a story bringing together three ideas, of which one, death occurring at an old people's home, had also crept into early drafts of *Endless Night*. Another was the 'picture theme': 'Doctor Murray is suspicious of certain deaths in Sunny Ridge. Mrs W presented picture to her shortly beforehand – did she always do this to a prospective victim? Did she add a boat every time to picture? Signing her victim's name underneath?' Third was the 'Child murder theme': 'mother of girl who had illegitimate baby and, perhaps, killed it', 'sister of Friendly Witch – a children's nurse – confined – she used to steal children and sacrifice them', 'Lady Peel – barren – had had abortion – haunted by it?' Mrs Perry, a sinister 'Friendly Witch', did come into *By the Pricking of My Thumbs*, as did the theme of child murder and child substitution. 'Behind the Fireplace – Oct. 1967', Agatha wrote firmly in her notebook, with the deceptively simple but sinister phrases: 'It was your poor child, was it? No – I'd wondered – The same time every day. Behind the fireplace – at ten minutes past eleven exactly.'

Those four days Agatha spent in New England in 1966 also produced her next plot, a 'forged will idea', *Hallowe'en Party*, the novel she wrote in the spring of 1969, in which a child who boasts of having seen a murder is drowned in a tub while ducking for apples. The party itself resembles an American rather than an English celebration of Hallowe'en, though the setting of a children's party had occurred to Agatha before. She was interested in children's innocence and its exploitation, in their ability, as in *N or M?*, to perceive or reveal the truth, and, as in *Crooked House*, and *They Do It With Mirrors*, children's capacity for evil. She knew that their beauty might be deceptive, while the phenomenon of identical twins fuelled her preoccupation with disguise, resemblance and the nature of identity. *Hallowe'en Party* draws on several of these themes, reintroducing, too, the notion of transformation of landscape, for, as in *Dead Man's Folly* and *Endless Night*, Agatha supplies a character who, given money and opportunity, will realise a vision of beauty. Like *By the Pricking of My Thumbs* and *At Bertram's Hotel*, *Hallowe'en Party* is muddled, not least because Agatha sought to include too many ideas. For that reason, too, it is, like all her later work, remarkable.

By mid-1969 Agatha was being heavily bombarded with requests to appear here, pronounce there, contribute a story, a column or a witty saying elsewhere, in large part because producers, publishers, journalists and promoters of various kinds were making early preparation for her eightieth birthday. She did not look forward to the onslaught. 'I suppose you and I will have to construct something about my "coming of age",' she wrote ruefully to Cork. '*No television*. Definitely.' One producer assured her that television techniques had changed but she was immovable. 'Entirely a personal idiosyncrasy,' she explained. 'I have to admit that I am *not* television-minded. ... I find it *useful* – for watching race meetings, occasional news, misleading weather reports (in common with newspapers)! But not, to me, *pleasurable*.' Her antipathy, she believed, might be because television was 'possibly the wrong size for me. Some things *are* like that. Either photographs the size of postage stamps – or blown up to the most hideous proportions.' Not only did Agatha 'find it difficult to get any feeling of reality when watching that static box', she was also filled with distaste for interviews that gave her 'a feeling one would like to apologise for being present as an onlooker when anyone's private and personal affairs are being questioned and probed – usually without any pretence of courtesy or good manners. ...' She admitted that she had enjoyed some television programmes: '*The Forsyte Saga* – and the thrill of seeing live men stumbling about on the moon – and the agony of fearing they will never get back.' She herself, however, had no wish to appear or to write for it.

Some aspects of the forthcoming anniversary did please her, the commissioning of a photograph for the National Portrait Gallery, for instance, showing her with Max, and the china horses presented by her Danish publisher. She was delighted by Mathew's decision to establish the Agatha Christie Trust for Children in 1969, and particularly fascinated by another exercise, also arranged by Mathew. Max had suggested she have her portrait painted and Mathew had approached Oscar Kokoschka. Though he no longer did much portraiture, Kokoschka, an admirer, agreed to paint Agatha, and they had eight two-hour sittings in London, at each of which he consumed half a bottle of whisky. Painter and sitter liked each other, not least because they found a common butt in a doctor who had recently observed that people aged eighty or more were useless and should be mercifully killed. Kokoschka's portrait is interesting. It is of a very old woman, whom Agatha gradually grew to resemble. As in his other portraits, the sitter's features resemble Kokoschka's own, especially the square shape of the back of the head. Yet it caught Agatha's appearance and bearing, indicating, for instance, her habit of tapping her fingers (now afflicted with psoriasis) on the arms of her chair. 'It's very frightening,' was her reaction, when Kokoschka allowed her to see it. 'At any rate,' she told Cork, 'I look like *someone*.' Majestic, she triumphed over Hollywood: 'He was a great admirer of my *nose* – so big and important. I see all the film stars are having their noses *reduced* in size. Anyway I'll stick to my Roman glory.' Mallowans, Kokoschkas and Prichards celebrated with luncheon at Boodles, the painter cabling Agatha beforehand with his requirements: three kippers and a pint of Guinness.

25

'an ordinary successful hard-working author ...'

In retrospect it seems as if Agatha had been installed at the pinnacle of international success for decades. In fact it was a long, if steady, climb. She became the acknowledged leader among mystery writers only in the early nineteen-seventies, the moment when her British and American publishers chose to promote her books more vigorously than ever. She herself had confessed to Max after the War that she must be included among the four most eminent detective storywriters, in her article for Russia; even in 1961, however, the Cork and Ober offices issued to staff a list of 'Christie' manuscripts which might now be destroyed.

Agatha's admirers would have thought this sacrilege. Her worshippers grew more numerous by the day, as did their demands. From the nineteen-forties she was inundated with requests for photographs, financial assistance, books said to be unobtainable in Malta, Japan, Brazil, Czechoslovakia, Surrey. Much of this correspondence was intercepted by her agents, although Agatha was always interested in what admirers told her, especially if they could point out slips or omissions. She answered some letters, including the zanier ones, herself. One that caught her eye was a diatribe, in verse, obviously from a madman, against the evils of life generally. It had been copied to various Heads of State. She annotated the envelope with possibly useful observations on the writer's state of mind. Some of the enquiries she received were startling; from New Zealand came a request for a photograph to be placed in a special room containing 307 calf-bound copies of her work. An engine driver from the Antipodes wanted to know how one paid for meals on the Orient Express, a Frenchman requested permission to publish extracts from *The Labours of Hercules* in a book about Britain, with 'The Capture of Cerberus' illustrating the Underground and 'The Arcadian Deer' a study of English tea-drinking. A Japanese computer expert needed help with his compilation on 'Mrs Marple's life', and the manager of the Sverdlovsk Film Studio a list of her books. Agatha, her publishers and agents had difficulty themselves in keeping track of her works, now translated and published all over the world. Indeed, Cork and Collins welcomed Gordon Ramsey's book largely as an aid to straightening out her bibliography.

She was sent innumerable questionnaires, not only by her own aspiring biographers but by those of people associated with her. 'Why did you select a charming old lady to be your second famous detective?' asked an admirer of Margaret Rutherford. 'No particular reason,' Agatha replied firmly, for she gave such enquiries short shrift. One especially imposing questionnaire came from an Italian magazine, interested in 'the phenomenological and social character' as well as the cultural and historical nature 'of the participation of women in societal life'. Asked about the cause of women's increasingly active role, Agatha attributed it to 'the foolishness of women in relinquishing their position of privilege obtained after many centuries of civilisation. Primitive women toil incessantly. We seem determined to return to that state voluntarily – or by listening to persuasion, and therefore forfeiting the joys of leisure and creative thought and the perfecting of home conditions.' Invited to assess the degree to which scientific and technological progress demanded the participation of women, she replied that: 'I should say it could get on fairly well without it.' 'Do the answers ... correspond to the general view of your country?' the document concluded. Agatha wrote tersely: 'Probably not.'

The volume of her sales, as well as the amount of her correspondence, was another measure of success. The UNESCO figures published in 1961 indicated the buoyancy and steadiness of sales of her books; radio and television companies, particularly in America where audience ratings were important, applied incessantly for the right to show her work. *The Mousetrap*, the longest-running play on the British stage, enhanced interest in the dramatic possibilities of her books, even if it could not always sustain the popular appeal of her other plays. Agatha's publishers and agents recognised her value; even her hardback books sold between forty and fifty thousand copies in the first weeks of publication. Their appreciation was demonstrated by the extent of the services they performed for her. Ober's office tracked down books and engravings published only in America, and 'the very nicest kind of maple sugar' to be sent in one pound packages every quarter. 'These chores for Agatha can be the very devil,'

Cork apologised to Dorothy Olding, but, as Billy Collins once told his colleagues during a particularly complex saga over repair work on her car, 'I know these arrangements are difficult, but Agatha Christie is a very exceptional author.' He was generous with Wimbledon tickets and books, providing Agatha with works from Collins's list for the local primary school at Galmpton, the village nearest Greenway, of which she was, as she put it, 'one of the managers', and sending Agatha at Christmas a package of books chosen on her annual sortie.

Contractual arrangements remained simple. There were no advances on royalties but the percentage on sales she received was high. In 1950 Dodd, Mead pointed out to Cork that it now exceeded the royalty paid to Bernard Shaw. Even so, Agatha's finances were erratic and she often found herself short of money, for while her earnings were huge, so were her taxes. Furthermore, her situation was so complicated that for the greater part of her professional life she did not know how she stood. Agatha was not unused to financial precariousness. The collapse of her father's business, the frugal years at the beginning of her first marriage and the difficult time after her separation from Archie had all been worrying. In 1938, just as she began to earn large and regular sums from her writing, there was another blow.

Agatha employed various professional advisers to look after her affairs, her solicitor, accountant, and Edmund Cork, who saw to contracts and, in consultation with her accountant and Ober, decided when it was sensible to transfer foreign earnings to Britain. The bulk of her income in the nineteen-thirties came from the United States; 'a non-resident alien author' was also, it appeared, not liable for American tax on contracts negotiated in the United States. Such income might be taxed only in Britain, when it fell due there. In August 1938, however, the Court of Appeals in the Second Circuit in America heard a case between the US Commissioner of Internal Revenue and Rafael Sabatini, a prolific and successful author, a British subject residing in London, and the Court decided that Sabatini was in fact liable for American tax. It was the imminence of this case which led the American Revenue Authorities to pay particular attention to Agatha's affairs and Harold Ober to engage Mr Reinheimer.

If the Revenue Board applied the Sabatini judgement to Agatha, she would clearly be liable for enormous amounts of additional tax. How much, no one could estimate. Her American earnings were substantial (*Collier's* had, for example, paid $27,500 for the right to serialise *Hercule Poirot's Christmas*) but the extent to which the assessment might be made retrospective was unknown. Reinheimer, moreover, could be expected to plead that the lapse of time between Agatha's receipt of such monies and the Revenue's taking this stand, together with the fact that, guided by experts, she had taken all reasonable steps to fulfil the Revenue's known requirements, certainly meant she should incur no penalty and might possibly limit the size of the actual bill.

Unravelling these complexities took a decade. Many of the documents were discarded or went astray. Dodd, Mead and Ober Associates did not keep great quantities of past records in expensive floor space in Manhattan; at the London end, few files survived wartime bombing and successive moves. As the lawyers' arguments unfolded, additional papers were created, confusing the issue until these, too, were lost in distribution between offices in different tax districts.

During the early years of these discussions Agatha's plight was severe. As we have seen, the American authorities withheld income until matters could be settled; after 1940 exchange control regulations made it difficult to transfer even the small amount they might concede. Agatha's problems were the greater because she needed American income to pay British taxation on accumulated earnings: 'If I could only get straight *here*,' she told Cork in 1941, 'I could live on very little and keep my head above water.' British banks would not make loans unless they were connected with the War effort and, apart from copyrights, Agatha's only assets were in property, which was then virtually impossible to sell. Early in 1948 a settlement was reached, but only for the years 1930 to 1941. (The sum was more than $160,000.) Further argument then arose over the details of interest levied by the Revenue, and after that there were talks with the British authorities as to whether tax should be paid in England on the money thus freed. Though the United States and Britain had signed a double taxation treaty in 1948, Agatha was still uncertain as to the proportion of any prospective American income she might retain, since there remained the bill for the years 1941–48. That question appeared to have been settled by the end of 1948, but then Reinheimer's settlement was thrown into disarray by another court action in America. P.G. Wodehouse, a friend and admirer of Agatha, had himself been subject to the Sabatini judgement, being another non-resident alien, and his lawyers pursued the matter until the appeals procedure was exhausted. In December 1948 the American Supreme Court heard the Wodehouse case; in mid-June 1949 they upheld the application of the Sabatini judgement. Wodehouse's lawyers requested a rehearing and it was not until October 1949 that the Supreme Court pronounced. The rehearing was denied. Wodehouse and Agatha at last knew where they stood. There were, in addition, large bills from lawyers and accountants.

That episode behind her, Agatha decided to forget it. She did notice, however, the large difference between the sums she was now earning from her work and the amount she actually retained. British basic tax and super-tax rates were exceptionally high; by the mid-nineteen-fifties a large proportion of her earnings went to the Revenue. 'Where *is* it all?!!' she wrote to Cork from Iraq in the spring of 1954. He pointed out that in that year, 1953–54, the tax for a married couple with no dependent children and with, say, earnings of £30,000 a year, taxable at higher rates, would be some £25,000. He proposed that, when Agatha's American negotiations were over, for they dragged on, her advisers might establish a Company for which she might write her novels under a service contract. Instead of paying tax at a top rate of over ninety per cent as she did at that time, she would receive an income from the Company. The Company itself would pay profits tax at the standard rate but not surtax. If shares were sold, they would be a capital gain, then not subject to tax.

Wary by now, Agatha observed that Cork did seem to be 'enmeshing himself in a legal net!' She added, 'I do hope it won't end in disaster.' Anxious not to do anything illegal and, indeed, not to shirk her responsibilities (she refused to contemplate moving to a 'tax haven'), she asked for legal opinions. Reassured, she agreed that the Company should be established. Meanwhile, at the end of 1954, the British tax authorities finally agreed to the terms of the American settlement. In 1955 a trust was formed, subsequently called the Christie Settlement Trust. Agatha gave the Trustees £100, which they used to purchase one hundred shares in a Company, Agatha Christie Ltd, established simultaneously. Agatha Christie Ltd undertook to employ Agatha thereafter. Her initial salary was roughly comparable to the income she had received, after tax, since 1950. These arrangements began at the end of 1955.

Two years later, in January 1957, another trust was formed, the Christie Copyrights Trust, to look after the copyrights of work Agatha had completed before the creation of Agatha Christie Ltd. To this second trust Agatha assigned rights to a large number of books and short stories, keeping a few for herself, largely for sentimental reasons. Agatha's advisers had drawn her attention to the question of death duties, which might in her case be impossible to meet; it was useless to predict how much these might be, since this would depend on decisions of the Revenue. There was an alarming precedent in the case of Bernard Shaw; on his death the Revenue had valued copyright on the most successful of his plays and multiplied by the number of his works, producing an enormous sum. Cork's nightmare was, for instance, that the Revenue would value Agatha's copyrights by multiplying the income from *Witness for the Prosecution* by the total number of stories she had written. That, including film rights, might come to £20 million or so. Setting up the Christie Copyrights Trust not only avoided such possiblilities but also permitted the Trustees to distribute capital sums to chosen beneficiaries. Agatha's consent was needed, and was never refused, and, while she did not seek to influence the distributions, she was pleased when the Trustees' thoughts coincided with her own. Relations and friends who needed help received sums from time to time, as did various charities. One of the disbursements Agatha particularly welcomed was to the Harrison Homes, an organisation providing accommodation for old people who enjoyed independence but needed somewhere safe and inexpensive to live. Carlo and her sister Mary had first spoken of the Homes to Agatha; she was pleased when the board asked whether they might name a new wing after her.

Agatha had interrogated her advisers at the time when the trusts and the company were founded. She feared the worry and cost of litigation and, after her American experience, had little faith in the permanence of treaties and legislation. She was right to be cynical. In 1957 there was another dispute, this time over the tax position on the copyrights Agatha had retained. This argument with the Revenue in large part depended on the outcome of a case between the tax inspectors and the executors of the estate of Peter Cheyney (himself an author of detective stories), who had died in 1951, and it took several years for that case to be settled and its implications disentangled.

It was like Jarndyce v. Jarndyce all over again. Only at the end of 1964 was the assessment delivered. Agatha's family and Cork agreed that she would be shaken by the size of the sum involved, some £100,000 to £125,000. In the spring they decided to appeal, to brief silk and to break the news to Agatha. Anthony pointed out that she would want to know whether she would be subject to cross-examination and whether the hearing would be reported in the press. Fortunately, the answer to these questions was no. Agatha's attitude was robust and sensible. Had she the time and energy, she declared, she would fight the case as far as the House of Lords, representing herself. She also suggested, only half-ironically, that the Company should give the retained copyrights to the Revenue to do as they pleased. Leaving her Trustees and advisers to deal with the matter, she took herself and Max off to Talloires and Lake Annecy, prolonging a holiday in Austria and Switzerland while she could enjoy it. In November 1965, after further uncertainty, she learned that the appeal had been lost and that somehow she had to raise more than £100,000 to pay off the assessment. 'Top Tax Counsel' had done their best but 'LAW-YERS!!!' she wrote to Cork in January, 'Next time we'll have the Bottom Tax Counsel. The result will probably be just the same and will cost less!' For Christmas Cork sent Agatha a picture of Hercules. 'It recalls the happier days,' she said in her letter of thanks, 'when one was on the upgrade instead of crashing downwards!'

Throughout 1966 and 1967 matters remained unresolved. There were the routine baffling income tax demands. 'I can't understand how one is supposed to live if you get £7000-odd income from Company and pay £5000-odd surtax out of it,' she wondered, 'as well as three demands for different kinds of income tax as well.' Cork tried to disentangle the muddle of notices sent by the Revenue but she was still disturbed. In March she asked for details of all her tax payments: 'I don't know what or *why* I am paying. And I find this worrying.' There were more large bills for legal advice 'Talk, talk, talk. Object, and no good comes of it. Lawyers!'

Cork assured Agatha that she would always have enough to live on. Not only was Agatha Christie Ltd entirely secure but since 1966 negotiations had been under way to strengthen the Company. A large public company, Booker McConnell, the agricultural and industrial conglomerate, had since 1964 owned fifty-one per cent of Glidrose Productions, the company in which the rights to all Ian Fleming's work, including the 'James Bond' books were vested. In the summer of 1968 a subsidiary, Bookers Books, acquired a fifty-one per cent holding in Agatha Christie Ltd (subsequently increased to sixty-four per cent). The Glidrose holding was transferred to Bookers Books and in time interests in similar companies were added, to make a flourishing Authors' Division. (It was thus, incidentally, that Booker McConnell decided to establish the Booker Prize for fiction in 1972.) In December 1968 Bookers Books acquired half of the Christie Copyrights Trust's interest in those copyrights they owned and in April 1972 the remainder.

The problem of meeting the special assessments was still unsolved but eventually a method was devised. Booker McConnell, the parent company, agreed to lend Agatha the necessary sum, the loan being secured by Agatha's own reserved copyrights. These arrangements were completely separate from those made between the Trustees of Agatha Christie Ltd, and Booker Books; indeed, Agatha herself saw to the payment of a full rate of interest on the loan. At last she was clear, if in debt, but that condition was familiar.

Throughout these trials Agatha's attitude was a mixture of airiness and resignation. Anthony was a comfort, patiently unravelling figures for her. Occasionally she panicked and wrote miserable letters to Cork, or suggested wild schemes, like lecturing in America or contriving some arrangement with *Collier's*. For the most part, however, she kept a sense of proportion, joking about the mess she was in and reproaching Cork only for giving her insufficient news: 'Your admirable habit,' she told Cork 'of (like sundials!) only recording the sunny hours (or news) makes me suspicious when I don't hear!' She worried unless she knew roughly how her finances stood: 'I must have *some* information .... And you are the Horse's Mouth!!!' The unexpected retrospective demands from tax authorities made her mistrustful, 'Don't get me into trouble by someone being "too clever" over things,' she pleaded. 'It makes me nervous!' When matters were finally sorted out, with her regular cheque from Agatha Christie Ltd, enclosed with a formal statement, she remained troubled. 'How am I to know even who it comes from?' she wrote unhappily to Hughes Massie and, remembering past encounters, 'If a tax man asked me ... I'd have to say "I don't know". For years all has been easily understood .... Now with the Private and Confidential and no other information it looks as though I'd been levying blackmail on someone who pays money into my account without saying who it is from or *why* ...' She appreciated that her advisers had sought to regularise her tangled affairs, calling herself 'the Hired Wage Slave', in fun, when she delivered a book and was happy. If she thought that decisions were being made without consultation – collections of stories assembled without her knowledge, or, as her memory became less reliable, 'forewords, blurbs, and things they may think up' slipped by – she could be resentful. 'I don't believe you realise in the least how much I mind,' she told Cork, in one exchange. 'It's misery to be ashamed of oneself. I'm not just a performing dog for you all – I'm the *writer.*'

Agatha admitted, and her family and advisers recognised, that this was no more than, as she put it, 'blowing off steam'. The interminable argument with the Revenue had frustrated her because she liked things clearly marked and ordered. She preferred to have her accounts straight; indeed, she liked an accounting. (She had a special one at the village shop in Churston, where others dealt in cash.) She wished to be tidy – and, with reason, after the untidiness into which others seemed to have plunged her affairs.

Instinctive generosity and a sense of humour carried Agatha through her financial difficulties and helped her brush off, with only slight exasperation, stories about 'the vast wealth' she actually lacked. She was also fatalistic; before their marriage she had confided to Max the fear that perhaps she took 'too detached a view of life'. Max sensibly told her that if her disposition was, in his words, 'to take an impersonal view', she should stop worrying and recognise its benefits. Those who were close to Agatha believed that, after the collapse of her first marriage, when she realised life could be 'unfair', she resigned herself to whatever fortune and misfortune came her way. She displayed a certain aloofness, a calm self-analysis, which the few who knew of her discussions with psychoanalysts in the late 'twenties thought that experience had given her. Her propensity to draw general conclusions from specific instances, to classify and discern patterns of behaviour, also gave her a sense of perspective and proportion. Max said Agatha 'saw things like a child'; there is advantage in that.

More troubling was another consequence of success on such a scale: the invasion of her privacy. There were attempts to take aerial photographs of Greenway and constant applications to see the house and garden. Rosalind and Anthony helped her fend off these requests, for they had moved to Greenway a year after Mathew's marriage, when he and Angela, and Agatha's first great-grandchild, Alexandra, took over Pwyllwrach. Rosalind

Agatha Christie

and Anthony lived in Ferry Cottage, at the bottom of the garden by the water's edge, but they spent much of the day at the main house, Anthony looking after the property and Rosalind seeing to the running of the house.

It was as well that Agatha had her family and friends to protect her, so unrelentingly importunate were many of her admirers. Some could not understand her irritation at particularly daft proposals and her refusal to open fêtes and sign piles of books in public baffled people. Agatha was adamant. 'Why should writers *talk* about what they write?' she asked Cork. Many did not know or refused to believe that she was shy. 'NOT on your life,' she told Cork, when French television asked her to present a self-portrait for '*Qui suis-je?*' Her secretary and friend Stella Kirwan had great difficulty in convincing the producer of a British television programme, *This is Your Life*, that Agatha would be horrified to be lured to a studio and suddenly confronted with her personal history. Though she grew less jumpy about references to the events of 1926, she preferred there to be no discussion. It was a private matter. Insidious references to it upset her: the occasion, for instance, when an American publisher invited her to complete Franklin Roosevelt's outline for a plot about a successful man's contriving his own disappearance. Her annoyance lingered, too, over the disclosure of Mary Westmacott's 'identity'. 'The people I really minded knowing about it were my friends,' she told Cork, when a *Sunday Times* columnist made much of the story. 'Cramping to one's subject matter. It's really all washed up. ... An author's wishes should be respected.'

Idiotic stories in the press were wounding, particularly when they were bizarrely at variance with the facts. 'I take exception to this,' Agatha wrote to Cork from Bayreuth, where she had seen a German magazine alleging that her dog had devoured a recent manuscript, 'which had decided me in future not to sip away at so many double scotch and sodas'. *Woman's Own* received a salvo, when they introduced one of her stories with a 'rare interview' with 'the world's most mysterious woman'. '"Track down" indeed,' Agatha expostulated to Cork. 'I am in *Who's Who* and am easily reached by post through my publishers. What do they suggest I am? A Bank Robber or a Bank Robber's wife? I'm an ordinary successful hard-working author – like any other author.'

Agatha would give interviews only if Cork recommended it or, even more rarely, if she was surprised by an especially tactful approach. 'A positive posse of journalists received me at

Amsterdam,' she told Cork in 1951, describing a journey to Syria 'How do they know these things! I was interviewed by three, had a "radio conversation" with another. ... Not so bad really as it passed the time – one has four hours there – and after you've eaten an enormous steak there isn't much to do!' 'An enormous bouquet of red roses' paved the way for another group a year or two later: 'I whispered hoarsely to them in French – their French was also a little sketchy, so goodness know what I actually said.' Photography was equally unwelcome. For her sixtieth birthday celebrations Agatha had gone to the studio of Angus McBean, a clever, sympathetic and fashionable photographer, with a flair, suppressed on this occasion, for surrealistic composition. He found her nervous and difficult to photograph but tried to emphasise what was youthful and dramatic in her appearance. Agatha was no longer photogenic; her face, which now showed its heaviness, was more interesting in motion than in repose. She was pleased with the results – 'He has taken out the wrinkles!' – especially compared with an album of pictures Collins sent after her party. 'It saddens me a good deal,' she confessed to Cork, 'and deepens my inferiority complex about my appearance.' After that there were few photographs, apart from those taken by Agatha's family and friends. These are often delightful; Agatha needed to be seen full-length, not simply as an immobile head and shoulders, and looked her best with flowers, or dogs, or Max. She became increasingly sensitive. 'Look here, Edmund, have I got to stand for this?' she wrote in 1953, on receiving a particularly unflattering photograph. 'Just about fit for the psychopathic ward is what I would say ... from now on, photography is OUT. I don't see why I should continuously be humiliated and made to suffer. Even the Post Office have been stupid and delivered it to my flat in spite of the form they have. Otherwise, I daresay, you'd never have let me see it!! Yours sadly ....' After that, only photographs by Walter Bird and Angus McBean were used for publicity, Cork doing his best to suppress the rest. Some slipped through, causing more distress, notably a set in *Paris-Match* in 1955, accompanying an interview Agatha had given to a journalist introduced by James Watts. 'Edmund,' she lamented, 'it's *awful*!' Though the photograph taken for the National Portrait Gallery pleased her, she had asked Cork to buy the copyright, fearing to see it reproduced unexpectedly. By the end of the 'sixties, she was hypersensitive: one letter, drafted but not sent, complained to the editor of a magazine publishing her stories about the other contents of the page announcing the series: 'It is occupied,' she observed, 'mainly by a large reproduction of a woman sitting at a table with a BALD HEAD – I have shown it to six separate people ... one and all have said "bald, of course". Don't you think that this is rather a gratuitous insult to an elderly woman? Especially as my hair, not white, but iron grey, can be vouched for by any hairdresser as growing thickly in a mop all over my head. ... I may mention,' she added for good measure, 'that on the facing page to this is an advertisement beginning: "If you have *greasy unmanageable hair* ..." ... Tactlessness could really go no further, could it?'

Agatha's work was largely self-promoting. Peter Saunders made a special effort to advertise her plays, devising a succession of ingenious wheezes for *The Mousetrap* in particular, but her books virtually sold themselves. The nineteen-seventies were to provide indisputable proof of this. Agatha, from the security of Winterbrook and Greenway, could enjoy the real fruits of her success: peace, privacy, the company of her family, friends and the dogs, delicious food and drink, and books. Her reading neither slackened nor became less varied: novels by Paul Gallico and Muriel Spark, Hammond Innes, Julian Symons, Norman Collins, H.E. Bates, Nancy Mitford and Gerald Durrell; 'Spine Chillers', as she called them; memoirs and biographies of Frieda Lawrence, Thomas Cranmer, Ivan the Terrible, Teilhard de Chardin; *Shaw on Shakespeare*, *The Life of Christ*; an enormous number of detective stories and encyclopaedias on crime, criminals, detection and drugs. She asked Collins for 'Ice Station Zebra' which 'everybody says is very good' – and was not put off by finding that *Ice Station Zero* was not about animals. Always she returned to her favourite classical litarature. During the War the 'Brains Trust' panel broadcasting on the wireless had been asked for a list of 'Great Authors' and Agatha and Max had exchanged answers to this question. 'I *should* add Shaw,' Agatha had written. 'I'm not sure about Kipling – you must wait about another twenty years to know. What about Masefield? Wells? Galsworthy?' She reread Dickens and Shakespeare and was never without a volume of poems. From Wallingford and Swan Court there were discreet expeditions to the opera and theatre: *King Lear*, *Oliver*, Mozart at Salzburg, *How to Succeed in Business*. She adored flowers and food; rich veal and egg dishes served in the restaurant at Swan Court, which she and Max sometimes enjoyed with Sybil Thorndike and her husband, who lived next door; bottled plums, blackcurrants, raspberries and strawberries in the country. Agatha was proud of her appetite: *A Murder is Announced* had been dedicated to friends at whose house she first tasted 'Delicious Death', an extremely rich chocolate cake, and, years later, on sampling a foaming meringue soufflé, its flavour enhanced with liqueur, she observed, 'But *this* is delicious Life.'

26

'It will not, I think, be long ...'

Agatha arrived at the height of her fame in 1970, her eightieth year. It was to be a strenuous one. She and Max had not been away to the sun at the beginning of 1969 and in the spring she struggled with a severe chill. To gather strength and escape the damp, they had a holiday in Cyprus in January 1970 and at Easter went to Austria for mountain air, where Agatha had her wish and saw the Oberammergau Passion Play. For the rest of the spring she tried to tidy up her new book, *Passenger to Frankfurt*, or, as she spelt it, 'Frankfort'.

She had begun to think about the plot in 1963, asking Collins to find a copy of *The Royal Family of Bayreuth*, by Friedelinde Wagner, the composer's grand-daughter, whom she, Max and Mathew had met at Bayreuth. Friedelinde had taken them behind the scenes of the Opera House and later to King Ludwig of Bavaria's opera house, and had told them anecdotes about her grandfather and Hitler. Agatha brooded on all this, fitting it to her ideas about world conspiracy and espionage. She also asked Collins for *Contributions to European History* and Cork for a list of 'Iron Curtain Coins, all of small size and small value', and the origins of the quotation 'For want of a nail, the horse was lost. ...' Her draft took up another thought, long germinating, for a book beginning in 'An Air Lounge' – a place which is no place, designed for arrivals, departures, exchanges. 'Passengers in Transit' was one of Agatha's working titles for the development of this idea, or 'Missing Passenger Story'. This plot acquired the title *Passenger to Frankfurt* in 1966, in the notebook Agatha kept on her American visit: 'Airport. Renata. ... Sir Neil at War Office of M14. His obstinacy aroused. Puts advertisement in. ... Hitler idea. Concealed in a lunatic asylum. One of many who think they are Napoleon – or Hitler – or Mussolini. One of them was smuggled out. H took his place. ... Branded him on sole of foot – a swastika. The son. Born 1945. Now 24. In Argentine? USA? Rudi, The Young Siegfried. ...'

Thus Agatha started to mix her old obsessions: disguise; people who *actually* are who they say they are, mixed up with people who are not; the hiding of people in the obvious place for them to be (a sort of 'purloined letter' notion); the international conspiracy idea; the advertisement in the newspaper device. These were intermixed with popular contemporary preoccupations – the true fate of Hitler and his entourage; the refuge they might have sought; the possibility of Hitler's return, reincarnated almost, as a son. She joined these with another theme, 'the Mrs Boynton character', another megalomaniac, sadistic mother: 'old lady Gräfin – in decay but she is a woman of power – Great riches – a Bertha Krupp – Armament heiress. ...' The draft brought together a tangle of fantasies, ideologies, fixations and recollections, some evolved via meetings with dotty prophets in California, some by Agatha's reading. 'Do you think I could have this series?' she asked Billy Collins, after seeing a review of the Fontana *Modern Masters* paperbacks. 'It would educate me to be up-to-date, and help my writing. Alexandra *must* have an intelligent great-grandmother!! If they could come *here* – not Greenway – I could commence study!! I know I am the daughter of the horse leech, saying "Give, Give, Give!"' There she was, plunging into Marcuse, Fanon and Chomsky. Agatha had always found intellectual speculation exciting; her discussions with Max and her family at Greenway had included Freud and Jung, Moore and Wittgenstein, as well as, years before, Dunne on time and Jeans on Relativity. It was now harder for her to concentrate; even so, some of what she now read disturbed her, the more because, from what she gathered elsewhere, it was peddled effectively and swallowed uncritically. Not that this was anything new. 'Trends and tendencies,' Mr Robinson says in *Passenger to Frankfurt*, 'coming again and again, repeating itself like a periodic table, repeating a pattern. A desire for rebellion.' In itself the desire was not reprehensible. What made Agatha shudder was its malevolent exploitation, the wicked taking advantage of the innocent or naïve. A long note in her draft for this book, marked 'Incorporate', illustrates her attitude: 'Idealism can arise from antagonism to injustice and to crass materialism – and is fed more and more by a desire to destroy ... those who get to love Violence for its own sake will never become adults. They are fixed in their own retarded development.'

This was the pin with which Agatha fastened her disjointed thoughts. 'Suggestions', she put in one note-book, 'Quotation or

Résumé of Stalin's Aims (From Svetlana's book?). ... African Régime – Nkrumah or Congo? Algeria? Ireland? Belgian Congo? Italian risings and terrorist activity. American universities. Black Power etc.' Her notes are fascinating, and moving. In large letters, with something of her middle-aged verve but more often with more of the child's hand that had first written in the 'Confessions', she set down her troubled thoughts. *Passenger to Frankfurt* was stuffed with fantasy but it echoed the real fears expressed by Agatha's friends and the people she met in London, Oxford and Washington, diplomats, journalists, politicians. In the late nineteen-sixties and early seventies there were constant reports of hijackings, terrorism, disaffected youth, drug-peddling, wars, coups and revolutions. Agatha described her book as an extravaganza and only the most gullible and paranoid readers saw it as more than that. It was, however, timely: a book that was confused but published at a time when everything seemed upside-down, views about human psychology and instinct as much as events in the external world. Agatha's novel proclaimed, moreover, the triumph of the ordinary over the exotic, or, more precisely, that appparently unglamorous people could mobilise their somewhat eccentric resources against ruthless and well-equipped criminals. Lady Matilda Cleckheaton, pleasantly perfumed, pale pink, wrinkled, with a touch of arthritis; the careless, idiosyncratic Stafford Nye; stalwart, imperturbable Horsham; Colonel Pikeway, self-sufficient and weary, his office suffused (as Max's and Stephen Glanville's office had been) with cigarette smoke; and plain Mr Robinson, whose tastes were simple but who was one of 'the great arrangers of money' – these were Agatha's archetypal heroes.

When the book was done, almost everyone – Cork and Dorothy Olding, Agatha's family – was dismayed. Collins, in particular, feared the book would be a disaster. Only Anthony liked it, apart from its soppy ending. They were all confounded. In the autumn, sales rocketed in Britain and, when the American edition appeared in spring 1971, it was as much of a sensation there. Agatha had not only dealt with universal and timeless themes; she had hit raw nerves.

Passenger to Frankfurt also soared upwards on the publicity for Agatha's anniversary. 'If the book is published as an 80th birthday book,' she had acknowledged to Cork, 'something ... will have to be done, I suppose. But I suggest – Keep it snappy! Not long tiresome "Profiles".' She escaped with only an effusive interview in the *Daily Mail*, by Godfrey Winn, who, to everyone's delight, was bitten by Bingo, the successor to Treacle, who had died of an epileptic fit at the beginning of 1969. Bingo was irredeemably neurotic. Rosalind had found him for Agatha, who insisted on a Manchester terrier from a breeder. It turned out that he had been so terrified as a puppy that he bit almost everyone in sight. Max's legs were a mass of scars, one visitor after another was nipped, and there were innumerable stories of Bingo's success in pouncing on those who crept through Winterbrook by a complicated route to answer the telephone or the doorbell. Only Agatha was immune. Bingo adored her, slept on her bed; she loved him, some victims believed, because he was loyal, spiritedly protecting her privacy, and because he needed only affection.

Agatha spent her birthday in Devon, in a summer of celebration. There were parties for friends at All Souls' and Boodles and a family feast at Greenway:

> Picnic on the Moor with 5 dogs and a super dinner last night:
>
> > Avocados Vinaigrette
> > Hot Lobster à la Crème
> > Blackberry Ice Cream and real blackberries and lots of cream, and special treat – half a large cup of neat cream for ME while the rest had Champagne.

Furthermore, Agatha reassured Cork, 'I'm still alive today!!!' She was obliged to ask Hughes Massie to deal with greetings from abroad. The flowers, enormous telegrams and cards had, she said, made her feel 'like a Prima Ballerina, indeed quite above myself. No proper modesty left.' She was particularly delighted with a present of something she had – surprisingly – never owned before, a gold pen, sent by Cork: 'Death to anyone who borrows it and doesn't give it back.' Last was a party at Collins, where Agatha confessed that she 'enjoyed myself *very much*!!!' She asked for copies of the photographs of herself cutting a huge chocolate cake, of herself with Max and her 'good-looking publisher!' and of the literary editors surrounding her in a group, with 'a little plan of names ... because it will be nice to keep it with the 80th birthday souvenirs.' It was a publication party too; by artful counting, *Passenger to Frankfurt* was advertised as Agatha's eightieth book for her eightieth year.

The New Year's Honours List for 1971 announced that Agatha was created a Dame Commander of the British Empire. It was her last change of name. Friends and neighbours continued to call her Lady Mallowan, but her new style completely foxed American admirers ('Dame Christie?' was one ingenious guess), who flocked to buy *Passenger to Frankfurt* when it appeared in March. Agatha and Max went to Paris for a few days in January but she now found it increasingly difficult to get about. She managed, nonetheless, to deliver her new book in May, a Miss Marple story called *Nemesis*. It was an elaboration of a 'National Trust idea', listed among the 'Projects 1966 Oct', when Agatha had mused on what Miss Marple might discover on a tour of country houses and gardens and what her fellow passengers might be like. ('Lawyer? A doctor and his wife? A queer clever girl ...?') *Nemesis* itself was begun in January 1971. It is touching to see that Agatha has written 'DBE' on the line above the title of her notebook, as if she were murmuring encouragement to herself. She started her notes with a 'Recap. Death of Mr Rafiel in *Times*.' Mr Rafiel was the old man in the wheelchair whom Miss Marple had helped in *A Caribbean Mystery*; he was to use her as Nemesis, to see that justice was done.

The notion of retribution had always interested Agatha. Her views fluctuated but by and large she believed that, whether people were innately wicked or had chosen evil, they should not go free. The fact that certain basic rules and conventions of behaviour had been broken – taking another's life being the most extreme case – should, she felt, be recognised; very few of Agatha's murderers are unpunished, although a number die before they can be brought to trial. Bringing the guilty to justice also relieves the innocent, she maintained, not just those who may have been wrongly convicted but also those afflicted by not knowing where guilt lies. Justice restores order, closes an incomplete circle. She saw her detective stories as morality plays, demonstrating that there was wickedness in the world, but that it could be found out and sin expiated.

'Justice', however, is not punishment, vengeance or retribution. It is fairness. Agatha often leaves punishment to the gods. She wondered a good deal about all this. She would have liked to have felt that the matter was simple and, as she grew older, became more strongly convinced that crime should be strictly punished, that attempts to 'rehabilitate' criminals were often futile (though not all efforts were as daft as those described in *They Do It With Mirrors*), that punishment could deter others and that a good many dangerous madmen were allowed to wander about (not at all a surprising opinion given some of the paranoid correspondence that, despite Cork's screening, found its way to her). Even in the mid-'fifties, however, she allowed characters in *Butter in a Lordly Dish* to wonder whether capital punishment allowed men to play at being gods, and possibly to make mistakes. By far the most convenient resolution was to leave retribution to providence, nature, fate, some divine power or the Eumenides, whom Agatha, after reading Aeschylus in the War, likened to the spirits summoned in Voodoo ceremonies. Miss Marple was not an embodiment of these avenging Furies, but the instrument of justice, picked by Mr Rafiel to investigate a crime that had happpened long ago. He had chosen an ideal person, shrewd, sensible and wise, to do what human beings can do: mete out justice to other human beings. It is interesting that Miss Marple also represented the absolute objectivity of justice to an unexpected set of readers: the Tupamaros guerillas, who had kidnapped the British Ambassador, Sir Geoffrey Jackson, in Uruguay in 1970. Not only did Sir Geoffrey find consolation in Agatha Christie's works during his long imprisonment, fastening on Miss Marple – and, indeed, Hercule Poirot – as fixed points in an uneasy firmament, but his captors were interested in discussing Miss Marple with him, venerating her as they did their own revolutionary leader.

Nemesis, like many of Agatha's detective stories, mixes the important and the mundane. The creeper which hides the victim's burial place resembled the tangle of white flowers – 'Polygonum baldschuanicum' – over the ruins of a greenhouse at Winterbrook, 'concealing', Agatha said meaningly to her friend Lady le Rougetel, 'a multitude of sins'. The motive for the crime, the passion of a forceful, possessive woman for an impressionable girl, was both a powerful and an ordinary theme. (It is, incidentally, nonsense to suggest, as some critics have done, that in extreme old age Agatha suddenly broached more daring subjects, for from the beginning her books explored complex and unusual sexual and emotional relationships, of a type familiar to anyone living in a village, let alone Chelsea in the nineteen-seventies.)

Nemesis contained a number of discrepancies and oddities but, considering Agatha's age and increasing shakiness, needed little work. There was more difficulty with the play she sent Cork in the early weeks of 1971, *This Mortal Coil*. Agatha had recently made vague notes for several plays, including 'Mousetrap II'; an idea about a 'mousetrap party in Soho', with hired waiters, which ended with the victim being poisoned, 'a mixture of 3 Act tragedy and "Sparkling Cyanide".' *This Mortal Coil* was based on one of these ideas, 'death duties', and Agatha's first rough outline indicates the thoughts that were now running through her mind: 'M sends money to Chancellor of Exchequer: "How do you spend conscience?"' The play's next title became 'Fiddle-De-Death', later, 'Fiddlers Five'. Agatha had great hopes for her play. 'We saw *Move Over Mrs Markham* in Oxford last week,' she wrote to Cork. 'Max thought it very silly. Good audience and lots of laughs. People *want* to be cheered up and are tired of nothing but nudity.' She set off to Paris, leaving Cork to do what he could. Peter Saunders declined the play but James Grant Anderson, the actor-manager, took it on tour in June. It was not a success.

Agatha was by then confined to bed. She had fallen at Winterbrook and damaged her hip; at the beginning of June it was found to be broken. She was operated on at the Nuffield Orthopaedic Hospital in Oxford, returning home shortly afterwards to convalesce. Billy sent books and Mathew and Angela music on cassettes. Rosalind, Anthony and Max did what they could to amuse her but she was bored, entertaining herself by dispatching argumentative letters to Billy about the proposed jacket for *Nemesis*, enclosing cuttings of book reviews complaining about other publishers' jacket designs. By Christmas she was walking, though she found it difficult to get about in London, where she went briefly to be measured for her waxwork at Madame Tussaud's. (Agatha gave them an *old* dress, being both practical and anxious not to part with clothes she liked and could still wear.) There was also Christmas shopping. 'Most years I find it rather fun,' she told Cork. 'But now I get tired and want to go home.' She discovered, however, that ordering by mail would help, supplying, for instance, a cuckoo clock, a 'modern tool box' for her nephew, 'a hammering apparatus for her great-grandson', and a 'perennial fountain for moistening the sitting room'.

The winter was hard. By now Winterbrook was exceedingly dilapidated: 'A lot of wind and rain and somewhere water is running or dripping,' Agatha wrote to Angela. 'The Hall light has crashed – so there must be SOS on Monday to a plumber *and* an electrician.' The garden was overgrown, the kitchen dark and difficult for Mrs Belson to work in. Max worried about the cost of keeping up the house, meeting his bills, his own and Agatha's old-age pension. They had acquired a Mercedes Benz at the end of 1971 and he was anxious about the cost of its maintenance. Agatha now asked Cork to reassure him by showing him the last Miss Marple book, 'Cover her Face' (published as *Sleeping Murder*). She remained in good spirits. Even the coal strike at the beginning of the year did not defeat her: 'My nose gets icy cold at 4.30 a.m.,' she told Cork. 'I now attach an egg cosy to it at this hour.' She arranged an expedition to Nice, so she and Max could find some sun, ordered opera tickets, took herself to *Sleuth*, went out to luncheon and dined with friends, amazing another octogenarian, with delicate digestion, by tucking into *osso buco* and ginger ice cream.

She also refused to admit defeat over '*Fiddlers Five*'. Allan Davis, a director who had seen the play in Brighton the previous autumn, made suggestions for improving it and in the spring and summer of 1972 Agatha amended the script, amalgamating two of the characters and changing the title to *Fiddlers Three*. She stoutly rebuffed some of Davis's bolder ideas: 'I do not want a play of mine to be one that deals with everyone in it doing swindles – or in thoroughly criminal surroundings. ... Swedes or Norwegians or Danes seldom look anything but English – and seldom talk with Scandinavian accents. My own sister-in-law is Finnish. ... I cannot see any reason for building up the Spanish Waiter's act – he'd do just as well as an English waiter. ...' *Fiddlers Three* opened at Guildford at the beginning of August and Agatha was there. It toured for a few weeks but failed to find a theatre in London, which was perhaps fortunate, for it would have disappointed those who remembered *Witness for the Prosecution* and who still trooped to *The Mousetrap*. Agatha nonetheless derived great pleasure from the performance for she was still enchanted with the theatre. Indeed, the only society, apart from the Detection Club, over which she agreed to preside, out of hundreds of requests, was the Sinodun Players, an amateur dramatic society at Wallingford. She continued to scribble notes for plays to the end of her life.

That summer, too, Agatha conscientiously delivered her next book, *Elephants Can Remember*. 'Mrs Oliver. Poirot,' she wrote, clearly this time, for her psoriasis had retreated. 'Does a problem come to P? Or to Mrs O?' Another old friend returned in this book as well, Mr Goby, the ubiquitous but elusive purveyor of information, who had first appeared in *The Mystery of the Blue Train* and returned in *After the Funeral* and *Third Girl*. Mr Goby was what in the United States would be a 'gofer', an errand boy, but he procured facts. As other people in Agatha's novels were arrangers of money, Mr Goby was an arranger of material, from dossiers and reference books. He provided the data from which Poirot derived his knowledge, the intellectual tools to take apart the engines of conspiracy. Into *Elephants Can Remember* Agatha also brought some favourite themes: the long shadow of old sins; the shame of an unresolved crime; complicated domestic crimes ('Wife kills husband? Husband kills wife? Sick women killing children? Sisters jealous of sisters-in-law. ...') 'All so long ago,' Agatha wrote in her notebook. 'Everyone will have forgotten. People don't forget things that happened when they were children. ... It's like elephants. Elephants never forget.' So Agatha rambled through her own childhood and her own fixations: 'Calls on Poirot. Asks about Josephine (Crooked House).' Ideas surfaced that had been set aside: 'Lunch for literary women. Mrs Oliver. Mrs Gorringe. Discussion between them. A child could do a crime; Hyde Park. Nurse with Pram. Talk of gas – to make a baby sleep...; 'Lizzie Borden family – father and mother killed – two daughters – devoted sister-in-law. ...' Old fixations resurfaced: 'Boys pull flies' legs off but they don't do it when they grow up. ... Mr G says Professor of Genetics or Biology and Jesuits have to take a child before 7. ...' Not unexpectedly *Elephants Can Remember* wandered about as well. It was nonetheless ingenious, full of forthright and often very funny passages, blunt about the physical deterioration of the old and endearing in its depiction of the relations between generations. It was the last novel Agatha wrote before her powers really declined.

She was now trying to put her literary affairs in order, looking over some of her notebooks, and trying to label pages where ideas for new detective stories had first emerged; the contents were so haphazard, that she abandoned the effort. In February 1972 she sent Cork 'the odd poems that I have collected. ... I think it best to transfer them to your care now because, at the age of 81, one might at any time leave this world rather suddenly: either as a result of motor crashes on our roads, heart attacks from doing a few of the things one has been told not to do – running upstairs – or opening the door to a long-haired young man who would bash one over the head just for the fun of it.' Cork, she wrote, could, 'after crying at my funeral and if my family agree, introduce them into the world.'

Three months later, she sent him *Akhnaton*: 'It seems to me to be particularly applicable just at this time, that is if anyone was willing to put some money into staging it – and it would no doubt be an expensive production – but there is such a furore over the Egyptian Tutankhamun.' She added one or two sentences to take account of recent discoveries and speculations – the fate of Nefertiti, for example – but otherwise thought it not at all dated. 'I like the play very much,' she observed, 'though I am quite prepared to accept the fact that no one will put it on the stage. If that does turn out to be the case, I would like to have it published.' Both *Poems* and *Akhnaton* were brought out by Collins in 1973, together with a detective story Agatha painfully put together. 'I'm so tired,' she told Mrs Thompson, who helped look after things at Greenway, 'and they're waiting for every word I write.' She also felt responsible to Agatha Christie Ltd, feeling, unnecessarily, that she owed them an annual book. 'Notes for November 1972 and Plans', she wrote, drafting the first few chapters as she had always done. ('Possible point: the wrong woman died. ... *Various ideas* ... *Next* make a list of possible characters. ...')

Tommy and Tuppence were among those with whom she toyed. The title of her next book was taken from a poem of Flecker. Agatha had noted in a plotting book some lines which sounded well, though their sense is obscure:

Pass not beneath, O Caravan, or pass not seeing.
Have you heard
The silence where the birds are dead, yet something pipeth like a bird??

She tried several titles: 'Postern of Fate; Doom's Caravan; Disaster's Caravan; Fort of Fear ...'; she settled on *Postern of Fate*.

Agatha found it harder than ever to concentrate – Max told Rosalind that writing this book nearly killed her – and she herself was uneasy. She asked Cork for a candid opinion and he tactfully suggested she have some help with editing. Max and Mrs Honeybone, who did typing for the Mallowans (and to whom Agatha had dedicated *Nemesis*) tidied it up, though Agatha's family – Rosalind in particular – was unhappy. But when *Postern of Fate* was published, in Britain at the end of 1973 and in the United States early in 1974, the notices were unexpectedly good and so were sales. It moved rapidly up the best-seller list and by February 1974 was in third place in the list compiled by the European edition of *Time* magazine.

Rosalind was firm. Worried about Agatha's health, she was also a stern guardian of her mother's literary reputation. She

asked Collins to press for no more books. Billy Collins agreed
that Agatha's health must be protected, though he left the question open by declaring that, while her mind was active, 'maybe it
is a help to her to be thinking out a plot, and surely we should
not definitely turn down the idea if she thinks she would like to
write another story.' For the time being, Collins agreed that the
next book would be a volume of short stories, from those hitherto
published only in America or in magazines.

There was no new story. In October Agatha had a heart attack,
which left her frail, although she managed to scrawl a note to
Cork on a scrap of paper: 'Heart much steadier and doctor lets
me get up and come downstairs every other day for short time
but otherwise still in bed. Boring!!!' She read a great deal; all the
newly reprinted Mary Westmacott books ('*Unfinished Portrait* I
think is one of the best after *Rose and the Yew Tree*'), a batch of
novels, including Yukio Mishima's *Spring Snow*, Brian Moore's
Catholics, and some non-fiction, *Mysterious Britain* and *The
World of Victoriana*. She also asked Cork to send a script of her
Autobiography: 'I have time on my hands and would enjoy reading it at leisure.' She played with memories – 'Dickens Menus:
Salmon (Martin Chuzzlewit) Lamb. Peas. Innocent Young Potatoes. Cool Salad. Sliced Cucumber. Tender Duckling. A Tart.'
She made notes for 'Suggested Tours by AM in Idleness: Wick-
ham (Elephants?) Pretty Spot. ... Lambourne. Views all along
road and bridges. ... Seven Barrows. ... East Hagbourne – interesting heads in Church ...?,' all the drives along the lanes and
over the Downs between Oxford, the Thames and the Berkshire
Downs. Some of these places came into a 'Possibilities and Ideas'
list she also made. One was for a set of ghost stories, based on
the 'white horses' cut into the grass of the chalky downland in
different parts of England ('perhaps in a party with White Horses
at which a Ghost Horse might appear suddenly ...?'). In another:
'Jeremy – discusses with friends. Murders. What difference would
it make to one's character if one had killed someone? "Depends
on what the motive had been?" "No. *No* motive. For no reason.
Just an interesting experiment." The object of the crime – Oneself.
Would one be the same person – or would one be different? To
find out one would have to commit homicide – observing all the
time oneself – one's feelings. Keeping notes – Needed A Victim.
...' And there was 'Cookery Story. About A Meringue? Trifle.
Skewer. ...'

None of these was developed. In December Agatha fell into

the French window at Winterbrook and badly split her head. She sat in bed, in her silk nightdress (all her nightdresses were made by the blind), her hair blood-caked, a sad figure now. The drugs she took for her heart had shrunk her into a little scrap and she ate only a very little. Frail, she remained the good sport she had been in Syria and Iraq, tottering to Wimbledon with Max, and managing to attend the Lord Mayor's Dinner. In July Max persuaded her to come to the polling station to vote in the referendum on Britain's membership of the European Community; her reluctance was not due to the physical effort the expedition required but to doubts as to where her duty lay. A natural conservative, believing in gradual progress on a loose rein, she was wary of political and bureaucratic schemes, as she put it in her letters to Max in the 'forties 'to make people happy and safe by force'. Max, on the other hand, was a romantic in politics; in 1945 he had spoken to Agatha of Russia's new golden age, 'like that of sixth to fifth century Greece', renowned 'not merely for their military genius but for their economics, their organisation and ... imagination. Apart from Stalin 'perhaps' and Michurin the agronomist, he had rhapsodised, 'we know of no individual Russians. It is a collective genius animated by a burning belief in their political foundation, which to them amounts to a religion.' Agatha was not wholly convinced then, nor, as *Passenger to Frankfurt* showed, later. Now she rallied her strength to argue with Max about the Community: it would be no more than a customs union and a regulator's paradise, she predicted, while he visualised it as a unified historial, cultural and intellectual Eden. Gamely, Agatha agreed to try it, and voted yes.

She also kept up the running argument with Billy over covers, this time for the jacket of Collins's recent volume of short stories, *Poirot's Early Cases*: 'He was a *little* man,' she protested. 'His smartly dressed lower half seems entirely unlike him and represents him as 6 feet high at least. I never remember him as prone to carry a little bag.' She had been upset, too, by the choice of stories for inclusion in this collection, although these had been explicitly cleared. By now her mind was fuzzy. She still hoped to recover her old wits, to write 'a series – ghost story or book built round the White Horse of Uffington', which (in a swipe at the new Local Government Act) 'was situated in Berkshire and is now being transferred with all the rest of us to Oxfordshire, which causes very bad feeling to the neighbourhood. ...' One of these days, she concluded, 'when I am quite myself again. ...'

Fragile and immensely aged, Agatha became, as the very old sometimes do, more and more like the child she had been, over eighty years before. Sometimes she was serene, sitting quietly at luncheon with friends, gently leafing through one of her books. 'Stop it, Agatha,' Max once said, as he caught her looking speculative. At other times she was eccentric, declaring, for instance, that today she would wear all her brooches, from the grandest diamonds to small ornaments children had sent her. She was often difficult, frequently upset by the indignities and dependence of her state. Once, to the horror of her family and friends, she seized the scissors and cut off locks of the fine hair of which she had been so proud. Then she would be calm again, resting in the garden in the sun, asking repeatedly for a sun-hat and bemusedly finding she had it on. She could be as interested and quick-witted as ever; just as she had once speculated about the true facts of the Bravo murder case and, in the early nineteen-sixties, about the alleged theft of a diamond bracelet by a British footballer visiting Colombia so she now greeted her solicitor with the words, 'I wonder what *has* happened to Lord Lucan?' From time to time she still pounced on an idea for a plot: one old friend, visiting the house at the end of Agatha's life, explained that she gave a shine to her decanters by rinsing them in Steradent. She noticed how Agatha immediately fixed on this remark as a possible device for a story. A pompous guest was stopped in his tracks when she expostulated, 'What is this nonsense about "training" for the theatre?' Another lofty conversation about the meaning of life was punctuated by her asking, 'Does there *have* to be a purpose?' and an All Souls' acquaintance, talking about the vulgarity of dahlias, was amused to hear her murmur: 'But pompom dahlias do go so well with Dresden.'

Physical and mental decline is sad. Agatha's family tried to protect her. She still saw old friends and, very occasionally, a pilgrim. One admirer who called at Winterbrook was Lord Snowdon, commissioned by the *Sunday Times* to take photographs to mark the release of Lord Brabourne's film of *Murder on the Orient Express*. They were interesting and sympathetic pictures but her family insisted that it had been made clear that none was to be published without Agatha's explicit approval. She was upset when, with no clearance, the pictures appeared, and even more hurt when her desultory conversation with her guest appeared as an interview in an Australian magazine. It was another reminder of the gulf between those who see people as exhibits, to be used, and those who prefer to let individuals themselves decide whether they wish to live, and die, by self-advertisement.

One of Agatha's few expeditions was to the première of *Murder on the Orient Express*. Despite her determination that this story, one of her most precious, should not be made into a film, she had succumbed to the blandishments of Lord Mountbatten, so persuasive that she briefly forgot her disenchantment with film-making and agreed to entrust her story to his son-in-law, John Brabourne. Agatha was impressed by the lavish production and thought Albert Finney a convincing Poirot, apart from his feeble moustache; otherwise she was unconverted. The last outing was to the annual Mousetrap Party.

Agatha now needed a great deal of looking after. Her bed at Wallingford was moved downstairs and Max, writing his own *Memoirs*, left the sanctuary of his library for an uncomfortable chair beside her. Neighbours and friends would sit with her and a night nurse was engaged, but Agatha was unhappy at being so intimately cared for by a relative stranger and once more the work of attending her fell to Max and the family. Barbara Parker, who had so efficiently looked after things at Nimrud, came at weekends, to give Max some rest. Friends came to sit with Agatha; delirious, she talked of preparations and journeys, going to find Max, travelling to Cambridge, bringing ladders to fetch down trunks, packing for 'the children'.

Now she turned to her memorial. Months before, she had addressed an envelope to 'Max or Rosalind', adding later 'or Mathew'. Inside was the instruction, '*Put on my Slate*: Sleep after Toyle, Port after Stormie Seas. Ease after Warre, Death after Life, Doth greatly please.' She asked for 'Bach Air in D from 3rd Suite played at my funeral, please. Also Nimrud (sic) from the Elgar Variations. Mathew to arrange.' In another envelope, she again gave the quotation from Spenser, adding a phrase from the Psalms: 'In Thy Presence is the fulness of Joye,' with the words, 'I would like these two things put on my Tombstone. Agatha Mallowan.'

Agatha did outlive 'the insufferable Poirot', for in 1975 Rosalind decided that *Curtain* should now be published. In it, Poirot returns to Styles, telling Hastings, 'I am very tired – and the exertions I have been through have strained me a good deal. It will not, I think, be long ...' There was also a new edition of *Come, Tell Me How You Live*, published the autumn of 1975.

That winter Agatha caught a cold. 'I'm joining my Maker,' she murmured and on January 12th, just after luncheon, she died at Winterbrook. Max telephoned the doctor who had looked after her for twenty years, listened to her talk of her dreams, been worried by Treacle and bitten by Bingo. He left his house immediately but before he reached Winterbrook Max telephoned again: 'She's gone,' and then, the doctor's wife thought, strangely, 'Don't say a word.' Max's warning was wise, for within hours the invasion began. The local, national and foreign press appeared in Wallingford, the telephone rang incessantly. Max was inundated with telegrams and letters from the family and personal friends, which he answered within the day, official tributes, and requests that were sometimes in poor taste (an American company wanted to market a commemorative Hercule Poirot 'moustache mug') or well-meaning but idiotic (like 'a letter from some quasi-lunatic who would like to handle all Agatha's records', Max told Cork).

Agatha was buried in her wedding ring, as she had asked, at Cholsey, the little church near Winterbrook. The service was private, a small reunion on a chill January day for Agatha's family and a handful of close friends. In May there was a memorial service at St Martin-in-the-Fields, with the music she had requested, the twenty-third Psalm and a reading from Thomas à Kempis, the book she kept by her bedside. Billy Collins, unwell himself, delivered an Address.

Some of Agatha's affairs were settled quickly. There was little money to leave – only small bequests here and there – and the treasures she had chosen for her friends were soon packed and despatched (though an enormous mother of pearl 'Damascus' chest and a Wedgwood bust of Mercury were more difficult to transport to Edmund Cork). A fund to which her admirers contributed was divided between the Little Sisters of the Poor and the Agatha Christie Trust for Children, two causes close to her heart. Other memorials took longer. There were difficulties, for example, over her tombstone, the lettering carved by a friend from archaeological days and embellished with cherubs by another. The stone slab was so heavy that a crane was needed to hoist it over the churchyard wall. It can be seen, tall and shining, from the London to Oxford railway, where the lines skirt Cholsey.

Agatha's most complex legacy was her work. *Sleeping Murder*, the last Miss Marple story, was published in 1976. Billy was not, perhaps, surprised to receive a letter from Rosalind regretting that she had not been shown the proposed design for the jacket. For to Rosalind now fell the task of battling to protect the integ-

rity of Agatha's creations: to ensure that Agatha Christie Ltd
kept a wholesome distance from proposals for games, strip car-
toons, toys, cookery books; and to consider what her mother's
wishes would have been with regard to the exploitation of the
enormous number of copyrights in every market in the world, in
an age when literary material was seized on for films, television,
mail order and book club sales, cable rights and video-cassettes.

It is difficult to make more than a rough assessment of the
total volume of Agatha's sales, since any calculation is complicated by the fact that her books are known to be published in at
least fifty languages, in countries which have different procedures
for making returns, when they make them at all. Statistics are
unreliable and often out of date. An indication of her success is
given by the fact that by 1980 UNESCO believed that some four
hundred million copies of her books had been sold, world-wide,
since she first published *The Mysterious Affair at Styles*. Nor can
we give a precise figure for the earnings from her work, though
the records of Agatha Christie Ltd, for many years now the
owners of the vast majority of her copyrights, show in the 1980s
an annual turnover of over a million pounds. The complexities
of the Christie estate make it impossible to establish the total
income from her work or to estimate trends. The figures that are
available do show, however, that the popularity of her work
continues to grow.

Rosalind also found herself fielding successive applications to
write an official biography of her mother. A number of self-
appointed biographers published volumes of their own, from the
gushing to the malicious, from pot-boiling romances to serious
literary criticism. As Agatha had cheerfully forecast, the more
lightweight efforts were overshadowed by her own *Autobiography*.
This was published in 1977, after a great deal of cutting and
correction by Philip Ziegler of Collins, Rosalind and Anthony.
Max (who, bereft, had married Barbara Parker in September
1977) conscientiously examined the proofs but his own health
was failing now. After an operation on his arthritic hip in July,
he had another heart attack and died in August 1978.

Agatha's books last because they are good, if sometimes hopelessly improbable, stories. The reader, once hooked, wants to
know what happens next. They deal with myths, fantasies, obsessions shared by people of every sort: quests and contests, death,
sex, money, murder, conspiracy, transformation, power, the
triumph of the simple over the complex, the importance of the

mundane as well as the cosmic. They construct a pattern, assigning facts and emotions to their appointed place as problems are resolved and guilt and innocence established.

This last quality helps us understand why Agatha's *Autobiography* is so interesting. It is an enchanting book, fluent, pungent, clear-eyed about the times and circumstances in which she lived, funny about herself and other people. With *Come, Tell Me How You Live*, it gives many clues to her life and her nature. It interests Agatha's insatiable admirers and people who do not like detective stories or care a fig for her mysteries. Some feel her *Autobiography* leaves nothing more to say; others, disappointed because she dwells on her childhood – and ignores her flight to Harrogate altogether – believe much remains hidden.

There is, indeed, always more to say, if only because no one can give a balanced assessment of themselves. Memory fails, especially of events in adult life; recollections are invariably coloured. A person who writes an autobiography approaches it, consciously or not, in one of several ways: it may be their presentation of themselves to the world or their exploration of how they became what they are, an unravelling process for the writer as much as the reader. Some autobiographies do both. Agatha's is one. To what extent she gives a 'true' picture of herself and a fair account of her development is something each reader must judge alone; this biography, authorised by her daughter and based on Agatha's private papers, may help that assessment.

Knowing now as much as we do of Agatha, her work and its origins, we can, I think, understand the purpose of her own *Autobiography*. It was not intended as a screen, nor to distract attention from aspects of her life she did not want to be discussed. Agatha described her experiences as best she could, in the 'Mary Westmacott' novels and in the narrative and characterisation of her detective stories. If some of her writing about herself is fantasy or wishful thinking, that is true of all of us when we talk about ourselves. Agatha was good at seeing patterns, astute, sensible, down-to-earth, affectionate and dry. In her *Autobiography* she almost succeeded in fitting everything together, as she had matched pieces of the Nimrud ivories and Max's pots. Some pieces she could not fit; others, being too close, she could not see. Perhaps we can perceive her more clearly, in this biography, as if by shaking a kaleidoscope, looking along its length. There, reflected and refracted in its mirrors, is another arrangement of the fragments.

Index

384

Index